A History of Australasian Economic Thought

T0383998

This overview of Australasian economic thought presents the first analysis of the Australian economic contribution for 25 years, and is the first to offer a panoramic sweeping account of New Zealand economic thought. Those two countries, both at the start of the twentieth century and at its end, excelled at innovative economic practices and harbouring unique economic institutions.

A History of Australasian Economic Thought explains how Australian and New Zealand economists exerted influence on economic thought and contributed to the economic life of their respective countries in the twentieth century. Besides surveying theorists and innovators, this book also considers some of the key expositors and builders of the academic economics profession in both countries. The book covers key economic events including the Great Depression, the Second World War, the post-war boom and the great inflation that overtook it and, lastly, the economic reform programmes that both Australia and New Zealand undertook in the 1980s. Through the interplay of economic events and economic thought, this book shows how Australasian economists influenced, to differing degrees, economic policy in their respective countries.

This book is of great importance to those who are interested in and study the history of economic thought, economic theory and philosophy, and philosophy of social science, as well as Australasian economics.

Alex Millmow is Associate Professor in economics at the Federation Business School, Federation University, Australia. Alex's research interests include the making of the Australian economics profession and the role of economic ideas in steering public policy.

Routledge History of Economic Thought
Edited by Mark Blaug

Co-Director Erasmus Center for History in Management and Economics Erasmus University, the Netherlands.

For a full list of titles in this series, please visit www.routledge.com/series/SE0124

A History of Australasian Economic Thought

Alex Millmow

Routledge
Taylor & Francis Group

LONDON AND NEW YORK

First published 2017 by Routledge

2 Park Square, Milton Park, Abingdon, Oxfordshire OX14 4RN
52 Vanderbilt Avenue, New York, NY 10017

Routledge is an imprint of the Taylor & Francis Group, an informa business

First issued in paperback 2019

British Library Cataloguing-in-Publication Data
A catalogue record for this book is available from the British Library

Library of Congress Cataloging-in-Publication Data
Names: Millmow, Alex, author.
Title: A history of Australasian economic thought / Alex Millmow.
Description: 1 Edition. | New York : Routledge, 2017. | Includes index.
Identifiers: LCCN 2017001822| ISBN 9781138861008 (hardback) |
ISBN 9781315716152 (ebook)
Subjects: LCSH: Economics–Australia–History. | Economics–
New Zealand–History.
Classification: LCC HB129.A2 M55 2017 | DDC 330.0993–dc23
LC record available at https://lccn.loc.gov/2017001822

ISBN: 978-1-138-86100-8 (hbk)
ISBN: 978-0-367-87269-4 (pbk)

Typeset in Times New Roman
by Cenveo Publisher Services

Contents

Acknowledgements

I would like to first thank the commissioning editors at Routledge, Emily Kindleysides and Laura Johnson, for suggesting that I undertake this study. John Lodewijks and Tony Endres made very useful suggestions about how I should tackle this major undertaking. Australian and New Zealand economic thought in the twentieth century is a broad canvas but I only had licence and means to paint a miniature. Some great Australian economists, namely, Max Corden, Geoff Harcourt, Joe Isaac, Marjorie Harper, Michael Schneider and Bob Wallace were shown the penultimate draft and all made extremely useful comments and corrections. None of the parties I have listed should be held responsible for what unfolds in the following pages.

I would also like to thank the Economic Society of Australia for providing some material assistance in undertaking this study. My dear friend, Philip O'Brien, did a wonderful job of editing and re-editing the drafts he was sent. Thanks to Joy Tucker for copy-editing the final draft.

Lastly, I would like to thank my colleagues at Federation Business School, particularly Anita Doraisami and Jerry Courvisanos, and, most especially, my family and beautiful wife, Amanda, for their support over the two years it took to write this book.

Preface

All the Defunct Economists...

The nineteenth-century essayist Walter Bagehot once remarked that 'No real Englishman, in his secret soul, was ever sorry for the death of a political economist.' It might be said that Bagehot's remark could also have applied to Australian and New Zealand economists in the early 1990s, given the community's disquiet over the broad-based economic reforms being undertaken at the time. In other times, the death of a major economist in either country was usually met with some regret: understandable in two countries where economic news is prominent in the media. There was, for instance, considerable sentiment when two of Australia's most illustrious economists, Fred Gruen and Herbert Cole 'Nugget' Coombs, died on the same day in October 1997. That was repeated, five years later, when two stalwarts of the Australian economics profession, Sir Leslie Melville and Heinz Arndt, died within days of each other, the latter tragically en route to the former's funeral where he was to deliver the eulogy. Equally, two leaders of the New Zealand economics profession, Sir Frank Holmes and Conrad Blyth, passed away within the space of 12 months in more recent times.

All six economists were celebrated for that fine tradition of engaging in public debate, fleeting back and forth between the worlds of theory and practice. For the most part, though, those hundreds of economists who worked in Australia and New Zealand over the twentieth century usually just faded away, unlamented not just among the populace, but even among the younger members of the profession. We might only recall their names, it seems, when leafing through the back issues of economic journals looking for an obscure reference. Alan Bollard, the biographer of A. W. H. (Bill) Phillips, tells how Te Papa, the National Museum of New Zealand, rejected the idea of exhibiting one of Phillips's original, fully restored MONIAC machines. There would have been more interest, he argued, had Phillips been a famous sportsman or mountaineer.

Of course, the mere fact that some economists have been published guarantees them a measure of posterity. Some of the greats in either country have done far better, having had theorems, diagrams, theses, professorial chairs, books, rooms, memorial lectures, libraries, foundations, fellowships and scholarships – even university buildings – named after them. This is fitting praise in two countries where economics and economic policy have had a strong influence in nation-building. This book attempts not just to honour the great but also some of those lesser mortals, who have added colour and spice, mixed with a tinge of disappointment, to the story of Australasian economic thought in the twentieth century.

Introduction

Ideas are the ultimate realities.

Edward Shann, cited in La Nauze, 1935

In February 1951 Professor Gerald Firth of the University of Tasmania wrote to a colleague with some bad news: Australia's then greatest living economist, a thrice-decorated ANZAC soldier, Lyndhurst Falkiner Giblin, lay dying in a Hobart hospital. 'I am afraid Giblin is in very poor shape,' wrote Firth,

> his memory has finally let him down, and he is furious about it. Nor does he suffer his physical infirmities with resignation, though God they are serious enough... he tends to be upset by serious visitors, and it is rather a problem to know whether to go up and see him – but I go and gossip once a fortnight or so, and he seems to like it. Very depressing, for he was a great man... people have been prophesying his end and for so long now that one cannot never [sic] be certain that he will not miraculously recover at least to a less feeble condition, [sic] But at present it is pretty grim.[1]

Giblin told an old student: 'everything is moving to zero: use of legs, arms, fingers, voice and mind'. He died five days later. One of his closest friends, Douglas Copland, who had known him as a mentor and counsellor, was so affected he refused to speak for three days. Roland Wilson (1951) hailed Giblin as 'the fabulous old man' of Australian economics. It was a fitting tribute, although Giblin had no economics degree. Copland (1958), too, lavished praise on Giblin for his innovative theoretical and applied work. While he shunned the term 'economics', Giblin believed that this new priesthood of social scientists had a duty to improve to the plight of the working man. For Australia, the shambling giant of Giblin is an appropriate place to begin our story since he argued that modern Australian economics began in 1924 (Coleman *et al.*, 2006).

In the year before Giblin's death, Copland, then Vice Chancellor at the Australian National University, had given an address to mark the 25th anniversary of the founding of the Victorian Branch of the Economic Society of Australia and New Zealand. The Victorian Branch was then the strongest in Australasia with Copland the driving force behind it. The idea of a society was modelled on the Royal Economic Society. It would quickly be followed by branches in all six states of the Commonwealth of Australia and in the main cities of New Zealand.[2] Copland, looked back proudly on the first quarter-century of the Society, noted how the economics profession, still small in size, had boldly 'gone over the top' in confronting public policy challenges. Copland noted that the distinguishing feature of interwar Australian economists had been their tendency of 'seeing the economy as a whole and of realising the possibility of instituting policy to counteract maladjustment within the economy' (Copland, 1951, 16–17). He had misgivings, though, about the new generation of Australians, believing them a little grandiose in their aspirations. He warned how the 'more extreme devotees' of planning were 'much too confident of their ability to control the powerful forces arranged against them' (ibid., 25). Apart from an illusion of their omniscience, they had not considered the degree of public acceptance needed for the new Keynesian doctrine, especially from the business sector. Events would bear this out. Maintaining the economy at overfull employment – that is, with more jobs than workers to fill them – created problems with labour discipline, supply bottlenecks and impeded the mobility of resources necessary for the creation of new industries.

Like many of his peers Copland keenly felt that he had not kept pace with the technical advances in the discipline, especially the formalism that came with the post-war quantitative revolution. This pattern of falling behind would prove to be a recurrent one felt by every generation of economists. Another high-profile Australian economist, Heinz Arndt, also regretted his lack of formal training in mathematics but was still a frequent contributor to the *Economic Record* (Hughes, 2002, 479). At the time the post-war generation of Australasian economists was Anglocentric, heading for Oxbridge or London to learn their trade. They would, in turn, feel left behind by advances in methodology and econometric power exhibited by younger peers who had begun to gravitate towards North America. One graphic example of this is Burgess Cameron of the Australian National University (ANU). After earlier training at Sydney University, he undertook a doctorate at Cambridge on Leontief input–output matrices and planning using Australian data. When he returned to the ANU he took the Economics I class, one renowned for its rigour. As Dean, Cameron recruited brilliant, young, mathematically trained economists which would eventually make ANU the leading economics school in Australia. By the late 1970s these younger economists were beginning to find Cameron's style of economics old hat and pushed for an end to his beloved first-year course. They also made 'pointed remarks' to Arndt about his inability to teach economics in the modern mathematical style.[3] The detractors were unaware that Arndt had encouraged John Harsanyi to break into game theory. Both men were taken off teaching and put out to pasture.

This entrée serves as just a small part of the rich, engaging tapestry of Australian and New Zealand economics in the twentieth century. I will add a little more. It's a little-known fact that in 1919, just before he wrote *The Economic Consequences of the Peace*, J. M. Keynes was the official examiner for students undertaking economics examinations at the University of New Zealand. He granted first-class honours to one student who would, not much later, became a professor of economics. In his examiner's report Keynes thought the scripts were overall 'very dull'. 'It would be better', he suggested, 'if Economics were treated as a more lively subject, one having a controversial relation to current events and which candidates were quite entailed to express their own sentiments, even at the expense of error and some foolishness creeping in' (cited in Blyth, 2007, 153).

It is hoped that this book has been written with the same verve, trying to capture some of the domestic wisdom exhibited by Australian and New Zealand economists over the last century. This book intends therefore to examine some of the contributions to knowledge by Australian and New Zealand economists in the context of their own economy. Craufurd Goodwin (2002), who has written two books on the history of Australian economic enquiry, suggested that if further study was contemplated on the subject it should consider a broader canvas than just surveying the work and thought of local economists. This book attempts such a task by considering how politicians, economic journalists and some social scientists exerted influence on economic thought or, at least, its dissemination. Goodwin (ibid., 3) also helped the future historian of economic ideas by asking one to consider how two vibrant economies were built far from Europe and, second, how economic and social justice was achieved in these two now ethnically diverse nations.

What this book is about

The aim of this book is to survey Australasian economic thought from the mid-1920s through to the end of the twentieth century. It is therefore a study of economic ideas and thought that sprang from Australian and New Zealand economists in that century. It considers the interplay of economic events and economic thought and how this could affect government policy. Sometimes Australian and New Zealand economic policy has been shaped by changes in economic thought. Sometimes radical departures in policy were triggered by events and necessity. Keynes said that the power of vested interests is not as powerful as that of the sweep of economic ideas, but this account will argue that, for Australia and New Zealand, it took some effort to overcome stubborn interests. Indeed, for New Zealand it has been argued that the influence of university economists on economic policy has been insignificant; vested interests argued that protection was critical for nation-building (Brooke *et al.*, 2016, 16). An expatriate New Zealand economist, when revisiting his homeland, aptly described economic policy there as 'government of producers, by producers, for producers' (Condliffe, 1969, 116). In this light the comprehensive neoliberal reforms that these two economies undertook in the 1980s might be interpreted as one group of newer, powerful interests supplanting older vested interests rather than a wave of economic ideas sweeping over the ramparts (Brooke *et al.*, 2016). In other words, the underlying distribution of wealth, or the pattern of rents and to whom they accrued, was more important in understanding trade and industry policy than calculating welfare losses from intervention and protection. Both Australia and New Zealand had a conservative social welfare function, a preoccupation with keeping the income shares between labour and capital constant (Corden, 1974, 107–12). Arguably this mentality sprang from their respective economic histories, especially the 1890s Depression and then the Great Depression and the response by the authorities with defensive or protective strategies (White, 1992).

A related task in this story is to outline the history and development of the academic economics profession in both countries. So, besides surveying theorists and innovators, this book will also cover the key expositors and builders of the profession in both countries. The period under review covers key economic events including the Great Depression, the Second World War, the pursuit of full employment, the post-war boom, the onset of the great inflation and the economic reform programmes both countries undertook in the 1980s. All of these events took place amid a growing mobilisation of economics expertise. It covers, therefore, the period of the Keynesian consensus to the neoclassical resurgence when economists in both countries concurrently argued for a completely new model for their economies.

In all these struggles, whether for greater or lesser control over economic activity or in encouraging freer trade, Australasian economists have, like prophets in their native land, never been popular within their own communities. This was consistent with two striking aspects of Australasian society, namely, a general distrust of markets and competition, and a strong preference for egalitarianism (Caves and Krause, 1984, 2). This distrust of the price mechanism led to a proclivity for regulation and control. In New Zealand, too, both governments and the people 'do not like the operation of free markets' because they were perceived as 'the economic bogey' producing instability of prices and an unfair distribution of income. Consequently 'pressure groups attempt to manage or even dispense with markets' (Blyth, 1964, 15). It meant that the efficiency version of the economists' competitive model never went further than 'their drawing board' (Blyth, 1966, 44).

This distrust went much deeper. In 1930 the Australian historian W. K. Hancock remarked that 'the Australians have always assumed that economic problems are simple, and have resented those classifications and rewards which suggest that some men have a higher class of intelligence than those of the majority'. In that light Hancock observed that 'Australians have always disliked scientific economics (still more) scientific economists' (86). The populace embodied that disdain for those 'exasperating calculators' by renouncing their argument that protection had reached its economic limit by 1928. A New Zealand observer (Leatham, 1939) also remarked how his countrymen 'distrust, even despise theory' and prided themselves on being practical. This meant that the social and economic philosophy underpinning policy in that country, at least until 1984, was makeshift, only loosely connected with intellectual influences. In New Zealand, finance ministers have played a significant role in shaping economic policy. Here one notes, in particular, Robert Muldoon who had his hand on the economic levers as Finance Minister during the period 1967–72 and again during 1975–84 when he also served as Prime Minister. An accountant by training, Muldoon exerted a formidable presence. He dismissed economic theory with his remark, 'We can do without the disruption of academic theories which, because they are non-specific, seem to make sense until they are applied specifically to the real world', and, in another instance, spoke of having 'no intention of letting efficient industries go to the wall for the sake of a theory' (cited in Brooke *et al.*, 2016, 16). He was emphatic that homespun, do-it-yourself economics was best and that 'you cannot take a blueprint from some other country, slap it on this country, and expect it to work' (Muldoon, 1985, 163). Muldoon's successor, the Labour Party's Roger Douglas, Finance Minister in the Lange Government from 1984–8, did precisely that. He had become frustrated with extensive controls and regulations that enveloped the economy and took a radical alternative to his predecessor's meddling; in one fell swoop the entire policy framework of the past half-century was unceremoniously dumped (Bertram, 2009, 558).

Australians, too, sometimes felt that economic problems could be solved by practical men instead of 'theorists'. When Giblin, for example, was about to take a position in Melbourne, after delivering some home truths about the Tasmanian economy, one local paper churlishly declared that he would not be missed.[4] In Western Australia, the leading economic authority Edward Shann faced pressures to remove him from his university position because of his role in an economic stabilisation plan and his work as economic advisor to one of Australia's banks. Australians who lived through the Depression never entirely forgave their economists for cutting wages in 1931. When Copland, the leading influence behind the 1931 stabilisation plan, died one newspaper marked his passing with the headline 'Wage cut man dies'.

In the early 1920s economics was a Cinderella science; by the end of that decade young students were flocking to enrol in it. The establishment of a formal association of economists in both Australia and New Zealand occurred in 1925; relatively rapid introduction of formal courses in economics followed. From there began the systemic study and teaching of economic science in both countries. Ideally, the Economic Society of Australia and New Zealand would serve as an umbrella organisation for economists in both countries until the 1960s when New Zealand economists, dissatisfied with the Society and ambitious for their own perspective, broke away to form their own association.

Economics in Australasia, of course, predates this arbitrary beginning of 1925. An earlier period when economics was better known as political economy, has been adequately covered by Peter Groenewegen and Bruce McFarlane (1990) in their national history of Australian economic thought and by Goodwin (1966). Both accounts looked at the Australian tradition of economic heretics, cranks and amateurs. Groenewegen and McFarlane focused on 16 twentieth-century economists up to the 1980s, four drawn from the interwar era, seven from the post-war period, four so-called economist-advisors and one statistician-economist. There were some striking omissions of both individuals and issues but, as the authors admit, their study could not be more comprehensive because of space limitations. Marjorie Harper (1991, 377) found their account too biographical and that they did not fully demonstrate where Australian economists had been theoretically imaginative. She believed that, despite this attempt, there was still 'a fairly open field' for more work in the history of Australian economic thought after 1950.

This book serves to address that gap but also dips into some of the economic thought that originated from New Zealand economists in the twentieth century. In doing so we will examine the proposition from one observer that the contribution of New Zealand-based university economists has tended to be 'imitative and marginal' (Easton, 1997, 279). We will discover that, in fact, sometimes interesting and important work could be undertaken in the periphery and, moreover, that theoretical work undertaken in the periphery need not be on peripheral issues. In short, this study argues that there is more than enough in terms of controversy, personalities and contributions to justify a survey of Australasian economic thought from the 1920s onwards.

Why this book matters

The upcoming centenary in 2025 of the Economic Society of Australia and its house journal, the *Economic Record*, will celebrate the establishment of economics as a professional pursuit within Australia and New Zealand. In 2016 the New Zealand Association of Economists celebrated the 50th anniversary of its house journal *New Zealand Economic Papers* (Buckle and Creedy, 2016). Nearly 100 years on, Australasian economics has serious bandwidth, having made significant contributions in the fields of macroeconomics, agricultural economics, econometrics, wage and labour theory, tax theory, demand analysis, economic history, immigration economics, the history of economic thought, tariffs and trade theory, the latter including the 'dependent economy model'. Some of the major theoretical innovations sprang from Australasian-based problems or circumstances such as handling (or mishandling) resource booms and the absorption of both immigration and capital flows. It was the same, too, with economic policy for practices and conventions uniquely moulded in Australasia: artefacts such as the basic wage, the Higher Education Contribution Scheme, the Superannuation Guarantee, the Productivity Commission, the Fiscal Responsibility Act and inflation targeting, to name a ready half-dozen. There was also the odd lonely theorist – such as, say, one Donald Lamberton – breaking new ground in fields such as information economics, or Harsanyi – on game theory.

Less inspiring in our story, though, was that both countries in the post-war era zealously practised comprehensive import licensing to deal with trade imbalances even though many economists were strongly opposed to it. J. O. N. Perkins (1977, 1) found that a dominant thread in macroeconomic policy in Australia was the 'remarkable disinclination to use the market'. Monetary policy, for example, relied upon quantitative controls on credit rather than changing interest rates (Wallace, 1974). That tendency, to disallow the price mechanism full play in the allocation of resources, was entrenched in markets for agricultural produce in both countries. Marketing boards made possible a baroque form of 'home price' supports, usually above world prices, to bolster and stabilise agrarian income (Sieper, 1982).

They were complemented by producer boards with monopoly powers controlling the export of agricultural exports. Ian McLean (1978, 14–15), a New Zealand politician with economics training, colourfully described his country:

> as a market economy where markets are seldom permitted to operate efficiently, together with a centrally-planned economy without a central plan. The allocation of resources is to a large extent determined neither by the market mechanisms nor government decision, but by historical patterns fossilised in institutional procedures.

Imitators or creators?

While this book offers a survey of Australasian economic thought from 1920s until 2000, funnelled through institutions such as the Economic Society and the Association of New Zealand Economists, it has been argued that the nationality of economic ideas is now almost a meaningless concept given that ideas have become 'essentially international' (Backhouse, 2002, 307). It is true, too, that the history of economics and economic philosophy in Australasia largely involves the transmission and cultivation of ideas from Europe and North America; in that respect, Australasia has been 'a net importer of economic theory by a very wide margin' (Johnson, 1971, 25). One of Australia's most respected economists, Sir Leslie Melville, reflected that, apart from Trevor Swan and Colin Clark, Australian economists had 'made little contribution to the theory of economics', but had, in some cases, been 'brilliant' at adaption (Cornish, 1993, 455). It is also true that Australasian economics is renowned for its capacity to draw upon the best theoretical and empirical work from abroad and to adapt and apply that knowledge to local economic and social issues facing policy-makers. Lodewijks (2001, 2) notes that, in terms of a cohesive theoretical tradition, there has been no Australian school of economics. Coleman (2005, 5) suggests that Australian economics is derivative, 'just a provincial receptacle for what is being produced overseas'. This echoes the view, too, of Clem Tisdell, one of Australia's most prolific economists, that, when it comes to economic thought, Australasia lived on borrowed ideas: 'There appears to be very little independent self-generated contribution... most of it is in applying overseas material, with a lag' (cited in Dollery and Wallis, 1996, 28). Tisdell also laments that there was a lag in responding to new pockets of economic research such as 'law and economics' or 'personnel economics'.

Corden has noted that, whatever its authenticity or originality, the Australian economics profession 'rates well and does not need to apologise for anything'; the fact that it was derivative did not make it any different from other economic professions (cited in Groenewegen, 1989, 103).

In his survey of Australian economic thought and economic policy, Corden (1968), too, was struck by the absence of research in areas such as transport economics or urbanisation; strange for an island continent with a high degree of urbanisation. Another gap was industrial economics until a compendium volume was prepared on the subject (Hunter, 1963), along with competition policy (Hunter, 1961). On urbanisation, Max Neutze, a New Zealand Rhodes scholar who undertook a doctorate at Oxford on location economics, came to the rescue, setting up the Centre on Urban Research at an Australian university as well as penning two books on urban economics. In some cases, branches such as law and economics or public choice theory failed to take root and had little practicable weight in shaping policy in Australia (Pincus, 2014). Monetarism and Austrian economics generally met with a lukewarm response from Australasian university economists.

Groenewegen and McFarlane (1990) argued that there was, though, an Australian school in terms of the research issues selected and the mode of analysis, but that it was fading away by the 1980s. We might still ask, though, whether there has been, at times, a reverse flow of ideas or practices from Australia and New Zealand to the rest of the world. Peter Lloyd (2014, 38) credits Australian economists with making a 'distinguished' intellectual contribution to the measurement and analysis of the costs of industry assistance more than any other country. Larry Krause (Caves and Krause, 1984) echoed this when Brookings did a survey of the Australian economy in the 1980s praising, in particular, the 'excellent work' of the Industries Assistance Commission. In more recent times there has been outstanding work assessing the net benefit of privatisation and also immigration. Most of that thought and analysis originated from the cloisters, with the occasional contribution from public service or 'inside' economists. We can add, though, one overriding fact: Australasian economists are renowned for being better at applied work than theory. Giblin put it this way:

> Australian economists are a peculiar tribe. Rarely are they nourished by the pure milk of the word. Mostly they have been advisers to governments for many years – permanently or intermittently, publicly or privately. Governments do not love them but are inclined to believe them honest… They are frequently more practical and realistic than businessmen… They are resented of course by sectional business interests. The word of complaint or abuse is 'academic'; but, in truth, they are the least academic of God's creatures.
>
> Cited in Hytten, 1960, 154

In other words, Australasian economists, certainly in the interwar years, were not ivory tower figures but a practically focused group intent, as many of them would say, upon 'making a difference' not just to the understanding of the real world but also to outcomes. This book will show that ethic has been carried on by later generations of Australasian economists.

The structure of this book

Apart from the Economic Society this book uses, as a narrative device, the *Economic Record*, one of the world's oldest economic journals and, for many years, the only outlet for Australasian economists. It was widely read, and the notes and announcements at the back of each issue announced the comings and goings of members of the economics profession there. In the twentieth century there has been a passing parade of Australasian economists. To help the reader we focus upon leading Australian and New Zealand economists as markers in the telling of the story of economic thought in this part of the world. Other characters, drawn from the parade, merit only a brief mention but always with an accompanying justification.

The first chapter sets the scope and limitations of this study emphasising that we are examining the economic thought of Australian and New Zealand economists in the context of their economy. It also discusses prior literature in the field. In Chapter 2 there is a brief survey of the idiosyncratic nature of economic life in Australia and New Zealand, including the unique institutions and conventions that characterised those economies. This is followed by some detail on the formation of the economics profession in both countries which took shape in a trans-Tasman body known as the Economic Society of Australia and New Zealand. It was a bi-nation society because the number of economists in either country at the time was small.

In Chapter 3 we discuss the first theoretical contributions and controversial propositions raised by Australasian economists to draw the attention of the outside world. Chapter 4 discusses how both countries dealt with the Great Depression and how Australian economists, in particular, were regarded by the international economics community as pioneers in economic stabilisation. New Zealand's response to the Depression was less coherent, even contradictory at times, but economists had announced their presence. Chapter 5 discusses how Keynesian ideas of macroeconomic management came to both countries. In Australia it was a clear, direct and authentic application of Keynesian approaches to policy guided by academic expertise. In New Zealand that process was more obscure, more a pragmatic and political response to an economic emergency. Chapter 6 surveys the contribution to economic thought by Australian and New Zealand economists during the war and immediate post-war years. These pioneering contributions to economic thought were repeated in the latter half of the 1950s, particularly in Australia. Chapter 7 recounts how Australia and New Zealand's growing research strength in economics in the 1950s came about through a combination of good fortune: by attracting human capital, more state funding and sponsorship from like-minded institutions, as well as a greater professionalism within universities towards encouraging research. Chapter 8 observes how the 1960s was a decade of growth and maturity for the economics profession in Australasia, with economists believing that their discipline was a force for good in society. This exuberance was cut short by the new challenge of stagflation and structural disrepair which Australia and New Zealand found themselves facing during the 1970s. This and some of the policy responses to it are discussed in Chapter 9.

Chapter 10 discusses the almost breathtaking economic reform processes of the 1980s and the involvement – or, in New Zealand's case, non-involvement – of university economists in that story. The last chapter discusses the change in professional economic opinion in Australia and New Zealand during the 1990s and how a new political economy was set in place in each country. It arrived with theoretical developments in certain areas and with some heated reaction to the neoliberal reforms.

Notes

1 Firth to Prest, 12 February 1951, Prest Papers, University of Melbourne Archives (UMA).
2 In 1970 a branch of the Economic Society was also established in Port Moresby in Papua New Guinea. That country was then an Australian protectorate and there was considerable coverage given to the economic concerns of that territory. One leading economist there was the Australian Anthony Clunies Ross, who occupied the chair in economics at the University of Papua New Guinea from 1967–75. Among the other staff were Ross Garnaut, David Vines and Chris Gregory (the anthropologist).
3 Arndt oral transcript 1990, Australian National University, p. 13.
4 The New Zealand economist, A. G. B. Fisher was more accurate in saying that Tasmania had suffered a 'disability... through the drain to the mainland of the best Tasmanian blood'. Fisher to Copland 1928, Copland Papers, National Library of Australia (NLA).

References

Backhouse, R. 2002, *The Penguin History of Economics*, London: Penguin.
Bertram, G. 2009, 'The New Zealand economy 1900–2000', in G. Byrnes (ed.), *The New Oxford History of New Zealand*, Oxford: Oxford University Press.
Blyth, C. A. 1964, *The Future of Manufacturing in New Zealand*, London: Oxford University Press.
Blyth, C. A. 1966, 'The special case: the political economy of New Zealand', *Political Science*, 18: 38–51.
Blyth, C. A. 2007, 'John Maynard Keynes: external examiner for the University of New Zealand, 1919', *History of Economics Review*, 46: 151–62.
Brooke, G., A. Endres and A. Rogers, 2016, 'Does New Zealand economics have a useful past? The example of trade policy and economic development', *New Zealand Economic Papers*, 50(3): 281–302.
Buckle, R. A. and J. Creedy, 2016, 'Fifty years of New Zealand economic papers; 1966–2015', *New Zealand Economic Papers*, 50(3): 234–60.
Caves, R. and L. Krause (eds), 1984, *The Australian Economy: The View from the North*, Sydney: Allen and Unwin.
Coleman, W. 2005, 'A conversation with Murray Kemp', *History of Economics Review*, 41: 1–16.
Coleman, W., S. Cornish and A. Hagger, 2006, *Giblin's Platoon: The Trials and Triumph of the Economist in Australian Public Life*, Canberra: Australian National University Press.
Condliffe, J. B. 1969, 'The economic outlook for New Zealand', *New Zealand Economic Papers*, 3(1): 5–14.
Copland, D. B. 1951, *Inflation and Expansion*, Melbourne: Cheshire.
Copland, D. B. 1958, 'L. F. Giblin and the frontier of research on the Australian economy', *Australian Journal of Science*, 21: 120–5.
Corden, W. M. 1968, *Australian Economic Policy Discussion: A Survey*, Melbourne: Melbourne University Press.
Corden, W. M. 1974, *Trade Policy and Economic Welfare*, Oxford: Clarendon Press.
Cornish, S. 1993, 'Sir Leslie Melville: an interview', *Economic Record*, 69(207): 437–57.
Dollery, B. and J. Wallis, 1996, 'An interview with Clem Tisdell', *International Journal of Social Economics*, 22(4): 20–48.

Easton, B. 1997, *In Stormy Seas: The Post War New Zealand Economy*, Dunedin: University of Otago.

Goodwin, C. D. 1966, *Economic Enquiry in Australia*, Durham, NC: Duke University Press.

Goodwin, C. 2002, 'Economic enquiry in Australia: reflections after 41 years', *History of Economics Review*, 35: 1–3.

Groenewegen, P. 1989, 'The development of economics in Australia: a tale of two centuries', *Economic Papers*, 8(1): 97–108.

Groenewegen, P. and B. McFarlane, 1990, *A History of Australian Economic Thought*, London: Routledge.

Hancock, W. K. 1930. *Australia*, London: E. Benn.

Harper, M. 1991, 'Review of P. Groenewegen and B. McFarlane', *A History of Australian Economic Thought*', *Economic Record*, 67(199): 377–8.

Hughes, H. 2002, 'Heinz W. Arndt: economist and public intellectual', *Economic Record* 78(243): 479–89.

Hunter, A. 1961, 'Restrictive practices and monopolies in Australia', *Economic Record*, 37(77): 25–49.

Hunter, A. 1963, *The Economics of Australian Industry*, Melbourne: Melbourne University Press.

Hytten, T. 1960, in D. B. Copland (ed.), *Giblin: The Scholar and the Man*, Melbourne: Cheshire.

Johnson, H. 1971, 'Reflections on the current state of economics', *Australian Economic Papers*, 10(16): 1–11.

La Nauze, J. 1935, 'Edward Shann', *On Dit*, 21 June.

Leatham, S. 1939, 'Policies and trends in New Zealand', *Economic Record*, 15(1): 39–53.

Lloyd, P. 2014, 'The path of protection in Australia since federation', *History of Economics Review*, 59: 21–43.

Lodewijks, J. 2001, 'Educating Australian economists', *Journal of Economic and Social Policy*, 5(2): 1–9.

McLean, I. 1978, *The Future for New Zealand Agriculture: Economic Strategies for the 1980s*, Wellington: Fourth Estate.

Muldoon, R. D. 1985, *The New Zealand Economy: A Personal View*, Auckland: Endeavour Press.

Perkins, J. O. N. 1977, 'Lessons of macroeconomic policy in Australia', in P. Drake and J. Nieuwenhuysen (eds), *Australian Economic Policy*, Melbourne: Melbourne University Press.

Pincus, J. J. 2014, 'Public choice theory had negligible effect on Australian microeconomic policy, 1970s to 2000s', *History of Economics Review*, 59: 82–93.

Sieper, E. 1982, *Rationalising Rustic Regulation*, St Leonards: Centre for Independent Studies.

Wallace, R. H. 1974, 'The changing role of monetary policy since 1956', *Economics*, September, 44–9.

White, C. 1992, *Mastering Risk: Environment, Markets and Politics in Australian Economic History*, Oxford: Oxford University Press.

Wilson, R. 1951, 'James Bristock Brigden: a tribute', *Economic Record*, 27: 1–10.

Wilson, R. 1976, 'L. F. Giblin: a man for all seasons', *Search*, 7(7): 307–15.

1   Setting the scene

The purpose of this short chapter is briefly to survey earlier efforts at documenting the history of Australasian economic thought. Prompted by the Australian Bicentenary in 1988, Groenewegen and McFarlane's *A History of Australian Economic Thought* (1990) remains, until now, the only attempt to cover the contribution to theory by twentieth-century Australian economists. A predecessor was Craufurd Goodwin's omnibus *Economic Enquiry in Australia* (1966), which covered Australian economic thought until around 1929, much of it covering figures drawn from the underworld.[1] It was lavishly praised for its comprehensiveness, with one reviewer saying that its quality 'puts Australian scholarship to shame' (La Nauze, 1966, 473). In that same year the economic historian Geoffrey Blainey wrote *The Tyranny of Discipline* (1966), which evocatively summed up how geography and remoteness had shaped the economic development of Australia. Other recent short accounts covering Australian, and indeed Australasian, economic thought appear in encyclopaedic handbooks such as Coleman (2015) and Cornish (2008). Heinz Arndt (1987) wrote a little-known encyclopaedic entry entitled 'Antipodean economics'.[2] The neglect of any 'comprehensive investigation' of New Zealand's scholarship in economic thought was first raised by Hight (1939). Since then there still has been no broad account of New Zealand economic thought except for a short working paper by Gary Hawke and Ralph Lattimore (2005). John Nevile and Paul Dalziel (2013) briefly surveyed New Zealand economic thought from a post-Keynesian perspective. Tony Endres has written extensively on the contribution of New Zealand economists, with a particular focus upon theoreticians during the interwar years. A collaborative paper (2016) written by Geoffrey Brooke, Endres and Alan Rogers, which surveyed New Zealand economists' thought on her trade and economic development until 1984, is an excellent start to gauge that country's contribution to economic thought in the twentieth century.

There was also an anthology, or survey, of the 'state of the art' of Australian economics undertaken during the late 1970s, a project commissioned by the Australian Academy of the Social Sciences. Fred Gruen regarded this as updating the work by Corden in his *Australian Economic Policy Discussion: A Survey* (1968), which had been prepared at the request of the American Economics Association. The Gruen project, comprising three volumes over the period

1978–83, was also completed for the benefit of economists working in related fields: partly for postgraduates but also for stimulating research in neglected areas. Some of the subjects surveyed reflected the prevailing concerns at the time of the study, such as 'Protection', 'Inflation' and 'Radical Economics'. The second volume included a chapter in which Gruen (1979) wrote, in part, upon the economic opinion of the Australian economics profession. Gruen's personal preference in the project was reflected in a survey on poverty and income redistribution. In a review of the third volume of Gruen's project, John Hatch noted that contributions by Australian economists in the theoretical domain was essentially duplicating the work done by overseas scholars. Economics as a subject, as Backhouse noted, 'travels well'. This meant that contributors to the volumes had to confront the problem of whether to empathise 'the great bulk of original theory, or the small and often relatively unimportant local contributions' (Hatch, 1984, 390). In 2003 the Gruen exercise was essentially repeated by McAllister *et al.* (2003). It is interesting to contrast the areas of economic theory surveyed over the past 30 years, a period when Australian economic policy underwent a philosophical change. Some areas such as international economics, labour economics, immigration and macroeconomics remain perennials but others such as radical economics were one-offs. By the new millennium the research focus had switched to new areas such as privatisation, competition policy and innovation while subjects such as inflation lapsed. Appendix 2 (this volume) presents the contents of these three major surveys of Australian economic thought. Norman (2007) has comprehensively looked at the contribution of Australian economists but strictly from a policy impact perspective.

Which economists should this book survey? John King's *A Biographical Dictionary of Australian and New Zealand Economists* (2007) suggests a taxonomy we might use: such a work should include major contributors who were born in Australasia or had made significant theoretic contributions while working there. Peter Groenewegen has a similar approach in defining what constitutes an Australasian economist (1989, 106). What, though, of Australasian economists who made all their notable work overseas, names such as John Harsanyi, Kelvin Lancaster, Arthur Smithies, Ronald Meek, John McMillan and Peter C. B. Phillips? Should we include them? King's approach suggests not. Others who did make contributions abroad, such as Geoff Harcourt, Max Corden and A. W. H. (Bill) Phillips, are included because they spent a fair part of their careers in Australasia – especially the first two. Indeed, it was sometimes argued that some economists such as Corden, Harcourt or the econometrician Adrian Pagan went abroad, and often, 'to improve their understanding of the economics of Australia' (Hatch and Rogers, 1997, 97). A captive of wanderlust in his youth, Bill Phillips yearned for the blue skies, mountains and clean air of New Zealand before returning there in 1970.[3] Another issue here is choice of material. Should we cover contributions to Australasian economic thought and policy or to the body of economic thought overall? The ambit of the book proposes to cover both aspects.

In selecting the most eminent twentieth-century economists from both Australia and New Zealand, we can refer to Mark Blaug's *Who's Who in*

Economics (1999) to disconcertingly discover that Australasian economists such as Max Corden, John Creedy or Peter C. B. Phillips are not listed under Australia or New Zealand simply because they were not born there. However, we are helped in our task by the respective economist associations in both countries, who have already identified their greatest twentieth-century theorists. Since 1987 the Economic Society of Australia has annually presented a Distinguished Fellow Award to one of its members who has made an impact or contributed towards the development of economics while based in Australia. At the time of writing there have been 29 recipients of this award.[4] Then, in 2004, the New Zealand Association of Economists announced its first four Distinguished Fellows. So far, there have been 19 recipients of this award for meritorious work undertaken in the twentieth century. Its belated nature means that theorists such as Richard Manning, who died in 1989, could not be honoured for his work on labour economics, search theory and international economics *inter alia*. Appendix 1 (this volume) lists the names of recipients and their areas of expertise for both societies. The two lists include figures specialising in econometrics, economic history, theory and applied areas of economics. As mentioned, the Economic Society award has a residency criterion, insisting that those elected did the bulk of his or her work in Australia, whereas the New Zealand award can go to New Zealanders plying their career abroad. This reflects the fact that many New Zealand economists went abroad to further their studies or take up appointments and never returned home. Take, as an example, Peter C. B. Phillips, one of the world's leading econometricians. Currently he is Professor of Economics at the Cowles Foundation for Research in Economics at Yale University. He took his first degree and Master's at Auckland University before leaving to study at the London School of Economics (LSE). As an Alumni Distinguished Professor he holds a part-time position in the Department of Economics at Auckland University, visiting there two or three times a year. The diaspora of New Zealand's finest economists is clearly evident when one sees that all but three Distinguished Fellows are living and working in New Zealand. One of those honoured, Peter Lloyd, has been recognised by both societies for his work on trade theory.

This book argues that Australasian economists were, for most of the twentieth century, a pragmatic, non-doctrinaire community of scholars, content not to challenge the fundamental parameters that underpinned their economies' conduct and performance. New Zealand economists were more free trade-orientated but aware that political realities trimmed their aspirations. Nation-building held sway before economic efficiency; responding to events, including economic crises, mattered more than theorising. Australian economists adopted economic theory and practice to suit their respective country's needs and discarded it when no longer relevant. Agricultural price supports were extensively employed to stabilise agrarian incomes (Weststrate, 1959). At the turn of the twentieth century Australian economists saw that the tariff, up to a point, could play a vital part in the overall development of their economy; they were more interested in trade liberalisation than free trade, *per se*. By contrast, in New Zealand all the economists were, from the outset, opposed to protection because of its impact upon the export sector, domestic living costs and overall efficiency. Import licensing and exchange control, first used in 1938 by New Zealand and by Australia in 1952, was regarded as a necessary evil by economists, much better than deflating economic activity to quell import growth. In New Zealand import licensing was used to protect the trade account but also as a form of mercantilism, to preserve foreign exchange and promote manufacturing (Brooke *et al.*, 2016). Economists in both countries regretted their use primarily because it pointed to a fundamental disequilibrium within the economy better addressed by a devaluation.

However, not all economists went by convention. In New Zealand, Bill Such and Wolfgang Rosenberg were ardent defenders of import controls, planning and industrialisation. Rosenberg also opposed New Zealand becoming a full member of the International Monetary Fund in 1961, suggesting that it would mean a loss of economic sovereignty – especially in maintaining a high level of economic activity (Hawke and Wijewardane, 1972; Tay, 2007, 580). Once New Zealand became addicted to foreign capital, Rosenberg feared that it would need to get involved in restructuring to engage in export-led development, which he saw as destroying everything that has put New Zealand in the vanguard of social achievement.[5] One of his books, *A Guidebook to New Zealand's Future* (1968), was savaged by a departmental colleague for its insistence upon nationalism and autarky (Wooding, 1968). Rosenberg's other departmental colleagues at Canterbury were also critical of his doctrines. After 33 years as an unrepentant defender of Fortress New Zealand, Rosenberg, perhaps his country's most publicly known heterodox economist, retired from the University of Canterbury urging his colleagues to 'turn on to a fairer road' (Tay, 2007, 23). It met with no response.

University economists were vocal enough if they felt the economy needed a policy correction or structural reform. In the post-war era the central banks of both countries convened regular meetings of university economists to evaluate the performances of their respective economies. Given that both economies were small, relatively closed yet highly dependent upon primary good exports to furnish sufficient foreign exchange to finance imports, any deterioration in the terms of trade usually triggered remedial action. It was only in the 1970s – with the breakdown of the Bretton Woods Agreement, rising and persistent inflation, stalling growth and poor productivity – that the first stirrings of major alternatives were voiced. Before then there was little collective agitation for wholesale economic reform, though some economists from the 1960s onward were beginning to quantify the static and dynamic costs of protection and, in New Zealand's case, an over-reliance upon farm exports.

Before the 1970s Australia performed more creditably than is commonly believed. On that score, the book will contest the now popular view that the post-Federation 'Australian Settlement', to use political journalist Paul Kelly's (1992) term, was inimical to growth and development over much of the twentieth century. By 'Australian Settlement' Kelly refers to the adoption of the White Australia policy, tariff protection, centralised wage determination, state paternalism and the imperial benevolence of being part of the British Empire. Kelly was adamant that 'Australia's economic problem is a 90 year problem' and dismissed the idea that it was a 1960s or 1970s phenomenon; 'The malaise', he insisted, 'stretched back much further, to the post-Federation settlement' (ibid.: 13).

While seductive to some, Kelly's panoramic sweep is misleading. It was true that there was a period of economic stagnation, but it dated from the 1890s Depression, not Federation. It ushered in a period of below average growth which was to last until the Second World War. Australia, for instance, endured an average rate of 14 per cent unemployment during the interwar era. New Zealand's experience during the interwar period told a similar story. Kelly's account, too, overlooks the fact that Australia enjoyed appreciable, though not spectacular, economic growth for nearly three decades after the Second World War; a period in which wage arbitration, protection and paternalism prevailed. Historically, Australia enjoyed a high rate of economic growth, along with low inflation and low unemployment. However, it was later argued that this growth rate was 'purchased' at the expense of future growth potential in that it derived from investment in the protected domestic market; this had the effect of locking up Australian industry in a fragmented, insulated setting. This pattern showed up in Australia's productivity growth rate, or growth of real GDP per capita, during the period 1950–73, when it was consistently inferior to the OECD average (MacFarlane, 2006, 13). For the period 1973–9 the real growth rate per capita averaged 1.3 per cent. The blame was attributed to a high rate of labour force growth and import substitution, which led, in turn, to rent-seeking behaviour in the private sector. In the post-war era Australia grew at over 5.5 per cent annually, higher than most other western countries. Between 1962 and 1973 the Australian growth rate was still 5.1 per cent (Caves and Krause, 1984, 3). However, the ANU economist Ross Garnaut noted that this was attributable to what Conrad Blyth (1987, 2) called 'pseudo growth', fed by 'tablets of demand management, or slow drips of protection'.

It was once a running joke that the number of unemployed in New Zealand was so few that the successive Ministers of Labour knew all their names! Weststrate (1959, 129) claimed that New Zealand's unemployment experience, of having more vacancies than unemployed until the mid-1960s, was unprecedented for any capitalist economy and related it to the country's institutional apparatus and the practice of wage stability. Rosenberg attributed New Zealand's low unemployment to the use of Keynesian economics and import controls, which allowed a higher level of economic activity. Nonetheless, New Zealand's post-war macroeconomic performance was comparatively inferior to Australia's, with poor productivity growth per capita due to import and exchange controls distorting the returns from capital goods; despite this the country recorded an average annual 4.3 per cent growth rate during the post-war boom. Australia and New Zealand enjoyed a similar growth trajectory in terms of real GDP per capita during the post-war period until 1970 when a divergence opened up between the two countries (Goldfinch, 2000, 14; Greasley and Oxley, 1999). In the 1970s relative economics decline was even more evident for New Zealand, with the economy growing by less than half the average of those in other western countries.

Kelly also overlooks that during the 1950s and 1960s Australia's population, fed by immigration, grew on average at 2.5 per cent, one of the highest growth rates in the world. From 1891 till 1947 Australia's population grew at an average rate of 1.25 per cent. In 1939 Australia's population stood at 7 million and was projected to be around 8 to 9 million by the end of the century (Wolstenholme, 1937). This remarkable change came about after the scare during the Second World War when Australian planners and politicians realised that their country was dangerously underpopulated and needed to depend on itself. Australia, therefore, embarked upon a massive assisted immigration programme and set out to expand the economy to provide jobs and rising living standards for that growing population. This raised the old chestnut of whether immigration was a net benefit in the context of raising per capita income in the long run; that answer was always in the affirmative (Withers, 2003, 78–9). In the post-war era economists such as Arndt, Belshaw, Bensusan-Butt, Corden and Karmel spent time researching Australian immigration economics. Later research drilled down into looking at how the benefits of immigration were distributed, including regional impacts, human capital and the net effect on demographic ageing. There were also short-run implications for employment, training, wages, public outlays and the foreign debt. The post-war immigration programme would initially depress growth in per capita income even with investment increasing from 18 per cent to 29 per cent of GDP, with only a tenth funded by foreign investment. A key concern here, using Salter's (1960) work on vintage capital, was to ascertain whether immigration would, by increasing the population growth rate, improve or modernise the capital stock, so offsetting any 'quantity based capital-dilution effect' (Withers, 2003, 80). In New Zealand economists like Belshaw mulled over the same issues (Brooke, Endres and Rogers, 2017).

During the 1950s there was some concern, expressed by economists and businessmen, that Australia was, if anything, growing too fast and thus endangering the trade account. And it is this problem, the external account, which was greatest commonality between the two countries throughout the twentieth century; that is, how to maintain a high rate of economic development without recourse to import controls. In New Zealand this predicament was termed 'the balance of payments-constrained economy' (Easton, 1997, 31). The problem was that the sustainable level of output and employment was constrained by the balance of payments, with export revenue and international borrowing dictating the level of imports which, in turn, set the domestic economic growth rate permissible. In that respect New Zealand authorities always kept a close eye on the ratio of foreign exchange reserves to imports (Zanetti, 1966, 7). In Australia's case there was a tendency for over-importation that could not be attributed to internal inflation or to the pace of development.

The vast majority of Australian and New Zealand economists did not seem unduly concerned by the growth performance of their respective economies until the 1960s. In his influential 1985 Edward Shann Lecture, Fred Gruen (1986) showed that Australia had recorded a 'mediocre' growth in per capita GDP from the 1960s onwards. Indeed, in the 1970s Australian economists begun to ponder why the country's growth record was so poor; Australia had slipped down the per capita domestic product totem pole from being fifth largest in 1950 to 13th in 1977.

The only consolation was that their country was ahead of New Zealand, which had fallen even further. While distance and small domestic markets were draw-backs, economists knew that other factors detrimental to economic growth were man-made. There had long been dissent by New Zealand economists about the distorting effects of import licensing, whereas their Australian counterparts accepted the paradigm of protection, wage arbitration and a marked degree of public regulation. Both countries' reputation as trading nations suffered in the post-war years due to the policies of insulation and import-substituting industri-alisation (Caves and Krause, 1984). They were the only two nations among the advanced economies not to experience a large increase in the export share of output (Garnaut, 2001, 149). It was commonplace to argue that Australia and New Zealand's economic growth was ultimately governed by international economic conditions. Yet, in the post-war era, both countries resorted to import controls to protect their foreign exchange reserves while there were rounds of multilateral trade reform everywhere else (Endres and Rogers, 2014). Although mooted as emergency measures, these import controls soon become almost permanent. It might be remembered, too, that both countries were suspicious of the post-war new economic order and, together with Soviet Union, did not sign the Articles of Agreement arising from of the Bretton Woods Conference. Leslie Melville, leader of the Australian team at that conference, recalls that this was a 'hangover' from the Depression for Australian and New Zealand politicians to view international financiers as sinister and likely to create financial trouble for both countries (Cornish, 1993, 449). Australia agreed to ratify the protocol in 1947 and New Zealand only did so in 1961.

Despite a mutual suspicion of global economic forces, both Australia and New Zealand were primarily concerned that their respective economies adequately met economic and social needs. This underscores the fact that Australians and New Zealanders have always had a clear appreciation that their economic and social destiny lay in their hands and that they had to develop attitudes and institutions to meet changing opportunities, needs and aspirations. That said, they were also individualistic enough to largely shun the idea of systemic economic planning in the 1960s when other countries were entranced by the idea. The peoples of both countries were security-minded and looked to their governments to provide basic social services. This meant a considerable degree of government intervention in both economies. Aiding this was what the Cambridge economist Brian Reddaway once called the 'Australian genius for improvisation'. This disposition, both to improvise and adjust, is one of the grand themes of Ian McLean's account of the economic history of Australia entitled *Why Australia Prospered* (2013). In this regard Australian economists were at the forefront in tweaking economic controls but also in introducing new institutions to meet new economic challenges. However, this could only go so far in improving economic performance.

It was, to repeat, only in the 1970s, in response to dispiriting macroeconomic performance, that a real stirring for economic reform, for an entirely new economic model, or paradigm, began. The inferior economic performance was due to either economy resorting to 'All the restrictive practices known to man'

(Butlin, Bernard and Pincus, 1982). In Australia, at least, that discontent was aired within the seminar and tea rooms of economics departments. In New Zealand, though, it has been said that it was economists within the Treasury and the Reserve Bank of New Zealand (RBNZ), rather than university economists, who led the call for more market-based reforms (Bertram, 1993). It is too early to make such a judgement, but certainly economists within the central banks in both countries were to have considerable influence with policy-makers.

Notes

1 It was followed by Goodwin's other publication, *The Image of Australia: British Perception of the Australian Economy from the Eighteenth to the Twentieth Century* (1974).
2 Arndt Papers, NLA.
3 In 2008 the New Zealand Association of Economists celebrated the work of Phillips, particularly the 50th anniversary of his famous Phillips curve article appearing in *Economica*, by hosting its annual conference in his honour, marking the occasion with the theme 'Markets and Models: Policy Frontiers in the AWH Phillips Tradition'.
4 Australia also has the Academy of the Social Sciences, with a division for economists and another for economic historians. To become a Fellow of the Academy an economist must be nominated by other fellows and then have their candidature put to the vote by the rest of the fraternity. Those elected are considered 'those who have achieved a very high level of scholarly distinction recognised internationally'. The equivalent body in New Zealand is the Social Sciences division of the Royal Society of New Zealand.
5 'Forty years of joy and sorrow for a New Zealand economist', Rosenberg Papers, Alexander Turnbull Library, Wellington.

References

Bertram, G. 1993, 'Keynesianism, neoclassicism and the state', in C. Rudd and B. Roper (eds), *State and the Economy in New Zealand*, Auckland: Oxford University Press.

Blaug, M. 1999, *Who's Who in Economics*, 3rd edn, Cheltenham: Edward Elgar.

Blyth, C. A. 1966, 'The special case: the political economy of New Zealand', *Political Science*, 18: 38–51.

Blyth, C. A. 1987, 'The economists' perspective on economic liberalisation', in A. Bollard and R. Buckle (eds), *Economic Liberalisation in New Zealand*, Wellington: Allen and Unwin.

Brooke, G., A. Endres and A. Rogers, 2016, 'Does New Zealand economics have a useful past? The example of trade policy and economic development', *New Zealand Economic Papers*, 50(3): 281–302.

Brooke, G., Endres, A. and Rogers, A. 2017, 'The Economists and New Zealand population: Problems and policies 1900–1980s', *New Zealand Economic Papers* 51(1).

Butlin, N.G., Barnard, A. and Pincus J.J. 1982, *Government and Capitalism: Public and Private Choice in Twentieth Century Australia*, Sydney: Allen and Unwin.

Caves, R. and L. Krause (eds), 1984, *The Australian Economy: The View from the North*, Sydney: Allen and Unwin.

Coleman, W. 2005, 'A conversation with Murray Kemp', *History of Economics Review*, 41: 1–16.

Coleman, W. 2015, 'A young tree dead? The story of economics in Australia and New Zealand', in V. Barnett (ed.), *Routledge Handbook of the History of Global Economic Thought*, London: Routledge, 281–93.

Coleman, W., S. Cornish and A. Hagger, 2006, *Giblin's Platoon: The Trials and Triumph of the Economist in Australian Public Life*, Canberra: Australian National University Press.

Condliffe, J. B. 1959 [1930], *New Zealand in the Making*, London: Allen and Unwin.

Condliffe, J. B. 1969, 'The economic outlook for New Zealand', *New Zealand Economic Papers*, 3(1): 5–14.

Copland, D. B. 1958, 'L. F. Giblin and the frontier of research on the Australian economy', *Australian Journal of Science*, 21: 120–5.

Corden, W. M. 1968, *Australian Economic Policy Discussion: A Survey*, Melbourne: Melbourne University Press.

Corden, W. M. 1974, *Trade Policy and Economic Welfare*, Oxford: Clarendon Press.

Cornish, S. 1993, 'Sir Leslie Melville: an interview', *Economic Record*, 69(207): 437–57.

Cornish, S. 2008, 'Economics in Australasia', *The New Palgrave Dictionary of Economics*, Basingstoke: Palgrave Macmillan.

Easton, B. 1997, *In Stormy Seas: The Post War New Zealand Economy*, Dunedin: University of Otago.

Endres, A. M. and A. Rogers, 2014, 'Trade policy and international finance in the Bretton Woods era: a doctrinal perspective with reference to Australia and New Zealand', *History of Economics Review*, 59: 62–81.

Garnaut, R. 2001, *Social Democracy in Australia's Asian Future*, Canberra: Asia Pacific Press.

Goldfinch, S. 2000, 'Paradigms, economic ideas and institutions in economic policy change: the case of New Zealand', *Political Science*, 52(1): 1–21.

Goodwin, C. D. 1974, *The Image of Australia*, Durham, NC: Duke University Press.

Greasley, D. and L. Oxley, 1999, 'Growing apart? Australia and New Zealand growth experiences 1870–1913', *New Zealand Economic Papers*, 33(2): 1–13.

Groenewegen, P. 1989, 'The development of economics in Australia: a tale of two centuries', *Economic Papers*, 8(3): 97–108.

Groenewegen, P. and B. McFarlane, 1990, *A History of Australian Economic Thought*, London: Routledge.

Gruen, F. H. G. (ed.), 1978, *Surveys of Australian Economics*, Vol. 1, Sydney: Allen and Unwin.

Gruen, F. H. G. (ed.), 1979, *Surveys of Australian Economics*, Vol. 2, Sydney: Allen and Unwin.

Gruen, F. H. G. 1986, 'How bad is Australian economic performance and why?', *Economic Record*, 62(177): 180–93.

Harper, M. 1991, 'Review of P. Groenewegen and B. McFarlane *A History of Australian Economic Thought*', *Economic Record*, 67(199): 377–8.

Hatch, J. 1984, 'Review of the Survey of Australian Economics: Volume 3', *Economic Record*, 60(4): 390–3.

Hatch, J. and C. Rogers, 1997, 'Distinguished Fellow of the Economic Society of Australia, 1996: Professor Emeritus Geoff Harcourt', *Economic Record*, 73(221): 97–100.

Hawke, G. and R. Lattimore, 2005, 'Scoping the history of economics in New Zealand', New Zealand Agricultural and Resource Economics Society Conference, Nelson.

Hawke, G. R. and B. A. Wijewardane, 1972, 'New Zealand and the International Monetary Fund', *Economic Record*, 48(1): 92–102.

Hight, J. 1939, 'Preface', *Economic Record*, 15: 3–6.

Kelly, P. 1992, *The End of Certainty: Power, Politics, and Business in Australia*, 1992, St Leonards, NSW: Allen and Unwin.

King, J. E. 2007, *A Biographical Dictionary of Australian and New Zealand Economists*, Cheltenham: Edward Elgar.

La Nauze, J. 1966, 'Review of *Economic Inquiry in Australia* by Craufurd Goodwin', *Economic Record*, 42(99): 472–4.

McAllister, I., S. Dowrick and R. Hassan (eds), 2003, *The Cambridge Handbook of Social Sciences in Australia*, New York: Cambridge University Press.

MacFarlane, I. 2006, *The Search for Stability*, Sydney: ABC.

McLean, I. 2013, *Why Australia Prospered*, Princeton, NJ: Princeton University Press.

Nevile, J. W. and P. Dalziel, 2013, 'Theorizing about post-Keynesian economics in Australasia', in G. C. Harcourt and P. Kriesler (eds), *The Oxford Handbook of Post Keynesian Economics, Volume 2 Critiques and Methodology*, New York: Oxford University Press, 412–35.

Norman, N. 2007, 'The contribution of Australian economists: the record and the barriers', *Economic Papers*, 26(1): 1–16.

Salter. W. 1960, *Productivity and Technical Change*, Cambridge: Cambridge University Press.

Tay, F. 2007, *125 Years of Economic Studies at Canterbury, New Zealand*, Christchurch: University of Canterbury.

Weststrate, C. 1959, *Portrait of a Mixed Modern Economy*, Wellington: University of New Zealand Press.

White, C. 1992, *Mastering Risk: Environment, Markets and Politics in Australian Economic History*, Melbourne: Oxford University Press.

Withers, G. 1978, 'The state of economics', *Australian Quarterly*, December: 74–80.

Withers, G. 2003, 'Immigration', in I. McAllister, S. Dowrick and R. Hassan (eds), *The Cambridge Handbook of Social Sciences in Australia*, Cambridge: Cambridge University Press, 74–93.

Wolstenholme, S. H. 1937, 'The future of the Australian population', *Economic Record*, 12(1): 195–213.

Wooding, P. A. 1968, 'Review of *A Guidebook to New Zealand's Future* by W. Rosenberg', *Economic Record*, 44(108): 541–1.

Zanetti, G. N. 1966, 'The New Zealand economy 1966: the failure of policy', *New Zealand Economic Papers*, 1(2): 5–15.

2 The professionalisation of Australasian economics

The pattern of economic life in the Antipodes

Addressing a group of American businessmen in the 1970s, an Australian professor of economics once opened his lecture with the remark that his country was, in many ways 'a potty little country, of little account in the world'. Richard Downing of the University of Melbourne went on to describe Australia the same way that poet T. S. Eliot described America, as 'a large flat country which no-one wants to visit'. The professor was half-joking but his remarks carried a touch of truth. Equally, *The Economist* once opened a story on New Zealand as 'small, far-off country of which most people know very little'.[1] For most living in the northern hemisphere New Zealand was literally out of sight, obscured from a map of the world, as Brian Easton joked, by the filing cabinet or pot-plant (1997). With half of its physical geography open pasture, New Zealand was eternally summed up by one of its famous economists as 'a remote farm' (Condliffe, 1940). Even much later Condliffe (1969, 10) was adamant that the 'grasslands will remain the foundation of New Zealand's economy'. In the post-war years New Zealand was a relatively straightforward economy (Gould, 1982, 66). It pursued a correspondingly simple array of economic objectives such as full employment, price stabilisation and maintaining an adequate level of overseas reserves. The appellation 'small' has been oft-used to describe Australia and New Zealand, though New Zealanders endearingly prefer to use 'wee' to describe their country. In terms of economics, they were always denoted as small, open, dependent economies representing no more than 2 per cent of world output. One cannot extend that same description to the contribution Australian and New Zealand economists made to world economics; they never represented an academic backwater.

Australia and New Zealand: traditionally commodity exporting economies

This narrative is told against the backdrop of the economic history of the two countries. Obviously each country's material progress, and the conditions underpinning it, attracted the attention of the local economics profession. The economic history of Australia and New Zealand is a story of chequered economic development but, overwhelmingly one of growth, prosperity and structural diversification in what were resource-driven economies. Their economic paths were remarkably similar in exporting staples such as wool, wheat, dairy products, meat, timber and metals to Britain. They were classic settler economies, dependent upon trade, capital and migrants from Britain, with London serving as their financial centre. Australia and New Zealand have often been regarded as commodity exporting countries. New Zealand encouraged farming on the premise that overseas markets would be limit-less and expanding. That tradition was damaged by the 1932 Ottawa Imperial Trade talks and by concurrent changes in British agricultural policy. Moreover, New Zealanders discovered that, in their bargaining with the mother country, they were more dependent upon Britain than she was upon them. Australia's commodity orientation might be gleaned from the fact that in the 1960s it had more of its labour force in manufacturing than did America – so much so that one local economist entitled his book *A Small Rich Industrial Country*, likening Australia to Sweden or Switzerland (Arndt, 1968). New Zealand, too, had a considerable manufacturing capacity at this time following the official policy of 'industrialisation in depth' (Greasley and Oxley, 1999). Either country therefore fell uneasily between the stools of maturity and underdevelopment (Blakey, 1958). Because of their indus-trial development and high material standard of living both countries could be considered mature or developed economies; but they could also be regarded as developing countries in the sense that they possessed resources yet to be exploited. Things have changed. One striking development is that the structural feature of high levels of protection that prevailed right through to the 1980s has vanished. At the time of writing, Australia and New Zealand were enjoying resource-driven export booms, not in wool or meat, but in iron ore and dairy products respectively. In both countries the pastoral wool industry is now in decline. Today the destination for these high-grade iron ore, coal and dairy products is China; that country is being provided with the wherewithal to make steel to build its cities, the power to live in them and also to nourish its population with dairy-based products. Both Australia and New Zealand recently entered into free trade agreements with China, a devel-opment which augurs well for their future.

In a sense things have come full circle. When the New Zealand Finance Minister, Walter Nash, a long-time member of the Economic Society, once asked the visiting English economist Colin Clark 'What is the future of New Zealand?' the cryptic response was that it all depended on the prices of her primary produce.[2] That observation, made in 1938, upheld the simple fact of economic life, that New Zealand's and Australia's living standards were dependent upon economic conditions in the global economy (Condliffe, 1958, 56). This made New Zealand acutely vulnerable since its high proportion of exports to total trade meant that any shrinkage in export income ensued a bigger direct proportionate loss in national income. It also meant a compulsion to find new markets. As Hancock noted, 'History had determined that the basic prob-lem which the New Zealanders had to face was the problem of markets' (cited in Sinclair, 1976, 133). In 1928 the value of her exports comprised 36 per cent of national income and 44 per cent of all production; pastoral and agricultural products constituted 96 per cent of exports. So it was pastoral prices by which prosperity or depression was transmitted to New Zealand. For Australia, certainly until the 1960s, wool prices were the key to either prosperity or adversity. This was not the end of the process, however; domestic prices were usually far more rigid than export prices, meaning that agricultural income would fall more than gross income. This decline in farm income percolated through the rest of economy; the rigidity in costs in the sheltered parts of the economy, along with wage arbitration, made it difficult to make adjustments in prices to conform to the reduction in demand for farm produce.

Australia and New Zealand: economic and financial institutions

Fluctuations in exports prices also had a monetary impact which was conveyed through the banking system. Rising export prices meant a boost to export income; deposits in banks would swell, allowing banks to increase their advances. A higher level of aggregate demand meant prosperity; falling prices meant falling bank reserves, credit contraction and, as a consequence, economic stringency.

To a large extent New Zealand's economic history has been a story of 'creaming off' some of the huge economic rents of the farming sector to support manufacturing and services (Blyth, 1966). Conrad Blyth supplemented that view by later arguing that New Zealand's planned industrialisation in the postwar era had been at the expense of real wages (Blyth, 1987, 19–20). No one in authority dared to point this out. In Australia the 1929 Brigden Report was equally evasive on that point.

A convenient factor in the telling of our story is that Australia and New Zealand had similar economic profiles and a common cultural heritage; both were white settler dominions of the British Empire. Undeniably, both were not just lucky countries, but rich countries, in terms of resource endowment, and underpopulated. In 1953 New Zealanders could boast of having the third highest standard of living in the world; this was the consequence of becoming one big farm, exporting pastoral products. It is also much more compact than Australia. The scale of Australia has to be understood; Perth is separated from Brisbane by a distance no less than that between London and Cairo or Ireland and Nova Scotia. In the 1950s Australia, like New Zealand, rode on the sheep's back with wool comprising half of its exports. It was only in the 1970s that both countries slipped from the top ten of per capita income countries (Goldfinch, 2000, 14). New Zealand had a portent of what was to come in 1957, and again in November 1966, when wool prices fell 40 per cent, setting off an external account crisis.

As outliers of empire, both dominions had security courtesy of British naval might until 1939. They also exhibited remarkable parallels in history, culture, location and governance, including economic institutions such as wage arbitration and tariff-making bodies. In Australia the Tariff Board was an independent body which reviewed all proposals for tariffs and gave advice to the federal government (Capling and Galligan, 1992, 80–4). New Zealand had its own Tariff and Development Board charged with similar charter and operation. When import controls were superimposed upon an already comprehensive system of tariff protection this made the two countries the most protectionist in the OECD group of nations. The British politician Hugh Dalton described this propensity towards 'conscious control over the economic system' as 'economic statesmanship', adding that *laissez-faire* 'was never taken very seriously' in Australia (Smith, 1929, vii). Victoria, for instance, had, for its size and standing, 'the largest and most comprehensive use of state power outside Russia' (Eggleston, 1932, 69–71). Shann would beg to differ, with Dalton's assessment, arguing that Australia's difficulties stemmed from too much state control of prices, wages and conditions of employment. It also accounted for the bad press Australian economic management received in London during the interwar era. Both countries' monetary arrangements were also similar. Their exchange rates were in parity with sterling and anchored to the gold standard until 1930. Given that neither country had effective central banks until the 1930s and that both were also huge borrowers in the London market, domestic monetary arrangements were virtually set by the London market. The sterling exchange standard meant that every pound of exports was deposited in the Australasian banks and, simultaneously, in exporters' accounts in either Australia or New Zealand (Tocker, 1924). These foreign exchange reserves were referred to as the London Funds. The sterling which paid for imports by Australia and New Zealand determined whether there was to be a credit squeeze or credit expansion in either country. An increase in imports reduced London Funds, meaning that the ratio of deposits to advances in Australasian bank accounts declined. Therefore the movement in the London balances, and the corresponding movement in the ratio of deposits to advances, was the key driver of the credit policy for Australian and New Zealand banks. Even when both countries established their own central banks, the state of their London Funds still exerted a strong influence upon monetary and economic conditions therein. Exchange rates and each country's foreign exchange reserves were dependent upon the net surplus of exports over imports, less the net sterling debt servicing cost, plus any new sterling loans.

In the latter half of the nineteenth century both countries were among the richest in the world on the basis of tiny populations producing a large proportion of the world's supply of wool. New Zealand also pioneered the export of frozen meat, cheese and butter, while Australia became a significant exporter of wheat. Their export income was a valuable part of their prosperity and was based, therefore, on staples whose price lay beyond their control; it was, moreover, subject to violent and unpredictable variations. This volatility in export earnings led to 'a brooding pessimism about its prospects' with regard to the external account and whether they would have enough foreign exchange reserves to maintain their fixed exchange rate (Corden, 1968). In addition there was, after 1945, a renewed bout of export pessimism based on the premise that the global income and price elasticity of demand for primary goods were both low. The post-war replacement of wool by synthetics and butter with margarine lent weight to that pessimism. There was also a certain bleakness in both countries about their capacity to actually expand export production. In Australia this bleak forecast found comic expression in 'Said Hanrahran', a 1921 poem by P. J. Hartigan about a mythical farmer whose fearful reaction to flood and drought was:

'If we don't get three inches, man,
Or four to break this drought,
We'll all be rooned' said Hanrahran,
'Before the year is out.'

In New Zealand, Bill Sutch was the major exponent of export pessimism and used it to justify diversification (Easton, 2001, 164–5). This diversification would be achieved from the 1960s by erecting a labyrinth of different export subsidy schemes (Endres and Rogers, 2014, 70). Geoffrey Blainey (1968) reminded us that this pessimism was, to some extent, self-inflicted, highlighting the case when Australia placed an embargo upon the export of iron ore. The embargo, which applied from 1938 was only relaxed in 1960.[3]

There are so many parallels between Australia and New Zealand that much that can be said about the one country, could apply, *mutatis mutandis*, to the other. However this presumption of sameness can sometimes be carried too far (Greasley and Oxley, 1999, 2). It certainly did not apply to economists' views about trade and development. Despite being closely integrated with Australia with a myriad of trade, capital and labour flows, after 1901 New Zealand survived by becoming more trade-dependent upon Britain (ibid.). Refrigeration made possible the almost complete reorientation of New Zealand's 'farm' towards the British market over the period from 1870–1970. By as late as 1965, 97 per cent of New Zealand's exports were pastoral (dairy, meat and wool), with 50 per cent heading to Britain. It represented around 20 per cent of national income. After another terms of trade shock in 1966 New Zealand mounted one of the most extensive diversification programmes of any OECD country (Easton, 1997).

Politically, Australia had a complex federal system of governance where, until 1942, the states were as economically and politically important as the national government. It was inevitable, however, that this division of powers would raise special problems in economic control and that changing economic circumstances would mean change in methods of that control. In particular, the demand for national economic control would expand the field of action of the federal government. New Zealand, by contrast, had a far simpler, unified system of governance and, as aforementioned, a far simpler economic structure. While the two countries were separated by the Tasman Sea – the distance between London and Moscow – it was even mooted before Federation that New Zealand might join as the seventh state. The idea, though, was never really popular across the Tasman Sea, which New Zealanders affectionately refer to as 'The Ditch'.

Australia and New Zealand: industrial arbitration

Another concern was both countries' arbitration systems, which were as unique as the kangaroo or the kiwi. This institutional arrangement lasted in each country for nearly 100 years. In brief, the system of industrial relations was based on three principles, namely, compulsory unionism, minimum terms and conditions of employment and compulsory arbitration. Constitutionally, the system's prime task was to prevent and settle industrial disputes through wage determination. However, that has not always been its main focus. At times the Commission found itself operating as a national wage policy-making body. In 1907 Justice Henry Bournes Higgins, the President of the Commonwealth Court of Conciliation and Arbitration, brought down the famous Harvester Judgement which held that an employer was required to pay a decent, fair wage that that would cover the basic needs of the average employee and his family. This wage was based on the needs of the worker and not on individual productivity nor the firm's ability to pay. The needs provision meant that wages were indexed to the rate of inflation in every quarter until 1953, when it was abandoned in favour of the firm's ability to pay. At the time, Australia was recovering from a strong bout of cost-push inflation. The Commission would only alter the basic wage when it judged there had been a change in the economy's ability to pay. Besides the basic wage, the Court also adjudicated upon 'margins' for skilled workers. The basic wage was the minimum wage for unskilled workers but also a significant part of all wages. The Court also invoked capacity to pay considerations when deciding on margins. When it was found that the purchasing power of the basic wage had slipped, the Court decided that price increases could not be disregarded. Moreover the Commission encouraged the idea of productivity-geared wage policy, an idea floated by Downing and Joe Isaac (1961) and before them, Peter Karmel and Keith Hancock. By this policy, the Court would lift the basic wage and 'margins' by small regular and foreseeable quarterly wage increases at a rate just below increases in average productivity instead of a double-digit rise every three or four years. This system of basic wage and margins persisted in Australia until 1967, when the newly re-titled Commonwealth Conciliation and Arbitration Commission introduced job-specific wages, though the basic wage still 'anchored' the whole system. In New Zealand the Court of Arbitration had also to consider 'general economic conditions'. One would expect that, amid all this, the opinion of economists would have played a prominent part. Far from it. The judges were lawyers, not economists and the whole process was entirely legalistic; nor were the judges under any obligation to consult economic experts. The Court would only hear economic advice if economists were called by either party, usually at national wage cases. In such cases, economists could be expected to be cross-examined by the opposing side. Sometimes, as we shall see, an advocate for either the unions or the employers would encourage economists to undertake research that might fortify or give intellectual support to the advocate's argument.

In fact, it was in wages policy that Australian economists made 'their most original contribution' (Corden, 1968). Their role as 'wage theorists' was already minted since a wage-making body already existed. Historically, Australia and New Zealand were small, mostly closed, economies reliant upon a predominant rural or export sector quite distinct from the rest of the economy. This meant there was a focus on the income distribution falling between the sectors (ibid., 9). One of the key outcomes of Australian wage theorists was to devise a recipe for sustainable wage rises which took into account not only inflation and productivity, but also movements in the terms of trade. This meant that the rest of the community shared in the gains and losses of the rural sector as affected by export prices. An improvement in the terms of trade represented an increased capacity to pay higher wages and vice-versa.

Australia and New Zealand: trade and capital flows

This imperial trading circuit of capital, people and trade flows was to continue right up until the 1960s, when both countries diversified their trade and capital flows. This became an imperative when Britain made known its intentions in the early 1960s about joining the European Common Market. As a portent of its future economic orientation, in 1957 Australia signed a major trade treaty with Japan, an act regarded as the most economically significant measure during the Menzies years (1949–66). The economist behind it, Sir John Crawford, had been aware of the potentialities of trade between the two countries since the 1930s. By contrast, New Zealand was a laggard and, in something of a jest, the Association of New Zealand Economists had, as its patron, Charles de Gaulle who, while President of the French Republic, was defiantly against British entry into the European Common Market. While the patron had been unable to attend meetings of the Association, 'the General' was toasted every year until 1970 (Holmes, 2011).

Australia was noted for maintaining high tariffs from the 1930s onward to encourage the development of what became, ultimately, an inefficiently wide range of manufacturing. New Zealand had a low tariff structure, though it went to extremes in 1938 by using import controls to maintain industry and the processing of farm produce. While the main rationale for import controls was to preserve exchange reserves, some argued that it was part of a coherent strategy to build up its manufacturing sector. This vulnerability of external reserves would recur at critical moments in New Zealand's economic history. When Colin Clark visited there and saw the newly introduced policy of 'insulation', of exchange controls and import licensing, he wrote that it was the clearest example yet of an economy ruined by protection. In 1938 New Zealand went further and, anticipating Britain's Beveridge Report of 1942, introduced a Social Security Act which established a welfare system to provide medical services, family allowances and unemployment benefits. This restored New Zealand's status as 'a social laboratory'; it had already begun to introduce price stabilisation measures for its major agricultural commodities.

The beginnings of formal economics instruction in Australasia

It was the need for economics expertise to meet the strains of recurring economic growth and development that was a dominant factor in the formation of the economics profession within Australia and New Zealand in the 1920s. The business and corporate sector wanted more commercially minded graduates to draw upon; economists answered the call. The fortunes of war, too, played a part as many of the profession had served as soldiers in the First World War. We might call them 'Anzac economists'. Uniting them was Douglas Copland, a galvanising figure, an economist who held lofty aspirations for his profession. Copland, whom we might call a New Zealander Australian, had wanted to go to war with his brothers but, much to his distress, a heart ailment made him ineligible to serve. He sunk his energies and patriotism elsewhere; he made his name in Australia as the driving force behind the establishment of a society that gave strength and recognition to the fledgling economics profession. Corden (2010, 461) has described Copland as the veritable 'George Washington' of the Australian economics profession. 'Washington' in the sense, too, that Copland was quick to prevent any disunity from developing within the profession. One instance of this was his advice to Giblin, whom he feared would write a critical review of a textbook written by two Sydney economists: 'We are out to put Australia on the Economics map, and there is not enough strength here to make any show unless it is all put in the common cause' (cited in Harper, 2013, 77). In less than five years this new profession would be challenged by an inquiry into the Australian tariff and how it related to economic development. This was quickly followed by the challenge of the Great Depression, where regions of recent settlement, such as Australia and New Zealand, suffered relatively more than the metropole economies. In both nations economists were thrust further into the limelight of public policy-making than their counterparts elsewhere in the world. They would demonstrate an imaginative flair and coherence in crafting a stabilisation package to deal with the crisis of falling export prices and overseas indebtedness. That response, particularly in Australia, caught the attention of economists overseas.

The New Zealand experience

It is instructive to recall that the development of economics as a university course was already well established in New Zealand by the mid-1920s, although with only five economics professors. It was true, as Heaton (1926, 237) remarked in an article in the *American Economic Review*, that 'Academic economics was much better in New Zealand than in Australia.' Keynes would marvel at the teaching prowess of a man, literally at the edge of the world, who turned out first-rate economists. His name was James Hight, Professor of Economics and History at Canterbury University College for nearly 30 years. Hight had a 'special position in the development of economic teaching and study in New Zealand' (cited in Endres, 1991, 173). Marshall and other classic economic texts provided the wellspring for the 'tough analytical theory' with which Hight's students were confronted. Hight regarded Marshall's tome as 'not only sound economics but also good literature' (cited in Millmow, 2015: 3). In Hight's world, economic analysis had to dabble in socio-historical developments, geography and politics

(Endres, 2009, 176–7). He was not interested in theory for theory's sake, but as a means to unravel domestic economic problems such as public finance, economic fluctuations or the role of the government within the economy.

Hight always felt that New Zealand would be attractive to economic researchers because it possessed a 'comparatively simple society', free from ethnic, racial and dynastic tensions. 'Economists', Hight suggested, 'should be interested in New Zealand not only because of its "experimental" economic legislation, but also because it is more possible there to measure the real effects of introducing some piece of economic machinery, some new institution' (Hight, 1939, 3–4). As a young student at Christchurch, Copland heard a visiting American professor describe New Zealand as 'a sociological laboratory', a country where social consciousness was well developed and where the state was pushing ahead with social experiments.[4] But New Zealand was also interesting because, as we have seen, it was a 'vulnerable' or 'dependent' economy whose prosperity was acutely sensitive to disturbances in global prosperity which were transmitted to it by changes in relative prices. Despite these propitious circumstances there had been a dearth economic research activity. It was Hight's enthusiasm and force as a teacher that got such research underway (Endres, 2009, 175). Hight encouraged his better students to investigate aspects of the New Zealand economy with accessible data (Tay, 2007, 15). It was reflective of what would characterise the Canterbury 'tradition' in economics – that is, the application of economic analysis to practical policy. Personalising this, Hight had already sat on public inquiries, one of which was a Royal Commission on the Cost of Living in 1912 that drew Keynes's attention, especially for its rejection of tariff protection (Fleming, 1989). The other characteristic of Canterbury economics was a pragmatic predisposition towards free markets and free trade (Tay, 2007, 13).

Like Australian universities, the New Zealand university model was based on British standards, but with a twist.[5] Four university colleges constituted the University of New Zealand, located at Auckland (Auckland University College), Wellington (University of Victoria), Christchurch (Canterbury College) and Dunedin (Otago University College). There were also two agricultural colleges at Lincoln and Massey that taught farm management which, coupled with economics, evolved into agricultural economics. The University was responsible for setting the curricula of the subjects taught as well as the conduct of exams and appointment of examiners. Here the practice of having exclusively overseas external examiners, usually from England, lasted until 1939 (Tay, 2007, 4; Blyth, 2007, 10). This gave New Zealand a substantial lead over Australia in professional economics education. For the subject of political economy, the external examiners included John Neville Keynes for some ten years; later, in 1919, John Maynard Keynes stood in (Blyth, 2007). Other examiners were Marshallians such as J. S. Nicholson, Henry Clay, D. H. McGregor and J. H. Jones (Blyth, 2008, 10). These examinations tested New Zealand students on mainstream British economics, the likes of figures such as Marshall, Pigou, Robertson and Hawtrey. A sampling of the textbooks Hight used at Canterbury included Marshall's *Economics of Industry*, Ingrams' *History of Political Economy*, Sidgwick's

Political Economy, Mill's *Political Economy* and J. S. Nicholson's *Principles of Political Economy*. Hight also included the works of J. H. Clapham in his economic history classes. From 1940 the examination system changed and the four university colleges could set both the syllabus and the exam. In 1961 the University of New Zealand was dissolved, with the creation of four universities from the four previous constituent colleges.

The introduction of a Bachelor of Commerce degree by the University of New Zealand in 1906 standardised the Economics syllabus and led to the appointment of full-time economists within the four-college system. Blyth (2008) likened it to a mini-revolution. Another leap forward was to create chairs in Economics at the four establishments. They were all filled quickly by New Zealanders. Economics was taught as a subject in Commerce and Business degrees but not as a degree in its own right. Economics was also taught within the Bachelor of Arts and, for a long time, economics was located within the Arts Faculty. Two Anzac economists, A. G. B. (Allan) Fisher and Ralph Souter, were on the teaching staff at Otago from the mid-1920s, while another Anzac economist, Harold Rodwell, took up a lectureship at Auckland in 1928. The Economics Chair at Otago was filled by Fisher in 1924; he had just returned armed with a PhD from LSE, supervised by Edwin Cannan. Fisher was actually Australian-educated and his move to Otago pointed to the trans-Tasman traffic of economists that continues to this day. In fact, in the interwar and the post-war periods, most of the economists in Australasia were, apart from the odd English import, native born.

Otago University College

During the interwar era Otago produced some excellent graduates, including Conrad Blyth, Ralph Souter and Colin Simkin, some of whom would make significant contributions to economics literature (Tay, 2007, 44–5; McLean, 2011). All three would go overseas to earn their doctorates, at Cambridge, Columbia and Oxford respectively. Simkin, a graduate from Otago, was the top economic Master's student for the whole country in 1936, earning first-class honours from his external examiner – who described him as 'a brilliant student' for his thesis on the evolution of banking, which was 'worthy of a doctorate' (McLean, 2011, 20). He soon moved to Canterbury as a lecturer, where he befriended Austrian-born philosopher Karl Popper, who had fled from the Nazis. Popper impressed upon Simkin the need for precise explanation and application of scientific method in his work, including mathematical and statistical techniques. Simkin was, after Hennie Popper, the second reader of drafts of what would become Popper's *The Open Society and its Enemies*. Unlike his elders, Fisher and Condliffe, Simkin invested time in the study of mathematics to deepen his understanding of economics. Keeping in touch with Popper, Simkin fulfilled his promise with an Oxford dissertation, later published, on the economic peculiarities of his native country. He had turned to Oxford because he was impressed with the work of John Hicks rather than Keynes (Hogan, 1999, 313). Simkin's long career would straddle three generations of Australasian economists, characterised by a trenchantly quantitative approach to teaching economics.

Canterbury University College

In Christchurch the two outstanding economists during the interwar era were Jack Condliffe and Douglas Copland; Horace Belshaw, John Riches and Harold Rodwell came not long after. Condliffe and Copland were fully trained in economics and both would, in time, achieve international recognition. Condliffe (1950, 20) recalled how he began studying economics 'in an old tin shed in a small remote college' and 'getting his teeth into Marshall's *Principles*'. Both Condliffe and Copland knew that they had the world at their feet and sought their fame abroad; New Zealand was just too small for them. This was, as we shall see, to be the destiny of many of New Zealand's most eminent economists. However, being an émigré economist did not always mean neglecting native heath as a topic of applied research. Copland, who had written a thesis on the local wheat industry, visited his homeland every year and remained interested in policy developments there. In 1932 he was called back by the New Zealand government to serve on an official committee formed to advise authorities on policies to deal with the Depression. Condliffe was widely known internationally for his focus upon global trade issues. His first job after graduation was as a public servant, where he also took a Workers Educational Association (WEA) class in economics that included future New Zealand prime ministers Walter Nash and Peter Fraser (Condliffe, 1969, 5). After he left New Zealand, in 1927, Condliffe held some impressive appointments, including a research directorship at the Institute of Pacific Relations and then at the Secretariat of the League of Nations, Geneva, where he wrote the first *World Economic Survey*. After that came a long appointment at the University of California, Berkeley. A patriot throughout his life, Condliffe wrote several books and articles on his homeland with his *New Zealand in the Making* (1959 [1930]) regarded as a classic.

Condliffe had enlisted to fight in the First World War, leaving his position at Canterbury. His autobiography (1973) reveals the fortuitous twists that life took for this Anzac economist. After being wounded on the Western Front, he was despatched to Gonville and Caius College, Cambridge, in 1919 on a soldier's scholarship. He recorded his early impressions of Cambridge for Hight, describing Arthur Pigou, his supervisor, as 'nervously apologetic but very agreeable in every way'. Condliffe attended Pigou's lectures which were:

> quite like his book, subtle and very abstract. He is keen in his argument, but very abstract all the time in his methods. Like a genuine mathematician he prefers to work from the unknown to the known... One of the most common jibes here is that he used to boast that he was never inside a factory and that he wrote a book on unemployment without ever mentioning the unemployed. But even he, while retaining Marshall's form and methods, is travelling a good way past the old conception of economics as a fairly fixed science.[6]

While Condliffe liked Pigou and respected his intellectual subtlety, he felt that his lectures were not of as much practical value as his contributions to theory and that his lectures should be supported by more popular and functional exposition of the subject.[7] For Condliffe, economic life was not always 'the smooth abstractions of the economic texts'; economic questions were inseparable from their political and social environments which were, in turn, the product of history and inertia (Tay, 2007, 15). For Condliffe (1973, 16) theory operated on hypothetical and unreal assumptions but could also be a powerful engine of analysis.

Condliffe told Hight that he was trying 'to get as much out of Cambridge as possible'.[8] In this he had been 'extraordinary fortunate' in meeting 'all the new school of economists'.[9] His 'most exciting experience' was listening to six lectures by Keynes, using the oven-hot proofs of *The Economic Consequences of the Peace* (1919) as he took his audience behind the scenes at Versailles: 'I shall never forget those long thin fingers, the ease and grace with which he handled great issues and the burning conviction with which he pressed his arguments against the treaty and particularly its reparations provisions.' Condliffe received a personal invitation from Keynes to attend his Political Economy Club.[10]

In his last letter from Cambridge he told Hight that what struck him about Keynes was his 'friendliness' to the students: 'He is a tall, ungainly man, loose limbed, very dark, his head thrust forward. Next to you he must have, I imagine, the finest brain among the men I have met.'[11] For Condliffe, then, Cambridge was a revelation: 'I had never lived in such an atmosphere of intellectual curiosity.' In his autobiography (1973, 10) he recalled that it had been indeed a 'privilege to live for a while in this island of detachment from everything sordid and trouble-some. I only had a brief experience… but it altered my whole outlook and I can never be sufficiently grateful for it.' Condliffe told Copland that, having seen the Cambridge Faculty at close quarters, he felt that their education by Hight compared well. He added: 'I am not saying we would not have had better training at Cambridge; but as an individual teacher the Doctor would be hard to beat.'[12] Interestingly, Condliffe revealed his penchant for being an applied economist rather than a theorist by describing 'the worship of the PhD degree' as 'the worst disaster that ever befell to social sciences and humanities' (cited in Tay, 2007, 14). This did not stop him from earning that accolade himself from his own university.[13] Condliffe would live to regret eschewing modern analytical tech-niques and, like many of his generation, feel alienated from the post-war sophis-tication of the discipline (Endres, 2009, 176). In short, while he was not 'a very sophisticated economist' (Adelman, 2013, 203), he did write one of the finest economic histories of his country in *New Zealand in the Making* (Condliffe, 1959 [1930]). Condliffe also had to endure the cruel fate of proclaiming the virtues of free trade at a time when the world had decidedly turned against it. In one instance, he drew 'one of the most revealing figures ever constructed in econom-ics', which displayed a wagon wheel showing the 'contracting spiral' of global trade due to protectionism during the interwar years (Lloyd, 2007, 64).

Horace Belshaw had gone to Cambridge in the early 1920s to undertake his PhD, examining the effects of the trade cycle on agriculture in small, dependent economies such as New Zealand. It was the first time Belshaw had actually been inside a university as his earlier studies had been completed by correspondence. In time, Condliffe would hail him as one of the world's leading authorities on agricultural credit (Endres, 2009).[14] Keynes, too, had a high regard for his abilities. Belshaw had a good sense of balance; he still taught WEA classes while a professor in Auckland and, during the 1930s, would catch the train down to Wellington, the nation's capital, to advise the government, especially J. F. Coates, the Finance Minister (Fleming, 1989). For one year, 1935, he took on the role of full-time economic adviser to Coates.

When Hight took the History Chair in 1920, Condliffe would, following Pigou's and Keynes's recommendation, take the Economics Chair there; Copland apparently came second. Condliffe eventually headed overseas. It was 'a great loss... because he was the best man there'.[15] Condliffe was not the only 'Anzac economist'. One of his army comrades, Albert Tocker, took up a post-war appointment at Canterbury University College in 1921, where he undertook graduate studies in economics. He prospered well at Canterbury such that, after six years as an assistant lecturer, he succeeded Condliffe to the Chair. Copland, however, felt he lacked his predecessor's 'breadth of vision and analytical power'.[16] John Riches, a Canterbury economics graduate who spent his career with the International Labour Office (ILO), knew that Tocker was a sincere exponent of laissez-faire doctrines in economics and was closely aligned with Canterbury business interests with whom he wrote a business digest. Tocker's first academic article, perhaps his best, was on the monetary arrangements in New Zealand and on the effect monetary impulses had on its trade cycle. It continued earlier work by Condliffe on how fluctuations in agricultural export prices were transmitted to New Zealand through the exchange rate.

When Ralph Souter returned to Dunedin he enrolled as a philosophy student in 1919. After obtaining first-class honours in both philosophy and economics, and being awarded a Rockefeller Scholarship to attend Columbia University, he undertook a doctorate under Wesley Mitchell. He briefly lectured there where one of his students, Milton Friedman, found his book, *A Prolegomena to Relativity Economics* (1933), 'almost unreadable, entirely abstract and filled with jargon' (Friedman and Friedman, 1998, 46). Mark Donoghue (2007) gives a more lucid appraisal of this scholar's work. Souter delivered 'a broad methodological attack on static mechanistic and atomistic developments in economics, including formalism' (ibid., 262). Souter planned another two grand volumes designed to deal with the problem of a general reconstruction of value theory to a closer consonance with the modern philosophy. One volume would deal with welfare economics and the other with the pure theory of money and interest. Souter planned an interim volume covering the territory of all three volumes.[17] However, his pen ran dry, despite returning to Otago in late 1936 to succeed Fisher in the Chair of Economics. He had apparently applied for the Chair in Hobart, but one of the adjudicators, Copland, felt that Souter's economics was too philosophical in orientation for students and, moreover, part of the duties of the Chair was to also advise the Tasmanian government on economic matters.

Victoria University College

In Wellington, Victoria University College was quick to establish a Chair in Economics in 1916. The College Council wanted a Chair established because, as one proponent, echoing Hight, put it: 'New Zealand had been called the world's economic laboratory. Our University Colleges should produce men trained to analyse economic phenomena, men who in years to come will be leaders of public opinion' (cited in Blyth, 2008, 32). Funding for the Chair and other teaching staff came from the Macarthy Trust, with the School of Economics established in 1912. The first occupant of the Macarthy Chair in Economics, established in 1920, was Barney Murphy, who had impressed Keynes with his examination scripts. Murphy, though, did not live up to expectations, publishing not one journal article over his 30 years in the Chair (Blyth, 2007, 153). He did, however, publish an economics principles textbook in 1924, just five years after graduating![18] Murphy's brief that came with the Chair was to teach 'economics, descriptive and analytic, with special reference to New Zealand conditions' (Barrowman, 1999, 42). He also consistently wrote for the financial press. Conservatively inclined, Murphy was a public advocate of free trade and the gold standard, becoming a figure who seemed always to be dragging his feet to new vistas in economic thought (Bertram, 2007).

Auckland University College

In Auckland the School of Commerce, which began in 1906, was initially led by Joseph Grossmann, who held the Chair in Economics and History from 1915. The Cambridge-educated Belshaw took over the Economics Chair in 1926 upon Keynes's recommendation (Blyth, 2008, 38). He was told not long after that a fellowship at Gonville and Caius College had been in the offing. Belshaw could easily have taken two offers of appointment in Australia but wanted to return home; it was to his country's benefit that he did. Belshaw told Copland that Cambridge was 'one of the finest departments of commerce in the world'.[19] It was Canterbury, though, with Condliffe as mentor, which gave Belshaw his first exposure to economics. He had worked with Condliffe on rural credit schemes with recommendations to avoid farmers becoming more encumbered by debt. Belshaw would, like Condliffe and Copland, be involved in some important assignments abroad; in 1944 he was appointed International Research Secretary with the Institute of Pacific Relations in New York, before going on to work with the Food and Agriculture Organization (FAO), concurrently holding a university appointment in California. In fact, Belshaw could have left New Zealand much earlier. Copland told him that, apart from not enjoying a greater status within their own country, New Zealand economists had greater opportunities for research abroad, including Australia.[20] It was a telling comment; New Zealand would forever export not merely butter, but also brains. By 1944 four of the country's best economists had left New Zealand for ever.[21] Condliffe believed that the loss of specialist human capital made the country the happy hunting ground of quacks.

One such example was the following that British engineer Major Douglas and his Social Credit economics reform movement enjoyed in New Zealand at the time, especially in influencing Labour Party doctrine – so strongly, in fact, that its effect would foment the call for a Royal Commission on Monetary, Banking and Credit Systems in 1955. The Chairman of the Royal Commission was Sir Arthur Tyndall, who had been Judge of the Court of Arbitration since 1940. While Frank Holmes served as one of the inquiry's secretaries, no economist sat on the Commission and, equally, no university economist presented evidence; the only point of interest was that Colin Clark turned up to argue the case that New Zealand's currency become a commodity currency.

Overall, New Zealand's small corps of professional economists was Marshallian in outlook, applying their skills with verve to domestic problems. They were a pragmatic bunch, with liberal attitudes to economic issues and subscribed to the view that the public sector had a role to play in economic development (Endres, 2010, 89). But they were a far more orthodox tribe on trade, development and labour matters than their Australian counterparts (Brooke *et al.*, 2016). In a small, homogenous country, such as New Zealand or even Australia, being an economic dissident meant ploughing a lonely furrow (Hatch and Rogers, 1997, 98).

The Australian experience

The University of Sydney

According to Robert Irvine, who held the first Chair in Economics in Australia at the University of Sydney (1912–22), visitors were struck by the initial lack of investigation and criticism of social and economic issues within the universities. The University of Sydney had a taken the lead in offering economics instruction, including the Bachelor of Economics degree established in 1913 even before an Economics Faculty was established (Groenewegen, 2010, xxiii). Sydney had acted after being urged by the local Chamber of Commerce, despite university leaders being against the idea. While the first Chair in Economics at Sydney had been established in 1912, its first occupant, Irvine, another student taught by Hight, was regarded as something of an 'outcast from the emerging body of professional economists' (Hancock, 2013, 188). Herbert Heaton, Director of Classes at the University of Tasmania, and later Lecturer in Economics at the University of Adelaide, was another who drew attention to the fact that there had been no scientific assessment of Australian economic problems prior to 1914. A decade later, Copland echoed Heaton in a lecture given before Section G of the Australian Association for the Advancement of Science (AAAS) by bemoaning the lack of interest in academic discussion of economic problems and that no recognised economist had been asked to enlighten government committees; nor was there any training of government officials dealing with economic issues. Copland looked forward to a time when 'the economist would be king in this and in every other country' (Harper, 2013, 60).

In his exhaustive survey of Australian economic thought, Goodwin (1966) found little original research during the period from Federation to 1914. Economists had said very little about issues such as land settlement, wage regulation, the tariff, social legislation and state-owned enterprises. There were extenuating circumstances to explain this. These issues were considered political and the opinions of economists were not welcome by the business community; economists were seen as socialistic and antipathetic to business. Universities, moreover, were inclined to see commercial education as unworthy of formal study (Copland, 1951, 12). As a scientific study, economics was regarded by university administrators as pretentious (Goodwin, 1966, 574). Australian economics needed a salesman to overturn these outdated views, to make economics business-relevant yet academically respectable.

In Sydney, Richard Mills occupied the Chair of Economics (1922–45) after his predecessor Irvine, who had been removed by the universities authorities for unseemly behaviour. A lawyer turned economic historian, Mills' doctorate from the LSE was entitled 'The Colonisation of Australia 1829–42'. He set about establishing economic expertise at Sydney (Groenewegen, 2010), as well as being involved in government committee work, but it came at a cost; he could only recollect: 'I wish I could have spent my life at research. Instead, I had to build a factory' (Randerson, 1953, 43). Mills recruited Frederic Benham from the LSE after asking the authorities there for a pure theorist not necessarily addicted to statistics but learned in the austerity of pure theory. When Benham arrived in Sydney he was probably the most thoroughly trained economist within Australia.[22] This was true enough, but did he, as one sceptic later asked, really understand the nature of the Australian environment and local values? During his six years at Sydney, Benham wrote *The Prosperity of Australia* (1928), using Cannan's theoretical framework. It was considered to be the first serious analytical study of the Australian economy. For Benham, the book's publication merited the award of a PhD from the LSE. In writing his monograph Benham, a staunch exponent of English classical political economy and a self-confessed 'diehard of laissez-faire', raged against Australia's web of wage regulation and protection (ibid., 245). With these views he might have been far happier in New Zealand than Australia; however, Benham enjoyed his time in Sydney being 'an ebullient and resolute spirit' and not thin-skinned to criticism (Black, 1962, 12). One of his students, Hermann Black, recalled how Benham had, in his room, a painting of a beautiful woman who he named 'Miss Free Competition' and that, after he had looked at the 'real' world, he would retire to his room convinced that nothing there was half as beautiful as his portrait.

Benham became embroiled in a theoretical dispute with Brigden about the economic effects of the Australian tariff. Benham told Cannan how his forthcoming book resonated 'closely with your teaching', and how he had to struggle 'in comparative isolation and darkness' getting his line of argument accepted. He continued: 'Hardly anyone in Australia is capable of thoroughly understanding the issues and declaring that one is right.'[23] Benham complained, too, how he had been abused by manufacturers and the gutter press for his stand against protectionism. His plea for greater wage elasticity antagonised trade unionists. Despite the poor reception, Benham had the last laugh as his textbook on economics (1938) was widely used in post-war Australian universities. But before Benham it was Marshall's *Principles* that fairly dominated the economics curriculum at Australian universities (Groenewegen, 2010).

The University of Melbourne

After Sydney had established the first Australian Chair in Economics, Melbourne, then the political and business capital of Australia, responded in kind. After the First World War, economics had become relevant since all the leading social questions revolved around economic issues; the war had disrupted trade and industry and had dissolved the pre-war international monetary system. Questions of currency, protection and finance were being discussed and the need for a scientific basis to these discussions was necessary. The University of Melbourne established a Faculty of Commerce in 1924, with Douglas Copland, still in his 20s, the outstanding candidate for Dean (Harper, 2013). Until then Melbourne offered just one subject in the field, namely, Political Economy, a legacy of the Hearn years (Harper, 2009).[24] Copland had arrived in Australia in 1917 after winning a lecturing position at the University of Tasmania. At the time only one economics subject, Political Economy, was offered there. Copland's application showed that he was a member of the Royal Economic Society and the American Economics Association. By 1920 he had become the Dean of the Faculty of Commerce at the University of Tasmania, the first established in the southern hemisphere. Never immodest about his ability, Copland recalled that, when he first came to Australia, he 'knew more about economics than any of the economists in Australia'. The creation of the Faculty at Melbourne and Copland's appointment as Dean were imaginative steps because he was, as Neville Cain (1973) put it, was not just 'the public relations man' for the coming science of economics but an outstanding administrator. The Melbourne Faculty of Commerce began with one department, one professor, one full-time lecturer and 323 students (Hodgart, 1975).

At Melbourne, Copland knew that he could not antagonise his business benefactors and that the economics research which the Faculty would engage needed to be practically focused (Copland, 1951). He was contemptuous of Sociology, believing it was underdeveloped and lacking empirical vigour (Harper, 2013, 95). He was always unapologetic about how his School of Economics would be perceived by his contemporaries, not least, in Sydney. Syd Butlin, Chair of Economics at Sydney (1946–69), always felt that their approach delivered a technical training in economics, whereas Melbourne was too closely affiliated with business (Butlin, 1978). Melbourne would, indeed, specialise in descriptive and empirical studies, an approach which allowed a thorough examination of the Australian economy during the interwar period (Copland, 1951, 12). The divide created a fair degree of animus between the two men.[25] Gerald Firth, who joined the department in 1938, would later tell his Sydney counterpart, Hermann Black, that he had 'a private axe to grind', namely, that he felt the 'teaching of economics in Melbourne may be developed along rational and intelligent lines' and that greater contact with the Sydney counterparts with regular meetings might help in that regard. Black responded favourably, telling Firth that the lack of any such previous cooperation did not lie with his Sydney colleagues.[26]

All this did not mean Melbourne made no original theoretical contribution – far from it – rather it was orientated towards the world of affairs. Despite his humble origins, Copland also had a remarkable degree of self-assurance, helped by having an article on the application of the Quantity Theory of Money published in the *Economic Journal* edited by Keynes. That link opened up a correspondence between the two which was far greater, incidentally, than the link between Giblin and Keynes. One Australian businessman even hailed Copland as the 'Keynes of the Commonwealth' (Millmow, 2015). Copland's strength, though, was always as a builder of institutions rather than as a theoretician. He would never, much to the disappointment of his teacher, Hight, write a major treatise. When once describing the ideal leadership of the Commerce School, he favoured an economist with a 'fair knowledge of economic theory' and a keen interest in the practical application of theory, as well as administrative capacity. He added: 'It would be a mistake to rely upon a pure theorist or one who is wholly interested in the application of theory.'[27] He told one of his favourite students to 'resist incursions into theory. You can let the theory work itself out gradually as your grasp of the main facts if the situation improves.'[28] That aside, Copland mattered because he was the great enabler; by his energy and actions he encouraged others to become first-class economists.

Melbourne's Research Chair in Economics was the gift of a pastoralist, R. B. Ritchie, established in honour of his son, who had been killed in the First World War. It was his other son, Alan Ritchie – who had undertaken the Cambridge Tripos just after the war – who was, in fact, the real impetus behind the gift. Ritchie had befriended Copland and it was from their interaction that the idea of a Research Chair arose. Copland welcomed it as likely to be 'one of the prizes of the profession, if not the prize in this part of the world' (cited in Harper, 2013, 99).[29] After an unsuccessful international search, which involved establishing teams in America and England, the selection committee turned to a local man. Before then, Copland asked the American economist Frank Taussig whether the Canadian economist Jacob Viner would be interested in coming to Australia for a few years.[30] Copland, however, was relieved when Giblin accepted the offer of the Chair since he had already demonstrated his ability on the work on the tariff by finding 'a way of measuring economic phenomena which baffled the rest of us'.[31] A grateful Giblin told R. B. Ritchie:

> It seemed to me a great thing that anyone should have sufficient faith in the application of science to economic problems to found such a chair. I believe this is the critical time when Australian problems most urgently need economic study and economics is just sufficiently advanced to make that study useful and profitable to the country.[32]

They were noble sentiments, but Alan Ritchie, as we shall see, would later become disappointed in the fruits of the venture.

Copland and Giblin would form a formidable combination at Melbourne. The old Tasmanian was wise, serene and a true scholar; a wonderful counterpoise to the energetic, well-connected and publicly minded Copland. They would represent the Melbourne School of Economics. Meanwhile, Copland had another piece of good fortune which would strengthen the professionalisation of economics throughout Australasia. In 1926 he had been appointed the Australasian representative for the Social Sciences for the Laura Spelman Rockefeller Memorial, which was funded by the Rockefeller Foundation (Harper, 2013). The scheme provided Australasian academics and teaching staff with the opportunity to undertake more research training or a qualification at an approved place of higher learning in North America or Europe. Once the trust was operational, Copland was instrumental in encouraging and facilitating more than 25 Australian and New Zealand economists to be awarded a two-year Rockefeller Scholarship (Millmow, 2015). The one strict condition of the award was that successful candidates had to return home.[33] As a preliminary to the new task, Copland was afforded the opportunity to examine how the Foundation operated in New York and Paris. It allowed him the chance to visit the leading economic departments in America, Britain and Europe and to develop networks with leading economists. Visiting Keynes in London, Copland was told that the training at Canterbury 'must be as good as it is anywhere'. Copland told a colleague 'How is that for our Australian friends!'[34] Privately, Copland came away thinking that Keynes was something of 'a spoilt prima donna'.[35]

The University of Adelaide

The University of Adelaide might well have established a Chair in Economics before Melbourne, since it had already established commercial education, but a controversy over comments made by Economics lecturer Herbert Heaton meant they were denied that distinction (Bourke, 1990). Heaton had apparently antagonised local business interests who were underwriting the university because they felt his brand of economics was politicised and too closely affiliated with the trade unions (Hagger, 2004, 12–13). Business interests wanted to see the practical use of commercial education and were wary of the political implications that came with an education in economics (Bourke, 1990, 69). Since the University failed to give Heaton his due, it meant that Adelaide was the only university in Australasia with no Chair in Economics until one was advertised in 1928. It made amends by establishing a Chair in 1929, with Leslie Melville, the Public Actuary for South Australia, elected to the post, notwithstanding the fact that he was the only economist within the department. Copland felt that business interests had considerable influence behind Melville's appointment and regretted that another applicant, A. G. B. Fisher, had missed out on the Adelaide Chair.[36]

The University of Western Australia

At the isolated outpost of Perth, Edward Shann was appointed the foundation Professor of Economics and History at the University of Western Australia

(UWA) in 1913, where he laid the foundations for economics education (Moore, 2011). Like Richard Mills, he had, in part, been educated at the LSE and was primarily an economic historian, rather than a theorist. The most significant formative part of Shann's life had been to live through the boom and bust of the 1890s and subsequently to write an economic history of Australia (1930) foretelling the next crash. Fate would compel him to live through his prophecy, but this time on a far larger scale than he imagined.

The University of Tasmania

It was Hobart, though, that had been the 'Edinburgh of the South' when it came to the establishment of economics in Australia (Coleman and Hagger, 2003). It was to be the first Faculty of Commerce established in the southern hemisphere. Hagger (2004, 148) rated the Tasmanian Faculty as the best School of Economics in Australia during the 1920s on the basis of four criteria: turning out first-class graduates, path-breaking research, providing advice to official authorities and 'spreading the light' – that is, informing the public about economic problems. It was true Tasmania could boast first-rate minds. Giblin, who was the Statistician for the Tasmanian Government, advised Copland on academic matters. Also assisting Copland was another Anzac economist, James Brigden. His story paralleled that of his compatriot, Condliffe. After being wounded in action he ended up, by the 'merest fluke', in a convalescent home near Oxford. One of the volunteer assistants there was Rita Cannan, wife of the eminent LSE economist. Intrigued by his conversation and occasional writing, she alerted her husband (ibid., 31). Another eminent visitor was Professor F. Y. Edgeworth, who taught political economy at Oxford and, like Cannan, gave Brigden tuition. Brigden was granted leave for a year to take a soldier's scholarship. A man, then, who had barely attended secondary school ended up going up to Oriel College, Oxford. While there, he undertook a Diploma in Economics and Political Science and later graduated in the Honours School of Jurisprudence. It was through Cannan that Brigden became interested in economics, although the article he wrote in the first issue of the *Record*, about diminishing returns in agriculture, would have gone against his mentor. Copland, as editor, had welcomed it, saying it would encourage 'a great respect for economic theory'.[37] It was rushed into print.

After graduating from Oxford, Brigden was appointed Director of Tutorial Classes at the University of Sheffield. While there, he was approached by Albert Mansbridge of the WEA to accept a similar position in Tasmania (ibid., 34). The WEA, established in 1913, was another significant pioneering factor in promoting economics in Australasia, with almost all of the economists under discussion involved with it (Goodwin, 1966). It was hard work teaching the principles of economics in the countryside to miners, labourers and farmers or, in the cities, to factory workers. With Copland's blessing, Brigden became a Lecturer in Economics and Industrial Relations at the University of Tasmania in 1923. When Copland moved to Melbourne in 1924, Brigden took his place. Brigden served on the Queensland Economic Commission on the Basic Wage alongside Mills. In its recommendations, the Commission broke new ground by putting forward the proposal that the Court include in its deliberations on the basic wage some reference to the capacity of industry to pay.

The Economic Society of Australia and New Zealand

There had been, in the 1880s, an Australian Association of Economists, but it was short-lived and Sydney-centric (Scott, 1990, 2). Business and commercial interests in Melbourne, the then financial and political capital of Australia, first canvassed the idea of forming an association of economic expertise, but it was to be academics who were the deciding factor. And it was at an academic forum of Australian scientists that the Economic Society emerged. At the 1924 Adelaide meeting of the AAAS there was, as Giblin put it, 'a gathering of the clans' with economists forming the Economic Society of Australia and New Zealand (Goodwin, 1966). Copland's energy and verve lay behind the formation of the Society. He saw its potential: 'It will be possible... for the economists of Australia to compare notes and map out the big problems of research awaiting treatment.'[38] It is interesting that these two bodies, the Australian and New Zealand Association for the Advancement of Science (ANZAAS) and the Economic Society, were the only two learned societies that spanned the Tasman for a lengthy period of time.

The objectives of the Society were to encourage the study of economics and to consider its application to Australia and New Zealand. It also sought to provide a forum for debate, to promote research through monthly meetings and to disseminate those findings. This ambit included publishing a journal, which put out its first issue, with bold gothic lettering, in November 1925 (Scott, 1990, 7). The first number had a production run of 1,150, a respectable figure compared to the *Economic Journal*'s run of 3,000 copies. Soon production reached 1,500 copies. Two issues were put out for each of the first two years, with the editors never short of submissions. The *Record* contained reviews of the latest economic literature, both domestic and overseas. It also featured a section on economic conditions for the business clientele who had invested in the venture. The journal was, therefore, no remote academic screed; it would, after 1956, contain surveys of the Australian and New Zealand economies until 1968. Before 1945, the *Record* was 'Australasian in subject matter, pragmatic in method, and policy orientated' (Butlin, 1966, 513). This was still the orientation of the journal by the end of the century – that is, an applied journal mostly focusing upon Australian economic issues. That intention is writ large in the journal's editorial statement.

Ninety years on, the aims of the Society have barely changed. It was, moreover, to be a Society for professionals and non-professionals, with no strictures on admission other than an abiding interest in economics issues. The contents of the pages of the *Record* were a window into the orientation of the profession in either country. In that regard, Fleming (1994, 10–11), using citation data drawn from the *Record* for the period 1925–46, found that, during the interwar period, Australasian economics was anglicised, drawing inspiration from the likes of Keynes, Pigou, Marshall, Hayek and, most especially for the Australians,

Cannan. However, Fleming found that Australasian economics showed signs of maturity, with local scholars citing each other as the *Record* addressed issues relevant to Australasia. That said, Fleming reminds us that mere citation data cannot substantiate claims of anglicisation without peering into the methods of research, empiricism and focus of enquiry of Australasian economists. The general impression of first decade of the *Record* was of the smallness of the body of stalwarts who made contributions at that time.

The structure of the Economic Society was federal, with a Central Council, headquartered in Australia, charged with managing its affairs. A President was elected every two or three years and, with just two exceptions, was always an Australian-based identity (Scott, 1990). There was representation from all the branches in all the main cities of Australia and New Zealand. The Melbourne and Sydney branches were the largest and most powerful in Australia, as was the Wellington Branch in New Zealand. Interestingly, the editorial board for the journal had five members with at least two drawn from New Zealand. This editorial arrangement would last for more than 60 years before it was expanded to comprise of Australasian economists from home and abroad. For nearly 40 years the *Record* was the only publishing outlet for Australasian economists.

The first editor of the *Record* was originally intended to be Herbert Heaton, but, after he had accepted a Chair at Queen's University, Canada, his place was taken by Copland, already the President-elect of the Society. It was, in any case, a propitious appointment, since Heaton lacked the tactfulness and guile of his successor. Mills was co-editor and promptly responded to Copland on every submission sent to him. There was also representation from New Zealand on the editorial board. Nonetheless, Heaton (1926, 235) graciously welcomed the appearance of the new journal as marking 'the beginning of the systematic study and teaching of economic science in the Antipodes'. Heaton (ibid., 248) intoned that, if the first issue of the *Record* was any guide, Australia would be well served 'both critically and constructively in its experiments by its economists'. Tocker felt the first number of the *Record* was better than the December issue of the *Economic Journal*: 'It hits on stuff that is new, interesting and badly in need of investigation. It'll do us a lot of good, give us information and stimulus, a forum, and bring us closer together.'[39] The debate between Brigden and Benham on the Australian tariff enlivened the pages of the first issue. Condliffe (1950, 27) praised his old colleague, Copland, for 'nursing to international recognition' the journal 'which has done more than any other single vehicle to give the economists of Australia and New Zealand an opportunity to publish their work'. Copland's editorship marked the start of a 52-year period of Melbourne holding that position. While the *Record* was modelled on the *Quarterly Journal of Economics* (*QJE*), the new journal was literally all things to all men, not just a specialist academic journal. Before 1945 half of the articles it contained were written by non-academics (Butlin, 1966). This would become a nagging concern for the journal. Richard Downing, editor of the *Record* for 20 years, complained about pandering to the business clientele, which he described as the 't.b.m.' – 'the tired business man'; they were, however, 'the majority of our subscribers'

(Brown, 2001, 180). From the outset, the journal had a bias towards applied economic research, an orientation it has consistently held. Another perennial concern, more evident after 1945, was the low level of representation or output from New Zealand economists (Buckle and Creedy, 2016, 6–7). That aside, the journal was the only social sciences journal in Australasia until the mid-1950s. Giblin (1947, 1) hailed the *Record* as a 'great achievement' for Australian economics which had 'started behind scratch in 1925'. He believed that 'in no other branch of studies, literary or scientific, has Australia produced a journal widely recognized and highly esteemed as in Economics'. This was praise indeed, but could it be sustained after 1945, when economics would become more formalised and quantitative?

Conclusion

After a long grounding in political economy, Australasian economics was ready to begin afresh with a small corps of dedicated economists. Economic instruction was now entrenched and systematic in the curriculum rather than having the haphazard status it had endured in the nineteenth century. Australasian economists had been mostly brought up on the English classical political economy tradition, with the New Zealanders, especially Condliffe, Copland and Belshaw, enjoying the better training. Whatever the perceived insularity and provincialism of Antipodean economics, their economists responded to a wide range of public policy issues that needed to be addressed. In undertaking that challenge, Australasian economists would not just improvise but be innovative. They developed both theoretical and policy innovations that would startle their peers around the world.

Notes

1 'Can the kiwi economy fly?', *The Economist*, 30 November 2000.
2 Colin Clark's interview with B. McFarlane and D. Healey, mimeo. Always outspoken, Clark told Nash that New Zealand farmers were the richest in the world and that they had 'an insatiable lust for money' (Sinclair, 1976, 168). At the time many farmers there were still in mortgage stress, but Nash had given dairy farmers guaranteed prices.
3 When one Australian Federal Treasurer, Harold Holt, was shown the scale of mineral deposits in Western Australia he remarked that it was a gift beyond our dreams.
4 Other Copland material, Lecture notes, Faculty of Economics and Commerce (FECC), University of Melbourne Archives (UMA).
5 Strangely there has never been a trans-Tasman university operating in both countries. However, Michael Porter, the Director of the Centre for Policy Studies at Monash University, tried in 1988 to establish a privately funded Tasman University in central Melbourne that would offer management education courses for Australian and New Zealand business executives. The venture never got off the ground.
6 Condliffe to Hight 9/2/19, Macmillan Brown Library (MBL).
7 Condliffe to Hight 26/1/1919, MBL.
8 Condliffe to Hight 19 3 1919, MBL.
9 Condliffe to Hight 18/7/1919, MBL.
10 Keynes to Condliffe, Condliffe Papers, Bancroft Library

11 Condliffe to Hight 10/12/1919, MBL.
12 Condliffe to Copland 20/6/1920, Copland Papers, NLA.
13 It was supervised by J. P. Clapham and was entitled 'The Economic Development of the Far East'.
14 Belshaw died in Rome while working for the FAO. His gravestone in Cimitero Acattolico in Rome records: 'Scholar, educator and international servant who left his New Zealand home to befriend the rural peoples of all nations'.
15 Copland to Brigden 9/3/1927. While in Hawaii Condliffe was sounded out to be the first Director of the Bureau of Economic Research in Canberra, which had been established by the Bruce Government.
16 Ibid.
17 Souter's application letter for the chair of economics, 5/9/1935, University of Otago Archives.
18 Since the 1920s Australia has had a modest tradition of producing textbooks for domestic students, starting with Mills and Benham, *The Principles of Money, Banking and Foreign Exchange and its Application to Australia* (1925), supplemented a decade later by Mills and Walker, *Money* (1935), which displayed the uses of monetary policy in dealing with the business cycle.
19 Belshaw to Copland 13/1/1926, Copland Papers, NLA
20 Copland to Belshaw 9/2/1930, Copland Papers, NLA.
21 They were Copland, Condliffe, Fisher and Riches.
22 Brigden to Copland 26/4/1924, Copland Papers, NLA
23 Benham to Cannan 29/12/1927, Cannan Papers, LSE.
24 William Edward Hearn (1826–1888) was an Irish-born academic and politician who was the first Dean of the University of Melbourne's Law School in 1873.
25 Noel Butlin Oral Trc, ANU.
26 Firth to Black 30/1/1940, Black to Firth 1/2/194,0 Black Papers, University of Sydney Archives.
27 Report on Faculty of Commerce, 1928 FECC, UMA.
28 Copland to Polglaze 10/12/1937, FECC, UMA.
29 The selection committee behind the chair was prepared to offer the position to Cannan but he replied saying he would find two years in Melbourne rather too strenuous. Keynes suggested they find someone within Australasia.
30 Copland to Taussig 5/3/1928, FECC, UMA.
31 Copland to Taussig 3/12/1928, FECC, UMA.
32 Giblin to R. B. Ritchie 2/5/1929, Ritchie Papers, UMA.
33 Benham would be Copland's first choice as a Rockefeller Fellow and, indeed, the only one not to return to Australia.
34 Copland to Wood 26/6/1926, Copland Papers, NLA.
35 Copland diary of his 1926 trip, Copland Papers, NLA.
36 Copland to Fisher, March 1929, Copland Papers, NLA.
37 Copland to Brigden 8/10/1925, Copland Papers, NLA.
38 Copland to Taussig 12/4/1924, FECC, UMA.
39 Tocker to Copland 22/1/1926, FECC, UMA.

References

Adelman, J. 2013, *Worldly Philosopher: The Odyssey of Albert O. Hirschman*, Princeton, NJ: Princeton University Press.
Arndt, H. W. 1968, *A Small Rich Industrial Country*, Melbourne: Cheshire.
Barrowman, R. 1999, *Victoria University of Wellington 1899–1999*, Wellington: Victoria University Press.

Benham, F. C. 1928, *The Prosperity of Australia*, London: P. S. King and Son.

Benham, F. C. 1938, *Economics: A General Textbook for Students*, London: Sir Isaac Pitman and Sons.

Bertram, G. 2007. 'Bernard Edward Murphy (1884–1959)', in J. E. King (ed.), *A Biographical Dictionary of Australasian Economists*, Cheltenham: Edward Elgar.

Black, H. D. 1962, 'Frederick Benham', *Economic Review*, 7: 12–13.

Blainey, G. 1968, 'The cargo cult in mineral policy', *Economic Record*, 44(4): 470–9.

Blakey, K. 1958, 'Economic Experiments in New Zealand and their Political Background', *Economic Record*, 34: 189–98.

Blyth, C. A. 1966, 'The special case: the political economy of New Zealand', *Political Science*, 18: 38–51.

Blyth, C. A. 1987, 'The economists' perspective on economic liberalisation', in A. Bollard and R. Buckle (eds), *Economic Liberalisation in New Zealand*, Wellington: Allen and Unwin.

Blyth, C. A. 2007, 'John Maynard Keynes: external examiner for the University of New Zealand, 1919', *History of Economics Review*, 46: 151–62.

Blyth, C. A. 2008, 'Early academic economics in New Zealand: notes on its history from the 1870s to the 1950s', Working Paper Series, Department of Economics, University of Auckland, No. 266.

Bourke. H. 1990, 'Herbert Heaton and the foundation of economics at the University of Adelaide, 1917–1929', in F. B. Smith and P. Crichton (eds), *Ideas for Histories of Universities in Australia*, Canberra: Australian National University.

Brooke, G., A. Endres and A. Rogers, 2016, 'Does New Zealand economics have a useful past? The example of trade policy and economic development', *New Zealand Economic Papers*, 50(3): 281–302.

Brown, N. 2001, *Richard Downing: Economics, Advocacy and Social Reform in Australia*, Melbourne: Melbourne University Press.

Buckle, R. A. and J. Creedy, 2016, 'Fifty years of *New Zealand Economic Papers*: 1966–2015', *New Zealand Economic Papers*, 50(3): 234–60.

Butlin, N. G. 1978, 'A fraternal farewell: tribute to S. J. Butlin', *Australian Economic History Review*, 18: 99–118.

Butlin, S. J. 1966, 'The hundredth record', *Economic Record*, 42(100): 508–19.

Cain, N. 1973, 'Political economy and the tariff: Australia in the 1920s', *Australian Economic Papers*, 12(20): 1–20.

Capling, A. and B. Galligan, 1992, *Beyond the Protective State*, Melbourne: Cambridge University Press.

Coleman, W. and A. Hagger, 2003, 'An Edinburgh of the South? Some contributions to fundamental economic analysis by Tasmanian economists in the 1920s', *Tasmanian Historical Studies*, 8(2): 10–27.

Condliffe, J. B. 1940, *The Reconstruction of World Trade*, New York: W. W. Norton.

Condliffe, J. B. 1950, 'The teacher and the influence', in R. S. Allan (ed.), *Liberty and Learning*, Christchurch: Whitcombe and Tombs.

Condliffe, J. B. 1959 [1930], *New Zealand in the Making*, London: Allen and Unwin.

Condliffe, J. B. 1969, 'The economic outlook for New Zealand', *New Zealand Economic Papers*, 3(1): 5–14.

Condliffe, J. B. 1973, 'Autobiography', manuscript.

Copland, D. B. 1951, *Inflation and Expansion*, Melbourne: Cheshire.

Corden, W. M. 1968, *Australian Economic Policy Discussion: A Survey*, Melbourne: Melbourne University Press.

Corden, W. M. 2010, 'Review of *Balanced Growth* by Ross Williams', *Economic Record*, 86(274): 461–3.

Donoghue, M. 2007, 'Ralph William Souter (1897–1946)', in J. E. King (ed.), *A Biographical Dictionary of Australasian Economists*, Cheltenham: Edward Elgar, 261–4.

Downing, R. and J. Isaac, 1961, 'The 1961 Basic Wage Judgement and wage policy', *Economic Record*, 37(80): 480–94.

Easton, B. 1997, *In Stormy Seas: The Post War New Zealand Economy*, Dunedin: University of Otago.

Easton, B. 2001, *The Nation Builders*, Auckland: Auckland University Press.

Eggleston, F. W. 1932, *State Socialism in Victoria*, London: P. S. King and Son.

Endres, A. M., 1991, 'J. B. Condliffe and the early Canterbury tradition in economics', *New Zealand Economic Papers*, 25(2): 171–97.

Endres, A. M. 2010, 'Marshallian economics in New Zealand, c. 1890–1940', in T. Raffaelli, (ed.), *The Impact of Alfred Marshall's Ideas: The Global Diffusion of his Work*, Cheltenham: Edward Elgar.

Endres, A. M. and A. Rogers, 2014, 'Trade policy and international finance in the Bretton Woods era: a doctrinal perspective with reference to Australia and New Zealand', *History of Economics Review*, 59: 62–81.

Fleming, G. A. 1989, 'The role of economists in New Zealand policy making 1912–51: economic advice structures in development', Working Papers in Economics, University of Auckland, No. 59.

Fleming, G. A. 1994, 'Some problems in interpreting citation practices in the economic record 1925–1946', *History of Economics Review*, 22: 1–15.

Friedman, M. and R. Friedman, 1998, *Two Lucky People*, Chicago: University of Chicago Press.

Giblin, L. F. 1947, 'The *Record* and its editors', *Economic Record*, 23(1).

Goldfinch, S. 2000, 'Paradigms, economic ideas and institutions in economic policy change: the case of New Zealand', *Political Science*, 52(1): 1–21.

Goodwin, C. D. 1966, *Economic Enquiry in Australia*, Durham, NC: Duke University Press.

Gould, J. 1982, *The Rakes's Progress*, Auckland: Hodder and Stoughton.

Greasley, D. and L. Oxley, 1999, 'Growing apart? Australia and New Zealand growth experiences 1870–1913', *New Zealand Economic Papers*, 33(2): 1–13.

Groenewegen, P. 2009, *Educating for Business, Public Service and the Social Sciences: A History of the Faculty of Economics at the University of Sydney 1920–1999*, Sydney: Sydney University Press.

Groenewegen, P. 2010, 'Marshall and Australia', in T. Raffaelli, (ed.), *The Impact of Alfred Marshall's Ideas: The Global Diffusion of his Work*, Cheltenham: Edward Elgar.

Hagger, A. J. 2004, *Economics in the University of Tasmania: The First One Hundred Years*, Hobart: University of Tasmania Press.

Hancock, K. 2013, *Australian Wage Policy: Infancy and Adolescence*, Adelaide: University of Adelaide Press.

Harper, M. 2013, *Douglas Copland: Scholar, Economist, Diplomat*, Melbourne: Miegunyah Press.

Hatch, J. and C. Rogers, 1997, 'Distinguished Fellow of the Economic Society of Australia, 1996: Professor Emeritus Geoff Harcourt', *Economic Record*, 73(221): 97–100.

Heaton, H. 1926, 'Progress and problems of Australian economists', *American Economic Review*, 26(2): 235–48.

Hight, J. 1939, 'Preface', *Economic Record*, 15: 3–6.

Hodgart, A. W. 1975, *The Faculty of Economics and Commerce: A History 1925–75*, Melbourne: Melbourne University Press.

Holmes, F. W. 2011, *The New Zealand Association of Economists: Memories of its Early Years*, Wellington: New Zealand Association of Economists.

Hogan, W. P. 1999, 'Colin George Frederick Simkin, 1915–1998', *Economic Review*, 75(230): 313–22.

Lloyd P. 2007, 'J. B. Condliffe (1891–1981)', in J. E. King (ed.), *A Biographical Dictionary of Australasian Economists*, Cheltenham: Edward Elgar, 62–5.

McLean, L. 2011, *A History of Economics and the Development of Commerce Degrees at the University of Otago 1871–2009*, Dunedin: Uniprint.

Millmow, A. J. 2015, 'John Maynard Keynes and the Keynes of the Commonwealth', *Australian Economic History Review*, (55)1: 1–19.

Mills, R. C. and Benham, F. C. 1925, *The Principles of Money, Banking and Foreign Exchange and its Application to Australia*, Sydney: Angus and Robertson.

Mills, R. C. and Walker, E. R. 1935, *Money*, Sydney: Angus and Robertson.

Moore, G. C. 2011, 'The campaign to arrest Ed Shann's influence in Western Australia', *History of Economics Review*, 54: 14–44.

Randerson, R. 1953, 'Masters of economics', *Australian Quarterly*, (25)1: 42–54.

Scott, R. H. 1990, *The Economic Society of Australia: Its History 1925–1985*, Melbourne: Economic Society of Australia.

Shann, E. 1930, *An Economic History of Australia*, Michigan: The University Press.

Sinclair, K. 1976, *Walter Nash*, Auckland: Auckland University Press.

Smith, N. S. 1929, *Economic Control: Australian Experiments in Rationalisation and Safeguarding*, London: P. S. King and Son.

Tay, F. 2007, *125 Years of Economic Studies at Canterbury, New Zealand*, Christchurch: University of Canterbury.

3   The practical Utopia
of economics

> There are said to be, in the far north and the far south, happy lands where econo-
> mists all give the same advice, where the government listens to it, where the
> public understands why the government has listened – and where, the cynic might
> add, the very prices of timber and wool play, as though by magic, their appointed
> part in the harmonious scheme.
>
> D. H. Robertson (1940)

Introduction

The Cambridge economist Dennis Robertson's peroration was a direct reference to the work of economists in Sweden and Australia during the 1930s. An
Indian economist, B. P. Adarkar, hailed Australia as a Utopia for practical
economists (Goodwin, 1974). There is no doubt that the decade of the 1920s
was a watershed period for Australasian economics in a formative sense, but it
was to be in the 1930s that its economists really made their name, becoming
the interest, if not the toast, of the international economics community. By that
time, the subject had gained 'a position of authority and respect' (Goodwin,
1966, 639). What drove this and how did Australian economics become so pre-
eminent so quickly? The answer was, of course, events and the response of
public policy to them. High authority, too, played a part believing that the new
discipline had something to offer clever and efficient administration. Aiding
this was a bias in Australasian economics towards 'empiricism and pragmatism'. Indeed, it was so entrenched that Leslie Melville felt it was sometimes
to the detriment of theoretical innovation. Echoing Giblin's earlier comment
about Australian economists, Melville recollected that '[e]ssentially we were
all pragmatists dealing with applied economics, applied to practical problems
that were developing very rapidly, and there wasn't much development till a
good deal later'.[1]

This penchant for practicality over theoretical innovation is important in the
telling of our story. It can, however, be oversold. While the attribute paid dividends in pushing economists into the limelight, it did not really mean that they
were slow in acclimatising to new theory or, as we shall see, even pioneering new
theoretical innovations. The policies which Australasian economists advocated

during the Depression and thereafter sprang from the very latest theoretical and applied research (Copland, 1951, 17). But before all that came an inquiry that undermined the case for free trade and unrestricted markets.

An analysis of the articles published in *Record* in the 1920s revealed that 30 per cent were on economic development, population growth, manufacturing and land settlement, reflecting the fact that both countries were undergoing economic development. Heaton (1926, 245–7) told an American audience that the predominant research interests of their Australian counterparts were the economics of federation, wage fixation and banking and currency policy. The problem, however, that really preoccupied the Australian economics fraternity in the 1920s was determining Australia's optimum population size and the standard of living that could be afforded (Cain, 1973).

In 1921 Australia had established the Tariff Board, a quasi-independent body to examine applications for tariff support, to develop its own criteria and make recommendations to government. New Zealand had its own Tariff and Development Board. They were the only countries to have such a body advising the government on trade policy. In 1926 the Tariff Board sanctioned the principle that a viable and efficiently operated firm be given enough protection to survive and earn a reasonable profit. It granted protection, therefore, to 'economic and efficient' production, something that was administratively difficult to quantify. Inevitably, there was discussion about the tariff and its worth to the nation. Pastoralists and other rural interests sought to quantify the excess costs of the tariff and highlighted the vicious circle of rising tariffs and rising wages that became known as the 'New Protectionism'. While passionately dedicated to protectionism, the Tariff Board was concerned about manufacturers clamouring for protection to compete against imports. This put pressure upon primary producers, who were already facing lower prices for their produce (Capling and Galligan, 1992, 89).

In 1927 Prime Minister Stanley Bruce commissioned a committee of economists to quantify the costs and benefits of the Australian tariff. Giblin, Brigden and Copland served on the committee, together with Edward Dyason, a Melbourne stockbroker, and Charles Wickens, the Commonwealth Statistician, who served as Chair; but it was Giblin, Brigden and Copland who did most of the theoretical sparring. Accounts of the drafting of the Report (Harper, 2013; Cain, 1973) suggest that it was a difficult process trying to reconcile different viewpoints and reach common ground. Brigden's earlier work foreshadowed just what the Committee would conclude; the compromise document was radical enough and would make waves.

The Australian heresy

Australian economists have always been renowned for their contributions to trade theory. In the 1970s Max Corden, Murray Kemp, Richard Snape and Peter Lloyd were widely recognised for their work on aspects of trade theory, both pure and applied. Kemp is interesting in that, as Australia's leading pure trade theorist, none of his work has a distinctly Australian focus, even though he was a research professor at the University of New South Wales for 38 years. Kemp came to international economics from initially dabbling in Keynesian and welfare economics. One of his most important papers was with Henry Wan, showing that forming a customs union would be Pareto optimal if the members of the union adjusted their common external tariff so as to keep its trade volumes with non-member countries at the pre-union level. Using the lecture notes he gave at a graduate class at the Massachusetts Institute of Technology (MIT), Kemp wrote a definitive text on the theory of international trade which drew the effusive praise of Paul Samuelson (1993). In that volume, Kemp led the mathematicisation of trade theory and examined the fundamentals of the Heckscher–Ohlin–Samuelson paradigm (Wan and Van Long, 1998). Kemp's text was superseded by compatriot Alan Woodland's advanced textbook on *International Trade and Resource Allocation* (1982).

Described as an 'old-fashioned' academic, Lloyd was interested in economic theory in order to understand the real world and contribute to policy advice. Like many Australasian economists, Lloyd was not interested in pursuing 'theory for its own sake' (Corden and Jayasuriya, 2006, 77). His first contribution to economic scholarship was a paper with Herbert Grubel (1971) on intra-industry trade. In what became the *Record*'s second most highly cited paper, they argued that intra-industry trade was a subject worthy of attention. The two authors immortalised their names by drawing up the Grubel–Lloyd index to measure this type of trade. Another path-breaking contribution was that of Snape, introducing product differentiation in an optimal tariff model with domestic monopoly. It foreshadowed the literature on product differentiation in international trade later described as 'the new international economics'.

These were just some of the worthy advances in orthodox trade theory, but the first major contribution that Australian economists would make was in disputing accepted trade theory. It still causes controversy today; one of Australia's leading economists, Ross Garnaut (2013, 39), recently remarked that his predecessors 'obliged the country's political preferences by developing a unique and analytically unsatisfactory "Australian case for protection"'. In another publication, Kym Anderson and Garnaut (1987) accused their predecessors of 'a dereliction of duty' in allowing protectionism to take root in Australia. There is, of course, a certain amount of revisionism in this view. Their predecessors were, at the time, famed for theoretically justifying the case for protection, albeit with qualifications. Moreover, what these Australian economists devised was analytically innovative and relevant for Australia's development. It is interesting to recall that, as late as 1965, a Committee of Economic Inquiry lent support to their findings (Downing, 1966). Australian tariff policy was still associated with the absorption of population. Now secondary industry had supplanted land settlement as the means of absorbing new population, the difficulties of rural production soon resulted in a steady extension of protection through devices such as the Home Price Scheme. Only the wool and meat industries were exempt from this distortion.

Protection all round

Interestingly, the groundswell for protectionism came from Tasmania, Australia's smallest and most disadvantaged state. Before long, protection became more than just a policy; it was 'a faith and a dogma' even among most of Australia's small band of economists (Hancock, 1930). As one historian put it, 'The standard of living was the sacred Australian cow and the tariff was its fodder' (Cotter, 1967, 249). Protection was popular even within the Country Party, which represented rural and pastoral interests. It was a case of 'protection all round' with only the wool and gold industries exempt from any assistance.[2] Copland confirmed that the total cost of assistance going to the primary industries was greater than the assistance accruing to secondary industry. Giblin warned, too, that there were definite limits to the way assistance could be rendered by putting the burden on the wool industry. He colourfully described the arrangement by picturing 'Australia as one enormous sheep bestriding a bottomless pit, with statesman, lawyer, miner, landlord, farmer and factory and all hanging on desperately to the locks of its abundant fleece' (cited in Capling and Galligan, 1992, 92). He added that there was no policy of controlling the assistance going to primary industry yet representatives of those industries were 'always the most trenchant critics of the tariff'.[3] Bruce complained to a member of the Tariff Board: 'We have gone Tariff mad!' (Capling and Galligan, 1992). He feared the cost of protection was making Australian industries uncompetitive, and commissioned an inquiry into the matter led by his favourite economist, Brigden.

It was Brigden who sparked the whole debate with an article in the first issue of the *Record* outlining the rationale for the Australian tariff. He had picked up Alfred Marshall's comment on the operation of the tariff in America that it relieved the pressure of population on inferior land. The tariff had slowed down the cultivation of less-productive lands because it diverted production away from increasing-cost industries such as agriculture to decreasing-cost industries such as manufacturing. Brigden applied Marshall's logic to argue that, without the tariff, Australian manufacturing could expand only when the standard of living of the worker had been reduced to that of the newest settler on poorer land (Harper, 2013, 152).

The Brigden Report 1929

The report on the Australian tariff was to mark the first genuine theoretic contribution made by Australian economists in the twentieth century. It made two distinct contributions to economic theory: first, by looking at the effects of the tariff upon income distribution and, second, by trying to quantify the excess cost of the tariff. The Brigden Committee was also 'the first major intrusion by a body of economists into the field of economic policy' (Goodwin, 1966: 35). Australian economists defended protectionism on demographic and development grounds. Interestingly, their contemporaries in New Zealand were never allowed to engage in a similar exercise. The writing of the Report was a fraught affair for the authors, largely due to doctrinal differences. It was fortunate, too, that Mills and Shann were not on the Committee because they were unrepentant free traders. Brigden and Giblin, representing the Hobart protectionist view, prevailed over the more sceptical Melbourne free trade view represented by Copland and Dyason. Copland, for instance, had a prejudice against the tariff, believing that successful and impartial administration of it was impossible. At one stage, during the writing of the Report, Brigden joked to Copland 'that while we were drifting towards free trade, you were defending protection' (cited in Harper, 2013, 157). Technically, the Report sought to estimate the excess cost of the tariff and identify who bore the incidence. It showed that the excess cost was justified if it was a modest amount and granted to industries with increasing returns. In that event, as demand increased and production expanded, the cost per unit would fall and the excess cost would fall in tandem. Giblin used a statistical technique by which several categories of production and income were measured and the costs of protected production gauged. This revealed that it was the change in the relative domestic price of manufacturing output which drove up the prices of labour and other materials to the rural sector, thus putting pressure on its profitability.

Without the tariff Australia would have had to invest in extensive rural settlement, but the income and employment from that additional primary production would not have been as great as the income and employment generated from a larger manufacturing sector. This meant therefore that the tariff maintained the present population at a higher standard of living than would be the case under free trade. In other words, the tariff was justifiable for Australia's economic development, welfare and population growth. Under free trade, diminishing returns in agriculture would not only skew income distribution to landowners but would drive down welfare levels and restrict the absorption of a growing population (Cain, 1974, 352). Brigden (1925, 45) concluded that 'protection had been as beneficial for Australia as free trade had been to Great Britain'. Before the Report was published, Brigden told his old master, Cannan, about the key findings and how these bore out the expressed views in his 1925 *Record* article.[4] Brigden's findings presaged the conclusions reached in the final report of the Committee's *The Australian Tariff: An Economic Enquiry* (Brigden *et al.*, 1929). The Report stated that the fall in income that would ensue from unimpeded rural development and population growth would be prevented because tariffs maintained real wages by redistributing rents from landowners to labour. An increased production of manufactured goods would increase the demand for labour, resulting in larger relative and absolute income accruing to labour. The Committee's finding, presented boldly on its first page, was to reject the orthodox contention that Australia could have maintained its present population at a higher standard of living under free trade. It went on:

> We have to recognise in the tariff as a whole, in spite of its undoubted extravagance, a potent instrument in maintaining at a given standard of living a larger population than would otherwise have been possible. It seems certain that without the tariff we would not have offered the same

field for immigrants and would not have been able to maintain our growth
of population.

Ibid., 84

The tariff, moreover, kept the terms of trade favourable by placing an implicit tax
on further rural exports (Coleman and Hagger, 2003, 15). Giblin would later
corroborate the Hobart view by calculating the amount of rural production that
Australia would have had to produce in order to generate an equivalent standard
of living. Such an effort would have driven down produce prices and would have
made Australia acutely vulnerable to world trends (Groenewegen and McFarlane,
1990, 122). Protection, Giblin concluded some years later, 'had turned out a
winner' (cited in Capling and Galligan, 1992, 100). The Committee found
instances where the cost of protection exceeded its benefits. Moreover, they were
keenly aware that the practice of tariff-setting had 'a demoralising effect upon
self-reliant efficiency' and would create covens of rent-seekers. They concluded
that the tariff had reached its upper limit and that any further increase would have
'to bear the most rigorous scrutiny of the cost involved' (cited in ibid., 95).
Putting forward sound principles for the Tariff Board to follow, the Committee
urged that rigorous examination of tariff assistance be undertaken by an agency
of independent economic advice. The Bruce Government (1923–29) went some
way in responding to this recommendation by passing legislation to establish a
Bureau of Economic Research.

When published the Report became a bestseller, the first economic work to do
so, facilitated by being an inexpensive paperback edition. It was also the first
comprehensive study ever undertaken of the Australian economy. In the foreword, Bruce hailed it as 'a free gift to the Australian people'. This was a reference
not just to the Report's practicality, but the way its authors had laboured without
compensation (Davidson, 1977, 146–7). The Report had been overshadowed by
events, namely, falling prices for wool and wheat, which had the effect of making
the margin of profitable land shrink all the faster and the case for the tariff
stronger (Harper, 2013, 158).

The authors of the Brigden Report were anxious to see how their overseas
counterparts would judge it. Jacob Viner praised Bruce for having commissioned
'a disinterested and non-political inquiry by competent and unbiased economists
into the merits of a policy to which his party and his country are so strongly
committed' (cited in Davidson, 1977, 147). However Viner was not convinced
that the authors had decisively argued their central thesis. Keynes, although not
entirely convinced by it, applauded the Report as 'a brilliant effort of the highest
interest' with a 'method of approach most original'.[5] Yet for all its endeavour, the
Brigden Report was, in effect, shelved when the incoming Scullin Government,
as an anti-depression measure, raised tariffs no less than seven times during its
first year in office (Capling and Galligan, 1992, 95).

As a sequel, Copland always remained sceptical of the theoretical underpin-
nings of the Brigden Report and would later spend a sabbatical studying the

issue. He wanted to find out whether there was any foundation in classical theory for the position taken by Australian economists. He felt that English economists had not considered the full implications for tariff theory arrived at in the Report. He told Keynes that English economists were all too ready to presume that the conditions favouring free trade in England were of universal application. Copland personally felt that British economists 'were not prepared to face the music when ideas at variance with their traditional notions are put forward'.[6] However, after further research surveying the classical writings for the point of view taken by Australian economists, Copland came away a little surprised at the origins of the economic philosophy behind the Brigden Report. He told a friend: 'We were quite wrong in thinking that we had developed a new point of view. Traces of the theory can be found in Marshall, Taussig, the Dutch economist, Pierson and in Sidgwick.'[7] Equally, Copland was also 'surprised' at the amount of support given to the Brigden Committee view when he addressed Keynes's Political Economy Club in Cambridge in 1933. Copland's seminar was 'successful beyond my greatest expectations' and he hoped to develop a good theoretical paper out of what he had heard in discussion. He found Keynes and his capacity for anticipating an argument 'amazing' in capturing the drift of the paper before anyone else.[8] In his closing comments, Keynes accepted Copland's argument of a transfer of resources from inelastic to elastic industries. He also complimented Copland for having 'provoked the best theoretical discussion at the Club in years'.[9] As such, the Brigden Report foreshadowed many of the insights of trade theory subsequently developed in the Heckler–Ohlin–Samuelson trade model, in particular, the Stolper–Samuelson theorem that a higher tariff would increase real wages if the import competing sector was more labour intensive than the export competing sector. Copland and Marion Samuelson deserve credit for leading the theoretical case. That theorem brought to light the potential for trade policy to result in distributional conflict between labour, capital and landowners.

The Brigden Committee and Copland's research into justifying modest protection were not the only contributions to trade theory developed during the interwar period. Roland Wilson, another Tasmanian who was taught by Copland and Giblin, brought out the distinction between the tradeable and non-tradeable parts of the economy and how capital inflow amplified that divide. It was a very pertinent topic since both dominions, especially Australia, were huge borrowers on the London capital market. In the 1920s Australia was regarded, rather unfavourably, as a somewhat 'brave' borrower of international funds in order to harness the development of its natural resources. While the idea of borrowing abroad would die very hard in Australia, London was becoming concerned about the extent of Australia's liabilities, lest it become the 'black sheep' of the British Empire. Wilson (1931, 3) wrote of how Australia's borrowings had been 'lavish' and, in that sense, too 'she had been lavish in the opportunities afforded the student of international capital movements' and how 'her financial vices became virtues' for the scientific investigator. In short, Australia had, in yet another context, 'turned herself into the social and economic laboratory'.

Wilson had the distinction of holding two doctorates in economics, one from Oxford, on the import of capital, and the other from Chicago, on the economic consequences of capital movements. He finished his Oxford doctorate at Chicago. His supervisor at Chicago for his second doctorate, Viner, hailed him as one of the two or three best doctoral students he encountered, though he was astounded when Wilson expressed an interest in returning home to Tasmania (Cornish, 2007, 311).[10] In his book, *Capital Imports and the Terms of Trade* (1931), Wilson had discovered that it was not necessarily true that a capital importing country such as Australia would experience a terms of trade boost and that, in any case, it was not all that important in terms of the balance of payments adjustment. Moreover, movement in the terms of trade were determined by trends in world markets; capital imports or foreign borrowing may or may not be associated with a rising terms of trade. Instead, Wilson focused on the difference between domestic and internationally traded goods. What was more important and far more likely for a small open economy such as Australia, he argued, was that capital inflow would push the prices of domestic goods up relative to international goods with the effect that the country incurred a trade deficit. This mechanism became known as the real exchange rate adjustment; it marked a singularly Australian contribution to trade theory, later known as dependent economy model (Metaxas and Weber, 2016, 492). Several other leading Australian economists would further develop this model.

New Zealand's reaction to the Brigden Report

How was this native wisdom received across the Tasman? New Zealand was, initially at least, never beholden to protection as much as Australia. This reflected the power of its farmers. New Zealand's economic development was characterised by rural activity, especially dairying. Consequently, tariffs were low by international standards (Endres and Jackson, 1993, 155) and New Zealand would even cut tariffs during the 1930s, although they were an important source of government revenue. Those tariff cuts were the outcome of the National Industrial Conference of 1928, when representatives of farmers, employers and unions were called together to discuss changes to reform the arbitration system (Fleming, 1989, 10–11). Economists, it was believed, would bring all parties together. Belshaw, Fisher, Tocker, Murphy and David Williams of Massey Agricultural College presented papers (Brooke *et al.*, 2016, 3). Underlying the conference was the knotty issue of the disparity between export prices and sheltered domestic prices and wages. In summary, exporters' costs were rising while their returns were falling. In this the economists failed, partly because of politics and partly because their recommendations were considered too theoretical (Fleming, 1989, 33). Tocker, Murphy and Williams, supporting the farmers, rounded on the arbitration system and wage regulation. Taking a more illustrative approach, Belshaw focused his attack on tariffs and how they accentuated the disparity between domestic and external prices. He pushed for a lowering of the tariff to foster efficiencies in domestic production. Belshaw drew upon Pigou's argument that protection was more an economic cost than a benefit when it came to preserving employment. All the economists emphasised that any increase in tariff levels would have zero economic benefit; a reduced tariff which would lower domestic costs and create less pressure for centrally determined wages to rise.

At the 1928 meeting of AAAS, Tocker gave a paper critical of arbitration in New Zealand, advocating its demise, but this was poorly received by his Australian colleagues. Copland conveyed this news to Justice Higgins of the Arbitration Court, adding: 'Arbitration, like any other institution, has its defects but it seems to me to be the height of absurdity and wickedness to insist upon all our troubles being due to this institution.'[11] In sum, while Australian economists were generally supportive of the nexus between arbitration and tariff protection, their New Zealand counterparts saw these institutional arrangements as putting unnecessary strain upon the export industries. Much later, Fisher took a swipe at the Brigden Committee. He had been not at all convinced by the logic of the Report and its whole method of approach, arguing that:

> It was a pity they had got away with it so easily… but really effective criticism demanded much more detailed work than anyone had time to give to the subject. The evil that they did seems especially clear when the attempt is made to estimate tariff costs for the separate states.[12]

Major Giblin's multiplier

When Giblin, as Ritchie Professor of Economics at the University of Melbourne, gave his inaugural public lecture entitled 'Australia, 1930' in April of that year he marked it with a theoretical bombshell, 'a landmark in economic thought' (Wilson, 1976, 310). Coleman and Hagger (2003, 19) have uncovered evidence that Giblin discovered the economic concept of the multiplier while based in Tasmania. He had been researching the effect of public works upon the economy, trying to unravel its aggregative effect, but now he came up with more concrete evidence.

It was under the aegis of a government agency, the Development and Migration Commission, that Giblin's multiplier, in its original form, came about. Copland had asked Giblin to calculate what the impact on population growth would be if a new railway were built in an area of new settlement, allowing a number of new farms to produce wheat for export. While there would be an expansionary effect on national income, Giblin was asked to quantify it, together with the associated effect on Australia's population. He approached the problem by modelling the new settlement as a disturbance to the economy. He calculated that it would have a direct and indirect effect upon Australia's population (Hagger, 2004), using a form of multiplier analysis in a mathematical expression to trace out the repercussions for the economy. What was critical was whether the railway could be made to pay if the indirect effects of the increased wheat production were taken into account. Giblin considered the direct and indirect gains from establishing the new farms and figured that the value of each new farm would be 700 pounds which would, in turn, merit an increase in population capacity of seven.

It was when Giblin calculated those indirect effects that he discovered a concept which became known as the multiplier. He reasoned that two-thirds of the income generated by each new farm would be spent on locally produced goods, thereby generating income for workers and employers. They, in turn, would spend two-thirds of that. Giblin's memorandum, entitled 'New Farms and Population', was dated August 1929. Giblin, who was said to be 'excited' by his discovery but unsure of its validity, passed it to Brigden to critique. Brigden saw the concept's potential and drew out the implication that with lower import propensity there would be a greater stimulatory effect. It was Brigden, too, who first recognised the significance of what he called the 'multiplier' working in reverse, with the cue being falling wool prices (Coleman, 2007, 20). In his Ritchie lecture eight months later, Giblin applied his new analysis to the contemporaneous drop of export income of 50 million pounds compounding to three times that amount. Giblin admitted some of the workings of the multiplier were 'obscure', adding 'I confess I do not see my way clearly through the tangle of price reaction that must follow the loss of income' (cited in Coleman *et al.*, 2006: 89). It seems that Giblin was ignoring his earlier work on the domestic investment multiplier associated with the railways construction. Moreover, as a hesitant Giblin confessed, it was his 'somewhat muddled belief that if this loss in export income was evenly spread through the community' (ibid.) the full multiplier process would not come into play. These oversights suggest that Giblin's understanding of his multiplier was underdeveloped.

Robert Dimand (1991, 16) is correct to say, therefore, that, with the exception of his Australian peers, Giblin's analysis 'vanished almost unremarked from the collective memory of the economics profession'. While Giblin had sent a bound copy of his 'Australia, 1930' lecture to the library at King's College there is no evidence any of the economists there, including Keynes or Richard Kahn, having read it. William Coleman, too, has ascertained that Cambridge economists were entirely unaware of Giblin's multiplier, implying that Kahn's employment multiplier, which was more fully developed in any case with savings as a leakage, was an innocent case of 'doubletons' (Coleman *et al.*, 2006, 94).

Was a grave injustice done to Giblin? Some felt so. Copland recalled 'The Cambridge boys never really conceded that Giblin was the pioneer.'[13] He told W. S. Robinson, the Australian mining magnate, 'The work we did on the multiplier before the Depression brought us to the conclusion that the addition of 1 million pounds of exports income would ultimately add three million to National Income.'[14] The matter resurfaced after 1945, when Copland raised the matter with Roy Harrod, editor of the *Economic Journal*, after his research assistant Ronald Barback's short note on the emergence of Giblin's multiplier was rejected. Copland was annoyed by Harrod's dismissal of the originality of the concept as a mere matter of 'fine shades both in the theory of theory and chronology'. Copland repeated that British economists had been 'much too coy' in giving Giblin recognition for his work.[15] Colin Clark, who declared he had been 'present at the birth of the multiplier' and worked on estimating its potency for the British Economic Advisory Council in 1931, was emphatic Giblin 'had been way ahead of the profession'.[16] In another place, he recalled,

> The evidence was satisfactory that Professor Giblin, in his inaugural lecture in Melbourne in 1930, first put the multiplier on the map. The multiplier appeared to have been in the minds of economists in Australia long before it had been thought of in America or Great Britain.

> Cited in Markwell, 2000, 34

Giblin never seemed peeved at non-recognition for his innovation, not least from Keynes. In 1933 he criticised Keynes's multiplier calculations in *The Means to Prosperity* (1933), informing him 'I have at times made similar computations here, eg on the total increase in income following from a given increase in export production' (cited in ibid., 36). As Peter Karmel (1960) clinically pointed out, Giblin's multiplier spoke, first, in terms of income not employment and, second, savings were automatically invested, with no recognition of an insufficiency of aggregate demand. While Giblin's multiplier was forgotten, another of his contributions would crystallise into a unique Australian economic institution.

Australia: fiscal federalism and the Commonwealth Grants Commission

While the Federation of the Australian states might have been a good idea from a constitutional perspective, economically it caused great angst among the weaker members of the union. A Royal Commission on Taxation (1920–23) had recommended that the Commonwealth government impose income tax and leave land tax and probate to the states. It was felt that the states should give up their income-taxing powers because they lacked uniformity and that this disturbed the flow of capital between the states. This recommendation was not implemented and states continued to levy income tax at different rates and on different definitions of taxable income. There was also the problem of the small states. Given her relative isolation, small size and equally small population, Tasmania faced daunting economic prospects. Western Australia and South Australia were, at the turn of the century, also adjudged to be in need of additional assistance, given their level of development. Ascertaining the net adverse effect of federation was problematic. South Australia, dependent upon wool and wheat exports, felt disadvantaged by the imposts from an artificial economic policy pursued by the Commonwealth, namely, tariff protection, wage arbitration and cabotage. Tasmania, too, needed fiscal assistance to survive and to be able offer the same social educational and welfare standards that would keep the Federation economically cohesive. The question, then, was how to calculate scientifically Tasmania's economic disadvantage. Giblin was the man who set about unravelling the puzzle. Brigden and Giblin had already served on a committee inquiring into state–federal finance and how Tasmania fared in the allocation of Commonwealth funds. They argued that, under the Federation, Tasmania was economically disadvantaged and should be accorded more federal assistance.

Giblin developed a theory of different scales of taxable capacity according to each state's economic development. If one could calculate a state's taxable capacity and how, in a Federation, some states were richer than others, then a system of special grants could be devised for those states most in need. These states needed to demonstrate a deficiency of taxation greater than for the average for the whole Federation. Another problem was how to prevent grants from encouraging wasteful public spending or allowing states to become lax in raising revenue. To control the process, Giblin argued for a body, similar to the Tariff Board, to be composed of professionals who would arrive at an unbiased opinion about per capita payments. He was rightly made a member of the Commonwealth Grants Commission when it was established in 1933. It was initially to be called the States Disabilities Commission, since it was established to look at the finances of the weaker states. It still operates today and, up until 1970, all its advice was accepted by the Australian Federal government. Its task remained to examine applications for financial assistance in the form of special grants. The inaugural Chairman of the Commission was Frederic Eggleston. Giblin and Eggleston discovered a way to work out how the Commission should distribute Commonwealth money between the states such that living standards would be equalised, a process sometimes known as horizontal fiscal balance. The emphasis on equality between the states continued through until the end of the century and many economists served on the Commission, following in Giblin's footsteps. Federal–state financial relations became even more convoluted after the end of the Second World War, when the Commonwealth decided to retain sole control over income taxation although this was subject to a new scheme of reimbursement to the states. Taxation raises the other key problem of fiscal federalism, namely, vertical fiscal imbalance – that is, that the Commonwealth had far more revenue-raising powers than the states.

In the 1980s a visiting American economist deemed that Australia had 'the most equalising federalist system in the world' in the sense that the Commonwealth gathered most of the tax revenue but made large grants to the states designed to equalise to provide the same level of service to every Australian (Gramlich, 1984). It was a tribute, in part, not just to Giblin and Richard Mills, but also to the work of Russell Mathews, whose *oeuvre* was taxation and fiscal federalism as the means towards an equitable society. Mathews was foundation Director of the Centre for Research on Federal Financial Relations established at the ANU in 1972 to sponsor research into the Australian federal system. A genuine believer in fiscal equalisation, which he believed bound the Federation together, Mathews decried the tendency towards fiscal centralisation, though he was in favour of a strong public sector, at both levels of government, to provide basic services. That is, that he wanted, like Mills, to see the relationship between the Commonwealth and states as a cooperative rather than imbalanced one (Barton and Grewal, 2000, 405).

New Zealand: land values and price stabilisation of farm produce

The predominant economic problem in New Zealand after 1921 was the lower returns accruing to farming industries following a glorious twenty-year boom for all farmers. There was a connection between export values and the value of farm land; a fall in export prices accentuated the disparity between farmers' incomes and their costs. The problem was compounded by the government dispensing loans to returned servicemen to buy land for farming. This had pushed up land values. Everything was satisfactory until export prices began to slip. Many farmers suffered a high rate of mortgage indebtedness in relation to the total productive value of their farms. Farmers, moreover, had little access to free capital since rural credit systems were underdeveloped. This was an issue where Belshaw, primarily an agricultural economist, would make his mark. It was also a testing ground for other young economists such as Rodwell and Condliffe. Land prices were subject to several variables especially farm product prices. This link between export prices and land values created a serious debt burden when commodity prices collapsed after 1921. It was later argued that this volatility would be eliminated by price stabilisation of farm produce prices (Weststrate, 1959, 176). This became a rationale for a guaranteed price scheme for dairy products which was introduced by a Labour government in 1935. Prior to that, the New Zealand government moved to establish a rural credit scheme which Belshaw had researched for a decade, including in some of his doctoral work at Cambridge. Belshaw felt rural readjustment would also have to involve more efficient farming practices, the rationalisation of some farm holdings, lower tariffs on agricultural inputs and a whole new approach to mortgage adjustment.

Conclusion

The research on estimating the cost of tariff assistance, together with Giblin's quantitative export multiplier analysis, bestowed on Australian economists an economy-wide perspective of the costs and benefits of external economic shocks. This would become useful when they adopted the doctrine of 'spreading the loss' after Australia's export income plummeted in 1929. So significant had been the achievements of Australian economists that they began to draw the attention of eminent economists abroad: Frank Taussig of Harvard wrote:

> I am greatly interested in the remarkable development of economics in the Commonwealth, and in the skill and courage with what [sic] your government applies economic science to the problems of your country. I wish I could say that work as good has come from the immensely larger number of American economists.[17]

In New Zealand the economists had, in contrast to their Australian counterparts, spoken out against the linkage between protection and wage levels and how this was affecting the country's economic performance.

Notes

1 Melville, TRC 182, NLA.
2 The expression of 'protection all round' is usually associated with the Australian politician John McEwen, who was a Country Party member, although the prevalence of comprehensive protection predates him.
3 Copland to F. Alford 6/6/1935, FECC, UMA.
4 Brigden to Cannan 13/8/1928, Cannan Papers, LSE.
5 Keynes to Giblin 28/8/1929, FECC, UMA.
6 Copland to H. Clay 31/5/1932, Copland Papers, NLA.
7 Copland to F. Alford 6/6/1935, FECC, UMA.
8 Copland to Wood 1/11/1933, Wood Papers, NLA.
9 Notes on discussion at Keynes Club, Cambridge October 1933, Copland Papers, NLA.
10 Wilson might have also disappointed his Australian mentors by deciding to pursue a career in the Commonwealth Public Service rather than academe. In 1932, he left a lectureship at Hobart to become the first trained economist hired by the Commonwealth Public Service. Again, in the post-war years, he was also offered the inaugural Research Chair in Economics at the ANU but declined. Like 'Nugget' Coombs, Wilson decided that he never felt deeply attracted to scholarship for its own sake. Of course, it could be said that Australia's Public Service benefited greatly when Wilson became Secretary of the Treasury in 1951.
11 Copland to Higgins 6/7/1928, FECC, UMA.
12 Fisher to La Nauze 17/11/1936, La Nauze Papers, NLA.
13 Copland to Downing 17/7/1959, Downing Papers, UMA.
14 Copland to W. S. Robinson 27/3/1934, FECC, UMA.
15 Copland to Harrod 10/10/1952, Copland Papers, NLA.
16 Colin Clark interview with B. McFarlane and D. Healey, 1977, University of Adelaide.
17 Taussig to Copland 13/12/1929, FECC, UMA. Taussig had made a series of references to various aspects of Australia's economic development in his textbook *Elements of Economics* (1911).

References

Arndt, H. W. 1968, *A Small Rich Industrial Country*, Melbourne: Cheshire.
Anderson, K. and R. Garnaut, 1987, *Australian Protectionism: Extent, Causes and Effects*, Sydney: Allen and Unwin.
Barrowman, R. 1999, *Victoria University of Wellington 1899–1999*, Wellington: Victoria University Press.
Barton, A. D. and B. J. Grewal, 2000, 'Russell Lloyd Mathews: an appreciation', *Economic Record*, 76(235): 401–11.
Blyth, C. A. 2008, 'Early academic economics in New Zealand: notes on its history from the 1870s to the 1950s', Working Paper Series, Department of Economics, University of Auckland, No. 266.
Bourke. H. 1990, 'Herbert Heaton and the foundation of economics at the University of Adelaide, 1917–1929', in F. B. Smith and P. Crichton (eds), *Ideas for Histories of Universities in Australia*, Canberra: Australian National University.
Brigden, J. B. 1925, 'The Australian tariff and the standard of living', *Economic Record*, 1(1): 29–46.
Brigden, J. B., D. B. Copland, E. C. Dyason, L. F. Giblin and C. H. Wickens (eds), 1929, *The Australian Tariff: An Economic Enquiry*, Melbourne: Melbourne University Press.

Brooke, G., A. Endres and A. Rogers, 2016, 'Does New Zealand economics have a useful past? The example of trade policy and economic development', *New Zealand Economic Papers*, 50(3): 281–302.

Brooke, G., Endres, A. and Rogers, A. 2017, 'The Economists and New Zealand population: Problems and policies 1900–1980s', *New Zealand Economic Papers*, 51: 1.

Cain, N. 1973, 'Political economy and the tariff: Australia in the 1920s', *Australian Economic Papers*, 12(20): 1–20.

Cain, N. 1974, 'The economists and Australian population strategy in the twenties', *Australian Journal of Politics and History*, December, 20(3): 346–59.

Capling, A. and B. Galligan, 1992, *Beyond the Protective State*, Melbourne: Cambridge University Press.

Coleman, W. 2007, 'Lyndhurst Falkiner Giblin (1875–1951)', in J. E. King (ed.), *A Biographical Dictionary of Australian and New Zealand Economists*, Cheltenham: Edward Elgar, 110–14.

Coleman, W. and A. Hagger, 2003, 'An Edinburgh of the South? Some contributions to fundamental economic analysis by Tasmanian economists in the 1920s', *Tasmanian Historical Studies*, 8(2): 10–27.

Coleman, W., S. Cornish and A. Hagger, 2006, *Giblin's Platoon: The Trials and Triumph of the Economist in Australian Public Life*, Canberra: Australian National University Press.

Condliffe, J. B. 1940, *The Reconstruction of World Trade*, New York: W. W. Norton.

Condliffe, J. B. 1950, 'The teacher and the influence', in R. S. Allan (ed.), *Liberty and Learning*, Christchurch: Whitcombe and Tombs.

Condliffe, J. B. 1959 [1930], *New Zealand in the Making*, London: Allen and Unwin.

Condliffe, J. B. 1969, 'The economic outlook for New Zealand', *New Zealand Economic Papers*, 3(1): 5–14.

Copland, D. B. 1951, *Inflation and Expansion*, Melbourne: Cheshire.

Corden, W. M. 1968, *Australian Economic Policy Discussion: A Survey*, Melbourne: Melbourne University Press.

Corden, W. M. 2010, 'Review of *Balanced Growth* by Ross Williams', *Economic Record*, 86(274): 461–3.

Corden, W. M. and S. Jayasuriya, 2006, 'Distinguished Fellow of the Economic Society of Australia, 2005: Peter Lloyd', *Economic Record*, 82(256): 77–81.

Cornish, S. 2007, 'Sir Roland Wilson 1904–1996', in J. E. King (ed.), *A Biographical Dictionary of Australian and New Zealand Economists*, Cheltenham: Edward Elgar, 310–14.

Cotter, R. 1967, 'War, boom and depression', in J. Griffin (ed.), *Essays in the Economic History of Australia, 1788–1939*, Brisbane: Jacaranda.

Davidson, F. 1977, 'Brigden, Vernon, Rattigan, Jackson', in J. P. Nieuwenhuysen and P. J. Drake (eds), *Australian Economic Policy*, Melbourne: Melbourne University Press, 146–58.

Dimand, R. W. 1991, 'Cranks: heretics and macroeconomics in the 1930s', *History of Economics Review*, 16: 11–30.

Downing, R. 1966, 'Summary of the Report', *Economic Record*, 42(1): 1–12.

Easton. B. 1997, *In Stormy Seas: The Post War New Zealand Economy*, Dunedin: University of Otago.

Endres, A. M. 1991, 'J. B. Condliffe and the early Canterbury tradition in economics', *New Zealand Economic Papers*, 25(2): 171–97.

Endres, A. M. 2010, 'Marshallian economics in New Zealand, c. 1890–1940', in T. Raffaelli, (ed.), *The Impact of Alfred Marshall's Ideas: The Global Diffusion of his Work*, Cheltenham: Edward Elgar.

Endres, A. M. and K. Jackson 1993, 'Policy responses to the crisis: Australasia in the 1930s', in W. R. Garside (ed.), *Capitalism in Crisis: International Responses to the Great Depression*, London: Pinter, 148–65.

Fleming, G. A. 1989, 'The role of economists in New Zealand policy making 1912–51: economic advice structures in development', Working Papers in Economics, University of Auckland, No. 59.

Fleming, G. A. 1994, 'Some problems in interpreting citation practices in the economic record 1925–1946', *History of Economics Review*, 22: 1–15.

Friedman, M. and R. Friedman, 1998, *Two Lucky People*, Chicago: University of Chicago Press.

Garnaut, R. 2013, *Dog Days*, Melbourne: Black Inc.

Giblin, L. F. 1947, 'The *Record* and its editors', *Economic Record*, 23(1).

Goldfinch, S. 2000, 'Paradigms, economic ideas and institutions in economic policy change: the case of New Zealand', *Political Science*, 52(1): 1–21.

Goodwin, C. D. 1966, *Economic Enquiry in Australia*, Durham, NC: Duke University Press.

Goodwin, C. D. 1974, *The Image of Australia*, Durham, NC: Duke University Press.

Gramlich, E. M. 1984 '"A fair go": fiscal federal arrangements', in R. Caves, and L. Krause (eds), *The Australian Economy: The View from The North*, Sydney: Allen and Unwin: 231–74.

Groenewegen, P. 2009, *Educating for Business, Public Service and the Social Sciences: A History of the Faculty of Economics at the University of Sydney 1920–1999*, Sydney: Sydney University Press.

Groenewegen, P. and B. McFarlane, 1990, *A History of Australian Economic Thought*, London: Routledge.

Grubel, H. and P. J. Lloyd, 1971, 'The empirical measurement of intra-industry trade', *Economic Record*, 47(120): 494–517.

Hagger, A. J. 2004, *Economics in the University of Tasmania: The First One Hundred Years*, Hobart: University of Tasmania Press.

Hancock, K. 2013, *Australian Wage Policy: Infancy and Adolescence*, Adelaide: University of Adelaide Press.

Hancock, W. K. 1930, *Australia*, London: E. Benn.

Harper, M. 2009, 'Economics before the Department of Economics: 1855–1944', in R. Williams (ed.), *Balanced Growth*, Melbourne: Australian Scholarly Press, 25–51.

Harper, M. 2013, *Douglas Copland: Scholar, Economist, Diplomat*, Melbourne: Miegunyah Press.

Hatch, J. and C. Rogers, 1997, 'Distinguished Fellow of the Economic Society of Australia, 1996: Professor Emeritus Geoff Harcourt', *Economic Record*, 73(221): 97–100.

Heaton, H. 1926, 'Progress and problems of Australian economists', *American Economic Review*, 26(2): 235–48.

Hight, J. 1939, 'Preface', *Economic Record*, 15: 3–6.

Hodgart, A. W. 1975, *The Faculty of Economics and Commerce: A History 1925–75*, Melbourne: Melbourne University Press.

Hogan, W. P. 1999, 'Colin George Frederick Simkin, 1915–1998', *Economic Review*, 75(230): 313–22.

Holmes, F. W. 2011, *The New Zealand Association of Economists: Memories of its Early Years*, Wellington: New Zealand Association of Economists.

Hytten, T. 1960, 'Giblin as an economist', in D. B. Copland (ed.), *Giblin: The Scholar and the Man*, Melbourne: Cheshire.

Karmel, P. 1960, 'Giblin and the multiplier', in D. B. Copland (ed.), *Giblin: The Scholar and the Man*, Melbourne: Cheshire, 164–74.

McLean, L. 2011, *A History of Economics and the Development of Commerce Degrees at the University of Otago 1871–2009*, Dunedin: Uniprint.

Markwell, D. 2000, 'Keynes and Australia', *Research Discussion Paper 2000–04*, RBA.

Metaxas, P. E. and E. J. Weber, 2016, 'An Australian contribution to trade theory: the dependent economy model', *Economic Record*, 92(298): 464–97.

Robertson, D. H. 1940, *Essays in Monetary Theory*, London: Staples Press.

Samuelson, P. 1993, 'Foreword', in H. Herberg and N. Van Long (eds), *Trade, Welfare and Economic Policies: Essays in Honor of Murray C. Kemp*, Ann Arbor: University of Michigan Press, vii–viii.

Scott, R. H. 1990, *The Economic Society of Australia: Its History 1925–1985*, Melbourne: Economic Society of Australia.

Wan, H. and N. Van Long, 1998, 'Profile Murray C. Kemp', *Review of International Economics*, 6(4): 698–705.

Weststrate, C. 1959, *Portrait of a Mixed Modern Economy*, Wellington: University of New Zealand Press.

Wilson, R. 1931, *Capital Imports and the Terms of Trade: Examined in the Light of Sixty Years of Australian Borrowings*, Melbourne: Melbourne University Press.

Wilson, R. 1976, 'L. F. Giblin: a man for all seasons', *Search*, 7(7): 307–15.

Woodland, A. D. 1982, *International Trade and Resource Allocation*, New York: Elsevier Science.

4 Ordeal by fire

Australasian economists and the Great Depression

Introduction

When Harvard University celebrated its Tercentenary in 1936 it invited eminent scholars from around the world to take part in a conference on Science and Letters convened by the President and Fellows of the University. The conference was held to represent all the major fields of learning and only two to three specialists in each field were to be selected. Three internationally eminent economists – Dennis Robertson, Wesley Mitchell and Douglas Copland – were each invited to give a separate address on the theme of the state and economic enterprise. Copland was invited because he had become something of an exalted figure in international economics.[1] He was one of 62 men of science and letters given an honorary doctorate at the proceedings. His citation read: 'A scholar hailed throughout the world as a successful practitioner of theoretical economics, a scholar who has applied his knowledge most fortunately for the recent history of Australia' (cited in Harper, 2013, 203). It was his crowning moment as a scholar; Copland went to Harvard representing not only Melbourne but also the University of New Zealand and the University of Tasmania, since those institutions, too, had 'played no small part in developing the study of economics in Australia'.[2] It was a remarkable achievement for the 13th child of a New Zealand family who, in the 1930s, was described as 'that skilful designer of cunningly mixed cordials for depressed economic systems' (Robertson, 1940, 118). Copland found his hosts, particularly American economists, irritating, since most 'fail to see the necessity for social control and they spend their time beating the air about the interference of the government with the economic law'.[3]

This chapter discusses how Australian and New Zealand economists responded to the Great Depression with innovative policy solutions. At the time, economists in Australia were rare birds and none were to be found in the civil service or economic agencies. That is, there were no 'inside' economists. It was the same in New Zealand. Australia would make the first move, appointing an economist to its central bank in 1931 and an economic advisor to the Federal Treasury in 1936. In New Zealand there were to be no 'inside' economists, certainly within the Treasury until after the Second World War (McKinnon, 2003, 162–3). A university economist, George Lawn, was hired by the Reserve Bank of New Zealand (RBNZ) to be its first economic advisor in 1937. For their part, Australasian university economists were a closely knit group and described to each other their thinking and work through correspondence, conferences and articles in the *Record*. Their advice on policy expedients drew praise from Keynes, among others, for rescuing Australia and New Zealand from the depths of the Depression without both countries defaulting on their sovereign debts. By 1935 both had balanced their domestic budgets. While these expedients were largely an improvisation of existing economic thought, Copland felt that there could be some claim to theoretical invention, especially on currency and exchange rate matters. Australia and New Zealand felt the Depression earlier and more keenly than Britain or America. Indeed, the causes of the Depression in both countries were similar. After briefly looking at the impact of the Depression in each country, we explore the contributions that economists made to extricate their countries from the crisis. A recovery in export prices helped, but this came later. New Zealand would follow a policy path in response to the Depression that Australia pioneered, but one also with a touch of deflation and hesitancy. Later, New Zealand would steal a move on Australia by taking a radical turn to the path of extensive intervention.

The Depression in Australia and New Zealand

While both countries were primary producing exporters, both recorded different phases entering and exiting the Depression. In a sense, New Zealand was dragged into the crisis by the mere fact that it lacked control over its London Funds. Although New Zealand had no balance of payments problem, it was infected by Australia's own problems of a sovereign debt and external deficit crisis because the sterling reserves of both dominions were intermingled within the same London banks (Wright, 2009, 48). It was clear that London looked with suspicion upon New Zealand's borrowings as much as Australia's. As a result, deflation was transmitted to New Zealand because of Australia's financial weakness (Greasley and Oxley, 2002, 703). This changed in 1934, with the creation of the RBNZ. There were subtle differences, too, between the two countries' paths through the Depression. There was a slight differential impact on per capita income; New Zealand's per capita fall in GDP over the period 1929–32 was 17.8 per cent while Australia's was 20.6 per cent. Indeed, it might be argued that the Depression was as nation-shaping an event in each country's history as was the ANZAC landing at Gallipoli in April 1915.

Australia

In the 1920s Australia had been favoured by high export prices and, in turn, the ease with which it could draw capital from London. Australia had borrowed heavily: 30 million pounds every year in the seven years leading up to 1930, courtesy of the Colonial Stock Act, which endowed dominion and colonial stock as trustee securities upon the London capital market. The borrowings were used to fund public works and land settlement. Although the average rate of unemployment still hovered around 10 per cent, many Australians still felt intoxicated by their country's achievements, its grand potential and grandiose plans for national development and immigration. Tariff protection was expanded and applied to all farm products. The easy prosperity unsettled Shann, who was completing his *Economic History of Australia* (1930). This followed on from a pamphlet he authored in 1927 entitled *Boom and Bust*, which foreshadowed the Depression about to engulf Australia. The reception for it and his *Economic History* had the effect 'of a shower of cold, acidic rain on the glooming warm optimism – an expectation of expansion unlimited'.[4] Shann's *Economic History* is still widely read today with its central message that economic progress, kindled by 'self-interest and hope', is inevitably checked by the 'apostles of restriction' and 'the cult of economic control' (Snooks, 2007). Around the same time, Copland had undertaken a study for the Commonwealth Development and Migration Commission on the control of the business cycle and unemployment. He had recommended the long-run planning of public works to synchronise fluctuations in economic activity.

Impact of the Depression

The Depression hit Australia in 1929, although there had been some forebodings with export prices faltering in 1927. The price of wool, for example, fell from 27 pence per pound in 1924/25 to 17.5 pence in 1928/29 (Hancock, 2013, 362). By 1930, the prices of wool and wheat, which at that time together accounted for 60 per cent of Australia's exports, had been halved. Overseas borrowing ceased, with London closing its market to Australasian borrowers even though New Zealand's external account was not in jeopardy. As far back as 1927 it had been necessary for the Commonwealth to assume a degree of liability for some loan policies of the states. The cessation of loan expenditure meant immediate retrenchment for thousands of workers and a drastic multiplier effect that Brigden had only just identified. Australia's national income fell from 630 million pounds in 1929/30 to 430 million pounds in 1931/32. Unemployment reached 32 per cent of the labour force by 1932. Australia also had to confront a balance of payments crisis due to the blow of lower export prices, suspended capital inflow and the need to meet overseas interest payments. Australia came off the Gold Standard and allowed its currency to depreciate. Copland likened the Gold Standard to a ship attached to an anchor in rough seas. Domestically, government revenues were hit with the effect of increased unemployment. The prospect of huge budget deficits also had to be faced. This meant immediate fiscal action, including reducing the interest on the internal debt, which required legislation, as well as devising new means of taxation. Despite what the Brigden Report had said about the limits of protection having being reached, the Scullin Labor Government raised tariff levels. Apart from external shocks, the overriding deflationary influence was a lack of confidence in the political and economic stability of Australia during 1930 and early 1931. The Scullin Government, which had assumed power just two weeks before the Wall Street crash of October 1929, split into factions about the economic approach to adopt in response to the Depression. In response to pressures from Britain, Scullin agreed to a Bank of England team being sent out to make an assessment of Australia's economic situation. The leader of that delegation, Sir Otto Niemeyer, informed his hosts that the nub of the problem was Australia's poor productivity growth rate, together with a reluctance to face austerity. He was entirely dismissive of the economic advice coming from the likes of Giblin and Copland (Millmow, 2010).

Australia's fundamental economic problem was how to reconcile high domestic costs with falling export prices. Its domestic price structure had been underpinned by overseas borrowing, which had increased the level of spending and wages. Since export prices had now fallen, but not the prices of sheltered products, Australian exporters were caught in a cost-price squeeze. So Australia had to reduce the cost structure of its protected and sheltered industries as much as possible. How was all this to be achieved and who would explain the predicament to the Australian people? It was Australian economists who responded to the challenge.

The response to the crisis by Australian economists

In May 1930 a handful of economists, gathered at the ANZAAS Conference in Brisbane, quantified the loss in national income and identified the nub of the problem facing the Australian economy, namely the disparity between domestic and international prices.[5] They agreed, in a memorandum, upon a course of action that could be put to the Commonwealth and the states. Their underlying philosophy was to 'spread the burden', to look for a way in which the community could adjust itself to the serious loss in income on an equitable basis without causing undue disturbance to the economy. According to Copland (1958, 121) it was Giblin who led the discussion upon the exposition of the loss of national income and of the need to share the burden equitably. Giblin was, at first, reluctant to devalue the Australian pound, which he felt would alleviate the pressure on exporters by raising relative farm prices. Import prices, expressed in Australian pounds, would increase, he argued. The objective was to restore the distribution of income to its balance before the Depression. The task, then, of readjustment was to close the gap between the prices of exportable goods and internal costs and to restore the real income of the export sector. These measures, Giblin proposed, would restore the balance between the prices of primary products and industrial products. New Zealand would shortly face the same challenge. Australia, facing a severe crisis and the morbid fear of defaulting on her overseas loans, had to act quickly. In Wellington, Barney Murphy poked fun at Australia's state of near bankruptcy, but Melbourne University economist Gordon Wood warned him that both countries were in the same cart and 'we will still find some fun in the mess'.[6]

Australian universities, as we have seen, had recently established Chairs in Economics just a few years before the Depression and the special problems of the Australian economy took pride of place as main focus of study. At Melbourne there had been research estimating the national income and the distributive effects of the tariff on society. Moreover, the establishment of the Economic Society took the examination of Australian economic conditions outside the universities and gave the studies a practical bias. In fact, university economists played a significant part in economic stabilisation by putting forward a plan for recovery (Millmow, 2010). This was foremost at Melbourne, where Copland, acting in consultation with Dyason, Giblin and Wood, outlined a 'middle way', a stabilisation package for Australia's predicament. This will be examined below in some detail because New Zealand's policy-makers would, after some lag, face the same set of circumstances.

New Zealand

For its part, New Zealand, despite the relative simplicity of its economic structure, could neither display nor marshal similar intellectual firepower until an extra Parliamentary Economics Committee was formed in 1932. Prior to this the government had called in businessmen to staff the National Expenditure Adjustment Commission on the manner in which the required policy of deflation would be implemented (Hawke, 1985, 5). John Riches, visiting his homeland, was astonished at the lack of intellectual leadership within the country and how the University of New Zealand seemed hampered by limited resources and inadequate staff. One could attribute the timid response to the small size of the profession there. Another more likely interpretation was that New Zealand did not seem to act in the concerted way Australia did simply because the gravity of the crisis, especially the external account, was not as acute. Indeed, for a while, it seemed that New Zealand had escaped the severity of the Depression, but, by 1931, it had gone the way of all primary producing countries. Prices for dairy products, some 94 per cent of New Zealand's exports, fell dramatically with the reduction in rural incomes percolating throughout the economy. From 1929–31 the country's real GDP fell by 16.6 per cent (Greasley and Oxley, 2002, 697). By 1931, the value of New Zealand's exports was just 63 per cent of the value they had been in 1928 (Weststrate, 1959, 126). New Zealand was going through what one economist called 'the particular purgatory reserved for those countries that ignored the terrors of compound interest during times of prosperity'.[7] Gordon Wood noted, too, how 'New Zealand feels the pinch much later but the effect was definitely far more severe since she is self-contained and has a much smaller domestic market.' During the 1920s New Zealand suffered severe downturns due to fluctuations in its export prices, but the early 1930s were to prove far worse.

At the height of the Depression unemployment climbed to 30 per cent. However, the worst of the Depression was relatively brief, with a sharp recovery commencing from 1934 as wool prices doubled and New Zealand's money supply increased as a consequence of the devaluation of the currency. This did not mean the mass misery was alleviated; the electorate would voice its displeasure the following year, with the governing coalition suffering a major defeat. Indeed, as Blyth (1966) argued, the Depression exerted a huge psychological impact upon

New Zealanders that would later resonate in the economic model under which they chose to live.

Stepping into the arena

Australia: The Premiers' Plan, 1931

As argued, Australia had to act quickly in response to the Depression and economists were at the forefront in urging action, and speaking with a common voice. Australia was, as Giblin put it, 'in a difficult hole'; her problems were compounded by a trading profile marked by a limited export basket of goods yet being acutely dependent on imports of capital and intermediate goods. Australia had to generate very quickly a trade surplus sufficient just to meet the yearly £30 million sterling interest debt. Copland estimated the transfer problem facing Australia in per capita terms as the highest in the world. Simply put, Australia faced two choices: stabilise the internal price level and let the exchange rate find its own level; or retain parity with sterling and engineer a lower level of domestic prices by engaging in deflationary policy.

The latter was the advice that Niemeyer had recommended when he made an assessment of Australia's situation on behalf of the Bank of England. By that time, Copland had already devised a third way and used the Economic Society as a sounding board to test business reaction. He read a paper entitled 'Economic adjustment and currency policy' to the Victorian Branch of the Economic Society in June 1930. It was his second airing of the so-called 'middle course' that he had first put forward at ANZAAS the month before. The paper, illustrated with lantern slides showing graphs and data, was received with considerable uproar among the 100 members present. Some were shocked by his prescriptions, with one member 'reduced to a state of mental decrepitude' by the graphs, data and suggested remedies. The meeting was adjourned to another date in July, where Copland again rehearsed his arguments.[8]

After receiving a copy of Copland's lecture (later published in the *Record*), Keynes replied that he had 'considerable sympathy with the line being taken', namely, price stabilisation via a fluctuating exchange rate as against outright deflation.[9] Keynes reaffirmed his support when he received an article from Copland on the subject of the Australian finances, adding:

> I only hope that you, and those who are thinking and working with you, will be able to steer your country along a wise middle course between the impracticable demands of the too orthodox and the dangerous demands of the too heretic.[10]

Copland's model of economic adjustment was inspired by Keynes's *Treatise* dealing with an open economy's adjustment to disequilibrium. Copland also drew upon his own work, *Credit and Currency Policy* (1930). The scheme entailed money wage cuts coupled with devaluation and some Treasury bill finance to tide over budget deficits but also to slightly raise the price level. Budgets had to be balanced before confidence would return. More than anyone else, Copland dismissed the idea that devaluation would place a huge strain upon budgets. This array of measures would depress real wages, he argued. Apart from the heresy of devaluation, there was also outrage at the price stabilisation or inflationary aspect to his plan. The strategy of the plan was to confine the loss of income by distributing that loss equitably and to prevent secondary repercussions from the decline in spending power; once equilibrium was restored an increase in economic activity could be secured by credit expansion. It was Giblin who pushed the credit expansion line, but it ran counter to conventional wisdom and private banks' obstructionism. Melville wrote in *The Adelaide Advertiser* that the price stabilisation proposals and the admission that the country would not be able to readily return to balanced budgets during the period of economic adjustment was yet another example of the Australian penchant for 'taking the easy road'. Copland, Giblin and Dyason fired off a quick rebuttal to Melville's 'hysterical' charges, emphasising how wage reductions were at the forefront of their strategy.

The first major and practical step in the recovery process was taken in January 1931, when the Commonwealth Arbitration Court reduced the basic wage by 10 per cent. This wage-fixing machinery, peculiar to Australasia, functioned well in the crisis because a wage cut was administered evenly. It gave Australia an effective form of wages control at a critical time. In a virtuoso performance, Copland appeared before the Arbitration Court as expert witness and was rigorously questioned on a memorandum he had submitted. Union representatives tried to discredit his argument that the loss of national income during the Depression required an across-the-board reduction in wages. Copland always saw the wage cut as an integral part to his 'scheme' of a package of stabilisation measures. He wanted these expedients – balanced budgets, lower interest rates, depreciation of the exchange rate and greater availability of bank credit – to be undertaken simultaneously. The rationale for a real wage cut was on the premise of a fall in national income of 10 per cent. Australia faced a choice between maintaining real wages and employing fewer workers or reducing the real wage and restoring the employment of who those who had been displaced by the fall in aggregate spending (Hancock, 2013, 392). Given the gravity of the situation, Copland was not interested in holding another inquiry as suggested by the unions: 'The duty of the country is plain, and it should be done,' he said (ibid., 386). He argued that the purchasing power of the nation was determined by the size of its national income. If a certain section of the community had its spending power reduced by 10 per cent, then this would release spending power elsewhere which would eventually increase the national dividend and ultimately increase spending (cited in ibid., 382). When asked whether his case comprised opinion or fact, Copland replied that it was built on 'logical argument', adding that 'Every professor of economics in this country believes that what I have put forward is correct' (cited in ibid., 398). Copland was essentially restating Say's Law, buttressed by the announcements that the wage cuts would not lead a reduction in the monetary volume of purchasing power but would, instead, be a transfer to employers thereby restoring their profits and incentive to produce. Not every economist supported his line of argument. The defrocked Professor of Economics at Sydney, R. F. Irvine, said that the crisis was due to international monetary factors and that a real wage cut would not help matters. As Hancock (ibid., 407) points out, Irvine's diagnosis did not address how Australia should adjust to its loss in real income stemming from the decline in the terms of trade and cessation of foreign borrowing. Another observer, Jerry Portus, agreed with Copland's diagnosis of the problem, but could not see how a wage cut would help Australia's export industries. However, Copland's evidence to the Arbitration Court was a tour de force and easily won over the bench.

As part of their role in explaining Australia's economic predicament, local economists had, for some years, contributed articles to newspapers. As public educators, Copland and Giblin reduced oblique economics to everyday discourse. Apart from Giblin's air of natural authority, Copland remarked upon his facility in communicating with the man in the street:

> Those of us who are handling economic doctrines have always to find a simple working rule for the average man as long as this working rule comes within, say, 10 per cent to 20 per cent of accuracy it can I think be accepted as satisfactory. Giblin is the most ingenious person I know in Australia for devising such schemes.[11]

In July 1930 Giblin put pen to paper with a series of ten commentaries addressed to the man-in-the-street about the facts of the Depression. They were entitled *Letters to John Smith*. Over a ten-day period, they explained to the working man why he must partake in sharing the burden.

The wage cut was immediate after a 30 per cent depreciation of the Australian pound initiated by the mercurial chief executive of the Bank of NSW, Alfred Davidson. Economically enlightened, Davidson had been convinced of the idea of depreciating the Australian pound by Shann and Copland. The Bank of NSW moved to 'raise' Australian pound to 130 for 100 pounds sterling and the other banks, including the Commonwealth Bank – which at the time was Australia's central bank – followed.

To deal with the deficits at both state and federal level, political action was required. In May 1931 the Commonwealth and the states commissioned a sub-committee, comprising four university economists (Copland, Giblin, Shann and Melville) and State Treasurers, to devise a plan that would save the Australian economy from liquidation. That plan has been written into Australian folklore as the 1931 Premiers' Plan, although it was initially called the Copland Plan. There had been, in fact, a veritable 'Battle of the Plans' between this variant and that of the expansionists at one time led by the Federal Treasurer E. G. Theodore. However, ordinary Australians, as well as overseas creditors, were in no mood for the credit expansion which lay at the heart of the Treasurer's plan. Another plan was named after the NSW Premier Jack Lang, with its centrepiece being a repudiation of Australia's international debt repayments until economic conditions improved. Facing an immediate budget deficit of 100 million pounds, the economists took as their guide the wage cut ordained by the Arbitration Court and pushed for 20 per cent in government expenditure, including interest on the internal debt. The Committee took the view that the interest on the public debt should also be reduced. As Chairman of the Experts Committee, Copland had to win over the support of the financial community. The reduction in rentier income, mortgage rates and rental payments were unorthodox measures, but the economists, by force of argument, and with a grudging, bereft Labor government in tow, had their plans accepted. Copland always insisted that the budgetary aspects of the plan were only part of a general and comprehensive plan of economic adjustment. When offering to brief readers of the *Economic Journal* about the plan, Copland told Keynes that Australia was lucky that a Labor government carried the programme through, since it would not had been achieved if they had been in opposition.[12] Keynes was delighted with Copland's offer, since events had been moving fast, and noted 'You seemed to have been working wonders, and it has been very gratifying to see what a prominent part the Economists have been able to play.'[13]

The educational aspect of the Premiers' Plan was interesting; by departing from classical economic prescriptions, the Australian economists were far ahead of their peers overseas. They had engaged in a nation-wide effort to bring some social equity into economic planning, with every class enduring a cut in income. Copland had been told by Keynes how impressed he was that Australian economists laid stress on the facts and then tried to fit the theory to the facts. When he visited America in 1936, Copland found the efforts of the Australian economists were less well known, his American peers, instead, marvelled at Sweden's economic policy, which was providing the 'middle way' between individual capitalism and state control.[14] This annoyed Copland; he told the Chicago economist Irving Fisher: 'Our economists and monetary advisors knew pretty well what they wanted, but I am quite sure that neither the Treasury authorities nor the Central Bank quite appreciated the nature and importance of the experiment they were conducting.'[15]

The New Zealand Economists' Committee, 1932–33

Hawke (1985) has argued, in his account of the Depression in New Zealand, that the government tackled the blight with some imagination and that, in the milieu of the times, 'devaluation was probably the peak of innovativeness'. Apart from an export promotion policy, it was also necessary to rehabilitate basic industry and the prosperity of the rest of the economy. The more active exchange rate policy was certainly emphatic because, at the time, there was no unsustainable excess demand for foreign exchange at the existing exchange rate. That is, the New Zealand balance of trade, unlike Australia's, was in surplus. As Endres (1990, 69) reminds us, the market was not dictating a devaluation as it had for Australia. The fact, too, was that no New Zealand economist had actually suggested devaluation until Copland's work on Australia attracted the attention of

Belshaw. Harper (2013, 191) reveals that Belshaw had been invited by Copland to Australia to attend a meeting with Australian economists around Christmas 1931. Belshaw was certainly the New Zealand economist most receptive to macroeconomic stabilisation alternatives, given his Cambridge background, as well as being well versed in the role of money and credit in the business cycle. Belshaw was a graduate of Canterbury University College, which upheld canons such as individual financial responsibility, lower tariffs, countercyclical public works, parity with sterling and a commitment to seek scale economies in the pastoral industries. Belshaw, however, had doubts about the School's commitment to fostering recovery in the export trades by merely deflating costs (Endres, 1990). The Canterbury School would be somewhat unsettled, therefore, by the recommendations of the Economists Committee.

The Committee had been appointed in 1932 'to examine the economic and budgetary condition of the Dominion' and options for reconstruction (Fleming, 1989, 16–17). The decision to appoint an Economic Committee came out of a meeting between the government, bankers and primary producers. By that time, export prices had fallen by 40 per cent. The Committee comprised four academic economists: Hight (chair), Tocker, Belshaw, Copland and one Treasury official, Alexander Park, 'obviously charged with keeping the academics in touch with reality' (Hawke, 1985, 6). Copland was on the Committee because he went home every summer to visit his extended family in New Zealand. Hight and Tocker were initially opposed to devaluation; they favoured lowering domestic costs and prices as the best way to relieve the hard-pressed farm sector. It was Copland, fresh from being portrayed as the mastermind of the Premiers' Plan, who became the 'intellectual force' behind the Committee's recommendations (Endres, 1988, 34). Belshaw, together with Copland, argued that a measured devaluation would reduce the extent to which internal deflation was necessary. In some quarters, Copland's advice was seen to be influenced by the Bank of NSW, while he was portrayed as an advocate of inflation which, at that time, was regarded as downgrading the value of the currency. Copland responded that this reflected the fact that his critics were simply 'unaware of the grave position' New Zealand was really in.[16] Devaluation was seen by Niemeyer and his local supporters as prejudicial to 'the whole fabric of national finance'. Copland also expressed astonishment at the influence and intransigence of the Treasury.[17] He found the exchange rate controversy 'amusing but I weep for my fellow countrymen'.[18] By this time Copland had won over Hight and Tocker, but not Park, to the 'Melbourne' view. Belshaw was astonished at Tocker's back-down and 'acceptance of interference with sacred laws. He is a strong on laissez-faire as ever but forgets his philosophy when he comes up against the specific problems of the present time.'[19] The Committee's report, delivered in March 1932, recommended adjusting the country's economy to reduced export prices. In addition to devaluation, the Committee proposed an 'equality of sacrifice' and recommended cuts in wages, dividends and interest rates. Civil servant wages and award wages had been reduced by 10 per cent in 1931, together with interest rate cuts and temporary mortgage relief. The Committee also recommended that the budget be balanced, though not before 1934/35. This outcome was achieved by tax increases, including income tax and a special emergency tax on unearned income. As in Australia, those citizens holding government debt saw it converted to a lower rate. The Report took a pragmatic line, arguing that the budget deficit was 'unavoidable', and urged that the banks finance the requirements of government. Public works were cut drastically on the basis that government borrowing would nullify reductions in costs and, especially, interest rates.

After helping draft the Committee Report, Copland fell ill and was forced by his doctor to relax, laid up in a Wellington hospital, where he read detective novels. He noted that one of his detractors, Murphy, did not come to visit him. The illness meant that Copland could not serve on the committee in Australia charged with reviewing the anti-Depression measures in place. Wellington did not immediately accept the Committee's recommendation. The Minister for Finance, William Downie Stewart, opposed devaluation, not just because of the budgetary implications that would ensue but, more importantly, because of concerns for international respectability. The Committee reconvened in January 1933 without Copland. It re-emphasised its original findings, but with added vigour given the deteriorating position of the farm sector. Shortly after, Wellington acted with a devaluation of 25 per cent. It required, however, the resignation of Downie Stewart to achieve it. Earlier, Downie Stewart and Treasury official Park had met Keynes in London, who told them to follow the Australian path; in contrast, Montagu Norman, Governor of the Bank of England, told his visitors to hold firm (McKinnon, 2003, 135). Now, with the dam about to burst, an observer informed Copland,

> It is a pity that our own government had not taken earlier notice of your recommendation – surely another case of a prophet not being without honour, save in his own country, however it looks as if at this rather belated hour the Government may yet adopt your gospel.[20]

The Economists' Committee reaffirmed that the economic welfare of the people was more important than upholding the exchange rate (Blyth, 2008, 50). That was as far as it went. The Committee was beholden to the view that a balanced budget was necessary for recovery and that no public works be authorised. Belshaw became an ardent defender of devaluation and saw the move as marking the first attempt at macroeconomic control (Endres, 1990). Reflecting upon what the Economists Committee had achieved, Belshaw wanted the devaluation to apply even when export prices recovered; he was urging, in fact, for an adjustable peg for the New Zealand pound which would soon fall within the domain of the newly established RBNZ (Blyth, 2008, 51). Underlying Belshaw's view was a faith that New Zealand would always find a boundless market, other than Britain, for its agricultural produce. In other words, Belshaw saw the devaluation as a 'growth-promoting mechanism' for the long term. However, the actual decision had been prompted by politicians who wanted immediate assistance for their rural constituencies (Belshaw, 1933, 764). Reflecting his research interests, Belshaw believed his country's growth potential was dependent upon agricultural expansion (Endres 1990, 72). It was a heroic position to hold in the 1930s, when protectionism prevailed. In the post-war years, Belshaw would find another version of this endless market when he extended his interest to the new field of economic development, with a particular focus on the Pacific region.

Copland's denunciation of the Niemeyer–Gregory position on the New Zealand pound was published in the *Economic Journal* in September 1932. The article had amused Keynes and his London acolytes with its wit and erudition (Harper, 2013, 192). Keynes felt that Copland had been too severe on Gregory, but Copland insisted that Niemeyer and Gregory '[have] made our work rather more difficult in Australia and apparently for the moment rendered it almost valueless in New Zealand', adding that 'Gregory was endeavouring to square economic truth with the truth as the bankers wanted it expressed' and 'I shudder to think what would happen to us if we had followed Niemeyer and bankers over the past two years.'[21] In a further retort, Copland told Keynes that Gregory's views had 'not helped the Australian and New Zealand economists to maintain their position against the forces of self-interest and prejudice that are always arrayed against us'.[22]

When news broke of the 1933 devaluation, Copland told a New Zealand agricultural economist how he would be 'guaranteed a welcome with the farmers anywhere in New Zealand but that the city people are still a little sore in the collar about me'.[23]

Like Australia, Wellington had already moved to cut outlays and public works; private and public sector wages had also been cut. These policies, though, were not alleviated by any credit expansion using Treasury Bills to fund the government deficit. As in Australia, there was little Wellington could do to increase public spending, since fiscal action would have put a strain on the London Funds and offshore lenders would have been reluctant to lend to the country. There was, in any case, a moral tone underlying the fiscal rectitude. Condliffe (1959 [1930], 61) called it 'a primitive morality requiring that adverse conditions be conquered by sacrifice and hardship'. It meant that New Zealand savagely cut back public works spending. Ironically, there would be less public spending there than there had been in the 1920s (Endres and Jackson, 1993, 150). Further, a regressive 'unemployment tax' designed to raise funds for unemployment relief was levied upon those lucky enough to have jobs. There was no talk of a public stimulus, rather a recycling of the Canterbury School view that public works crowded out private sector activity (Endres, 1990, 75). Even Belshaw was guarded about using deficit finance to trigger recovery, although he held it in reserve if devaluation did not get approval. While devaluation and a healthy money supply growth would eventually pull New Zealand out of the Depression, at the time it was considered that salvation would only come with a recovery in export prices brought about by an improvement in the global economy.

Despite calls for trade expansion by the Australian Delegation to the Ottawa trade talks, officials were to come away sorely disappointed. Indeed, what emerged from it was something of a shock to New Zealanders; the end of the

assumption of a limitless and expanding market. That vulnerability was emphasised by A. G. B. Fisher, who criticised the devaluation and domestic cost-cutting
strategy exercised by both countries.

Dissent from Dunedin: Fisher on the Report
of the Economists' Committee

Fisher mocked Copland's 'equality of sacrifice' mantra saying that it was a
'magic watchword' to justify the wage cut (Fisher, 1932, 76–7). Apart from his
disinterest in public affairs, Fisher always seems to be at loggerheads with the
economic thought of his contemporaries. Belshaw sensed that Fisher seemed
'temperamentally disposed to disagreement',[24] while Copland complained that he
was not a 'team player'. There was more to Fisher, however, than just crankiness.
His objections to the Report were far more nuanced than those of other critics. He
preferred internal inflation with bank credit to devaluation on the premise that, as
a mechanism, it would facilitate resources transfer out of 'old' industries, blighted
by depressed prices, into newer industries with higher prices (Endres, 1988, 41).
Belshaw and Copland could not convince him that this expedient would be ineffective or realistic even if the banks were compliant. As for the exchange rate,
Fisher proposed that it be floated. His main argument, though, was that the
'perverse' substitution effects of the devaluation would increase the supply of
resources going to the agricultural sector. Fisher could see no logic in curing 'a
farm depression' by just increasing the number of farmers (Endres, 1990, 71). He
said the same, too, about Australia, where farmers were equated 'as the sacred
animals of the Hindoos'.[25] He had a point; the world economy had lurched into a
period of protectionism with quotas soon to be set on agricultural production.
There was no answer to Fisher's critique, since the Committee had just focused
upon the short-term income effects of devaluation and had not concerned itself
with expenditure switching elasticities or production implications.

Fisher anticipated some of the arguments that Australian economist Max
Corden would make, much later, when he scrutinised the excess costs argument
within the Brigden Report. Fisher's dissent over the Report of the Brigden
Committee brought to the forefront the debate between Copland, with his short-
run practical response to the Depression, and Fisher, who entertained a broader
long-run perspective. Fisher felt, for instance, that the wage cuts did not take
account of the ongoing structural changes within the economy. In short, while
the Committee's argument was versed on an aggregative approach, Fisher saw the
economy through a micro lens with an emphasis upon structural change, of industries expanding and contracting. He also queried the fatalist attitude that the
Depression was an Act of God. He did not think that manipulating wage rates and
exchange rates were the proper response. Specifically, income adjustments with
devaluation and a wage cut blinded the Committee to the substitution effects of
its recommendations. In a nutshell, Fisher sensed that the fall in export prices for
pastoral and agricultural goods was not just a short-term, cyclical phenomenon,
but indicative of long-term changes in global demand as nations became

materially richer. He was therefore unconcerned by the fall in wholesale prices in the agricultural sector; that, in itself, was the product of rising productivity coupled with a declining growth in demand.

All this was the precursor to Fisher's monograph *The Clash of Progress and Security* (1935), which argued that economic progress was about competition and attracting labour and resources to their most efficient use. This was bound to threaten the security of some people's livelihood, he argued, but security in the sense of protecting labour or capital in any given employment, was incompatible with structural change and material progress. Fisher felt that that the path to economic progress was through educational opportunities and the freedom of newcomers to enter all trades and professions. Material progress meant continuous change in the demand for goods and services due to rising real income, he argued. This impelled the flow of resources into new and expanding industries, especially the secondary and tertiary sector; the prejudice in favour of expanding primary production was in defiance of long-term global trends. Fisher felt the relentless expansion of agriculture, land settlement and associated scientific research was misguided, since the demand for agricultural produce was inelastic. Fisher's ideal for economic policy was to propose the best possible use of resources and that meant a willingness to accept structural change.

Fisher would draw support from both London opinion and even Keynes (1935, 195) who, in commenting upon the Monetary Committee's Report in 1934, warned that New Zealand had 'already gone further than is prudent' by devaluation and that expanding her volume of exports risked adverse terms of trade. Fisher also had doubts about the ability of the Committee or any policy-makers to set the exchange rate. A flexible exchange rate would be better, he argued, and would allow the price adjustments to take place that would facilitate structural change (Endres, 1988). The year after his book was published, Fisher moved to Perth to take up the chair at UWA and, 18 months later, he became the Price Research Professor of Economics at the Royal Institute of International Affairs, otherwise known as Chatham House. While he would rarely return to New Zealand, he maintained an interest in the dominion's economic affairs and remained a close friend of Finance Minister Walter Nash. As part of the New Zealand Legation, he sat behind Nash at the 1944 Bretton Woods conference in New Hampshire, which constructed the post-war international economic architecture.

Basking in the limelight

One of the reasons why Australian economists succeeded in dealing with the Depression was that they had given a great deal of attention to its effects upon national income and the volume of employment. The Economists' Committee had noticed that the New Zealand situation was just as bad as Australia's, but that there had been a tendency to suppress it.[26] That said, the two countries shared the same strategy of devaluation and internal deflation, requiring balanced budgets, wage cuts and proportionate cuts in rent and interest. Beyond that, the strategy was to await a revival of export prices to deliver full recovery. There was little attention directed at domestic expansion; however, Australian economists quickly began to see that this was a major flaw in the Premiers' Plan. Copland (1951) would only express remorse when two of his closest colleagues, Dyason and Giblin, died a few years apart. Both, he said, had misgivings about the severity of the 1931 Premiers' Plan and put the case for more public works and credit expansion. Their protests had been dismissed, he said, and this had been a grievous error. However, even if some economists had 'seen the light' about reflation, they would not have been able to influence economic, let alone public, opinion. Voters were not ready at that time for such an adventure, opting instead for security, confidence and certainty. There was also a prejudice against public sector spending, especially among those with memories of the roaring 1920s. Consequently while private investment spending fell by 70 per cent between 1928/29 and 1931/32, public investment fell by 75 per cent over the same period. One can imagine the combined effect of this upon economic activity.

It was Copland (1934) who informed the world about Australasian economies' response to the Depression. Copland was awarded the signal honour of being invited to give the second Alfred Marshall Memorial lectures at Cambridge in the autumn of 1933.[27] The opportunity sprang from Copland's original suggestion that he give some lectures about the impact of the crisis upon Australia and how its institutions responded.[28] Keynes told Copland that the Faculty wanted to present his observations as that year's Marshall lectures. Copland was overjoyed at the news and used the lectures and accompanying book, entitled *Australia in the World Crisis 1929–1933*, to merit the award of a Doctor of Letters from Melbourne University. He told Gordon Wood:

> The book represents the contribution I have made during the past three years… I am just a little reticent about submitting them because people will say it is not dignified and my economist friends will pretend that I have stolen their ideas![29]

Copland was emphatic that the combination of reductions in money costs and credit expansion was indispensable, more than anything else in explaining the Australian recovery in 1933.[30]

All this frenetic public activity by economists raised the profile of the Australian profession. However, it came at a cost. Giblin's appointment as Acting Commonwealth Statistician and Copland's multifarious activities meant that their research work languished. Melville was recruited by the Commonwealth Bank to be its first economic advisor and Edward Shann was hired by the Bank of NSW to do likewise. When the Lyons government equivocated about sending Copland to the World Economics Conference in June 1933, he blew his top:

> I am getting very cynical about the attitude of governments towards economists – so much so that I have quite decided that I shall do no more work for governments without proper recognition. During the past two years, my life

has been completely disorganised by government work. It has been... a thankless task, an unpaid job and one that requires very great nervous energy. It was not a matter of working out the plan, but of getting politicians to agree to it. The community seems to be quite unaware of the fact that the economists of Australia produced a plan for Australia while other countries were drifting.[31]

Copland got his wish and he was joined by Shann, representing the Bank of NSW. Shann spearheaded the Australian economists' first foray into economic diplomacy by trying to encourage Britain and America to attempt some monetary injection that would result in 'an expansion of consumers' demand' (cited in Markwell, 2000, 310).

The last words of acclamation for Australian economists during the Depression should go to Keynes. In a commentary in an Australian newspaper in June 1932, he noted that Australia had made far greater adjustments to the crisis than any other country except Germany, before adding that the Premiers' Plan had 'saved the structure of the Australian economy'. These are well-known comments. Less well-known is that when Copland visited Cambridge in 1933 he was shocked to find out that none of the college libraries subscribed to the *Record*.[32] He petitioned Keynes that members of the Royal Economic Society be made aware of the *Record*. Later, Keynes wrote to Copland to inform him that members of the Royal Economic Society could now access copies of the *Record*. To mark the occasion, Keynes put out a statement to members praising the achievement of the Australian economists behind the Premiers' Plan:

Experience seems to show that when countries are plunged into economic difficulties they either, as a rule, do nothing whatever or else proceed to extravagant extremes. The advice of those counsellors who believe that reasonable remedial measures within the existing structure of society will not be in vain are generally ignored. But Australia has given the rest of us a lesson in accepting and positively carrying into effect advice which was experimental and unorthodox and at the same time a severe dose to swallow down, yet was not violent or revolutionary or destructive.

We all know how satisfactory the results have been. Their colleagues in the rest of the world are envious and proud of Australia's economists who have not only been successful in getting their advice accepted but have been shown, in the event, to have been lacking neither in practical wisdom nor in scientific insight.[33]

Copland was delighted, but quickly reminded Keynes that the *Record* was published not just by the Economic Society of Australia but also New Zealand:

We are rather proud that we are almost the only Society in this part of the world which unites Australia and New Zealand, but my New Zealand friends are very touchy and I have to be constantly on the watch not to offend them.[34]

Conclusion

Overall, the public reputation of Australasian economists was established and made secure by their response to the Depression. Economists had arrived on the scene. Moreover, the work on economic rehabilitation in Australia and New Zealand, extending over three years, was successful and was acclaimed as an important contribution to economic theory and practice.

Notes

1 The noted American economic commentator Walter Lippmann felt that Copland's place should have been taken by Keynes since 'he was a man of far greater recognition'. See Goodwin, C. 2014, *Walter Lippmann*, Harvard University Press p. 52.
2 Copland to Vice Chancellor M. Miller 15/6/1936, FECC, UMA.
3 Copland to C. L. Baillieu 3/11/1936, FECC, UMA.
4 'Professor Shann - An Appreciation' *The Melbourne Herald*, 26 May 1935.
5 It was interesting to note that no New Zealand economists attended that conference.
6 Wood to Murphy 1/6/1931, Wood Papers, NLA.
7 Wood to Isles 5/4/1933, FECC, UMA.
8 Minutes of meeting of the Victorian Branch of the Economic Society 27 June 1930 and 10 July 1930, Economic Society of Australia and New Zealand (Victoria Branch) Papers, UMA.
9 Keynes to Copland 20/8/1930, Copland Papers, NLA.
10 Keynes to Copland 19/11/1930, Copland Papers, NLA.
11 Copland to P. D. Phillips 22/11/1934, FECC, UMA.
12 Copland to Keynes 3/7/1932, Copland Papers, NLA.
13 Keynes to Copland 12/8/1931, Copland Papers, NLA.
14 'Harvard notes' 1936, Copland Papers, NLA.
15 Copland to Irving Fisher 23/11/1935, FECC, UMA.
16 Copland to Wood 4/3/1932, Wood Papers, NLA.
17 Copland to Belshaw 31/3/1932, Copland Papers, NLA.
18 Copland to Giblin 30/3/1932, FECC, UMA.
19 Belshaw to Copland 12/1/1933, FECC, UMA.
20 T. Gibbs to Copland, 19/1/1933, FECC, UMA.
21 Copland to Keynes 26/4/1932, Copland Papers, NLA.
22 Copland to Keynes 19 /7/1932, Copland Papers, NLA.
23 Copland to I. W. Weston 25/4/1932, FECC, UMA.
24 Belshaw to Copland 20/7/1932, Copland Papers, NLA.
25 Fisher to Cannan, 4/10/1934, Cannan Papers, LSE.
26 Copland to Barrett 28/6/1932, Copland Papers, NLA.
27 Another honour bestowed on Copland was an invitation by Irving Fisher to join the Econometric Society. Thirty years later, in 1963, Trevor Swan was invited to give the Marshall lectures at Cambridge, but his lectures, although delivered, were apparently never written up.
28 Copland to Keynes 19/5/1932, Copland Papers, NLA.
29 Copland to Wood 27/9/1933, Wood Papers, NLA.
30 Copland to P. Jacobbsen 27/4/1934, Copland Papers, NLA.
31 Copland to A. Grenfell Price, 7/6/1932, FECC, UMA.
32 The Marshall library only had a full set of the *Record* by 1937.
33 Statement by Keynes, 11/4/1934, Copland Papers, NLA.
34 Copland to Keynes 21/5/1934, Copland Papers, NLA.

References

Belshaw, H. 1933, 'Crisis and readjustment in New Zealand', *Journal of Political Economy*, 41(6): 750–76.

Blyth, C. A. 1966, 'The special case: the political economy of New Zealand', *Political Science*, 18: 38–51.

Blyth, C. A. 2008, 'Early academic economics in New Zealand: notes on its history from the 1870s to the 1950s', Working Paper Series, Department of Economics, University of Auckland, No. 266.

Brooke, G., A. Endres and A. Rogers, 2016, 'Does New Zealand economics have a useful past? The example of trade policy and economic development', *New Zealand Economic Papers*, 50(3): 281–302.

Coleman, W. 2007, 'Lyndhurst Falkiner Giblin (1875–1951)', in J. E. King (ed.), *A Biographical Dictionary of Australian and New Zealand Economists*, Cheltenham: Edward Elgar, 110–14.

Coleman, W., S. Cornish and A. Hagger, 2006, *Giblin's Platoon: The Trials and Triumph of the Economist in Australian Public Life*, Canberra: Australian National University Press.

Condliffe, J. B. 1940, *The Reconstruction of World Trade*, New York: W. W. Norton.

Condliffe, J. B. 1959 [1930], *New Zealand in the Making*, London: Allen and Unwin.

Condliffe, J. B. 1969, 'The economic outlook for New Zealand', *New Zealand Economic Papers*, 3(1): 5–14.

Copland, D. B. 1930, *Credit and Currency Control, With Special Reference to Australia*, Melbourne: Melbourne University Press.

Copland, D. B. 1934, *Australia in the World Crisis 1929–1933*, New York: Cambridge University Press.

Copland, D. B. 1951, *Inflation and Expansion*, Melbourne: Cheshire.

Copland, D. B. 1958, 'L. F. Giblin and the frontier of research on the Australian economy', *Australian Journal of Science*, 21: 120–5.

Endres, A. M. 1988, '"Structural" economic thought in New Zealand: the interwar contribution of A. G. B. Fisher', *New Zealand Economic Papers*, 22: 35–49.

Endres, A. M. 1990, 'The development of economists' policy advice in New Zealand 1930–34: with particular reference to Belshaw's contribution', *Australian Economic History Review*, (30)1: 64–78.

Endres, A. M. 1991, 'J. B. Condliffe and the early Canterbury tradition in economics', *New Zealand Economic Papers*, 25(2): 171–97.

Endres, A. M. and K. Jackson 1993, 'Policy responses to the crisis: Australasia in the 1930s', in W. R. Garside (ed.), *Capitalism in Crisis: International Responses to the Great Depression*, London: Pinter, 148–65.

Fisher, A. G. B. 1932, 'The New Zealand economic problem: a review', *Economic Record*, 8: 74–87.

Fisher, A. G. B. 1935, *The Clash of Progress and Security*, London: Macmillan.

Fleming, G. A. 1989, 'The role of economists in New Zealand policy making 1912–51: economic advice structures in development', Working Papers in Economics, University of Auckland, No. 59.

Giblin, L. F. 1930, *Letters to John Smith*, available at http://nla.gov.au/nla.obj-52859319/view?partId=nla.obj-103172306#page/n0/mode/1up

Goodwin, C. D. 1966, *Economic Enquiry in Australia*, Durham, NC: Duke University Press.

Goodwin, C. D. 1974, *The Image of Australia*, Durham, NC: Duke University Press.

Greasley, D. and L. Oxley, 2002, 'Regime change and fast recovery on the periphery: New Zealand in the 1930s', *Economic History Review*, 54(2): 697–720.

Hagger, A. J. 2004, *Economics in the University of Tasmania: The First One Hundred Years*, Hobart: University of Tasmania Press.

Hancock, K. 2013, *Australian Wage Policy: Infancy and Adolescence*, Adelaide: University of Adelaide Press.

Harper, M. 2009, 'Economics before the Department of Economics: 1855–1944', in R. Williams (ed.), *Balanced Growth*, Melbourne: Australian Scholarly Press, 25–51.

Harper, M. 2013, *Douglas Copland: Scholar, Economist, Diplomat*, Melbourne: Miegunyah Press.

Hawke, G. R, 1985, *The Making of New Zealand: An Economic History*, New York: Cambridge University Press.

Heaton, H. 1926, 'Progress and problems of Australian economists', *American Economic Review*, 26(2): 235–48.

Hight, J. 1939, 'Preface', *Economic Record*, 15: 3–6.

Hodgart, A. W. 1975, *The Faculty of Economics and Commerce: A History 1925–75*, Melbourne: Melbourne University Press.

Keynes, J. M. 1935, 'Report of Monetary Committee 1934', *Economic Journal*, 45(177): 192–6.

McKinnon M. 2003, *Treasury: The New Zealand Treasury, 1840–2000*, Auckland: Auckland University Press.

McLean, L. 2011, *A History of Economics and the Development of Commerce Degrees at the University of Otago 1871–2009*, Dunedin: Uniprint.

Markwell, D. 2000, 'Keynes and Australia', *Research Discussion Paper 2000–04*, RBA.

Millmow, A. J. 2010, *The Power of Economic Ideas: The Origins of Keynesian Economic Management in Interwar Australia 1929–1939*, Canberra: Australian National University Press.

Robertson, D. H. 1940, *Essays in Monetary Theory*, London: P. S. King.

Shann, E. 1930, *An Economic History of Australia*, Michigan: The University Press.

Snooks, G. D. 2007, 'Edward Owen Giblin Shann (1884–1935)', in J. E. King (ed.), *A Biographical Dictionary of Australian and New Zealand Economists*, Cheltenham: Edward Elgar, 247–50.

Weststrate, C. 1959, *Portrait of a Mixed Modern Economy*, Wellington: University of New Zealand Press.

Wright, M. 2009, '"Mordacious years": socio-economic aspects and outcomes of New Zealand's experience in the Great Depression', *Reserve Bank of New Zealand Bulletin*, 72(3): 43–60.

5   How Keynes came to Australasia

Introduction

This chapter looks at the arrival of and reception given to Keynes's *General Theory* in both Australia and New Zealand. At the outset it can be said that the coverage of Australian reaction, to this episode in economic thought, is more comprehensive than it is for New Zealand; indeed, there is remarkably little literature on just how this revolution in economic thought and, ultimately, practice unfolded in that country. In short, we do not readily know how New Zealand's leading contingent of economists, including Belshaw and Souter, initially regarded Keynes's new insights and theoretical perspective.[1] We have seen that they still subscribed to the Canterbury School of thought about public works expenditure. The word 'multiplier' would not be heard there until 1936. By contrast, Australian economists, especially Giblin and Copland, had begun to have misgivings about the Premiers' Plan, especially about cutting public investment, when export prices refused to rise. Yet there never seemed any remorse from the adherents of the Canterbury School about public spending.

At the official level, the New Zealand Treasury had just one figure, Bernard Ashwin, who, while an accountant, knew a little economics. The RBNZ did have George Lawn as a full time Economic Advisor from 1937, who would soon have the ear of Finance Minister Nash (Blyth, 2008, 53). Someone else who had Nash's attention was the economist Bill Sutch. An intriguing character, Sutch had, like Souter, a PhD from Columbia University, then a bastion of institutionalism. Sutch had written a thesis on wartime price fixing in New Zealand. His supervisor J. M. Clark considered him 'one of his best graduate students... well-grounded in economic theory... very quick and keen in his ability to catch a point in discussion and react to it'.[2] After completing his doctorate, Sutch embarked upon an extensive tour of Europe, the USSR and Asia. Before he joined the 'Brains Trust' of Finance Minister Gordon Coates, Sutch had applied for a Rockefeller Scholarship to study monetary theory at Cambridge. Sadly, his application was rejected because, at the time, he had no position to which he could return.[3] Meanwhile, at the RBNZ, Lawn would quickly introduce the Governor to economic statistics and intelligence (Fleming, 1989, 23). Giblin, who had been elected to the Commonwealth Bank Board in 1935, was already doing the same thing. Moreover, the Commonwealth Bank soon had three highly qualified economists within its employ: Leslie Melville who was the official Economic Advisor to the Bank, 'Nugget' Coombs and the Cambridge-educated J. M. 'Pete' Garland. Forgoing an academic career, Roland Wilson became the first professionally trained economist in the public service working as an assistant statistician with the Bureau of Census and Statistics (Cornish, 2007).

We mention economic officialdom because, as J. K. Galbraith reminds us, the Keynesian revolution was really a 'mandarin revolution' – that is, an intellectually powered one. In New Zealand the influence of university economists waned after 1932, with the Treasury more receptive to dealing with bankers and businessmen (Martin, 2015, 85). There was, though, one exception to that in 1934 with the Report of the Monetary Committee. In his history of the New Zealand Treasury, McKinnon (2003, 170) notes how there was little of the excitement and activity that there was in Australia, where university economists met to discuss and plumb Keynes's new book; they were helped by having scholars who had just been to Cambridge (Millmow, 2015b) and whose presence filtered through to shape Australian post-war economic policy. There was, by contrast – barring the imaginative mind of Belshaw – seemingly little intellectual ferment over Keynes's new theoretical model within the New Zealand economics profession (Nevile and Dalziel, 2013, 413). Brooke *et al.* (2016, 16) suggest that this disconnect of academic economists from policy extends right through most of the twentieth century.

However, New Zealand was not to be upstaged. A Labour government took office there in late 1935 and introduced Keynesian-like policies, including increased public sector spending. Copland called it 'vigorous economic radicalism', but it became better known as insulation. This new policy was designed to protect the economy from the effects of instability that went with dependence on primary production (Simkin, 1946). This initiative was a response to the 'psychological shock' of the Depression, but it is important to discern, if we can, whether there were economists' voices behind these major turns in economic policy.

The arrival of the Keynesian revolution in Australia is usually explained by the outbreak of the Second World War and the necessary mobilisation of resources, including economic expertise. While Keynes heralded America as the new economic and social testing ground where his new doctrines could be tested, Australia would prove the far more receptive host. Australian economists were ahead of their counterparts overseas in adopting Keynes's insights into demand management, not just to prosecute the war but also to avoid any recurrence of depression (Millmow, 2010).

Fertile ground: the Australian reaction to Keynes's *General Theory*

Australia would be at the forefront of a new revolution in economic thinking partly because of the worldly experience and knowledge of its economists. While most of them were employed by universities, they were uncommonly influential in their access to policy-makers, having already proven their worth in 1929 and, most importantly, in 1931. Australia could also boast of having two emissaries from Keynes who had been caught up in the excitement of the publication of the *General Theory*.

The relatively warmer reception of the *General Theory* in Australia also derived from the fact that Melbourne had a strong connection with Cambridge due to the work of Giblin and Copland. Both had been in correspondence with Keynes (Millmow, 2015b). Copland had a brief glimpse of Keynes's new 'Utopia' when visiting him at his home in Tilton, Sussex, in 1933. Keynes told him of a scenario where the rate of interest would fall to zero in order for investment to equal savings, and where 'Men will no longer live on interest, but merely on their capital.'[4] Giblin had become an expansionist by 1933, openly advocating the positive effect of public works expenditure. He reviewed Keynes's *The Means to Prosperity* in the *Record*, noting that, for Australia, the multiplier effect of public spending was three-fold. Giblin posited a scheme whereby to protect a country's exchange from this stimulus there had to be an international bank prepared 'to issue gold notes to the value of 5000 million dollars, and distribute them to countries in proportion to their gold reserves in 1928. All countries agree to accept gold notes as gold for all purposes except circulation'. The gold notes would be returned to the Bank on an agreed scale, when prices rose to an agreed level.

The Keynesian revolution, if we may call it that, made considerable headway into the Australian economics profession before the Second World War (Cornish, 1993b). Downing (1972) and Melville (Cornish, 1993a) were emphatic that most of the Australian economics profession were, more or less, Keynesian in orientation by 1939. Markwell (2000, 26) observed that in Australia the reception of Keynes's new approach generally 'declined with age and increased with the extent and recentness of direct contact with... Cambridge economics'. This rule of thumb could help explain how Ronald Walker and Richard Downing underwent a rapid conversion to the economics of Keynes. Yet Melville felt that his two Melbourne colleagues, Copland and Giblin, were 'not altogether convinced' of Keynes's new schema though beholden to his policy prescriptions (Cornish, 1993a and b; Macintyre, 2015, 289). They were much too pragmatic to accept the 'extravagant' promise of over-full employment after the war. Copland was distracted, too preoccupied with university administration, to dissect the *General Theory*. After a cursory reading of the latter Giblin complained that he had reservations about accepting the assumptions underpinning Keynes's theoretical framework: 'In so many places I cannot get the convincing picture of things happening just so – there are so many alternatives and qualifications to be thought out' (cited in Markwell, 2000, 33). Giblin would meet up with Keynes in 1938 and was 'proud' to think that he may have put him right on some theoretic issues. He did concede that 'Economic thinking has been revolutionized by his work' (Markwell, 2000, 32). According to Groenewegen and McFarlane (1990), Melville became the most committed to Keynes's doctrine but was not uncritical of ideas such as the euthanasia of the rentier. Melville's conversion to Keynes bemused Colin Clark, who recalled that in 1930 he had been a rigid upholder of deflation, free trade and the Gold Standard.[5]

The Rockefeller Foundation, and Copland's effective dispensation of it, resulted in four young Australian economists (including Ronald Walker, J. M. Garland and Jean Polglaze) attending Cambridge during the 1930s, while another two, Syd Butlin and Keith Isles, undertook the Tripos and Downing completed a diploma in economics (Millmow, 2015a).[6] During that same period, just one New Zealand economist, John Ord Shearer from Otago, went to Cambridge on a Rockefeller Scholarship to study problems of monopoly.[7] Walker and Butlin undertook their studies while Keynes was developing the *General Theory*. Both were supervised by Dennis Robertson and were, therefore, more observers than participants in the 'Keynesian ferment of the early 1930s' (Schedvin, 1978, 243).

The six Australians returned home and made a lasting contribution to Australian economics in the post-war era, helping in the propagation of Keynes's new aggregative approach to economic management, notably Walker, Isles, Downing and Garland. Jean Polglaze was one of the few professionally trained female economists in Australasia during this time, while Butlin came away from Cambridge wary of the idolatry of Keynes, an adulation Copland had noticed in 1933.[8] Walker and Isles undertook thesis work at Cambridge, with the latter looking at the relationship between monetary policy and wages policy. From early on Walker adapted a proto-Keynesian view that deficit budgets and public outlays were quite defensible when private spending was lagging (Cornish, 1991; Cain, 1984, 83).

Armed with a rare Cambridge doctorate (the second awarded after Belshaw), Walker would become the most authentic and ardent Keynesian in Australia, certainly before 1939 (Cain, 1984). Indeed, he penned a lucid review of the *General Theory* for the Australian press a month after its publication.[9] Within it he attacked the Commonwealth Bank for selling bonds to the public for fear that the economy was expanding too rapidly. Walker's Cambridge dissertation, later published as *Australia in the World Depression* (1933), was notable for focusing upon the relationship between wages and unemployment, specifically the case for wage cuts as an anti-Depression measure. In a theoretical contribution, he found that the 1931 wage cuts were only indirectly helpful in effect and that central bank credit and a positive mood among entrepreneurs had been far more powerful agents in explaining the recovery that began from 1932. Walker emphasised that the crucial dynamic was the way in which entrepreneurs reacted to economic developments. Admittedly, he felt that wage cuts would be useful during the recovery stage (Cornish, 1991).

Most Australian economists would eventually accept Keynes's theoretical framework, but Melville (1939) and Arthur Smithies (1936), freshly back from Harvard with a doctorate supervised by Joseph Schumpeter, put their qualifications and reservations into the public domain. Schumpeter rated Smithies highly and would have been astounded that his charge could only find employment within Australia at the Federal Treasury (Coleman *et al.*, 2006).[10] Melville's concerns about Keynes focused on the theory of interest rates and expectations, the marginal efficiency of capital construct. He also felt that Keynes's consumption function should make provision for a term for wealth. Smithies' concerns about Keynes, enunciated in the *Record*, revolved around the marginal propensity to consume and the supposed futility of money wage cutting.[11] To that end, Smithies told Copland that, after reading Keynes, he felt 'there were some pretty serious weaknesses in his argument'. Copland agreed, responding that the Australian experience of 1931 showed that, apart from reducing real wages, it was, indeed, possible to get some benefit from that expedient.[12] Three of Australia's youngest minds on economics had all focused on wage cuts and whether they were beneficial or not in a depression setting. Smithies would cross swords with Walker in the *Record* on the matter of wage cuts.

Walker and Smithies, probably the two most gifted theoreticians in Australia at the time, applied for the Adelaide Chair of Economics but were denied by Keith Isles, who had been 'desperate' to return to Australia.[13] When asked about Isles's qualities as a scholar, Copland recorded:

> He went from Cambridge rather full of the importance of theory – not a bad fault. He just missed getting into the inner circle of young dons in Cambridge. That may well have been a blessing in disguise because I thought I detected in him an exaggerated idea of the importance of theoretical disputations.[14]

Unlike the other two, Isles did not have a doctorate, but his Master of Science degree for his dissertation on 'Wages Policy and the Price Level' was supervised by Keynes. An earlier work, published in the *Record*, mooted an early version of the Phillips curve, suggesting that wholesale prices moved in tandem with the rate of unemployment.

In 1938 Downing eloquently wrote of the 'dazzling light' of the *General Theory* and going off to Cambridge 'to bathe in the new dawn of economic understanding with men who at last knew how to make the economy serve and enrich, not dominate and impoverish the people who lived by it'.[15] Another convert to Keynes was the LSE-trained H. C. Coombs (1981, 3) who later described the experience absorbing the *General Theory* as the 'most seminal intellectual event' of his life. Coombs would later become Governor of Australia's central bank (1949–68). However, his early exposure to Keynes was one of frustration. At first, he was not 'impressed' by the new book, though he felt Keynes's 'practical implications' were important (ibid., 30). He sounded like Giblin when he complained: 'At each stage there seems to be effects working in opposite directions so that net results are a matter of probability and are therefore unsatisfactory material to work on.'[16] His colleague, John La Nauze, an economics lecturer at Adelaide, found the task of interpreting Keynes 'a pain in the neck'. Fisher also confessed to having problems 'digesting' the import of Keynes. He held out hope that Keynes would soon 'provide a text for some general reference upon the conditions for a moving equilibrium'. He also confessed that the more he read it, the more he disliked it.[17]

Cambridge interlopers

In addition to postgraduates returning to Australia, some of Keynes's colleagues visited Australia during the 1930s. The first, Brian Reddaway, one of Keynes's top students, had been encouraged to take a two-year sojourn in Australia as a Research Fellow at the University of Melbourne. Reddaway would play a leading part in disseminating the content of the *General Theory* to his hosts. He presented his findings at a meeting of the Shillings Club in April 1936; these were quickly published in the *Record*, one of the earliest reviews of the *General Theory*. The Shillings Club was directly modelled upon Keynes's Political Economy Club at Cambridge. Reddaway (1936), just 23 years of age, accurately conveyed the meaning of the *General Theory* to the gathering in a paper entitled 'Is the idea of a fair rate of interest a mere convention?' The review, which reduced Keynes's system down to a system of simultaneous equations, was, as Reddaway was told much later by Warren Young, the progenitor of John Hicks's IS/LM framework of analysis. The savings–investment dichotomy of *A Treatise on Money* (Keynes, 1930) was retained, but the difference between the two aggregates now determined output, not the price level. The policy import was that unemployment could be reduced by increasing aggregate demand up to a point when supply constraints came into play; it was investment that determined savings, not the converse, and, more importantly, they equalised not through variations in the price level but through changes in output. Robert Dixon (2009, 248) considers that Reddaway's interpretation of Keynes was a unique Australian contribution to the annals of economic thought. Cain (1984, 367) felt the review gave 'a flying start' to Keynesian planning and that 'Australian economics had come of age'.

Reddaway's name, though, is more famous in Australian economic folklore for a wage decision brought down by the Full Bench of the Arbitration Court in 1937. The arguments put forward for a wage rise were more Giblin's than Reddaway's, even if the subsequent award was christened 'The Reddawage'. Simply put, Reddaway's submission reflected his hosts' emphasis on welfare and distributional equity – that is, gains in national should be shared just as equally as losses had been. Three arguments were put forward to justify a higher real wage. First, there was greater productivity per capita. Second, there had been an increase in efficiency since firms were working close to capacity, meaning that overheads were now spread over a larger output. Lastly, there had been an increase in export prices. In short, there had been an increase in real national income greater in proportion than the numbers employed. Another justification was the fear that if the boom was unchecked it would lead to the over-expansion of industry, rising land values and, ultimately, some check in the form of a recession or another depression.

Another Cambridge visitor at this time was Colin Clark, Keynes's favourite statistician. He took a year's leave to meet Copland's invitation to do a term of teaching at Melbourne involving economics, statistical method and public finance. His visit in 1937/38 coincided with Reddaway's stay in Melbourne. Not an early riser, Clark was taken aback at the practice of 8 a.m. lectures. Like

Keynes, Copland quickly appreciated the worth of his visitor: 'He is a rare find in that he has an unerring instinct for the right figure. Apart from his knowledge of economic theory, he is one of the most ingenious persons with statistics I have ever come across.' To another economist Copland reported that Clark 'is able to work out interesting methods of measuring economic phenomena... his contact with Australia will probably be quite valuable for him.'[18]

Clark always felt that his new-found Australian colleagues taught economics as a true and applied science, seeking practical solutions to economic ills. To that end he hurriedly co-authored a book with Jack Crawford, another applied economist par excellence, on the *National Income of Australia* (1937). It provided the first empirical 'test' of the multiplier concept, in this case the income multiplier (Coleman, 2015, 287). It would become the calculus on which Keynesian economic policies were based.

Clark created a stir on his visit to New Zealand. He came to the conclusion that New Zealanders, particularly farmers, were lightly taxed compared with their peers in other countries.[19] He also felt that New Zealand's national income was understated. There was criticism by Tocker of Clark's calculations of New Zealand's national income, arguing, in fact, that New Zealanders were overtaxed. He wrote to Clark seeking advice on the disparity between his figures and the official ones.[20] Clark suggested that the low tax take was due to widespread evasion or 'swindling'.[21] Clark, though, had seen enough of New Zealand, particularly its protective edifice and subsidised prices for primary produce, which he felt was economic planning gone crazy. He blamed politicians and popularisers. Clark seized on the reaction by one New Zealand politician, William Endean, to his visit, writing a magazine piece lamenting how the country had become 'a veritable museum of economic errors'.[22] In the article, Clark satirically listed 'fifteen fine specimens, all collected in New Zealand soil', including 'Mercantilism', 'Artificial prosperity', 'Malthusianism', 'Physiocracy' and 'the productive and unproductive fallacy'.

After his New Zealand sojourn, Clark found Australia far more inviting and spent a term teaching at UWA. He told his friend Paul Douglas at the University of Chicago that he took the position because of the 'opportunity of seeing this rather isolated country with a peculiar set of economic problems of its own'.[23] In a paper on 'The economist and rearmament', Clark, making use of his estimates of national income, argued that rearmament could be financed by taxation when there was full employment and by borrowing when there was unemployment (Petridis, 2011). In this regard he differed from Copland, who felt that state government expenditure had to give way to increased Commonwealth spending. Clark said that both could increase because he believed there still was enough slack in the economy to accommodate them. On his high horse, Copland admonished Clark for misrepresenting his views and for breaking a convention: 'I always take the view that... economists in this country should not start squabbling in public amongst themselves... The economists of England have to some extent rendered themselves futile before the public by indulging in controversy.'[24] While he regretted his dissent, Clark emphasised that their views were dissimilar and involved 'a question of judging in what phase of the trade cycle we now are'.[25]

Clark was fast building a reputation as a controversialist. A. G. B. Fisher spoke for many when he remarked 'that Clark's brilliance as a statistician is combined with a rather dangerous rashness'.[26] Clark (1986, 19) later claimed, for instance, that it was he, not Walker, who was largely responsible for introducing Keynesian economics to Australia. While Cornish (1981) agreed that Clark was indeed 'a leading expositor' of Keynes's *General Theory*, he emasculated his effectiveness by refusing to be involved in post-war reconstruction work and entertaining outlandish views such as opposing centralism and pushing the idea of Australia, or at least Queensland, becoming a rural Utopia of small farms.

In February 1938 the Premier of Queensland, Forgan Smith, offered Clark a seven-year appointment as Director of the Bureau of Industry, State Statistician and Financial Advisor to the Treasury.[27] It sounded onerous but Clark still found time to conduct his own research. He had been recommended to the Queensland Premier by Hugh Dalton, later Chancellor of the Exchequer in Britain's Attlee Labour Government. Forgan Smith wanted Clark's services to prepare Queensland's case for increased public borrowing allocations. In taking the Queensland position he turned his back on Cambridge. Clark conveyed the news to Keynes, who had always feared that Australia, with all its promise for a young economist, would snare away him from Cambridge. Clark explained why he was staying on in Australia:

> Economics ranks after cricket as a topic of public interest... People have minds which are not closed to new truths, as the minds of so many English-men are and with all the mistakes Australia has made in the past, I still think she may show the world, in economics... in the next twenty years.
>
> Cited in Millmow, 2012: 59

Clark may well have added that the local authorities had a positive outlook about the need to collect economic statistics.[28] The Bureau of Industry, for instance, had been established by the Queensland Government to 'acquire and disseminate economic information' (Clark, 1986, 18). Even earlier in 1923 the Commonwealth statistician Charles Wickens had, when estimating national wealth, spoken of 'human capital', stating that, for Australia, it was three times the value of material wealth, whether private or capital (Castles, 1998).

Meanwhile, Keynes was still not prepared to give up on Clark, telling him 'I do not know what we should do without you' and later 'We have not yet forgiven you for your desertion... So do come back and rule... a genuine Department of Applied Economics.'[29] Clark, who always felt 'a bit of a misfit' in Cambridge, could only sing of the joys of remaining in Queensland.[30]

> When you leave England for Australia you get a strange feeling you have somehow jumped ten years into the future, and when you come to Queensland

you jump ten years further. Queensland is a predominantly rural and small enterprise economy, with a very equalitarian distribution of income and property, very generous social services, compulsory Trade Unionism, and all matters of wages hours and working conditions judicially controlled by the Arbitration court, which now has such prestige that both sides always accept its decision.[31]

These were heartfelt words and Clark would spend the next 15 years furthering Queensland's economic development, becoming, in fact, a zealot for the state's fiscal autonomy. He literally sowed his seed in Australia by raising, with his wife Marjorie, a large family, seven of whom were born in Australia. He would, like other émigrés, regard himself as an Australian economist. The tradition of Australian economics, moreover, began to influence his approach to economic science which materialised in his book *The Conditions of Economic Progress* (1940), a companion volume to his earlier works, but this time looking at international comparisons of national income. The first edition of the book was noteworthy for dismissing the preference English economists had for engaging in speculation and theoretical reasoning rather than a science-based approach to the collection and examination of facts as the proper basis of economics. The inductive approach was where Australian economists thrived, he observed. 'There is room', Clark (ibid., 333) intoned 'for two or three economic theorists in each generation, not more… the rest of us should be economic scientists, content steadily to lay stone on stone in building the structure of ordered knowledge.' While he had begun it in Cambridge, the book was mostly written in Melbourne and Brisbane. It represented his third major contribution to economic science.[32]

Despite having its key findings in its first pages, it was a large, rambling, somewhat disordered work that partly mystified its reviewers. Clark discussed the role of capital in economic progress in an attempt to gauge the driving forces that determined the level and development of economic welfare in selected countries. The ambition of the book was to analyse the reasons for different rates of growth between nations. That said, one reviewer was struck by it having 'a certain vagueness to its purpose' partly caused by Clark's reluctance to employ any theorising (Rothbarth, 1941). It provided evidence of the gulf in living standards between rich and poor nations, concluding that most of the world was 'wretchedly poor'. Clark also unveiled his new three-fold classification of national income between primary, secondary and tertiary sectors of the economy with each related to the level of material progress. Fisher had earlier discussed this, but Clark maintained his definition and coverage of it was superior. Clark had been imaginative in computing the comparative real income of various nations in terms of international units of constant purchasing power. Other reviewers thought it more praiseworthy; Giblin (1940, 262) equated Clark's statistical genius with turning 'straws into bricks'. Arndt regarded it as Clark's best work for making seminal contributions in empirical macroeconomics, for returning to the classical problem of economic growth and development and for putting forward the first statistical evidence of 'the gap' in living standards between poor and rich nations (cited in Higgins, 1989, 302; Arndt, 2000).

Australia and New Zealand: two major monetary inquiries in the 1930s

Remarkably, Australia and New Zealand staged major inquiries into their monetary systems in successive years. Both forums allowed academic economists to display the latest wisdom and advice. Moreover, of all the interested groups given a forum at each inquiry, it was economists who made the most impact. The recommendations of the Monetary Committee in New Zealand (1934) and the Royal Commission into Banking and Monetary Systems in Australia (1936) lent respectability to the idea of an effective central bank in the former and a strengthened central bank in the latter. Both reports provided a good description of the monetary and banking system in each country.

New Zealand

The Monetary Committee's brief was to inquire into the monetary system and whether any improvements could be made to it, but allowed economists to review the effectiveness of anti-depression policy in New Zealand. Economic guidance would be aided by greater social direction of economic forces and materialise by establishing new agencies such as a Reserve Bank to control currency and credit for the common good. Belshaw wanted a Currency Exchange Board, as an interim measure, intent on preventing a return to parity with sterling. There was a definite if uncoordinated movement towards economic planning. The overall strategy was that depreciation of the exchange rate and cost reductions would narrow the internal and external price disparity and become a platform for recovery.

Reviewing the Monetary Committee Report, Keynes said New Zealand now had to sit tight and await a recovery in export prices. The other aspect of the report that drew his attention was the Committee's damning appraisal of the proposals put forward by Douglas Social Credit, a movement which had strong local support. Belshaw (1933, 30) had already dismissed the creed for ignoring the fact that prosperity in New Zealand was ultimately determined by the state of her export markets more than anything else. Keynes felt the Committee's probing examination and dismissal of the evidence given by adherents of Social Credit, including Major Douglas, coincidentally in New Zealand on a lecture tour, was the definitive rebuttal. He was wrong, however; Social Credit infiltrated the doctrinal basis of the Labour Party and would inevitably compel another inquiry into the monetary system.

Australia

While the Royal Commission into Banking and Monetary systems was prompted by political players it provided a forum for advocates of monetary reform. The

Commission's brief was to inquire into the monetary and banking systems at present in operation in Australia, and to report whether any, and if so what, alterations are desirable in the interests of the people of Australia [as] a whole, and the manner in which any such alterations should be effected. Richard Mills was one of the Commissioners, as was the Labor politician, Ben Chifley, a future treasurer and prime minister.

For the first time, macroeconomic goals were enunciated in a public forum. The contributions from economists revolved around the priority that should be given to the competing goals of exchange rate stability and economic activity. Eleven economists, including Fisher, Reddaway and Walker, presented evidence to the Royal Commission, which began at the same time that Keynes's *General Theory* was published. Fisher stressed the more microeconomic role of the central bank, namely, to ensure an efficient distribution of the nation's savings. This, together with avoidance of inflation, would lead to the optimum use of economic resources. He also argued that the Depression in Australia was the consequence of over-expansion of credit in the wrong areas, especially primary industry. Fisher was sceptical of the use of credit to achieve full employment. Most commentators, including the economists, held that the Commission's hearings and findings would lead to modern central bank practices. The economists argued for achieving economic stability and, to varying degrees, pursuing full employment. Most advocated preventing economic fluctuations through counter-cyclical monetary and, in some cases, fiscal policy. The use of liquidity controls on banks was mooted. To that extent, most would have welcomed the report's key finding that '[t]he Commonwealth Bank should make its chief consideration the reduction of fluctuations in general economic activity in Australia, thereby maintaining such stability of internal conditions as is consistent with the change which is necessary if economic progress is to take place' (*Royal Commission*, 1937: 210–11). Another key recommendation was that the Commonwealth Bank have greater leverage over the London Funds to ensure that Australia's reserves were at the appropriate level.

The submissions by the younger economists, particularly Walker and Reddaway, confidently displayed an appreciation of Keynes's new vision. Walker was probably the most astute in urging the prevention of the recurrence of deflation, but also inflation, though mitigation of the first should take priority. He also showed the greatest technical command of Keynes's theoretical system by invoking a number of key constructs (Cornish, 1991, 62). Melville saw the exchange rate and the level of foreign reserves underpinning it as fulfilling the role of economic management. The exchange rate would serve as a 'compass' by which authorities could steer the economy. It meant pegging the exchange rate and guiding the economy along that course with appropriate domestic policies. This became the general view of the economists, namely, that domestic economic activity was no longer dictated by the exchange rate. Rather, the exchange rate would be kept stable only as long as domestic economic activity was being maintained. The Commission's preference was for the prevention of domestic economic instability and the maintenance of high employment. While the Commission conceded, therefore, that 'reducing fluctuations in general economic activity' was not as precise as exchange rate stability, it felt it was a stance of 'fundamentally greater importance'. The same paragraph went on to say that this entailed expanding credit when the economy was in need of stimulus and the reverse when the economy was overheating, with the exchange rate generally kept stable. The economists' evidence was more influential and enchanting than any other group, especially that given by bankers. It was said that Chifley became a 'Keynesian-of-the-first-hour' after listening to the evidence and drafting the final report. Reddaway felt otherwise, informing Alan Ritchie that the Commissioners, bar Mills, were insipid; only Mills had 'any pretensions to economic intelligence', finding himself 'having to clear matters for the other members, because they don't even know enough to be able to frame their questions properly'.[33]

Copland did not present evidence to the Commission and revealed to Davidson the reason why:

> I am supposed to have so committed myself on banking policy that I am not considered eligible to serve on a Committee of Enquiry into banking, Yet I think I may fairly claim that I have more authority to speak on banking matters than any other Australian economist, other than Melville.[34]

It suggested that Copland wanted to be one of the Commissioners and so, in a fit of pique, withdrew. Copland knew his professional standing among his peers, or at least keeping abreast of new developments in theory, was lacking because he was being overtaken by pressures of university administration.

Radical expectations: New Zealand's policy of insulation

After four years of unmitigated deflation the first Labour government in New Zealand's history came into power in 1935, led by Michael Savage. The rural lobby voted for Labour because they had promised guaranteed prices for dairy farmers. The Savage Government entertained some radical expectations of economic management. There had, since the economists committee, been a drift to higher protection. Brooke *et al.* (2016, 6) found that that trade and tariff policy had been primarily used to secure income distribution. Aiding that had been the prior creation of single-desk producer-controlled marketing boards to secure the economic and political power of the agricultural lobby.

Copland was right when he told Keynes: 'New Zealand seems to be the only one British country where politics are really exciting. They have what they all will regard as a first class revolution in putting into office a Labour government with an enormous majority.'[35] What was to come was New Zealand's version of the 'New Deal', with policies to nationalise the central bank and to use its credit resources to guarantee dairy farmers a fixed price for their produce. It would be a template, Belshaw (1937, 170) predicted, for the other pastoral sectors of the economy. He found it difficult though 'to see how the farmer can benefit without loss to the rest of the community in the long run' (ibid., 184). The Dairy Board was able to borrow from the RBNZ at a concessional interest rate. It was akin to planting a time bomb; by 1983 the Board's debt had risen to $NZ900 million (Bassett and Bassett, 2006, 100).

Finance Minister Nash, the key theoretician behind the Labour Party platform, declared that he wanted 'a balanced economy for every section of the community' (Sinclair, 1976, 127). Workers were promised full employment at high wages. Apart from a greater provision of social welfare in the form of education and health services, there were commitments to authorise public works financed by loans and taxation. Lastly, there was to be a greater use of protection to encourage the development of manufacturing. That is, import control was a latent part of the Labour Party's policy.

Copland felt that the programme was too ambitious but not inflationary, sensing that national income would rise with the stimulatory measures. Income certainly rose, but so did imports while the export sector was inevitably squeezed by rising costs. He suggested that 'the real test in the long run will be whether the government can exercise a rigid control over private enterprise and yet keep capital in the country'. The package was spearheaded by Nash who commanded 'an unusual display of economic knowledge for a Cabinet minister'.[36] Fisher and Sutch were his economic advisors, with the latter mostly responsible for this package of measures (Easton, 2001, 130). Fisher felt that Nash sometimes fell prey to 'woolly thinking' (Hawke and Lattimore, 2005). A later example of this was at the Bretton Woods Conference in July 1944, when Lionel Robbins complained that Nash 'has shown a tendency to be about three bars behind the band' (cited in Conway, 2014, 230). Another instance was when Nash took issue with Condliffe in the revised edition of *New Zealand in the Making* (1959 [1930]), when the economist wrote of the 'doubtful economic validity of the secondary industry development behind exchange control'. Nash defended the expansion of manufacturing, asserting that it had added greatly to national income and the standard of living 'without in any way harming primary production or jeopardising our external trade relationships'.[37]

In 1935 the New Zealand government showed no awareness that the experiment could come to grief. Copland felt the Savage Government was overconfident in its ability 'to regiment private enterprise, eliminating the middle man and constraining the rentier whilst engaging in redistribution through taxation'.[38] Initially, Wellington had accumulated considerable reserves of foreign exchange, sufficient for a year's supply of imports before a considerable decline in overseas assets commenced. Towards the end of 1937, following the reflationary and adventurous programme of the Savage Government, a run-down in assets was compounded by a flight of capital (Weststrate, 1959, 273). This episode brought home to policy-makers the profound importance of 'the foreign exchange constraint', a constraint that was to dominate economic policy until the 1980s (Hawke, 1985). The simple problem was that export proceeds were insufficient to meet the country's import requirements and its international interest payments.

For New Zealand's economic planners, that constraint signalled the need for more and more controls. Meanwhile, to avert the crisis, Nash had to go to London to beg for a loan and sign a memorandum assuring Westminster that the import controls were not to be used for industrial development (Martin, 2015) The experience of 1938 and the new policy of exchange and import controls made New Zealand 'a laboratory for economic experiment perhaps as interesting to those who were looking on afar as to those who were engaged in carrying it out' (Copland, 1939, 27).

There were economic justifications for the change in strategy; factors such as the rise in economic nationalism, agricultural protectionism, more competition in sources of supply and the belief that New Zealand faced steadily contracting demand for the products in which it specialised. Sutch would become the greatest proponent for the argument that New Zealand's primary products faced a secular decline in price (Easton, 2001, 184). As Brooke *et al.* (2016, 7) emphasise, trade and commercial policy was, by this time, all about saving foreign exchange, not earning it. The negative aspect to import control which most economists articulated was that it was chronically inefficient, fostered monopoly behaviour and led to the creation of high-cost domestic producers. The original purpose of import licensing, to protect foreign exchange, was supplemented by a latter justification, to develop local manufacturing.

In a sense, New Zealand had no choice; it needed exchange and trade controls to stave off bankruptcy, but also to generate the foreign exchange needed to import raw materials and capital goods. Belshaw felt the resort to protection was an attempt basically to self-levitate the economy; it would all, he suggested, come to grief. By bottling up cost pressures with inefficient industry, the ongoing credit expansion meant creating inflationary pressures. There was no safety valve. Belshaw predicted that costs would overtake the guaranteed prices which farmers received. He concluded: 'Having attempted to insulate ourselves by guaranteed prices and import controls… we are now in a position to have private little trade cycles of our own' (Belshaw, 1939b).

In the absence of the first best response of a devaluation, Belshaw (1939a) proposed another solution to the exchange crisis – one drawn from the country's economic history. He proposed that the authorities build an external stabilisation fund by using taxation to skim off prosperous returns when export prices were high. These taxes would be used to buy foreign exchange and investment securities. This would quarantine the economy from the stimulus of high export prices and, in turn, high real income working itself through the economy. At that juncture, public works would be wound back. Conversely, when export prices were low, and prosperity declined, securities could be sold and foreign exchange accessed from the fund to meet the country's overseas bills. At the same time, public works and expansionary budgetary policy could be employed. A list of public works projects could be drawn up and acted upon whenever the economy needed a counterbalancing action. Belshaw's schema would allow his country to overcome its perennial problem of simultaneously achieving economic development and stability. However, this counter-cyclical budgetary policy had to be supplemented with some adjustment of internal costs to external prices. This raised the old problem of adjusting internal prices and costs; the best resort was to consider altering the exchange rate rather than guaranteeing export prices or adopting import controls. Devaluation would restore equilibrium in the domestic price structure and reduce real incomes to a level consistent with the productivity of the economy, as measured by the terms of trade and efficiency of domestic industry. However, devaluation was not as attractive as first thought. New Zealand had an inelastic demand for imports, while both the supply of her exports and the demand for them was inelastic in the medium term (Weststrate, 1959, 280–1). Copland suggested that insulation was possible, though it would degrade real income; over the long term it would enfeeble the economy because foreign investment would be scared off by restrictions on capital movement and weakness of currency (ibid., 272).

The effects of import control on the standard of living, industry and agriculture were disguised somewhat by the outbreak of the Second World War in September 1939. Before that, there was a critique of insulation and it came, again, from Dunedin. Ralph Souter felt that 'a small, vigorous nation' such as New Zealand did not need state socialism (Endres and Donoghue, 2010). Instead, calling upon his Marshallian apprenticeship, Souter proposed a form of economic chivalry; just how it would actually dispel the external account problem was not made clear. Souter was not enamoured of the pump-priming by the Savage Labour Government and, instead, rather wanted 'a diffused moralisation of the economy as the only effective means of economic stabilisation' (Souter, 1939). Underpinning this was a rejection of urbanisation and industrialism which Souter felt had led to the estrangement of the people from the countryside. Barney Murphy was another trenchant critic of import controls, particularly the choice of which industries to foster. He fired off broadsides in the press about industry ministers making visits to factories 'and having their boots kissed (metaphorically) by obsequious manufacturers, and their faces kissed (literally) by enthusiastic female employees' (cited in Brooke *et al.*, 2016, 8).

Conclusion

The timing of insulation was, as mentioned, fortuitous since it facilitated placing New Zealand on a war footing – that is, the instruments of control were already in existence. The next logical step was to build a war economy. To facilitate this the government established an Economic Stabilisation Commission in 1942 with 'a web of controls' over prices, wages and rents (Martin, 2015, 88). Ashwin, of the Treasury, chaired the Commission, with representation from the unions and farmers. The Commission and the mentality that underpinned it would exert a strong influence over economic policy-making well into the post-war era. Australia, too, slipped fairly easily into a war footing, given the relatively smooth acceptance of a Keynesian statecraft. Almost the entire Australian economic profession was drafted into war administration duties.

Notes

1 Belshaw spent most of 1936 on a Rockefeller Scholarship, visiting Cornell and other universities to study agricultural credit schemes and the capitalisation of agriculture.

2 Reference by J. M. Clark 2/5/1932, FECC, UMA.
3 Rockefeller application of Bill Sutch 1932, FECC, UMA.
4 'Notes from Cambridge 1933', Copland Papers, NLA.
5 Clark to Harrod 3/5/1945, Clark Papers, LSE.
6 Another Australian, Jack Horsfall, a graduate from Melbourne, went to Cambridge and studied under D. H. Robertson and Colin Clark. He decided to stay in Britain and, in a stockbroker's office, undertook statistical research work for Keynes. After the war he worked for *The Economist* before being recruited to become the first editor of the *Australian Financial Review* (Noonan, 2002, 20–1).
7 Shearer spent 1930 at Cambridge researching the problems of monopoly and their control.
8 Mention must be made of the LSE-trained Merab Harris at the UWA, who carried much of the economics teaching between 1934 and 1941 while the professorial chair was vacant (Weber, 2011, 21).
9 'Employment, interest and money; Mr Keynes again', SMH 14/3/1936.
10 Smithies would work in the Treasury for a few years. He won a post at the University of Michigan and that, together with an American wife, spelt the end of involvement with Australia. He never looked back, becoming a prolific publisher and eventually rising to become head of the Economics Department at Harvard.
11 Taking a sabbatical from the bank, Melville would write a manuscript entitled *The Unstable State: An Enquiry into the Nature of Non-Equilbrium Economics*. He never sought to publish it.
12 A. Smithies to Copland, 17/4/ 1936, and Copland to A. Smithies, 23/4/ 1936, FECC, UMA.
13 Isles to Copland, 31/7/1937, FECC, UMA.
14 Copland to Sir W. Mitchell 28/10/1938, FECC, UMA.
15 Graduation address Downing Papers, UMA.
16 Coombs to La Nauze 9/9/1936, La Nauze Papers, NLA.
17 Fisher to La Nauze 26/3/1937, La Nauze Papers, NLA.
18 Copland to B. Ruml 13/12/1936, Copland Papers, NLA.
19 'National income and taxation', *The Christchurch Press*, 17 February 1938.
20 Tocker to Clark 19/2/1938, Clark Papers, University of Queensland (UQ).
21 'The national income: Mr Colin Clark replies to Prof Tocker: widespread tax evasion alleged', *The Christchurch Press* 2 April 1938
22 'The Country would be better off without the Economics of the Universities and Their Products', *Tomorrow*, Clark Papers, UQ.
23 C. Clark to P. Douglas 23/12/1937, Clark Papers, UQ.
24 Copland to Clark April 1938, Copland Papers, NLA.
25 Clark to Copland 27/4 1938, Copland Papers, NLA.
26 Fisher to La Nauze 8/10/1938, La Nauze Papers, NLA.
27 'Keynes and others: a personal Memoir', Clark Papers, UQ.
28 'Australia certainly does provide rich material for the economist who likes to "test" his theories.' (Benham, 1928, vii).
29 Keynes to Clark, 24/2/1940, Clark Papers, UQ.
30 Clark to Harrod 5/5/1945, RES, LSE.
31 Clark to Keynes, 10/11/1941, Clark Papers, UQ.
32 Clark had written to Reddaway asking for a bright student to undertake the indexing of the books. Reddaway suggested Alan Prest, a gifted young Cambridge student. When he had completed it, Prest told his older brother, Wilfred, who was at Melbourne University, that Clark's book was 'quite good, if one can trust his statistics'.
33 Reddaway to Ritchie 22/10/1936, Ritchie Papers, UMA.
34 Copland to Davidson 11/4/1935, Copland Papers, NLA.
35 Copland to Keynes 4/12/1935, Copland Papers, NLA.

36 'Notes on New Zealand', 6/8/1936, Copland Papers, NLA.
37 Nash to Condliffe 14/8/1956, Condliffe Papers, Bancroft Library.
38 Ibid.

References

Arndt, H. 2000, 'Colin Clark', *History of Economics Review*, Supplement, 1–5.

Bassett M. and J. Bassett, 2006, *Roderick Deane: His Life and Times*, Wellington: Viking.

Belshaw, H. 1928, 'The economic position of the farmer in New Zealand', *Economic Record*, 4(1): 53–70.

Belshaw, H. 1933, 'Crisis and readjustment in New Zealand', *Journal of Political Economy*, 41(6): 750–76.

Belshaw, H. 1937, 'Guaranteed prices for New Zealand exports', *Economic Record*, 13(1): 168–88.

Belshaw, H. 1939a, 'Stabilisation in a dependent economy', *Economic Record*, 15(3): 40–60.

Belshaw, H. 1939b, 'Guaranteed prices in operation', *Economic Record*, Supplement, October.

Benham, F. C. 1928, *The Prosperity of Australia*, London: P. S. King.

Blyth, C. A. 2008, 'Early academic economics in New Zealand: notes on its history from the 1870s to the 1950s', Working Paper Series, Department of Economics, University of Auckland, No. 266.

Brooke, G., A. Endres and A. Rogers, 2016, 'Does New Zealand economics have a useful past? The example of trade policy and economic development', *New Zealand Economic Papers*, 50(3): 281–302.

Cain, N. 1984, 'The propagation of Keynesian thinking in Australia: E. R. Walker 1933–36', *Economic Record*, 60(171): 366–80.

Castles, I. 1998, 'Scientists, economists and statisticians', Academy of Social Sciences in Australia, Canberra.

Clark, C. 1940, *The Conditions of Economic Progress*, London: Macmillan.

Clark, C. 1986, 'The bureau of industry', in D. Fraser (ed.), *Administrative History in Queensland*, Brisbane: Royal Australian Institute of Public Administration.

Clark, C. and J. G. Crawford, 1938, *The National Income of Australia*, Sydney: Angus and Robertson.

Coleman, W. 2007, 'Lyndhurst Falkiner Giblin (1875–1951)', in J. E. King (ed.), *A Biographical Dictionary of Australian and New Zealand Economists*, Cheltenham: Edward Elgar, 110–14.

Coleman, W. 2015, 'A young tree dead? The story of economics in Australia and New Zealand', in V. Barnett (ed.), *Routledge Handbook of the History of Global Economic Thought*, London: Routledge: 281–93.

Coleman, W., S. Cornish and A. Hagger, 2006, *Giblin's Platoon: The Trials and Triumph of the Economist in Australian Public Life*, Canberra: Australian National University Press.

Condliffe, J. B. 1959 [1930], *New Zealand in the Making*, London: Allen and Unwin.

Conway, E. 2014, *The Summit*, London: Little, Brown.

Coombs, H. C. 1981, *Trial Balance*, Melbourne: Sun.

Copland, D. B. 1939, 'The economics of insulation', *Economic Record*, Supplement, 15: 25–31.

102 How Keynes came to Australasia

Copland, D. B. 1951, *Inflation and Expansion*, Melbourne: Cheshire.

Cornish, S. 1981. 'Full employment in Australia: the genesis of a white paper', *Research Paper in Economic History*, Canberra: Australian National University.

Cornish, S. 1991, 'Edward Ronald Walker', *Economic Record*, 67(1): 59–68.

Cornish, S. 1993a, 'Sir Leslie Melville: an interview', *Economic Record*, 69(207): 437–57.

Cornish, S. 1993b, 'The Keynesian revolution in Australia: fact or fiction?', *Australian Economic History Review*, 38(2): 43–68.

Cornish, S. 2007, 'Sir Roland Wilson 1904–1996', in J. E. King (ed.), *A Biographical Dictionary of Australian and New Zealand Economists*, Cheltenham: Edward Elgar, 310–14.

Dixon, R. 2009, 'Contributions to economic theory', in Williams R. (ed.), *Balanced Growth: A History of the Department of Economics, University of Melbourne*, Melbourne: Australian Scholarly Publishing Press.

Downing, R. I. (1972), 'Review of M. Keynes (ed.) *Essays on John Maynard Keynes*', *Economic Record*, 52(137): 111–12.

Easton. B. 1997, *In Stormy Seas: The Post War New Zealand Economy*, Dunedin: University of Otago.

Easton, B. 2001, *The Nation Builders*, Auckland: Auckland University Press.

Endres, A. M. and M. Donoghue, 2010, 'Defending Marshall's "masterpiece": Ralph Souter's critique of Robbins essay', *Cambridge Journal of Economics*, 34(3): 547–68.

Fleming, G. A. 1989, 'The role of economists in New Zealand policy making 1912–51: economic advice structures in development', Working Papers in Economics, University of Auckland, No. 59.

Giblin, L. F. 1940, 'Economic progress', *Economic Record*, 16(2): 262–70.

Groenewegen, P. and B. McFarlane, 1990, *A History of Australian Economic Thought*, London: Routledge.

Hancock, K. 2013, *Australian Wage Policy: Infancy and Adolescence*, Adelaide: University of Adelaide Press.

Hawke, G. R, 1985, *The Making of New Zealand: An Economic History*, New York: Cambridge University Press.

Hawke, G. and R. Lattimore, 2005, 'Scoping the history of economics in New Zealand', New Zealand Agricultural and Resource Economics Society Conference, Nelson.

Higgins, C. 1989, 'Colin Clark: an interview', *Economic Record*, 65(93): 296–311.

Keynes, J. M. 1930, *A Treatise on Money*, New York: Harcourt Brace.

Keynes, J. M. 1936, *The General Theory of Employment, Interest and Money*, London: Macmillan.

Macintyre, S. 2015, *Australia's Boldest Experiment*, Sydney: New South.

McKinnon M. 2003, *Treasury: The New Zealand Treasury, 1840–2000*, Auckland: Auckland University Press.

Markwell, D. 2000, 'Keynes and Australia', *Research Discussion Paper 2000–2004*, RBA.

Martin, J. R. 2015, 'An age of the mandarins? Government in New Zealand 1940–51', in *The Seven Dwarfs and the Age of the Mandarins*, Canberra: Australian National University, 81–106.

Melville, L. G. 1939, 'The place of expectations in economic theory', *Economic Record*, 15(1): 1–16.

Millmow, A. J. 2010, *The Power of Economic Ideas: The Origins of Keynesian Economic Management in Interwar Australia 1929–1939*, Canberra: Australian National University Press.

Millmow, A. J. 2012, 'When Australia turned its back on Colin Clark', *History of Economics Review*, 56: 59.

Millmow, A. J. 2015a, 'John Maynard Keynes and the Keynes of the Commonwealth', *Australian Economic History Review*, 55(1): 1–19.

Millmow, A. J. 2015b, 'Australian economists at Cambridge in the 1930s', *History of Economics Review*, 61: 44–57.

Nevile, J. W. and P. Dalziel, 2013, 'Theorizing about post-Keynesian economics in Australasia', in G. C. Harcourt and P. Kriesler (eds), *The Oxford Handbook of Post Keynesian Economics, Volume 2 Critiques and Methodology*, New York: Oxford University Press, 412–35.

Noonan, G. 2002, 'Australian Financial Review: the early years', MA thesis, University of Sydney.

Petridis, R. 2011, 'Depression, war and recovery: Western Australian economics 1935–1963', *History of Economics Review*, 54: 45–69.

Rothbarth, E. 1941, 'Review of *The Conditions of Economic Progress* by Colin Clark', *Economic Journal*, 51(201): 120–4.

Reddaway, W. B. 1936, 'The General Theory of Employment, Interest and Money', *Economic Record*, (12): 28–36.

Royal Commission on the Australian Monetary and Banking Systems 1937, Canberra: Australian Government Printer.

Schedvin, C. B. 1978, 'Sydney James Butlin', *Economic Record*, 54(1): 143–6.

Simkin, C. G. F. 1946, 'Insulationism and the problem of economic stability', *Economic Record*, 22(1): 50–65.

Sinclair, K. 1976, *Walter Nash*, Auckland: Auckland University Press.

Smithies, A. 1936, 'Wages policy in the Depression', *Economic Record*, 11(2): 249–68.

Souter, R. W. 1939, 'How do we want the New Zealand economy to behave', *Economic Record*, 15: 7–16.

Walker, E. R. 1933, *Australia in the World Depression*, London: King.

Weber, E. J. 2011, 'Wilfred E. G. Salter: the merits of a classical economics education', *History of Economics Review*, 54: 111–30.

Weststrate, C. 1959, *Portrait of a Mixed Modern Economy*, Wellington: University of New Zealand Press.

6   War, reconstruction and economic theory

Introduction

At the start of the Second World War, Keith Isles, Professor of Economics at the University of Adelaide, gave some 'fatherly advice' to colleague John La Nauze about research: 'Stick to your theoretical interests. It is time some of us did some work that is of more than local interest',[1] and, in another letter, 'Write on something that is of wider and more permanent interest than mere local war-time econs.'[2] The pages of the *Record* during this period were replete with aspects of war economics. In Adelaide, Isles admitted that he had lots of theoretical work to do but that he had lacked the time to complete it because he had been 'hopelessly overworked... according to English standards'. Isles also told La Nauze that because of the mobilisation of economists for wartime administration, and given there was only a small talent pool to draw from, there were only a few university economists still free to fully attend to their research.[3] Pigou had once said economists were cloistered people since contact with their subject was indirect, through the printed page; it would be difficult, though, to say this of Australian economists during wartime. In 1942 Isles was seconded to the Rationing Commission, having not lived up to his own high expectations with just a few articles on war finance. While administration, rationing and industrial organisation for the war effort occupied the time of university economists, there were, in fact, some remarkable contributions from Australian economists, particularly Clark and Walker. In a sense, the war gave impetus to applied research. There was also an attempt at building the first econometric model of the Australian economy. It was undertaken by a chain-smoking prodigy named Trevor Swan, who worked in the Department of Post-War Reconstruction, but would not be published until after his death. Older sages, such as Copland and Giblin, despite heavy administrative responsibilities, still found time to write about post-war economic prospects.

The purpose of this chapter is to survey this outpouring of economic thought during the war and immediate post-war years. The chapter will tend to dwell more on Australian economists than their New Zealand counterparts simply because there is more literature extant upon the former (Fleming, 1989). In New Zealand, only the RBNZ and Treasury hired economists such as William Sutch, who served as a ministerial advisor to Nash. Australia, in contrast, had a team of hitherto university economists in the Finance and Economic Committee (F and E) offering advice on war finance and related matters. We will also address economic practice and policy, since both countries continued to pioneer economic experiments such as the commitment to full employment in the post-war era, led mostly by Australian economists. This will be first, before turning to the contributions of individuals.

War finance and economic thought

Australia: putting the nation's economists to work

Australia's and New Zealand's participation as combatants during the Second World War presented problems of administration and resource mobilisation. However, this also opened up new opportunities for economic wisdom, especially in macroeconomic management and policy. Australia's increase in its defence effort presented problems for its federal style of governance and for a Treasury hidebound by traditional attitudes about public finance. However, Australia smoothly switched to a total war economy because the economists serving on the F and E Committee were uncommonly influential. The Committee had come into being as the idealisation of a central thinking agency (Whitwell, 1986). It included Brigden, Copland, Coombs and Melville, with Wilson as chair. All of these men were 'inside' economists, since Giblin had just resigned his Ritchie Chair at the University of Melbourne and Copland, on leave from Melbourne, would never return there. The Committee, under Giblin's serene leadership, convinced the Menzies Government that, before resorting to taxes and borrowing, the war effort could be met by putting the nation's idle resources to work. This was not the advice offered by the Treasury but Menzies could see its attraction. Coombs was later adamant that the Committee gave the 'economic planning of the war' a Keynesian pedigree. While Giblin is credited with leading the way, Walker, who had written a book on war economics in late 1939, should also share in the plaudits. Singing the book's praises, Copland said the 'great virtue' of Walker's approach was that it got 'behind the veil of money' and put the defence problem 'in real terms'. Walker spoke about resource allocation in wartime and how economics and economists could make a positive contribution. When peace prevailed, he argued that wartime controls should continue since he feared that depression might return if federal expenditure eased off (Cornish 1990, 63). The F and E Committee advised the government to shepherd resources by borrowing until the economy reached full employment. It was Giblin, then, who encouraged the authorities to attempt more with fiscal policy. Giblin demonstrated how Australia, with 10 per cent unemployment, could painlessly increase its defence budget without facing any resources pressures. Instead of a heavy-handed resort to economic controls that would intimidate business, Giblin felt that expenditure could be raised through credit expansion. The Treasurer, Percy Spender, made it clear in a submission to Cabinet how borrowing for defence would be from the central bank, thus sparing private enterprise from a greater tax burden. Once capacity and full employment were reached, however, taxation would assume its rightful place and prevent any inflation. Cornish (1993) identified this as the moment when a Keynesian revolution in economic policy 'arrived' in Australia because academic wisdom overruled the advice coming from Treasury.

Further signs of the new wisdom were evident when the Australian government began to implement a variant of Keynes's deferred consumption plan as a means of financing the war. Their advice followed that laid out by Keynes in his pamphlet *How to Pay for the War* (1940). Giblin communicated with Keynes about calculating 'the gap' between expected war expenditure and the resources needed that could be marshalled by taxation and loans. After considering the options, Giblin devised a deferred tax credits or compulsory loans plan, set within a national programme of uniform taxation which gave the Commonwealth a dominant position within the Australian federal system. When Japan declared war, on 7 December 1941, Australia had to move to a total war footing and the Committee drew again upon a Keynesian framework, advising even more severe fiscal measures. However, the new Curtin Labor Government did not warm to the idea of suppressing the consumption standards of low-income earners who would, as a result, bear the brunt of financing the war. Soon Australia resorted to the use of direct controls, including rationing and price and wage controls set within a National Economic Plan (Coleman *et al.*, 2006, 194). As such, an authentic Keynesian framework was discarded due to political exigencies. The war was soon being financed by central bank credit, with inevitable inflationary consequences bottled up by controls and rationing. Every Australian economist could see this. Brigden, although wary of credit finance, could see justification in funding the war effort in this manner. However, by 1939 he had noted that this expedient was predicated on the notion that wages would not increase once the unemployed were soaked up. He had noticed that 'each degree of increase towards full employment is accompanied by increases in wage rates and labour costs' (cited in ibid., 187). In a note written in 1944, entitled 'Crisis in democracy', Giblin was equally alarmed by this prospect, fearing that trade union militancy would push wages ahead of productivity, a development that had been 'looming in the distance for the last, perhaps, sixty years' (Coleman *et al.*, 2006, 226; Macintyre, 2015, 289–90). Brigden left the conundrum with the Secretary to the Treasury, S. G. MacFarlane, who later raised the matter with Keynes and got a fairly agnostic answer.

It was Copland who, as Commonwealth Prices Commissioner, was charged with controlling the inflation dragon with bluster and controls. Halfway through the war the F and E Committee languished, with its members returning to their official posts (Maddock and Penny, 1983). Coombs was made Director of Rationing and Brigden made Secretary of the Department of Supply. The work done by this small band of economists was recognised when a future prime minister, Menzies, noted in 1942 that '[i]n the economic history of the last fifteen years nothing will be more notable than the rise to influence and authority of the professional economist' (p. 6).

New Zealand: policy-makers not economists

In 1942, New Zealand passed the Economic Stabilisation Act equipping its government with a similar array of controls. The Economic Stabilisation Commission was to make recommendations to Finance Minister Nash regarding whole aspects of the economy during wartime and the post-war era. It is remarkable that no economists initially served upon it, confirming the general finding by Fleming (1989, 31) that economists were not regarded as essential to the New Zealand's wartime government (Martin, 2015).

Copland drew out another lesson of wartime economics, namely, that, given a clear and generally accepted objective, policy-makers could erect an economic structure far superior to that which was known during the dark days of the 1930s. This was a powerful sentiment when mixed with the collective view, shared by Australian economists, that capitalism had to be moulded to meet certain ends and could no longer be left to its own devices. Underpinning this was a marked shift in the philosophy of the economists. Unregulated capitalism, they argued, was prone to erratic expectations, uncertainty and turbulence. To counter this there needed to be a pledge by government to maintain aggregate demand to secure full employment. However, the F and E Committee economists felt there also had to be a change in underlying social attitudes within the community to bring this about (Whitwell, 1986). One milestone in this regard was to make full employment a political ideal in both countries.

Full employment idealism

The Australian economists inducted into war service, particularly those in the Department of Post-War Reconstruction, led by Coombs as Director-General, were given the task of drafting the White Paper on Full Employment. Gerald Firth and James Nimmo did most of the early drafting. They were emboldened by the appearance of the British White Paper on Employment Policy issued in May 1944. Firth, the senior author, was an English economist who had come to Melbourne as a Ritchie Research Fellow before being seconded to the public service. Prime Minister John Curtin wanted Australia to match the British government's 1944 White Paper on Employment Policy, which promised 'high and stable employment'. A year later an Australian White Paper, *Full Employment in Australia*, was tabled in the House of Representatives. As Selwyn Cornish (1981) noted, the document underwent a huge amount of redrafting, eight times over 12 months, with input from economists, together with contributions from Prime Minister Curtin and Federal Treasurer Ben Chifley. There was some later squabbling about the authorship of the final document between Copland and Coombs. Copland, at this stage, was the Economic Advisor to the Prime Minister; Curtin despatched him to examine attempts at full employment policy in America, Canada and Britain.

Full Employment in Australia was a more circumspect and considered document than its British counterpart. It had clauses on fiscal balance, the mobility of resources, productive efficiency, distribution, wage stability, inflation, the stabili-sation of farmers' incomes and concerns about the external account. Yet these safeguards would be scarcely honoured (Cornish, 1993). The main criticism by economists of the White Paper was its undue emphasis on maintaining full employment at all costs, particularly at the expense of resource mobility. J. S. G. Wilson (1946) reminded planners of the need for a flexible economy, including some unemployment, which enabled price signals to fulfil their role in allocating resources. There was also concern about the role in the White Paper given to public expenditure in setting the pace, private expenditure following in its wake. Both these issues would flare up in the post-war years, with substantive dissent expressed by some economists.

In 1944 New Zealand passed the Employment Act for the purpose of promot-ing and maintaining full employment. The English economist Dudley Seers, who briefly resided in New Zealand after the war, stated in a pamphlet entitled *The Challenge to New Zealand Labour* (1946) that he wanted the government to establish a staff of economists to furnish data to an inner economic cabinet.[4] Interestingly, Seers (ibid., 35) felt that, because local economics graduates 'have been taught by gentlemen of the old school', it would be better if New Zealand hired economists from abroad and that the staff be headed by an economist of international repute. Seers' other main point of the pamphlet was to remind the New Zealand Federation of Labour about their responsibilities in ensuring a wages policy compatible with full employment. Both Australia and New Zealand had earlier committed themselves to full employment in the 1944 Canberra Pact. This would fortify the Australasian case for arguing that, in the new post-war order, every nation should commit itself to full employment before trade liberali-sation was considered. That campaign, led by Australian economists, especially Coombs, was known as the 'international full employment approach'. It took the form of establishing an international agreement where nations would pursue full employment and thereby expand trade opportunities.

The 'Australian view' challenged the American dogma that full employment could be achieved by establishing a regime of free trade which dismantled all obstacles. The employment approach was Australia's and New Zealand's formal response, *in toto*, to Article VII of the Mutual Aid Agreement between the United States and Britain and her Dominions. Basically, the Americans wanted a reduc-tion in all forms of discriminatory treatment in international commerce, particu-larly the reduction of tariffs and other trade barriers – including imperial preferences. This would particularly affect New Zealand's dairy exports to Britain. Giblin feared that, under a policy of pure free trade, 'Australia would stand in danger of being given the permanent role of hewers of wood and drawers of water' (cited in Maddock and Penny, 1983, 42–3). By the same token, the F and E Committee economists agreed that a return to protectionism would contract trade and lead to a loss of income and employment.

Simply put, Australasian prosperity depended on exports, which were depend-ent upon a buoyant world economy. To bring that about, the F and E Committee economists wanted a universal commitment to full employment, especially by the major economic powers, which would underpin more global trade. This commitment to securing a high level of economic activity was considered far more important than reducing trade barriers. Without that assurance, which became the negotiating position for Australia and New Zealand, both countries would have faced a recurrence of balance of payments problems. In cases where external deficits threatened, Australia and New Zealand would have to abandon their full employment policy. While the trans-Tasman stance was seen as something of an irritant to negotiations on post-war reconstruction, Turnell (2001) reveals that it was not just economic 'posturing' but a theoretically considered case about the realities of global trade. It was Coombs who took the bit between his teeth and added strength to the Australian pitch. Basing his arguments within the orthodox canons of trade theory, Coombs drew attention to the explicit assumption of full employment which underpinned the theory. If that was not the case, he argued, then the theory became 'largely irrelevant' (Macintyre, 2015). Moreover, he argued that it was national income or the level of employment that was more important in determining demand than the elimination of trade barriers. If there was no universal commitment to full employment then nations would revert to exporting their economic problems as in the interwar period. It followed, then, that global trade would be better promoted if the focus was upon the maintenance of income rather than tariff levels (Turnell, 2001, 7). One might interpret this as yet another contribution to trade theory by Australian economists (ibid., 14–15). In effect Coombs was simply reminding US delegates that the model of the economy within the *General Theory* was a closed one and that the influence of international payments and trade, which Australia knew well about, had received scant attention.

While the Australians were proposing a strong Keynesian line, Keynes himself privately objected to their approach on the grounds that the Australians were promising to be 'not only good but clever… the main task is producing first the intellectual conviction and then intellectually the means. Insufficiency of cleverness, not of goodness, is the main trouble' (ibid., 9). He felt, moreover, that it was hard to estimate what the post-war economic environment would look like. The trans-Tasman economies also wanted the right to protect their small manufacturing sectors. This dilemma was compounded by their having joined fledgling international institutions such as the IMF, which had ruled out commercial trading policy. Although New Zealand was told that it could still use import licensing, it was not persuaded to become a signatory to the IMF Convention until 1961; its decision not to join was criticised by some as redolent of a 'Little Englander' insularity (Gould, 1982, 90). It reflected again the strong prejudices of Social Credit elements within the Labour Party, wary of incurring more foreign debt and being captive of international banks, even though A. G. B. Fisher, who now held an executive position at the IMF, was brought back to Wellington to convince them otherwise. A later study of the episode by Hawke and Wijewardane (1972) found that the decision had cost more than benefited New Zealand.

At several international conferences at and before the war's end, the Australian and New Zealand delegations sought to have the full employment approach inserted into the agreements being forged on trade and capital flows. Alas, because of American intransigence and British weakness in pressing the employment argument case, only watered down versions of the Australian resolutions were ever adopted (Cornish, 1993).

As it transpired, both trans-Tasman economies were to find the post-war environment bountiful with full employment, buoyant export prices, rising real incomes and swelling coffers of overseas assets. This would bring its own problems. New Zealand would become a working man's paradise with more vacancies than people to fill them. There was also a strong demand, with rising prices, for its wool, meat and dairy products (Condliffe, 1959 [1930], 112). Dairy prices, for instance, rose by 50 per cent in the first few years after the war. Both economies retained aspects of wartime control, including rationing, price and resource controls and import licensing. This, and the pent-up demand from the war, left both economies taut with inflation and awash with liquidity. So prosperous was New Zealand that Nash took the currency back to parity with sterling and even donated a gift of foreign exchange to the British government.

The aftermath of the Korean War wool boom would see both Australia and New Zealand prosper, with the latter becoming the world's third richest economy per capita (Gould, 1982, 22). That status did not necessarily translate into a higher quality of life because of oppressive controls and even restrictive laws on trade and business hours. In his adopted home of Queensland, Colin Clark, who had a liking for an ale or two, attacked the 'wowserism' of restricted liquor trading hours aided and abetted by limited competition in the brewery industry. In that respect he bemoaned the lack of effective anti-trust legislation in Australia. With an Edwardian attitude to women in the workforce, let alone the economics profession, Clark would be astonished to learn that it was to be a woman, Maureen Brunt, who first addressed the need for Australian companies to adhere to something akin to trade practices. In 1962, she was to publish, with Peter Karmel, path-breaking research into the structure and behaviour of Australian industry. The foreign investment that poured to nestle behind the tariff wall led to small-scale, regionally dispersed inefficient enterprises. Economies of scale were not reaped because of the Australian state governments encouraging decentralisation while being inactive on restrictive trade practices (Butlin *et al.*, 1982, 127–8). Karmel and Brunt's (1962) pioneering work showed the high degree of entrenched market power, collusion and the extent of restrictive practices operating within the Australian economy. That work, together with University of New South Wales (UNSW) economist Alex Hunter (1961) shining a light on restrictive practices in the business sector, was significant in signalling the need for some pro-competition law in Australia and even in New Zealand (Fels, 2007, 205). Brunt would offer an economist's approach to trade practices and concepts such as markets and competition (Norman, 2007, 10). She was a hands-on economist, serving not only with the Trade Practices Commission but also as a lay member of the High Court of New Zealand, specifically on competition cases from 1990–2000. Meanwhile, for Clark, there were other, more colourful features of his productivity during the war years to which we now turn.

Contributions to theory

While they were mobilised for the war effort a number of Australian economists continued to make significant theoretical contributions during and immediately after the war.

Colin Clark

Even while holding down his trinity of jobs for the Queensland government, as well as an appointment with the Commonwealth Department of War Organisation of Industry, Clark could still find time to make some controversial contributions to theory and forecasts. Some of his output first took shape in the monthly bulletin *Economic News*, which he edited on behalf of the Bureau of Industry. During Clark's employment there, from 1938–51, some 143 issues were published on a range of economic and social topics (Clark, 1986). While he had drifted away from working on national accounting, it could be said that, by the time he left Queensland in 1952 to take up an appointment at Oxford, he was, with the exception of Copland, Australia's most controversial economist. Clark had resigned, with regret, from the Queensland public service over differences about economic policy – essentially whether Queensland should develop manufacturing in its urban centres or support its rural industries. In what became his last letter to Keynes, Clark reported that his relationship with the Australian elite had soured:

> As a prophet of greatly improved terms of trade for primary produce I ought to be very popular in Australia, but I am not. Everybody has his mind set on making Australia a manufacturing country. Not many people have realised that if we exclude imports of manufactures, we shall lose our ability to export primary produce… The interests of the rest of Australia differ from those of Sydney and Melbourne, but these two cities have a strong political pull. Queensland and the rest of Australia are the States which have the greatest interest in export trade and also have the greatest possibilities of further development.[5]

Before Clark's resignation from his Queensland post in 1952, he had been prolific in his writing. In 1938 he published a study exposing the true state of Soviet economic performance. He then issued, as discussed earlier, a forward-looking postscript to his *Conditions of Economic Progress* (1940), which was predictive work built on some of the figure-work of his previous study. The central thesis of his work *The Economics of 1960* (1942) was that the course of economic development over the next two decades would be little affected by wars and revolutions or, indeed, any political or social upheaval. It was a stunning prognosis to be issued amid total war. Underpinning his analysis was the assumption that there would be no further global war. Clark foresaw how greater trade and full employment would enfeeble economic nationalism. He characterised economic history as comprising periods of capital satiation and capital hunger; he forecast that when the war ended it would be followed by a period of capital hunger. There would then be a resumption of international trade and investment and a big shift away from primary production to manufacturing. This meant that the terms of trade would rise in favour of commodity-exporting countries such as Australia and New Zealand. Clark prophesied the rise of India and China, that this transformation would be bigger than the Industrial Revolution and that the West should not impede this progress by resorting to protectionism. We now know that Clark was premature in his hunches, just as English economist G. D. H. Cole felt that he was too optimistic in his prophecy that economic forces would deliver nirvana by 1960. Cole was sceptical, too, about the veracity of Clark's statistics, just as Austin Robinson (1943, 239) was 'exasperated' about the absence of information on how he had arrived at his projections and admonished him for this lack of courtesy. Cole (1942, 69) concluded that 'this statistical pamphlet is less as an essay in prophecy than as a pointer towards a sane world economic policy'.

Clark became famous for his rule that the tax share of GDP should not exceed 25 per cent of GDP. It had prosaic origins. Queensland's Ned Hanlon, one of the four state premiers whom Clark advised, suggested that the scale of Australia's post-war expenditures on social goods and reconstruction would be so onerous that it reminded him how excessive taxation had been the undoing of empires in the past. In 1945 taxation accounted for 30 per cent of Australia's national income. Clark went back to his databank of statistics and, after some calculations, arrived at the contention that at full employment the maximum rate of taxation was 25 per cent of net national product; he submitted his paper to the *Economic Journal*. If a nation went beyond that limit, Clark predicted that, after a lag, inflation would ensue. In other words, high and rising taxation reduced savings and incentive and, in turn, efficiency and productivity, thus giving impetus to inflation. The remedy for inflation, Clark (1945) believed, was a large reduction in government expenditure followed by reductions in direct and indirect taxation. Much later, Clark was adamant that Keynes agreed with his contention. What Keynes actually told Clark was: 'This statistical inference is rather precarious, nevertheless as a practical proposition I should be strongly disposed to agree with your... main conclusions, namely, the 25 per cent taxation is about the limit of what is easily borne.'[6] Interestingly, in an earlier letter on Clark's first draft, Keynes qualified his views on the 25 per cent limit, which he found 'an interesting and fruitful subject'. He advised Clark: 'There is, however, a virtuous correlation by which an increase in government expenditure, particularly if it leads to a deficit, raises prices and so reduces the budgetary problem. Surely this is a highly relevant element in the situation.'[7] Keynes also felt that Clark had to take into account the effect of an improved standard of living in raising the limit. Clark, however, never deviated from his 25 per cent limit.[8] He would later use it as a proximate cause of Australia's post-war inflation, suggesting that, failing an appreciation of the exchange, one purgative available would be to allow a wage rise (Clark, 1950). That would raise unemployment, kill the boom and return the public finances to a more sober footing. When the Australian government cut taxes in 1952, Clark welcomed it because the tax ratio to GDP was then 30 per cent. He took the opportunity to attack those 'who adhere to an economic doctrine which I can only describe as "bastard-Keynesianism" (for Keynes himself never said anything of the sort) to the effect that a depression is the only time when you are permitted to reduce taxes'.[9]

Clark also continued his research on the optimal size of a city. Filtering into his thinking was his conversion to Roman Catholicism and the belief that large cities bred crime and alienation. Clark favoured rural development and decentralisation; when it came to the ideal size of a town he had arrived at the 'drastic conclusion' that a population of 200,000 was the level at which cities 'could be free from traffic congestion even if every family had a car, and could give nearly all the commercial and cultural facilities which a modern community requires'.[10] Beyond that size, civic pride suffered, amenities became uneconomic and transport gridlock made larger cities intolerable.

Another contribution of his was to formulate an econometric paper on a system of equations explaining the trade cycle in America during the period 1921–41. A Keynesian-inspired model, it gave emphasis to changes in inventory investment which depended on the rate of change in output. In the introduction to his article, Clark lavished praise upon Swan's comparable 1943 macroeconomic model and how he had expressed his variables in terms of which Keynes would approve.

Trevor Swan

Swan had won first-class honours and the University Medal at Sydney and Coombs, alerted to his brilliance, had quickly recruited him. As early as 1943, in a paper entitled 'The principle of effective demand: a real life model', he produced a ten-equation quarterly econometric model of the Australian economy, only the second time that a quantitative macroeconomic model had been built and some five years before Lawrence Klein's effort. Swan used a slide-rule and scatter diagram to derive his model.

Swan did not bother having his paper published; it was published posthumously in 1989. As mentioned, Clark (1949) had lavishly praised Swan's model as true to Keynes's method of estimation, showing consumption, investment and imports as functions of national income, with exports, public expenditure and tariff levels as exogenous variables, making it possible to 'explain' movements in national income over a ten-year period. The model also came with lags and expectations to add to its Keynesian authenticity. Swan claimed it made the first use of the Keynesian 45 degree diagram of aggregate demand and aggregate supply that Samuelson popularised (Butlin and Gregory, 1989, 372).[11] In a blaze of creativity, Swan was to make two more outstanding contributions: one in trade theory, the other in growth theory.

Ronald Walker

Walker matched Clark's productivity by writing four volumes in a decade, all concerned with unemployment and wartime economics – the latter meriting the award of a Doctor of Letters from Cambridge. In 1942 Walker, like many of his colleagues, joined the war effort, becoming Chief Economic Advisor and Deputy Director General of the Department of War Organisation and Industry. Before this appointment, he had put the finishing touches to *From Economic Theory to Policy* (1943), which tried to narrow the gulf between theory and policy. Walker argued that there was too much 'theoretic blight' within contemporary theory where chosen assumptions were either in conflict with the observable facts or where models abstracted from important facts. It was essential that policy advice be grounded in solid foundations. He set out, therefore, to determine how economic theory could be tailored to become more useful for policy formulation (Cornish, 1990, 63).

Walker even took aim at Keynes for building 'a theory on concepts which cannot possibly be checked against concrete facts', at his penchant for a 'laborious shadow sparring' mode of presentation and for not presenting a more realistic model of business behaviour (Whitwell, 1986, 62–3). As an example, he cited the apocryphal tale of how a copy of *The General Theory* in the parliamentary library in Canberra was only marked and scored in the practical and policy parts of the book, which, in any case, were few and far between.

Cornish (1990) credits Walker with anticipating the Public Choice School approach to economics by demonstrating how resources were sometimes allocated using non-market criteria. Walker claimed that there were instances where alternatives to the free market were sought by well-organised agents using the political process. Agents would then use market or non-market channels, depending upon how well organised they were in pursuit of their goals. Walker obviously welcomed the idea of economists advising governments. It was a role Australian economists relished so much that Arndt (1996) claimed – partly from personal experience – that, in the post-war period, 'inside' economists, such as Coombs, excluded university economists from policy influence. University boffins still mattered when it came to policy development. In the post-war era Walker was lost to Australian economics because of his diplomatic career, but he did not welcome the mathematical nature of the discipline, thinking it of little worth (Cornish, 1990, 66). In New Zealand the observation by one figure of authority was that, in the early 1950s, there were not enough economists in the public service while the country's academic economists lived in a world of their own (Webb, 1953, 30). Malcolm Fisher (1954), a New Zealand economist studying at Cambridge, lamented this paucity of economists within the public service and suggested more networking between inside and university economists.

Douglas Copland

Although an economist-advisor and never a theoretician, Copland continued to make valid contributions to post-war economic policy, showing originality in his observations of economic life. As a foretaste of his post-war views, he gave the 1944 Godwin lectures at Harvard, entitled 'The Road to High Employment'. As evidenced by the title, Copland felt that full employment might be hard to reconcile with efficiency and liberty. Essentially, he felt that trying to keep the economy at over-full employment would cause strains and would necessitate placing more controls on the economy. It was Copland who claimed the mantle of Keynes rather than the younger set of economists, whom he described as neo-Keynesians (Millmow, 2013). He suggested that 'the over-enthusiasm for the Keynesian theory and its extravagant expectations in a theory of full employment would have been disowned by the Master' (cited in ibid.: 190). Thus Copland could not understand Coombs's policy of continuously generating more jobs than there were people to fill them. He later told his protégé Downing:

> It is a mistake in these matters of public policy to seek for perfection or to make definitions of ultimate policy. If we can get unemployment down to an average of 4 or 5 percent in our first efforts we shall have done a pretty good job.[12]

A related challenge of the Australian economy in the post-war age was in accommodating economic development with a heavy immigration programme. Copland (1948, 43) felt that the post-war economic forecasts had been too pessimistic and that the 'obsession with security' and the need to guarantee a high level of aggregate demand was no basis on which to develop the nation.

He argued that the post-war boom was more due to accident than design, the main reason for the buoyant level of economic activity being due to the legacy of the war economy and reconstruction. It was not, Copland argued, 'a good ground on which to claim the success of a full employment theory of full employment' when that condition was inevitable (ibid.: 13). Copland (1948) feared that the objectives of post-war reconstruction were not been achieved. Australian policy-makers were becoming complacent because good times were masking underlying weaknesses within the economy; Australia was not investing enough in basic industries to secure vigorous and sustained growth. Copland (1949) felt that too many resources were being used in consumption at the expense of heavy industry, construction and transport. He described Australia as 'a milk bar economy'.[13] The phrase earned such currency that some local small retailers objected that they were being blamed for the nation's economic ills.

Copland also recycled Belshaw's idea of creating a stabilisation fund for booming wool exports as a means of quarantining revenue pouring into the economy. This device, while not welcomed by graziers, would check the inflationary potent of high export prices by cutting the connection between export prices and money incomes. It was also a better option, Copland felt, than fiddling with the currency.

Despite his reputation as a promoter for the economic profession, Copland came across in the post-war years as a windbag, sometimes flip-flopping on his views and acutely sensitive to his declining authority. The leadership of the economics profession was passing to younger hands, not least Coombs, who described Copland as a 'somewhat pedestrian' economist (Macintyre, 2015, 391). Some vindication came Copland's way, though, over Australia's zealous pursuit of full employment and its implications for price stability. With his ear to the ground, his research assistant told him:

> You will be interested to know that nearly all of the post-war reconstruction people who adopted such an exaggerated definition of full employment are now openly saying that some unemployment seems to be necessary in order to maintain internal stability. They are particularly worried about the difficulty of holding down money wages. It has taken them a long time to learn the lesson that you were driving at right through the post-war period, but I think we have now heard the last of the over-full employment doctrines.[14]

Colin Simkin

In his inaugural address as Professor of Economics at Auckland, entitled 'Insulationism and the problem of economic stability', Simkin (1946) emphasised how self-sufficiency, even with full employment, came with a depressed level of real income. This was due, he said, to the allocative inefficiency caused by distorting prices, controls on the free flow of capital and neglect of the principle of comparative costs. Monopoly elements and vested interests, too, were fostered under the new regime. Simkin defined insulationism as comprising four main instruments: counter-cyclical fiscal policy, guaranteed prices for agricultural output, exchange controls and, lastly, import controls. This machinery was guided by 'a clumsy and rather arbitrary system of state regulation'. Drawing inspiration from Hayek's *Road to Serfdom* (1944), Simkin warned that this economic edifice risked the creation of a massive and capricious bureaucracy (Brooke *et al.*, 2016, 9).

In a subsequent article (Simkin, 1948, 31), while sympathetic to the goals of security, social justice and economic independence, Simkin argued that the execution of New Zealand's insulationism had been marred by the controls falling far short of their objectives. He noted how there did not seem to be any great intellectual conviction behind insulation other than a pragmatic, opportunist response to a perennial concern. Moreover, 'It was difficult to discern any important influences upon its [Labour Party] policy either from socialist theoreticians or from professionally-trained economists' (ibid., 30). That is, insulation had not been grounded in any theoretical consideration. He went on to note, too, how his colleagues were essentially 'isolated from public affairs' and this was more marked than in any other advanced economy.

In his 1946 lecture, Simkin had suggested three alternatives: first, that New Zealand join the IMF and use the Special Drawing Rights as a partial stabilisation fund; second, that New Zealand adopt a uniform tariff that would allow the dictate of comparative advantage to have some force; and, third, that import licences be abandoned, licences being put out to competitive auction where they are needed. As Brooke *et al.* (2016, 10) note, Simkin's lecture was 'a far sighted critique that fell on deaf ears'. The Labour Party entertained ancient prejudices against international capital which ruled out New Zealand joining the IMF. Condliffe (1959 [1930]) would later come to the same findings when reviewing the record and doctrinal influences behind the first Labour Government (1935–49). Most of New Zealand's economists had been discredited for advocating real wage cuts together with budgetary stringency during the Depression.

Conclusion

Australian economists like Copland and Coombs certainly showed their practical side in high-level appointments to buttress the war effort and equally so in advising upon post-war institutional arrangements that would make for a better world. Amid their war administration duties, some – like Colin Clark, Ronald Walker and Trevor Swan – found time to make significant theoretical contributions of some note. Two New Zealand economists, Colin Simkin and Conrad Blyth, undertook active wartime service with the former, upon peacetime, making a significant contribution outlining a new sustainable economic path for his country. Overall, though, Australian economists were far more involved in war administration than their New Zealand counterparts.

Notes

1 Isles to La Nauze 24/12/1940, La Nauze Papers, NLA.
2 Isles to La Nauze 31/3/1940, La Nauze Papers, NLA.
3 Isles to La Nauze 28/3/1944, La Nauze Papers, NLA.
4 Paper presented to Wellington Branch of the Economic Society 9/11/1945.
5 Clark to Keynes 18/2/1946, Royal Economic Society (RES), LSE.
6 Keynes to Clark 9/3/1945, RES, LSE.
7 Keynes to Clark 10/1/1945, RES, LSE.
8 'Keynes and others: a personal memoir', Clark Papers, UQ.
9 'Sir Arthur Fadden is on the right lines', *The Courier Mail*, 19 August 1952. Interestingly, Clark's use of the term 'Bastard Keynesianism' predates Joan Robinson's more famous use, but the context is somewhat similar.
10 Clark to Keynes 10/1/1945, RES, LSE.
11 Interestingly, Swan was not made a Fellow of the Econometric Society.
12 Copland to Downing 1/11/1944, Copland Papers, NLA.
13 In Australian parlance a milk bar was a suburban corner shop selling all manner of consumer perishables. In New Zealand a corner shop is known as the 'dairy'.
14 R. Mathews to Copland, 3/8/1956, Copland Papers, NLA.

References

Arndt, H. W. 1996, 'Economic research and economic policy', *Australian Quarterly*, 68(3): 93–8.

Brooke, G., A. Endres and A. Rogers, 2016, 'Does New Zealand economics have a useful past? The example of trade policy and economic development', *New Zealand Economic Papers*, 50(3): 281–302.

Butlin, N. G. and R. G. Gregory, 1989, 'Trevor Winchester Swan, 1918–89', *Economic Record*, 65(191): 369–77.

Butlin, N. G., A. Barnard and J. J. Pincus, 1982, *Government and Capitalism*, Sydney: Allen and Unwin.

Clark, C. 1940, *The Conditions of Economic Progress*, London: Macmillan.

Clark, C. 1942, *The Economics of 1960*, London: Macmillan.

Clark, C. 1945, 'Public finance and changes in the value of money', *Economic Journal*, 55(220): 371–89.

Clark, C. 1950, 'The budget and the basic wage', *Economic Record*, 26(51): 179–85.

Clark, C. 1986, 'The bureau of industry', in D. Fraser (ed.), *Administrative History in Queensland*, Brisbane: Royal Australian Institute of Public Administration.

Cole, G. D. H. 1942, 'Economic forces and world order', *Nature*, 150(3794): 69.

Coleman, W., S. Cornish and A. Hagger, 2006, *Giblin's Platoon: The Trials and Triumph of the Economist in Australian Public Life*, Canberra: Australian National University Press.

Condliffe, J. B. 1959 [1930], *New Zealand in the Making*, London: Allen and Unwin.

Copland, D. B. 1945, *The Road to High Employment: Administrative Controls in a Free Economy*, Melbourne: Angus & Robertson.

Copland, D. B. 1948, *Back to Earth in Economics*, Melbourne: Angus & Robertson.

Copland, D. B. 1949, 'Balance of production in the Australian post-war economy', *Economic Record*, 25: 1–6.

Copland, D. B. 1951, *Inflation and Expansion*, Melbourne: Cheshire.

Cornish, S. 1981. 'Full employment in Australia: the genesis of a white paper', *Research Paper in Economic History*, Canberra: Australian National University.

Cornish, S. 1990, 'Edward Ronald Walker', *Economic Record*, 67(196): 59–68.

Cornish, S. 1993, 'The Keynesian revolution in Australia: fact or fiction?', *Australian Economic History Review*, 38(2): 43–68.

Fels, A. 2007, 'Distinguished fellow of the Economic Society of Australia, 2006: Maureen Brunt', *Economic Record*, 83(261): 204–7.

Fisher, M. 1954, 'Review of "Economic Stability in New Zealand" by R. S. Parker', *Economic Journal*, 64(256): 828–30.

Fleming, G. A. 1989, 'The role of economists in New Zealand policy making 1912–51: economic advice structures in development', *Working Papers in Economics*, University of Auckland, No. 59.

Gould, J. 1982, *The Rakes's Progress*, Auckland: Hodder and Stoughton.

Hawke, G. R. and B. A. Wijewardane, 1972, 'New Zealand and the International Monetary Fund', *Economic Record*, 48(1): 92–102.

Hunter, A. 1961, 'Restrictive practices and monopolies in Australia', *Economic Record*, 37(77): 25–49.

Karmel, P. and M. Brunt, 1962, *The Structure of the Australian Economy*, Melbourne: Cheshire.

Keynes, J. M. 1940, *How to Pay for the War: A Radical Plan for the Chancellor of the Exchequer*, London: Macmillan.

Macintyre, S. 2015, *Australia's Boldest Experiment*, Sydney: New South.

Maddock, R. and J. Penny, 1983, 'Economists at war: the Financial and Economic Committee 1939–44', *Australian Economic History Review*, 23: 28–49.

Martin, J. R. 2015, 'An age of the mandarins? Government in New Zealand 1940–51', in *The Seven Dwarfs and the Age of the Mandarins*, Canberra: Australian National University, 81–106.

Menzies R. G. 1942, 'The Australian economy during war', *Joseph Fisher Lecture in Commerce*, Adelaide: Hassell Press.

Millmow, A. J. 2013, 'Douglas Copland's battle with the younger brethren of economists', *Australian Economic History Review*, 53(2): 187–209.

Norman, N. 2007, 'The contribution of Australian economists: the record and the barriers', *Economic Papers*, 26(1): 1–16.

Robinson, A. 1943, 'Review of "The Economics of 1960" by Colin Clark', *Economic Journal*, 53(210): 238–42.

Seers, D. 1946, *The Challenge to New Zealand Labour*, Christchurch: Christchurch Cooperative Book Society.

Simkin, C. G. F. 1946, 'Insulationism and the problem of economic stability', *Economic Record*, 22(1): 50–65.

Simkin, C. G. F. 1948, 'Wartime changes in the New Zealand economy', *Economic Record*, 24(1): 18–31.

Swan, T. W. 1989, 'The principle of effective demand: a "real life" model', *Economic Record*, 65(190): 378–98.

Turnell, S. 2001, 'Full employment and free trade: an historical episode of Australian intellectual leadership', Economics paper No. 0102, Macquarie University.

Walker, E. R. 1939, *War-time Economics, With Special Reference to Australia*, Melbourne: Melbourne University Press.

Walker, E. R. 1943, *From Economic Theory to Policy*, Chicago: Chicago University Press.

Webb, L. S. 1953, 'The making of economic policy', in R. S. Parker (ed.), *Economic Stability in New Zealand*, Wellington: New Zealand Institute of Public Administration.

Whitwell, G. 1986, *The Treasury Line*, Sydney: Allen and Unwin.

Wilson, J. S. G. 1946, 'Prospects of full employment in Australia', *Economic Record*, 22(1): 99–116.

7   A coming of age for Australasian economics

Introduction

The early 1950s saw a changing of the guard in Australasian economics. In a matter of a few years, Australia lost Dyason, Wickens, Brigden, Giblin, Mills and Wood. New Zealand, too, suffered the early deaths of two of its Anzac economists, Souter and Williams. Other luminaries, such as Walker and Clark, had moved overseas. There was now a new, better-trained generation to replace the old guard, but this did not inspire Copland. When Mills died, Copland dryly observed 'Practically all his generation of economists are gone now and I don't think Australia is any the better for it.'[1] Both countries, especially Australia, would also draw precious human capital into the profession from immigration. The *Record* reached its 50th issue and would soon have a new editor to replace Copland and his deputy, Alf Weller, who had been labouring away, almost anonymously, since 1946.

Australia's low standing in the economics world was a little baffling. Despite a strong beginning and already making a mark in world economics literature – on tariffs, income distribution and macroeconomic stabilisation – Australia could not attract any eminent economists from Britain or America to apply for two prestigious research chairs, one in Melbourne, the other at the newly established ANU in Canberra, created by the Australian government as a centre of research excellence. The ANU would have economists spread in the Research School of Social Sciences (RSSS) and the Research School in Pacific Studies (RSPacS) and, after 1960, in the Faculties where undergraduates were taught. While there was then a world-wide shortage of economists, the lack of interest from overseas applicants still said something about Australasia's place in the economics world. It was reflected, too, in the authorship of articles appearing in the *Record*, with very few contributions from the northern hemisphere. Mark Perlman, a young American economics student who went to Melbourne to write a doctorate on the arbitration system, found the prevailing culture 'very provincial'. Geoff Harcourt (2001) could have told him that while the Melbourne department was Cambridge-orientated, the city itself was 'stuffy, snobby, sectarian'. Kurt Singer, a German émigré economist working in Sydney, found that his hosts had little interest in ideas (Arndt, 2000, 74). New Zealand was considered even more dowdy and one-dimensional, despite being third-richest country in the world at the time.

There was a certain naivety or amateurishness about the manner in which Australasian universities approached research during this period. Quite simply, professors were under no expectation to publish, and, when they did, it was usually in the *Record*. Belshaw had been astonished at the productivity of his counterparts at Cornell University when visiting there in 1936. Plainly, Australasian economics had to regather its strength and address itself to new challenges. Besides becoming more research-active, universities also had to increase their teaching to meet the likely increase in the post-war demand for economists. One way of doing this was to send their best and brightest to England or America for further training. By the end of the decade Australasian economics could boast some pockets of research strength. This chapter addresses how that came about. It was achieved, in short, by some fortune, by each country attracting human capital, by more state funding, by sponsorship from like-minded institutions and, not least, by a greater professionalism within universities about encouraging research.

Gentlemen and players: the post-war economics profession in Australasia

In 1948, when the new Vice Chancellor of Adelaide University, A. P. Rowe, complained, after an evening stroll around the campus, about how all the buildings were in darkness, he was informed, 'What you do not seem to know, Mr Vice Chancellor, is that this university goes home to tea' (Rowe, 1960, 33). Five years later Adelaide would, under Peter Karmel's leadership, assemble a gathering of young lions, most with overseas qualifications, making it the best economics research department within Australasia. One might have called it 'Karmel's kindergarten', so many younger economists wanted to work under him. In the tea room, Eric Russell reminded his colleagues of the limitations of the discipline. Of the 14 members of staff ranked as lecturer or above, 11 went on to hold chairs at other Australian universities.[2] In the collegial atmosphere of the departmental tea room, conversation, ideas, even workloads, were freely discussed. There was slumber at other universities.

At other universities, the lack of productivity was not entirely due to indolence or complacency. Syd Butlin (1948) of Sydney University blamed it on a lack of time; academics were too busy teaching. Moreover, there was no division between research and teaching. This applied equally to New Zealand academics; Simkin and Belshaw had heavy lecturing commitments. Professors were usually encumbered with so much administration that innovative theoretic research, or the preparation to engage in it, was near impossible. Equally encumbered, Butlin undertook research in the borderlands between economics and economic history (Butlin, 1978, 105–6). It was a wise choice since he would lament the mathematical methodology creeping into modern economics. His brother Noel was fully committed to economic history and was, much later, honoured by the Economic Society. Based at the ANU Research School in Economics (RSE), Butlin proved to be the great auditor of Australian economic history. His compilation of national income estimates for Australia going back to the days of European settlement, when combined with the official estimates, allowed a clearer picture of the dimension and nature of Australian economic growth. It was Noel Butlin who planted into the Australian consciousness the idea that the late nineteenth century was the watermark of Australian living standards. Moreover, Butlin showed, in a seminar entitled 'The Unimportance of Wool', that 'my whole theme at the time was cities are the places where you look for Australian economic history not amongst the bloody gum trees and the sheep'.[3] His other key contribution was to show the positive role the public sector had played in Australia's economic development (Snooks, 2007, 40). Butlin also brought the tools of the historian and demographer to peer into aboriginal society before and after white settlement. A lecturer in economic history at Sydney, John McCarty (1964) posited that Australia did not have its own theory of economic growth. McCarty resolved the matter by saying that Butlin's work, together with applying Canadian economist Harold Innis's staple approach, provided the answer. McCarty would go on to make its own contribution and become the first holder of the Chair in Economic History at Monash in 1968.

Another reason for the poor research productivity in Australia in the post-war years was simply that some academics were diffident about publishing their research. Two of Australia's greatest economic theorists, Trevor Swan and Eric Russell, were prime examples of this attitude, the latter believing that once a problem had been addressed there was no need to get into print (Harcourt, 1977, 468). It took eight years, for example, for Swan's famous diagram on external and internal balance to see light of day and, when it did, it was within an anthology of readings for economics students (Arndt and Corden, 1963). Russell's work on a sustainable wages policy for Australian workers and his enlightened views on foreign investment were belatedly published.

The relative isolation of posts such as Hobart, Dunedin and Perth was another factor. Economics research required expensive libraries and travel. There was little money, too, for research scholarships, though Melbourne seemed more blessed in this regard than any other Australasian university. This was consistent with the anti-intellectualism that pervaded both countries, with economic 'theorists' often lampooned by the media, even by prime ministers. Arndt complained that when economists have 'gone into the arena' their views have been dismissed as 'impractical', 'politically biased' or even 'foolish'.[4]

One episode illustrating the amateurishness of Australian economics at the time concerned the Ritchie Chair at Melbourne University. It had remained vacant since 1940, much to the chagrin of Alan Ritchie. A failed attempt to fill it led to Benjamin Higgins of McGill University negotiating a two-year term from 1948. He had been enticed into accepting the post by his friend, Richard Downing. Downing had even considered asking Michal Kalecki, then working in the ILO, to apply since 'he would have been an invaluable though a very uncomfortable person to have round'.[5] Melbourne proved a fruitful tenure for Higgins, albeit just less than two years; he published *What Do Economists Know?* (1951) following a suggestion by Ritchie that he explore the scope and method of economics. Higgins also wrote on macroeconomic balance. Like Clark and Reddaway, Higgins (1989) endured the daunting experience of appearing as an expert witness before the Arbitration Court during the 1949 Basic Wage Case. He subsequently wrote an article about wage-fixing under arbitration, arguing that high export prices warranted an increase in the basic wage. Like Perlman, Higgins was shocked by the poor living standards of what was purportedly the working man's paradise. When Higgins resigned from the Chair, the selection committee reconvened to consider those Australasians worthy of consideration: Clark, Melville, Simkin, Belshaw and Copland.

While it was Giblin's dying wish that Copland take the Chair, he was compromised by being a member of the selection committee. Simkin was considered a good theoretical economist, but there was doubts about whether he would measure 'to be an elder statesman type';[6] he was considered not to be interested in public policy. Copland felt Simkin would be 'too interested in speculations on economic theory [rather] than in attacking the problems of the Australian economy and that I have a good many doubts about the permanent value of much of the theoretical work that is being done'.[7] Another New Zealander who had not made the shortlist was Edward Neale. He was later described as 'not a spectacular person' who had specialised in demographics (Belshaw, 1961, 99). Internationally, those under consideration by the selection committee were the British economists Tom Wilson and Donald McDougall, together with Downing, who had only just left Melbourne to work at the ILO in Geneva.

Eventually, the committee offered the job to Downing. Copland welcomed this, telling Downing that the 'official economists have not pursued a sufficiently or vigorous line, and that we have not been alive to the problems of the Australian economy'.[8] By that, he meant that the emphasis of economic policy should be on long-run development instead of short-run stability. The dilemma between growth and stability also fixated economists like Belshaw (1953) in New Zealand. Since the end of war, Copland had felt that the Federal government's economic advisors were too cautious, too timid, about the Australian economy's ability to handle a faster rate of economic growth. They were, moreover, too keen to order price stability before growth. Copland wanted the university economists to take on the influence which 'inside' economists enjoyed. There was a personal element in all this about who claimed intellectual leadership of the Australian economics profession. Copland had developed an enmity towards Coombs, who, from 1949, was Governor of Australia's central bank and the apparent spokesman for the new generation of economists. Both, then, would, in the post-war years, conduct a feud over economic policy – specifically, concerning Coombs's preference that rapid economic growth and economic development should have priority over macroeconomic stabilisation (Copland, 1951, 9; Macintyre, 2015, 391–2). Underlying these differences was the disparagement, from what Copland called 'the younger brethren', that the stabilisation plan devised by Australian economists to deal with the Depression had been in error, by being both deflationary and placatory to the private banks (Millmow, 2013a). Copland regretted, too, that the sense of unanimity among the economists that had existed in the interwar period had broken down. He felt that this lessened the effectiveness of university economists in the policy arena. It formed part of Copland's vendetta with Coombs over the leadership of the profession, but, more particularly, over economic policy. About to depart for an overseas posting in 1953, Copland was happy to pass on the struggle to his protégé Downing, telling him that:

> Little Coombs is busy maintaining his prestige and building his Empire... I have kept the pot boiling on the facts of economic life... I have enjoyed exploding the heresies of the pretentious but, all in all, none of that has done much good for economists.[9]

Rather weirdly, Copland took up an appointment as High Commissioner to Canada. It reflected an aspect of his character that one of his closest friends, the Australian business magnate W. S. Robinson, had noticed, 'Douglas has a grand brain but he lowers himself to the level of the politician by his appetite for power.'[10]

Downing was a little apprehensive about the honour bestowed upon him: 'I must say that the state of economics in Australia doesn't sound very attractive – there seems to be an awful lot of cliques.'[11] He also felt a little intimidated by the long shadow cast by Giblin, but he would become, in his time as Ritchie Professor, the great narrator of economics in Australia (Millmow, 2013b). Downing's specialisation was social economics, including wages policy, poverty, housing and pensions for the aged. He would be the last Economics Professor elected to a Chair at Melbourne without having an international reputation based on publications. As part of his duties, Downing was expected to take over the editorship of the *Record*, a position he held for nearly 20 years from May 1954 until May 1973.

Finding an occupant for the first Research Chair in Economics at the ANU was just as chastening (Cornish, 2007). Arthur Smithies told W. K. Hancock: 'I have been completely at a loss to think of anyone who would be willing to go to Australia and whom I would recommend' (cited in Coleman *et al.*, 2006, 221). It might have said something, too, about the attraction of living in a remote capital city like Canberra, a former sheep station set in the Australian bush. After several rejections from some of the world's leading economists, including the likes of Cambridge economists Austin Robinson and Nicholas Kaldor, the selection committee, which involved Hancock and Copland, chose Trevor Swan, even though he had no higher or overseas degree. He did, however, have extensive experience at higher levels of the Commonwealth Public Service, his speciality being economic problem trouble-shooting. Even though Copland and Hancock shared some doubts about the decision, it would prove an inspired choice; in a short period of time Swan would astound his colleagues with some path-breaking research. When asked much later who was Australia's greatest economic theorist in his lifetime, Downing choose the mercurial Swan, noting that 'perhaps he is enough for a small country'.[12] John King (2007, 271–5) regards Swan as '[p]robably the greatest economist ever to have lived, worked and died in

Australia... his originality and analytical ability was clearly equal to that of Meade, Modigliani, Samuelson and Solow'. Yet perhaps Downing's words cast a spell on Swan because his output, after a brilliant first decade, dwindled, suggesting that he may have lost interest in the value of growth models (Butlin and Gregory, 1989, 375). The last theoretical paper Swan (1963a) published expressed a degree of disillusionment with theoretical growth models and their application. An ANU colleague Robin Gollan accurately described Swan as 'the sort of person who needed to have problems put to him for solution and that wasn't the situation he found himself in at the university'. Nor did Swan attract many graduate or doctoral candidates to his office from the 1960s onward: 'They were never good enough.'[13]

Disgruntled with working at the Food and Agricultural Organisation of the United Nations, Belshaw returned to academe, taking the Macarthy Chair at Victoria believing he still had something to offer in terms of intellectual leadership.[14] In his inaugural lecture, 'his third incarnation as an academic economist', he declared a new interest in a broader, integrated economics as a springboard into development economics.[15] He had no interest in model-building, which he equated with 'a clever sort of intellectual meccano'. Belshaw informed his friend Condliffe that the competence of the economics lecturers had improved, 'but there has been a disturbing emphasis on over-abstract mathematical economics and the currently sterile welfare theory which by spurious purism has thrown out the baby with the bath'.[16] Belshaw wanted to redress the balance by working in applied economics. Five years later he recycled the same complaints, but added that 'the modern dynamic equations are not applicable' to development economics or even Keynesian economics.[17] His new focus was on underdevelopment and on encouraging the establishment of the idea of mixed economies which would foment world peace and avert political extremism, particularly communism. New Zealand, he argued, would also prosper from its development and concomitant increase in purchasing power. The country should put more resources into agriculture, ridding itself of protection and imperial preferences, which he said were all 'a misguided sentimentalism'. Belshaw retained an interest in macroeconomic balance, but he was wary of over-full employment, seeing it as inflationary. He also wanted to keep the country's immigration rate aligned with the economy's absorptive capacity and recommended that New Zealand join the IMF to access more capital. In his *magnam opus Population growth and levels of consumption in New Zealand* (1955) Belshaw articulated a more considered view on New Zealand's population dilemma. Channelling Keynes, Belshaw, a self-confessed 'mildly optimistic neo-Malthusian', proposed what has been called a 'stable population Keynesianism' (Brooke *et al.*, 2017: 16). Belshaw felt that excessive immigration would warp capital formation, leading to capital widening rather than capital deepening. He was sceptical about claims that population growth was a boon for aggregate demand, seeing it as more likely to result in inflationary pressure and sectoral shortages. Belshaw's schema had limited appeal with his colleagues and, more importantly, the vested economic interests weighing upon economic policy. Simply stated, these interests all favoured population expansion, as did politicians (ibid.: 19).

Building the post-war economics profession

In the 1950s the only two Australian economists regularly cited in the British press were Douglas Copland and Colin Clark. Both men had left Australia by 1953; Clark was the new Director of the Agricultural Research Institute at Oxford. In the post-war era both were outsiders to conventional opinion about the Australian economy. A diehard free trader, Clark, as we have seen, wanted Australia to reject protectionism and manufacturing to become a net agricultural exporter, supported by a huge immigration programme that would facilitate a regionally dispersed population. If it did not do this, he argued that Australia would bear the contempt of the rest of the world. The Australian Council of Trade Unions (ACTU) advocate R. J. L. Hawke, who had studied economics at UWA, would later lampoon it as 'The economy of the peasant plots' (Hawke, 1962, 184).[18] Clark did eventually return to Australia in 1969 as a research fellow at Monash, but, arguably, he was not the creative force he once had been.

Copland was a proponent of balanced growth and saw some role for a protected manufactured sector. After 1945 he wanted Australia to break out of the sterling bloc, to recruit capital from the United States and to develop export markets in Asia – a view similar to Clark's. Both were, together with Belshaw and Ronald Walker, pioneers in the new field of development economics; both wanted to use growth and development as the buffer against the lure of communism. To counter the appeal of planned economies, Copland was one of the first economists to advocate that rich economies give 1 per cent of their GDP in aid to less developed countries (LDCs).

With the departure of Copland and Clark, the field was clear for Coombs and others to reinvigorate the local economics profession. As Governor of Australia's central bank, Coombs felt that it would be 'a good idea' to expose the bank's economists to discussions with leading exponents of economic thought and practice. The first guest was Erik Lindahl (in 1952), followed by Thomas Balogh (1954), Erik Lundberg (1955), Raymond Goldsmith and James Meade (1956), B. H. Beckhart (1957), Bill Phillips (1959), Ronald Henderson and P. C. Mahalanobis (both 1960) and, in 1962, Arthur Smithies, the Australian-born economist then at Harvard. These guests also gave lectures before the Economic Society, with some making contributions to the *Record*. Visits such as these to the bank continued even after Coombs's retirement in 1968, with the bank's research staff coordinating the visits of distinguished economists, including Ronald Henderson, Gunnar Myrdal, Nicholas Kaldor, Sir Donald MacDougall. Harry Johnson, Anne Krueger, John Helliwell, David Laidler, David Rowan and Michael Parkin (Schedvin, 1992, 426–7). The influence those visitors had on the local profession as well as economists within the bank would be considerable.

Between 1952 and 1966 Coombs took this interaction a step further by assembling a panel of leading Australian economics professors to meet annually at the bank's headquarters in Sydney to discuss the economy's problems and prospects. Heinz Arndt recalled that Coombs wanted academic economists to obtain more background information about what was going on in the economy so that when they talked in public they made more sense.[19] J. M. 'Pete' Garland and the irrepressible Austin Holmes participated in these meetings, with the latter setting the agenda and sometimes ruffling the feathers of the academics (Sanders *et al.*, 1986, 509). Their collective views on the state of the Australian economy would appear in the *Record*. For Australia, at least, there was no schism between university economists and economists working with Treasury and the Reserve Bank of Australia (RBA). Of course, this could be interpreted as the bank simply snuffing out any dissent about official economic policy (Hieser, 1964, 47). The RBNZ also conducted annual meetings of university economists to seek their support, as well as to keep academics informed of all aspects of economic policy. These regular surveys of the Australian and New Zealand economies ran in the *Record* from 1956 until 1967. All this emphasised the practical and policy orientation of the Australasian profession infusing the pages of the *Record*, a journal at the time read by public servants and businessmen (Butlin, 1966, 511). After 1950 the *Record* produced more academic contributions, with a commensurate decline in Australasian issues and also 'a downturn in the philosophical and practical content of economics' (Butlin, 1966: 514).

The RBA's forums with Australian economists provided an opportunity for Swan's 'analytical brilliance' to dominate the discussions (Arndt, 1985, 27). In the first meeting, he had ominously advised that: 'Unless we can learn to live in the twilight between inflation and deflation we had better reconcile ourselves to a permanent system of economic controls of wartime range and detail, or else abandon altogether the objective of full-employment' (cited in Brown, 2001, 175).

Some of the economists who wrote those commentaries had recently returned from studying abroad, usually England. Only a handful of Australian universities taught economics in the immediate post-war era (Williams, 2009). None of them offered doctoral training in economics, nor, indeed, did the University of New Zealand (Condliffe, 1950, 25). Melbourne only established guidelines for the PhD in 1946, with Kenneth Rivett the first PhD in economics graduating in 1954. When the ANU was established in 1946 and Swan appointed to the Research Chair in Economics, the university struggled to attract young minds. There was still in Australia something of a 'colonial tradition' whereby the finest social sciences postgraduates headed overseas to complete their education (Williams, 1965, 310). Karmel and Don Cochrane, for example, had gone off to Cambridge in 1947 to undertake doctorates and, when they returned, both would become responsible for building up strong economics faculties at Adelaide and Monash University, respectively. Earlier, in wartime Canberra, a young Peter Karmel, bored with the 'distressing sameness' of his public service job, told his old professor in Melbourne, Wilfred Prest, how he had read Hayek's *The Road to Serfdom* and found 'a lot of truth in it'. Karmel added, though, that he still had a hankering for 'planning', though sometimes the drive towards government planning was 'based on fairly irrational premises'.[20] He made the interesting observation that the economics profession needed something akin to a publicity office, making the public aware of the good economists were doing.[21] While at Cambridge, Cochrane made a classic contribution to econometric technique in association with the American Guy Orcutt. Another Melbourne-trained graduate, the econometrician Geoffrey Watson who studied at Cambridge, would also have his name immortalised in a statistical check for autocorrelation. He did not return to Australia. The immediate post-war period, 1945–60, was a time, then, when 55 Australian and seven New Zealand economists descended upon the London–Oxbridge triangle which dominated British economics at the time (Backhouse, 2002, 34–5).[22] Two of the Australian contingent who went to Cambridge during the immediate post-war period made pioneering contributions with their doctorates but did not capture the intellectual rent due them. Duncan Ironmonger's book *New Commodities and Consumer Behaviour* (1972), on a characteristic approach to consumer demand representing a pioneering effort in theory, sprang from his Cambridge doctorate submitted a decade earlier. Alan Barton's dissertation entitled 'A contribution to the theory of the multi-product firm' anticipated later work on the boundaries and internal organisation of multi-product firms. Cornish and Harcourt (2013) describe the work as 'remarkable for its creativity and breadth'; Barton was too self-effacing to get it published.

This phalanx of economists returned to Australasia and would shape post-war economics. They were buttressed by the arrival of several British economists who headed up the new university economic departments within Australia: David Rowan, followed by Alex Hunter at the UNSW; Ian Bowen at the UWA; Brian Tew at Adelaide; and Frank Davidson, who took one of the two new chairs at La Trobe University in Melbourne in 1967. David Bensusan-Butt, who had compiled the index for Keynes's *General Theory*, spent 20 fruitful years at the ANU.

Unlike today, very few Australasian economists went to North America to complete their economics training during this period: Murray Kemp, Maureen Brunt (destined to become Australia's first woman professor in Economics at Monash in 1966), John Nevile, Reg Appleyard and Noel Butlin were the exceptions. Australasian agricultural economists – John Dillon from Sydney, Frank Jarrett from Adelaide, Wilfred Candler from Massey – all went to study at Iowa State University in the 1950s, followed by Roger Mauldon from UWA in 1962. Candler did a doctorate on linear programming, while Dillon specialised on game theory; both were supervised by the world-renowned agricultural economist Earl Heady. Jarrett was the first appointee to the Economics Faculty at Adelaide with doctoral studies in Agricultural Economics.

In addition to building economics departments, these scholars brought back expertise to Australasian economics. Cochrane, for instance, wrote upon the new art of econometrics for the *Record* in a 1949 article entitled the 'Measurement of economic relationships'. Alf Hagger, too, was regarded as the figure 'most singly responsible for the advent of the post-war quantitative revolution in Australian economics' and established the first course in econometrics given there (Wells, 2011, 101). As such, the role of overseas education for Australasian economics cannot be overlooked. Cambridge, Oxford and the LSE were to exert considerable influence upon the professionalisation of Australian economics in the immediate post-war period.

In 1952 Melbourne acquired, at considerable expense, the MONIAC or Monetary National Income Analogue Computer to help educate its students on the stocks and flows of a monetary economy. Wilfred Prest, who held the Truby Williams Chair at Melbourne, had visited the LSE and seen a demonstration of it. MONIAC was the brainchild of Bill Phillips, a New Zealand ex-serviceman undertaking a sociology degree at the LSE, specifically financed by a New Zealand government rehabilitation grant which required recipients to return home after completing their studies.[23] The soft water of Melbourne played havoc with the machine when it was first turned on, resulting in spillages everywhere. Later, when someone had the idea of adding salt, the machine performed normally. It was only used in lectures for a few years and wheeled out for exhibition on special occasions. At the University of New South Wales (UNSW) a young tutor called Paddy McGuinness inadvertently sent their machine haywire by pressing the wrong buttons, thus mixing up the coloured water essential for its operation (Groenewegen, 2011, 101).[24]

Nearing the end of his career in 1967 Phillips took the new Chair in the RSEs at the ANU, working alongside Trevor Swan. Part of his duties was to supervise Adrian Pagan and Alan Preston who became, in turn, leading econometricians. Following his retirement from the ANU in 1970 due to ill-health, Phillips moved to Auckland where he resumed teaching, taking a postgraduate class in mathematical economics. Phillips had always wanted to go to university but the Depression prevented this; he turned instead to electrical engineering. At the LSE he spent most of his time studying monetary theory. He approached James Meade with blueprints to build a machine showing the monetary dynamics within an economy. Meade took him on and promised that if the machine was built and operable it could be demonstrated in one of Lionel Robbins's seminars at the LSE.

This was achieved in a memorable seminar before an audience where many had come along more to laugh than listen. Meade interceded on Phillips's behalf, writing to the New Zealand authorities in London asking that he be given more time to finish the prototype of his machine (Barr, 1988. 311). The LSE gave Phillips money to build it which, when completed, left Meade delighted. Phillips's employment status at the LSE was secured after an article in *Economica* which Robbins declared 'put him on the international map as an economist of profound grasp and originality' (cited in ibid., 315). In another act of generosity to Britain, the New Zealand authorities, quite aware of what Phillips was trying to achieve, generously waived any hold upon him. A few years later, Prest offered Phillips the Chair in Applied Economics within his department at Melbourne. Phillips declined, saying he had too many continuing and exciting projects under-way to leave London.[25]

Phillips had only resisted the charm of Australia because it was so far away from London. Gerald Firth, revisiting his homeland, noticed an asymmetric distance problem:

> One of the most striking impressions, talking to these people, is how much further away we seem to them than they do to us. It might be a good idea to encourage more frequent visits to the Antipodes by English economists. I'm sure it would broaden their minds.[26]

Travel to Australasia in the 1950s was a major undertaking; taking up an academic job position there was an even bigger gamble. Prest had only come to Melbourne in 1938 after Copland told him: 'If you were anxious to blaze a new trail in a new environment, I have no doubt that Australia would suit you.'[27] In 1946 Heinz Arndt undertook the same challenge and left the University of Manchester, where he was an Assistant Lecturer, to take a post at Sydney, though he barely knew where it was; John Hicks assured him that, in about five years, he would soon would have a Chair. Arndt achieved that task in four years with a Chair at Canberra University College, later to merge with the ANU. His inaugural lecture in Canberra was on 'The unimportance of money', which sought to downgrade the efficacy of monetary policy for economic management (Coleman *et al.*, 2007, 174). In his earlier career in England, Arndt, under the influence of Paul Rosenstein-Rodan, wrote *The Economic Lessons of the Nineteen Thirties* (1944) which put him 'on the world map of economists' (Drake and Garnaut, 1995, 2). Then a Fabian socialist, Arndt had written a pamphlet supporting the nationalisation of private banks and was 'proud to be the first socialist Professor of Economics in Australia' (Coleman *et al.*, 2007, 115). A federal politician and former student of Arndt's petitioned Prime Minister Menzies to cancel the appointment, but it was waved away.

Some of the economists who came to Australasia were fleeing Nazi Germany and war-torn Europe; these included Max Corden, Jan Kmenta, Helen Hughes, Fred Gruen and Kurt Singer – and, for New Zealand, Wolfgang Rosenberg, who made for Canterbury, and Harro Bernardelli, who took up refuge in Otago (Lodewijks, 2011). After being educated at Sydney University, Kmenta, the only person teaching econometrics in Australia at the time would, like Harsanyi, leave for America because there was more 'excitement' there about this new art (Lodewijks, 2005, 623).

Another refugee from the Nazis was the aforementioned Karl Popper, who wrote *The Open Society and its Enemies* (1945) while at Canterbury College.[28] Facing a long, potentially boring internment in their new home, Gruen and Singer used their time to educate themselves about Australia (Chapman, 1998, 187). Another later refugee was John Harsanyi, who fled Hungary in the wake of the communist revolution there. Other economists who arrived in Australasia in those years came, as now, to take up professional appointments. Some did well, others struggled. Singer, whom Keynes had described as 'the mystical economist from Hamburg', found career promotion hard going during his time at Sydney. He represented a novel, confusing experience for Australian students, given his wide cultural background. In an article in the *Record* entitled 'Robot economics' he introduced his Australian colleagues to von Neumann's growth model before describing how to deconstruct it (King, 2007, 254). Harsanyi undertook his Master's at Sydney, where a sympathetic Arndt suggested that he apply game theory to the arbitration system marking its first empirical application to Australian conditions (Coleman *et al.*, 2007, 191–2). However, Harsanyi – now working at the University of Queensland – would find that his early explorations in game theory, including one on generalising the concept of the bargaining equilibrium and the other on cardinal welfare, individualistic ethics, and interpersonal comparisons of utility, went unrecognised in Australia. Harsanyi acknowledged Arndt's assistance in both articles, even though the latter admitted he was a 'new-born babe in the theory of games'.[29] Arndt had been his referee for a Rockefeller Scholarship, telling the authorities 'there is a great deal to be said for enabling someone in this country to go abroad and specialise in the theory of games'.[30] Harsanyi spent time at Stanford studying under Ken Arrow. He did well at Stanford: so much so that Arndt joked that, 'When you come back, nobody in Australia will be able to understand you,' before adding 'the knowledge you will have acquired will be a great boon to mathematical economics in Australia.'[31] Arndt was prescient in the sense that when Harsanyi returned to Australia he took up an appointment at the ANU, but in the Philosophy department. Tragically for Australian economics, it was not long before he was enticed back to America, with Arrow locating a professorial chair for him. In his autobiographical notes as a Nobel laureate, Harsanyi recalled his years in Australia as ones of relative isolation simply because game theory was relatively unknown there.

Arndt would quickly establish a friendship with Richard Downing and become his offsider in editing the *Record* for nearly 20 years (Hughes, 2002, 483). They attempted to read every paper submitted, though if too technical they were passed on for judgement to Melbourne academics such as Sam Soper and Roy Webb, or Colin Simkin in Auckland. As the senior New Zealand member of the Editorial Board, Simkin had considerable power in advising upon articles from or about New Zealand. Downing would later have some suspicions about his role: 'I understand approximately that he dispenses everything but high level economics and that all other economists in New Zealand resent his attitude deeply.'[32] Downing refused to believe it and felt that the small number of articles by New Zealand economists reflected their productivity rather than Simkin's rigorous censorship. When Simkin stood down, Frank Holmes and Rex Bergstrom took up the editorial role. Downing sought to widen the journal's appeal by persuading university economists to divert their theoretical works to the *Record*; he need not have worried since most, at that time, did not rate overseas economics journals any higher than the *Record*. Downing never doubted that the journal's comparative advantage lay in the study of Australasian economic problems and that its first duty was to its readers, who funded the journal, rather than its contributors (Arndt, 1976, 296). To reconcile the two audiences, Downing gave the journal a blend of applied and practical articles mixed with the theoretical. To counter the problem of what he called the 'the worst kind of academic blight' he asked authors of mathematical articles to explain in English the question being dealt with and the outcomes generated, or at least relegate the maths to an appendix (ibid., 297). As late as 1963 Downing was flippantly telling an English academic: 'It does seem indeed necessary that people should be able to understand mathematics although I know of no evidence of any contribution to economics from the mathematical side.'[33]

Sometimes Downing found it was difficult to obtain submissions from his colleagues. When he invited Gerald Firth, who held the Economics Chair at Tasmania for nearly 30 years, to contribute, he was told:

> Since the only reason why people seem to publish nowadays is to get a better job or preserve their reputations, I should prefer to wait until (if ever) I have scratched some stuff together that will stand up a bit longer than this seems to have done.[34]

Ten years later, Firth was telling Arndt:

> We continue to find it damned difficult to make any serious impression at the research level... Half of us lack the modern econometrical techniques to make quantitative studies plausible. The other half is too busy refining techniques which are too refined already for the data available.[35]

Firth was being too modest as he toiled away on the new emerging problem of stagflation. His preferred research approach was to believe that the only effective job is the short term ad hoc guestimate. Ironically, on the staff of Firth's department was the econometric whiz Alf Hagger. Perhaps Firth preferred words to Hagger's equations, and policy advice to rigorous analysis, but even he saw the need to give students some quantitative training.

While neither Downing nor Arndt was an economic theorist, it was under their watch that the *Record* contained some striking post-war contributions to economic literature. Jumping ahead a few years ahead, the two collaborated with Alan Boxer and Russell Matthews on a futuristic report entitled *Taxation in Australia: Agenda for Reform* (Downing, 1964). It had been commissioned by the Social Science Research Council, the forerunner to the Academy of the Social Sciences in Australia. The Report made a comprehensive analysis of taxation in Australia. It considered broadening the tax base by removing exemptions and deductions. It also proposed an annual wealth tax rather than a capital gains tax (Freebairn, 2009, 229). Another of its findings was to propose a national superannuation scheme, something which Downing had first mentioned in 1958 (Brown, 2007).

Whatever the merits of the Report, it struck the English economist David Bensusan-Butt, now at the ANU, as rather timid and unimaginative, though he did not want his words to be taken too seriously. He had expected, given the intellectual firepower behind it, something more daring, but its authors had turned out to be,

> the mildest antiquarians... There is not an ounce of dynamite among them... To have Bentham announced and Burke led on; to be promised Lolita and given a reading from the Golden Bowl; to be warned of a bomb and handed a currant bun – these upset one's calm.
>
> Bensusan-Butt, 1964, 226–7

Boxer and Mathews were not to be put off by such wit. Boxer served on the 1972 Commonwealth Taxation Review Committee (Asprey Committee) – ironically, sitting alongside Bensusan-Butt. One of the major tasks of that review was to examine the long-run effectiveness of the tax system as a weapon of income redistribution. It was Bensusan-Butt who first put forward the idea of a broad-based consumption tax, but it would take over 25 years to come to fruition, with John Freebairn theoretically buttressing the case in the 1990s. Mathews would chair the 1974 Commission of Inquiry into Taxation and Inflation, bringing to the public's attention the extent to which inflation was distorting the income taxation system and the fact that indexation of the tax scales could alleviate it.

Another outburst of original theory, 1956–9

The 1956 November issue of the *Record* was a striking one.[36] Among its contents was article on economic development by Belshaw, one by Simkin on the New Zealand Royal Commission on Banking and a provocative book review by Clark berating Australian economists for giving in to public opinion on the tariff. At the time, Clark was the only Australian economist in favour of unadulterated free trade. That issue included what would become its most cited article, Trevor Swan on his growth model. There was also an article by Meade on Australia's experience with external and internal balance and a radical solution to help reconcile the two objectives. Meade had just spent a fruitful sabbatical at the ANU in 1956, later telling Arndt (2000, 100) that his time in Canberra had been one of his 'happiest memories'. His sabbatical was part-funded by Australia's central bank.

The mid-1950s onwards marked a remarkable profusion of theoretical work in Australian economics, with advances in growth, trade and wages theory and contributions by leading theorists such as Swan, Salter, Corden, Russell, Karmel and Donald Whitehead. Whitehead, had earlier persuaded employers to move from a position of arguing that award wage rises could not be afforded to one of relating them to average level of productivity. The problem with this formula was that, with money wage stability, there would be a drift to profits. Whitehead was reluctant to recommend money wage increases, fearing they were inherently inflationary. Later, he articulated his independent line of thinking in *Stagflation and Wages Policy in Australia* (1973), arguing that stagflation was caused by the authorities trying to curb a wage push inflation by conventional fiscal and monetary policy. Only an incomes policy could liberate economies from this vice, he argued, but, so far, no workable policy had been devised. A perhaps neglected visionary, Whitehead, who would become the Foundation Dean at the School of Economics at La Trobe University in 1967, laid out an institutional package for Australia's wage determination system, not least his favoured resort of a productivity-geared wage policy which, had it been implemented earlier, would have given Australia price stability.

Growth theory

Swan's neoclassical growth model demonstrated how resources and technical change had combined over time to produce rising living standards. It had a long appendix defending the use of capital in a production function. The end result was to show that only technical change could change a growth trajectory. Swan's (1956) paper was preceded by an article on the same topic in the February issue of the *Quarterly Journal of Economics* by Bob Solow.[37] John Pitchford (2002, 382–3), then a doctoral student supervised by Swan, recalls the seminar where his mentor first aired his theory. This was on the determinants of savings and investment; Noel Butlin, the presenter, was entirely upstaged by Swan. After hearing Swan's interjection, Meade moved that what had just been put forth was of great consequence. Swan retired to write up his comments and, when published, it marked the last of his most significant output. The timing of the discovery assumes importance since Solow was awarded the 1987 Nobel Prize in Economic Sciences 'For his contributions to the theory of economic growth'. Swan was barely acknowledged, though Solow paid him a warm tribute much later.[38] Peter Dixon later commented that Swan's diagram of economic growth was superior, and more comprehensive than the Solow version, a view shared by Swan's daughter, Barbara Spencer (2010) and her co-author, Bob Dimand.

Swan might have also qualified for the Nobel Prize for his earlier work on economic control in a small, open economy. Australian economists at that time had a preoccupation with the external account; there had been three balance of payments crises during the 1950s. Graphic evidence of this was seen soon after the Korean War boom with a blowout in the trade deficit due to the slump in wool prices, higher wages and excessive expenditure. Import controls were imposed, setting off a debate among economists as to whether devaluation or tariffs were not a better alternative. These controls had no effect on the root cause of the trade deficit. Relatedly, there was also pessimism about Australia's export growth and that commodity-based economies were facing a long-run decline in their terms of trade. Swan felt that the White Paper on Full Employment had not addressed the effect that real expenditure and domestic costs could have upon the external account (Metaxas and Weber, 2016). Building on the work of Roland Wilson, James Meade's book *The Balance of Payments* (1951) and Sidney Alexander's concept of absorption, Swan's (1963a) approach to internal and external balance was innovative. In short, it argued that the real exchange rate and macroeconomic policy affected both the internal and external balance and that policy instruments should be assigned only after deciding what combination of macroeconomic problems the economy was facing.

At the 1955 ANZAAS conference, Swan encapsulated Meade's findings with a powerfully explanatory diagram. It became known as the 'Swan diagram' and modelled the real exchange rate or cost ratio (defined by the ration of an index of the prices of imports and exports to an index of Australian wages) necessary to ensure external balance as well as the level of real expenditure required for internal balance. Two interpreting lines represented a country's internal and external balance. The external balance current account deficit or surplus sloped downwards and the internal balance employment–unemployment curve sloped upwards. Internal balance could be maintained with a high cost ratio as long as expenditure was kept low. Conversely, external balance could be maintained with a high cost ratio as long as real expenditure was kept high. At the intersection point were the cost ratio and level of expenditure required to achieve both internal and external balance, although it would be rare for an economy to be in such a position.

Further, Swan proposed four zones of economic unhappiness or disequilibria arising from his model. Restoring internal and external balance meant a mix of altering the cost ratio or the real exchange rate (or put simply, Australian wage levels) and expenditure levels. It was here that Swan confirmed Meade's finding that two policy instruments were required for two economic targets to avoid policy conflict.

When Meade came to Australia in 1956 he found an economy in a classic Zone IV disequilibrium, beset by a trade deficit and inflation caused by excessive spending. Eight Australian economists, orchestrated by Peter Karmel, had earlier issued an 'Economists' Manifesto' urging the Menzies Government to raise income and sales taxes, together with increasing interest rates, to contain excess demand. It was badly received by the press, with one Sydney evening tabloid announcing 'The theorists are at it again' and recommending that 'no one should take the slightest notice of them' (Coleman *et al.*, 2007, 183). Meade also recommended deflationary policy, together with devaluation, but also suggested a radical alternative – floating the currency. It was Swan, though, who turned the tables on Meade by using Roland Wilson's earlier work on the small country case. In a small country such as Australia, Swan noted that a depreciation raises the price of exports and imports proportionately, leaving the terms of trade constant; however, an improvement in the trade balance still occurs because the price of traded goods rises relative to non-traded goods. Put another way, a real depreciation shifts production from non-traded to traded goods and consumption from traded to non-traded goods. Corden and Salter made major refinements and improvements to the Swan model. Salter's (1959) version of the dependent economy model was more elegant because he aggregated exportables and importables into a single internationally tradeable good which simplified the analysis, reducing it from three goods – exportables, importables and home goods – to only two goods – internationally tradeable goods and home goods (Weber, 2011). For this reason, the number of relative prices under consideration fell from two to one. The supporting diagram had home goods on one axis and internationally traded goods on the other and a production possibility frontier spanning them. The slope of the production possibility frontier indicated the relative price between home goods and traded goods, a point which is now the real exchange rate. It was a theoretical advance on Swan, and Corden was to make a further improvement to it.

Wilfred Salter had the rare ability to blend theory with empirical and policy suggestions in the right proportion. He showed this in preparing the empirical work for Eric Russell's representations before the Commonwealth Court of Conciliation and Arbitration in the 1959 National Wage Case (Weber, 2011). Salter's published Cambridge doctorate on *Productivity and Economic Progress* (1955) was a work on the development of vintage models and of how technical progress was embodied in new capital good spending. In a growing economy, he argued, two main forces shape the adaption of new technology. First, improving technical knowledge expands the realm of the technically feasible and, second, changes in factor prices affect the choice between alternative techniques. Salter had already shown antecedence in the area by undertaking an honours thesis on factor productivity in his home state of Western Australia. Strangely, Salter walked away from academic research to work within the prime minister's department (Weber, 2011). He felt that only in the public sector could one have the resources to mine the income and output data he needed. Australia was impoverished when he died tragically young working as an economic advisor in Pakistan. While Swan (1963b, 487) wrote that Salter's name would always be associated with 'unfulfilled renown', his memory lived on not just in what he helped table before the Arbitration Court, but also what became known as the 'Salter effect', which was embodied in the growth forecasts of the Vernon Report. This was the idea that productivity growth was more likely to occur when output growth is rapid because the capital stock will embody the latest technology.

In a variation of the trade pessimism theme, Eric Russell and James Meade (1957) looked at the Korean War and its convulsive effect on the Australian economy and how this had all quickly turned sour. Using the 'dependent economy model' they showed how an export boom and a rising terms of trade would mean either a rise in real rents or a fall in real wages if internal balance and external balance were to be maintained. If real wages were made constant, then either internal or external balance would be adversely affected. Moreover, rising money wages would create cost pressures for the protected sector, causing it to contract. Here was the progenitor for the later work by Australian economists on the phenomenon known as 'Dutch disease'.

Trade and tariffs

Max Corden, a graduate of Melbourne, was one of 12 Australians who went to study at the LSE in the 15-year period after the war. Corden felt that luck was a steady companion in his illustrious career, starting off with his family's flight from Nazi Germany and eventual resettlement in Melbourne. There was more luck when he won a British Council scholarship to study at the LSE. Corden had, however, already shown great promise, having an article accepted, without revision, by the *Review of Economic Studies* on the economics of newspapers. Another 'turning point' in his life was to have Meade as his supervisor, pivoting his research work towards international economics; yet another piece of fortune was to have the Canadian economist Harry Johnson as his mentor (Snape, 1996). Corden never looked back. One of his most influential papers, written while he was still studying at the LSE – but very much with Australia in mind – examined the excess costs of the tariff using the Brigden Report as his reference. Corden found the Brigden Report to be 'interesting, but confusing' (Coleman, 2006). He wanted to, as he explained, 'sort it out' or 'de-confuse' it.[39] The Report became a rich seam of material and ideas upon which Corden would draw. One might say that he found his comparative advantage unravelling Australia's protectionist apparatus. In an original journal article, he used partial and then general equilibrium analysis, accompanied by diagrams, to show the production and consumption cost of protection. Interestingly, the article, later considered a classic, drew international attention, but only after Harry Johnson cited it.

After arriving back at Melbourne, Corden gave a noteworthy paper on protection at the 1958 ANZAAS Conference. In this, he proposed that the existing system of import licensing and made-to-measure tariff structure, under a fixed and overvalued exchange rate, be replaced by a uniform tariff. Moreover, made-to-measure tariffs merely provoked more rent-seeking. Though by no means a free trader, Corden was gently urging Australian authorities to consider abandoning import restrictions in favour of a gradual move towards a uniform tariff. A longer-run alternative to tariffs was export subsidy, he argued, and, beyond that, devaluation. Under Corden's plan, consumers would have a greater choice in what imports they really wanted: 'There are few good reasons for the tariff rate to be higher on one product than another' (Corden, 1957). The idea had been earlier discussed by Arndt, Karmel and Russell, but Corden investigated it much more thoroughly. Corden's work was followed not long after by Australia lifting import controls in 1959/60, but this was guided more by macroeconomic factors and pragmatism than by concerns about comparative costs. Interestingly, his work had little impact on the New Zealand policy-making authorities (Endres and Rogers, 2014, 75). In Australia, Corden's work on tariffs was at the forefront of research and policy relevance. He set the ball rolling on the great tariff debate. Not all economists supported Corden's stance; Hagger and Firth (1959), for instance, felt that both devaluation and the uniform tariff option were 'comparatively ineffective' when matched against import controls. They also questioned Corden's assumptions about trade elasticities, arguing that he had over-estimated the cost of import controls and under-estimated the costs of moving to a uniform tariff. Other economists pointed to the political difficulties of the change. Meanwhile, in New Zealand the tariff debate, certainly on the policy level, had barely started; the Wellington Branch of the Economic Society of Australia and New Zealand (ESANZ) decided at its 1958 annual forum to posit the question: 'To what extent and how can the New Zealand economy be insulated?' Two economists, Frank Holmes from Victoria University and Len Baylis from the RBNZ, joined a panel of businessmen and unionists to discuss it.[40]

When Clark visited Australia in 1962 to take part in a forum on economic growth, he told his audience that Australian economists had grown comfortable and complacent under 50 years of protectionist sentiment, but that they now had to change their ways. He predicted that they 'are going to have to work extremely hard, and face a good deal of unpopularity, to catch up with their duty of educating public opinion' (Clark, 1962, 29). Clark would live to eat his own words.

Some administrators within the Australian Tariff Board were becoming interested in Corden's work, especially in the 1960s when he studied the costs of distortion within the import-competing manufacturing sector due to the differing levels of tariff assistance accorded certain industries. It helped that Corden was a good communicator and an advocate of gradualism in economic policy.[41] Later, he would focus upon the *modus operandi* of Australia's tariff system and the 'logic' underlying it. He found the Board's statement on policy to be 'vague and question-begging'. Clearly, the Tariff Board did not employ economists. Corden came away somewhat dissatisfied with Australia's tariff system, believing it to be 'fundamentally irrational' and explicable only in terms of political and pressure groups (Corden, 1997, 125).

Later, when the Vernon Report investigated, *inter alia*, the cost disabilities which Australian manufacturers faced relative to other manufacturing countries it recommended a buffer. By that time, Corden, drawing upon the work of the Canadian economist Clarence Barber and his own work differentiating apparent and effective protection, expounded and quantified the true effect that protection had upon resource allocation (Corden, 2005). He found, of course, that the effective rate of assistance was much higher than nominal tariff rates. More importantly, he discovered that the variability of rates of assistance across industries was larger than thought. It was this finding which was to change Australian perceptions about tariff protection and industry assistance (Lloyd, 2014, 31). The 1965 Vernon Report was, therefore, the first official report by any country to make use of effective protection statistics and present empirical estimates for certain industries.[42] Corden's spadework began the journey on what he called 'the road to reform'. He likened his work to dealing with a social 'disease' with the aim of reducing its incidence (Corden, 2005). The new Chairman of the Tariff Board, Alf Rattigan, signalled a major turn in tariff policy in 1967 by stating that tariffs were no longer expected to maintain full employment or to maintain external balance; rather the primary objective of tariff policy was 'to encourage the efficient use of resources in protected industries and a high level of economic growth' (Rattigan, 1969, 25). In doing so Rattigan (1986, 274) drew attention to the high level of effective protection afforded to manufacturers, a move which had them up in arms.

Protection and capital inflow

Corden (1967) also shone a light on the cosy relationship between protection and capital inflow whereby he demonstrated how foreign companies benefited from tariffs. Other economists researching Australia's tariff policy and its effects on foreign investment included Arndt, Swan, Warren Hogan and Rodney Deane of the RBNZ. Foreign investment into Australia and New Zealand became a lively research topic, especially the question of whether it was a net benefit or not, and, in what circumstances. Arndt, for one, changed his earlier views on the consequences of foreign investment, seeing it in a more favourable light. It was an emotive issue in the mid-1960s, with populist, chauvinist attitudes predominating the debate about the scale of foreign ownership – especially within the manufacturing industry. Deane's work sprang from his doctorate, undertaken at Victoria University; he found that foreign direct investment (FDI) only began in earnest when New Zealand introduced import controls in 1938; Deane also found that the foreign investment projects usually involved under-utilisation of capacity and higher production costs (Bassett and Bassett, 2006).

Around the same time, the Canterbury-trained Don Brash, who would eventually become Governor of the RBNZ (1988–2002), was undertaking a doctoral study of American investment in Australian industry. Interestingly, Brash had, under Rosenberg, completed a Master's thesis in 1961 on foreign investment with results that were directly refuted by his ANU doctorate five years later. Brash admitted that his Master's was 'very much a left wing perspective' on foreign investment (Tay, 2007, 36). His doctoral thesis, on the other hand, argued that, on balance, the benefits of foreign investment outweighed the costs to the Australian economy. Brash found that overseas investment led to an increase in real incomes due to the redistribution of income away from the foreign company via external economies, taxation revenue, technology transfer and the positive effect on the terms of trade. Brash's (1966) work was published on the recommendation of one of the examiners, Charles Kindleberger. One work by an Australian scholar begged to differ with Brash. G. D. McColl (1965) argued on fairly unconvincing grounds that the influx of foreign capital had an adverse effect on the economy and should therefore be restricted.

Wages theory

On another battlefront, Coombs (1959) foreshadowed how rising inflation and unemployment might occur simultaneously. The context was that Australia and other western economies in the late 1950s were grappling with the problem of creeping inflation that threatened to become far more insidious. This was especially the case in Australia and New Zealand, whose economies were beset by excess demand and a marked degree of economic concentration. This propensity for prices continually to move upward was an entirely new economic problem and it worried Coombs. If rising inflation became entrenched and started to influence economic behaviour it presented policy-makers with a dilemma: whether to choose to contract or expand demand.

In short, Coombs anticipated the importance of inflationary expectations which would, in turn, encourage greater wage demands. The way to defuse the problem, he suggested, was to make institutional changes that would increase the standard of living without an increase in money wages (ibid., 348). In the same issue of the *Record*, where Coombs's article had appeared, were three other contributions on inflation. However, the editors, Downing and Arndt, had hoped that the issue would also have included the paper 'Wage changes and unemployment in Australia, 1947–1958' which Bill Phillips had given to the NSW Branch of the Economic Society. This basically portended for Australia what would later become known as a Phillips curve. Phillips had been expressly brought out to

Australia in 1959, at considerable expense, by the Commonwealth Bank because of Coombs's interest in macroeconomic stabilisation and, most particularly, because of Phillips's article that had appeared in *Economica* a year earlier. Phillips told his hosts that the central problem facing western economies was economic stability – in particular, whether it was possible to prevent continually rising prices of consumer goods while maintaining buoyant levels of activity. He asked whether Australia could prevent money wages from rising at 2 per cent a year while maintaining high levels of economic activity and employment. He deduced that, for Australia, there was a long-run inflation and unemployment trade-off. Assuming productivity growth of 2 per cent and steady exchange rates, he concluded that inflation would hover at 1.5 per cent, with unemployment at 1.7 per cent. Any attempt to reduce unemployment below that figure would lead to considerably higher rates of inflation. If Australia wanted wage rates to rise no faster than productivity then this meant having an unemployment rate between 3 and 4 per cent, at the time a completely unacceptable figure.

Phillips had promised the article to the *Record* but did not submit it, possibly because Eric Russell, who was an expert on Australian data about wages, employment and prices, had clinically shown that Phillips's data was non-homogeneous, thus making completely unsound any attempt to fit a curve to them (Harcourt, 2001, 304). In other words, there was no stable relationship to be found between changes in wage rates and unemployment. As Harcourt (ibid., 43) recalls, Phillips never claimed that the curve had been anything other than 'an interesting empirical relationship', yet, by being grafted onto the Keynesian model, it was used to undermine it when stagflation arose.

It was not just Coombs and Phillips who were worried by persistently rising inflation. In that same issue of the *Record*, Alan Boxer and Karmel offered separate contributions. Karmel couched his analysis in terms of three intriguing questions facing a mixed, open economy like Australia. First, is price stability compatible with full employment? Second, is the rate of growth of the economy affected by the level of economic activity? And, lastly, what exactly are the desiderata for an expanding economy? This broad canvas allowed Karmel (1959) to articulate an ideal wages policy for Australia. He drew upon the work which Salter and Russell had just placed before the Arbitration Commission in the 1959 Basic Wage Case. Salter and Russell's contribution was to stress the importance of money wages growth being determined by overall productivity plus prices. Bob Hawke, as ACTU advocate, had also asked his old classmate, John Nevile, to compile aggregative data showing the wage and profit factor shares for non-farm income in the belief that this would strengthen the union case for wage rises (Lodewijks, 1994, 19). It was likely that Nevile was the first to observe that, under Australia's centralised wage fixation system, there was a direct connection between economic growth and unemployment (Milbourne, 2001, 226). The emphasis on the wage–profit divide was to become of particular interest to Australasia simply because of the centralised wage fixation arrangements in both countries. Russell had earlier maintained that Australian workers were entitled to share in rising productivity and that the Arbitration Commission should take this into account in determining the capacity of the economy to pay (Harcourt, 1977, 241). Now with Salter's understanding of economy-wide productivity trends, Russell proposed that money wages be linked to average growth in overall productivity plus prices. This would mean that, over time, higher productivity industries would prosper while lower productivity industries would drop out. It would mean that wages would rise at the maximum rate permissible. These beneficial systemic macroeconomics effects of higher productivity and rising real income for all workers would be lost, though, if wage bargaining was decentralised with wages governed by different sectoral productivity growth rates

In an open economy, Russell (1965) held that money wages would have to move proportionally in line with trends in overall productivity modified by the terms of trade and prices. The successful recipe for cost stability was that average real wages move in line with effective productivity, defined as domestic productivity adjusted for changes in the terms of trade. This formula would, as mentioned, tend to wipe out low-productivity industries while encouraging high-productivity ones. By that formula, the relative income shares going to farmers, employers and workers would be maintained. For instance, if wages were tied to domestic productivity but import costs were rising, then overall costs would rise, leading to an increase in the price level if Australian businesses maintained a constant mark-up to maintain profit share. This would mean that real wages were rising less than productivity and that the share of wages in national income would slip. If the unions persuaded the Arbitration Court to grant a wage rise in excess of productivity and inflation, the wage share would rise. The Court, though, seems to have preferred a middle road strategy, one that reconciled the more extreme claims of unions and employers rather than any expressed concern with distributive shares.

Some of this economic research on wages had obvious implications for New Zealand. The Court of Arbitration followed the same ground rules of trying to keep the income shares in balance. However, it was remarkable that, with the exception of Phillips, most of this theoretical innovation and dissemination of policy came from Australian wage theorists.

Building the means for independent economic research

New Zealand

By 1960 the New Zealand economics profession was hosting annual two-day economics conferences of its own accord. One of the common subjects discussed at those first conferences was free trade between Australia and New Zealand. An Association of Economists took shape in October that year (Holmes, 2011). The idea had been first mooted at the 1956 ANZAAS meeting in Dunedin, with the RBNZ a key backer. The Bank was apparently dissatisfied by what the Wellington Branch of the Economic Society, the largest in New Zealand, had to offer, even though it presented eight public lectures a year. It was at one of the economics conferences that the plan for an association began to take shape; Simkin and

Belshaw eagerly backed the move. The Association's aim was 'to promote collaboration and discussion amongst professional economists in New Zealand' (ibid., 4). In its foundation year, the Association comprised just 37 members, reflecting the relatively small number of economists working at universities or within the public sector. By 1963 the Association entertained plans of launching its own journal. By 1970 the Association's membership had risen to 215 and could boast holding two conferences per year. The Economic Society did not seem overly concerned by the development until, perhaps, it was too late to make redress.

Belshaw had long lamented the lack of serious, independent economic research being undertaken in New Zealand. He would become the guiding spirit behind the creation of the New Zealand Institute of Economic Research (NZIER), which was established in 1958 after Belshaw secured some business backing. The RBNZ and Nash, who was now Prime Minister, were eager to assist in the venture. While Belshaw was considered 'the founding father' of the Institute, it should not be overlooked that the RBNZ had told the 1955 Royal Commission into Banking that New Zealand lagged behind other countries in conducting long-term systematic economic research that was helpful to both government and private enterprise. The Royal Commission included the establishment of a body such as this as one of its recommendations, but stressed that it should be a completely independent body. The Commission also felt it appropriate that the body be based in the political capital of Wellington and be affiliated with the Economics Department at Victoria University College. Funding would come from universities, business, trade unions and the RBNZ.

Conrad Blyth came back from Cambridge, where he had been a Fellow at Pembroke College, and became the Institute's first Director. The first reports from the Institute focused primarily on New Zealand's low economic growth rate and strategies to alleviate this. In the era of 1960s-style 'growthmanship', these reports particularly targeted abysmal growth rate, as well as dealing with inflationary and balance of payments pressures. With help from the mathematician Graham Crothall, Blyth built one of the world's first computable general equilibrium models which was published in *Econometrica* in 1965 (Easton, 2009). Another focus was to reduce the country's dependence on the British market, with a narrow range of commodity exports. Industrial economics, investing in more accurate national income statistics and the possibilities of free trade with Australia were early research tasks undertaken by the Institute.[43] In 1984 the Institute's future came under threat when the RBNZ removed its funding, possibly related to the changes in New Zealand's economic policy at the time.

Australia

Like Belshaw, Copland made a bequest to Australia in the form of a long-lasting economics research institute. It was a body that would enshrine his commitment to an apparatus that would align the interests of business with those of nation-building. In his 1936 Harvard address, Copland had made the point that there was a greater measure of public enterprise and public control in market-based econo-mies than commonly thought. Market-based economies had to become mixed economies with large public sectors and significant amounts of public invest-ment, he argued, in order to survive and meet the demands of a civilised society. Independent research into the underlying economic factors shaping Australia's future was achieved with the establishment of the Committee for the Economic Development of Australia (CEDA) in 1960. The new bipartisan, non-profit body would examine issues such as growth and productivity, taxation, investment patterns, education, demography, the labour force, the interplay of financial markets and investment, potential export markets and the perennial problem of Australia's balance of payments. As an independent economic research institute, CEDA would be a union between the private and public sectors; Copland called it a 'marriage of practical experience and theoretical know-how'. In this way, he ensured that research conducted by scientific experts would be grounded by having the work discussed with leading businessmen before the reports were released.

Rivalling CEDA was Melbourne University's Institute of Applied Economic Research, formed in 1962 under Professor Ronald Henderson, who arrived from Cambridge to take the helm. Downing and Prest, who were aware of their Department's relatively poor research effort, were instrumental in establishing the Institute and securing Henderson's services as Director (Drake, 2009, 110). Before that, Henderson, on an earlier visit to Melbourne, had been asked to write a memorandum on the structure and purposes of an independent research insti-tute. He suggested it should be modelled along the lines of an amalgam of the Department of Applied Economics at Cambridge and the National Institute of Economic and Social Research and that it should publish advice on macroeco-nomic policy for Australia (Ironmonger and Perkins, 1995). Its aim was to increase knowledge of the structure of the Australian economy so as to improve the basis for economic policy. In 1968 the Institute began publishing the *Australian Economic Review*, a quarterly that dealt with local economic trends, forecasts and informed comment (McDonald, 2006). Its arrival meant that the *Record* would no longer commission surveys on the Australian and New Zealand economies, freeing up space for more theoretical contributions. Later, Henderson, with colleagues from Melbourne, would be commissioned by the Whitlam Government to undertake a major study into poverty in Australia (Ironmonger and Perkins, 1995, 287).

Another major research development around this time was the establishment of the Australian Agricultural Economics Society. It was designed to promote research, discussion and policy evaluation in areas related to agriculture, food, natural resources and economic development. It also established its own research outlet, the *Australian Journal of Agricultural Economics* (*AJAE*). These academic pursuits were preceded by the Commonwealth establishing the Bureau of Agricultural Economics (BAE) in 1945. This body had come about largely through the efforts of John Crawford, who had previously assisted Sydney University's Faculty of Agriculture's foundation Professor R. D. Watt (1955) to temper the 'romance of Australian land industries' with sober counsel on questions of economic and environmental viability. After visiting American universities and the US Department of Agriculture in the late 1930s, Crawford had seen the value of agricultural economics research and how it could promote productivity in rural industry. He became convinced of the need for an official body in Australia. Fittingly, he became the founder-director of the BAE. His first concern was to provide a rational basis for price stabilisation and 'orderly marketing' by focusing upon costs of production affecting supply levels (Arndt, 2000, 20).

Crawford was, together with Clark and Belshaw, one of the first Australasian economists to see how industrialisation of Asian economies would be a boon for Australian and New Zealand agricultural exports.[44] As an applied economist, he was sceptical about theoretical research, especially when it was not connected to empirical analysis of practical issues (Garnaut, 2007, 75). Crawford did not have a high opinion of modern economic theory, 'so much of it being exercises in mathematical logic'. He liked to uphold the view of the English economist, Ian Little, that 'Economic welfare is a subject in which rigour and refinement is probably worse than useless. Rough theory, or good common sense, is, in practice, what we require' (Arndt, 2000, 37). Despite holding these views, Crawford, with his undoubted leadership and administrative ability, was appointed the first Director of the RSPacS at the ANU in 1961 (Arndt, 2000, 34).

Heinz Arndt himself, after a chance encounter with the Swedish economist Gunnar Myrdal, had broken new research ground with studies into Asian development, especially Indonesia (Hughes, 2002, 484–5). Arndt's departure to the RSPacS in 1963 allowed Burgess Cameron to become head of the Department of Economics in the Faculties. Aided by John Pitchford, Cameron moved ANU Economics away from the Oxbridge model of scholarship towards a more American model, with a stress on quantitative and modelling skills. In 1971 the ANU introduced the country's first Master's coursework programme in Economics and, besides local faculty, the department hired a veritable *Who's Who* of Australian economists from around the country, including Donald Whitehead, Eric Russell, Maureen Brunt, Ronald Henderson and Fred Gruen – each of whom gave lectures in their area of expertise.

The establishment of agricultural economics

New Zealand

We have seen that many of the first generation of Australasian economists had begun to undertake applied research work on agricultural and resource economics issues. Agricultural economics had always been one of the major subject areas appearing in the *Record* (Perlman, 1977). Agricultural economics, when formally taught, provided the testing ground for the post-war quantitative revolution in economics, including econometric model-building. It was the New Zealanders, though, who stole the lead here. Agricultural economics evolved out of farm management and economics. Both Lincoln Agricultural College and Massey

Agricultural College were established in the interwar years to help farmers on management and marketing matters. Massey appointed David Williams to teach agricultural economics. Lincoln's thrust into farm management and agricultural economics was initiated by the appointment of Albert Flay in 1928. Flay came from an agricultural science background rather than economics, but he was to become a pioneer in local agricultural economics (Hawke and Latimer, 2005).

With the New Zealand government eager to increase agricultural exports, it funded the establishment of the Agricultural Economics Research Unit (AERU) at Lincoln College in 1962. Bryan Philpott, who held the chair in agricultural economics at Lincoln, was made the first Director. He was a quixotic mix of econometric model-builder, agricultural economist and old-style believer in Keynesian economics and indicative planning (Holmes, 2000). A returned serviceman, he had been a wool-classer before he attended university where, appropriately enough, he worked on econometric demand functions for wool. Philpott noted how New Zealand faced an impasse in its trade policy; the country could not abolish import controls unless it found new markets, but it could not do so unless it abolished import controls. In other words, New Zealand had to look for more markets to sell its primary produce but be prepared to accept imports in return.

During the 1960s the New Zealand government wanted agricultural exports to increase by 4 per cent in volume terms every year. Philpott address the related problems of increasing exports of dairy, wool and meat products (Driver and Greer, 2012). He pioneered the use of econometrics and operations research to arrive at demand and supply projections and their likely reaction in world markets for agricultural products. Under his watch, AERU became an incubator for economics talent, including many who would later take professorial chairs such as Robin Court, Robin Johnson and Bruce Ross. In one of his early research papers, Philpott criticised the idea of increasing agricultural production by a set amount every year on the basis it made the economy vulnerable to putting 'all its eggs in the one basket'. He estimated the labour and capital inputs needed to engineer that increase in output and income distribution effects, but expressed doubts whether the growth in daily exports would find ready markets (ibid., 4)

A Christchurch-born economist, Rex Bergstrom, stood out, with five articles in *Econometrica* – the first derived from his Cambridge doctorate, in 1955, being on estimating the British demand for New Zealand pastoral exports.[45] He had earlier sent off some of the first econometric articles to appear in the *Record* on New Zealand export supply functions. He became known as that country's 'first econo-metrician' and was, after Bill Phillips, the second New Zealander to be elected a Fellow of the Econometric Society in 1971 (Tay, 2007, 22). In one 1962 contribu-tion in *Econometrica*, he introduced a new era of mathematical sophistication to econometric modelling. Bergstrom made his mark on continuous time modelling with another major contribution in *Econometrica* in 1966 that was deemed 'foun-dational and profound' by one of his students (Phillips, 2005). Bergstrom then turned to the development of macroeconomic models on cyclical growth bringing together real and monetary phenomena in a growing economy (ibid.). His last four years in Auckland before he departed for England in 1970 were spent building a complete macroeconomic model of the UK economy in continuous time and the consideration of its use for forecasting and policy analysis.

Another New Zealander, Malcolm Fisher, had, under Simkin's supervision, undertaken postgraduate work using demand theory, identification theory and regression techniques to conduct an empirical measurement of the demand for cheese. In 1950 he travelled to Cambridge to undertake a PhD in econometrics supervised by Richard Stone. Like many of his counterparts, Fisher found employment abroad; he taught at Cambridge for over 20 years, culminating in a Fellowship at Downing College. He returned to Australasia, when, much to his surprise, he was offered a Chair as foundation Professor of Economics at the new Australian Graduate School of Management at UNSW.

Auckland, with Simkin in command, had begun to build a Department with 'a bent for theory and econometrics' (Hogan, 1999, 316). Under his watch, Auckland would develop the 'reputation of being fairly severely mathematical and theoretical, scorning political economy as mere journalism'. Simkin was instrumental in arranging and filling the first Chair of Econometrics in Australasia with Bergstrom, who had returned from Cambridge with a doctorate. Auckland became, therefore, 'the shining beacon of quantitative economics' in New Zealand, with the firepower of Bergstrom, Bert Brownlie and Fisher (Tay, 2007, 20). Simkin had also introduced the econometric work of Jan Tinbergen and Trygve Haavelmo to New Zealand economics. This led Bill Phillips to conclude that, by the late 1960s, Auckland was a leader in the quality of econometrics taught. To that end, Bergstrom, with the aid of his book on the use of economic models (which one reviewer considered more for mathematicians than economists), trained successive generations of New Zealand economists in advanced econometrics, including Peter C. B. Phillips. It would mean that Canterbury and Auckland, up to the 1970s, were offering the equivalent to what was being offered in the most advanced courses in economic schools in Britain and America. New Zealand economists made easy pickings modelling and estimating econometric demand and supply functions for their country's exports of dairy products, meat and wheat, with their output appearing in *Econometrica*.

In Christchurch, Bert Brownlie, who had taken the second Chair in Economics at Canterbury in 1965, was also keen to expose students to the more quantitative methods being taught overseas. Brownlie went a step further by opening up economics education to those non-commerce graduates who had an edge in maths and statistics to undertake a two-year Master's course in economics without a prior undergraduate degree in economics. This was called the 'Knight's move' (ibid., 40). Interestingly, three of the Distinguished Fellows of the Association of New Zealand Economists came to economics by this route.[46] Brownlie was also instrumental in introducing economics to students within the Faculty of Science. This resulted in a number of scientists majoring in economics and going on to successful careers in that subject.

Brownlie studied applied econometrics before the days of computers and statistical packages. He directed most of his output to the *Record* (ibid., 39). As a result of his teaching, by the late 1960s Canterbury was the largest supplier of economists with quantitative skills. Auckland and Canterbury, in fact, stole the lead over Australian departments of Economics in devising economic models and testing for the verification of hypotheses. By contrast, Australian universities had neglected macroeconomic model-building and econometric capability. At UWA, the new head of the economics department in 1972, Douglas Vickers, was appalled by the training in econometrics provided to students. One senior lecturer told him that he did no research because 'all that could be said in his areas of interest had already been said' and that his position was his 'Shangri La' (McClure, 2011, 8). At the University of Queensland economics students had been taught by rote as late as the 1960s: 'an absolute scandal' according to one of its graduates, Jonathan Pincus.[47] One point of inspiration, though, was that Professor of Economics there, John Gifford, proved an early exponent of the theory that inflation was solely caused by monetary impulses rather than cost-push factors. In the final exam, Pincus tore Gifford's peculiar views on inflation to shreds but, because it would endanger the award of a first-class honours degree, Gifford's colleagues, including Helen Hughes, who was a lecturer there, deliberately misplaced his exam script (Lodewijks, 2007, 437). Coming just behind Pincus was the econometrician Adrian Pagan, who would later describe his education there as a 'poetic economics program' (Skeels, 2016, 1057).

Australia

Since Australia was primarily a pastoral-based economy it is surprising that agricultural economics was not offered as a major or formal part of economics education there until well after 1945 (Campbell, 1985). Agricultural economics, taught at American universities, was an important part in the story of Australasian economics simply because it would prove the training ground for many Australian economists: names such as Keith Campbell, John Dillon, Alan Lloyd, Alan Powell, Ross Parish and Fred Gruen. James Belshaw, the younger brother of Horace, instigated agricultural economics courses in Australia after researching similar programmes in Europe and America. In 1954 he proposed the idea that the New England University College, an offshoot of Sydney University, should establish a Faculty of Rural Economy. Agricultural Economics was soon offered at what became the University of New England (UNE) and would soon be regarded as 'Australia's major centre for academic training in Agricultural Economics' (Jordan, 2004, 161).

It was, though, Sydney which stole the lead in Agricultural Economics by establishing the first Chair in that subject, with Keith Campbell as original incumbent in 1956. The Commonwealth Trading Bank, given its stake in the rural economy, funded this position and also funded similar chairs in Melbourne, Adelaide, UWA and UNE (Bearman, 1985). The grant to the Sydney Chair stipulated that it should enable research to be undertaken and the results disseminated. There was much ground to cover; research enquired into the behaviour of commodity markets, rural credit, soldier settlement schemes and the efficacy of assistance such as home price arrangements, reserve prices and statutory market-ing authorities. These assistance schemes were part of the protection all round complex designed to compensate farmers for high domestic costs due to imports tariffs and wage regulation (Campbell, 1985). It was in tackling these issues that Australasian economists began to see the excesses and inefficiencies of rural regulation. Campbell did for agricultural economists what Copland did for econo-mists, namely, forming a scholarly society and with it a prestigious journal.

An extraordinary cluster of young, ambitious economists, including Fred Gruen, John Dillon, John Freebairn, Alan Lloyd, Alan Powell and Ross Parish, had, following Keith Campbell's lead; all found employment at the Division of Marketing and Agricultural Economics (DMAE) within the NSW Department of Agriculture. This ensemble of economists made for 'a special place... an academic nest within a government service organisation' (cited in Dillon and Powell, 1998, 194). The department even had its own journal called the *Review of Marketing and Agricultural Economics*, which, being refereed, was much more than a house journal. It also predated the *AJAE*. With agricultural and resource economics becoming a part of the economics curriculum at many Australian universities, the DMAE provided the human capital; it was responsi-ble, in fact, for filling no less than 12 chairs within academe. Dillon, who like Parish had been taught at the University of Sydney by the doyen of Australian agricultural economists, Keith Campbell, would become the foundation Professor of Farm Management at UNE in 1965. Dillon not only made UNE a leader in Agricultural Economics but was a great promoter of the discipline. Dillon (1972, 81) held that the training agricultural economists underwent, including an integral understanding of markets and quantitative methods, made them 'the best equipped of any Australian professional group' to deal with economic and envi-ronmental problems.

Apart from introducing practitioners to econometrics, agricultural economics gave the student an awareness of production and their interaction with household resources and objectives, together with an emphasis on gathering strong empiri-cal support. Parish (1969, 3) argued that agricultural economics was a seamless part of economics and its tools of analysis could easily be extended to everyday issues – from consumer protection to health insurance – and, as a result, strengthen the whole profession. His argument refuted the charge that Australia was over-investing by sending its best to study agricultural economics at American universities (ibid., 2). Keith Campbell (1985, 45), along with Edwards and Watson (1978, 198–9), disagreed with the perception that Australian gradu-ates of American agricultural economics programmes all came away transfixed by market solutions as the cure to economic problems rather than intervention.

Perhaps the best personification of this was Fred Gruen. Having experienced Chicago, where he enrolled to undertake his doctorate, he was of the view that the more rigorous training provided by American universities was superior to anything English universities offered and argued that this gave those who went there the advantage of transferring into other areas of research. Naturally enough, Gruen published much of his earlier research on applied aspects of technical progress to agriculture; he came to prominence with research on the application of superphosphate to pasture improvement, which merited the award as the best paper in the *Record* for its year (Gruen, 1960). In the subsequent year, in the *Journal of Farm Economics*, Gruen asked whether technological improvement could, in fact, lead to the relative immiserisation of the farming sector (Gruen, 1961a). He wrote a witty review of assistance flowing to the Australian dairy industry entitled 'Crying over spilt milk' (Gruen, 1961b).

After five years at the ANU, Gruen was elevated to the Foundation Chair in Agricultural Economics at Monash in 1964 – a position that was part funded by the RBA. He bought a farm outside Melbourne for the experience and joked how he was usually one lecture ahead of the students and one fence ahead of the cattle. More seriously, Gruen had to formally assure the University Council that maintaining the farm would not intrude upon his professional activities.[48] At Monash, Gruen worked with Alan Powell on a US government-funded research project on long-term projections of agricultural supply and demand in Australia. He moved to the RSSS at the ANU in 1972, where, showing his versatility, he broadened his research focus to include macroeconomics and socio-economic issues. His other contribution to Australian economics was as an intellectual leader, with the establishment in 1979 of the Centre for Economic Policy Research at the ANU, which was charged with examining macro-economic challenges besetting the Australian economy (Corden, 2007).

One might say that American agricultural and general economics training recast the shaping of the Australian economics profession since agricultural economics laid stress on price, resource allocation and partial equilibrium theory and was not concerned with income and employment theory. As the Keynesian consensus receded in the mid-1970s, those with a professional training basis in price theory reaped the rewards. Indeed, Parish (1969, 3), who pioneered the use of microeconomic theory to everyday, real-world problems, suggested that – for Australia, at least – 'the pendulum had swing too far to the macro-side, and that research and teaching in microeconomics had reached a pretty sorry state'. This was a thinly veiled attack on the post-war influence of British economics upon the Australian profession.

Wolfgang Kasper (2000), Helen Hughes and Ross Garnaut would all independently recycle that attack against those Cambridge-educated Australian economists who had trained students without alerting them to the structural rigidity of the economy. Garnaut (2001, 3) spoke of 'a long-term tendency of the Australian economics profession to blur the conclusions that have emerged from economic scholarship – the development of "The Australian case for protection"' and the 'idiosyncratic view of many Australian labour economists that the demand for labour is not much affected by its price'. Garnaut omitted Swan, Clark, Arndt, Corden and Simkin from his attack since they, at least, had pointed out how tariffs, restrictive practices and other distortions were restraining Australian economic development.

Meanwhile, conventionally trained economists such as, for example, Karmel or Downing were still addressing rural and pastoral issues such as assistance policy, reserve price schemes or the development of Northern Australia. Corden

(1968, 47–9) tells how, after reviewing an official Committee of Enquiry into the Australian Dairying Industry (1959–60), Karmel and Downing came down against assistance, in the form of an elevated home price for dairy products, simply because it detracted from productivity and allocative efficiency. They argued that more assistance was just compounding the problem: a view little different, in fact, from what Gruen and a team of agricultural economists includ- ing Ross Parish had concluded, namely, that assistance to the dairy industry was a waste of resources and did little to alleviate the low income status of farmers in that industry.

There was an encore performance in 1960 when Alan Powell and Keith Campbell gave evidence before the Wool Marketing Committee of Enquiry on the feasibility of a reserve wool price scheme favoured by Australian graziers. At the time, wool represented 37 per cent of Australia's exports but was facing competition from synthetics. Powell and Campbell (1962, 385) concluded that, since a wool authority was unlikely to have advance knowledge of shifts in the demand for or the elasticity of wool, such a scheme would become 'a lottery with, say 10 per cent of Australian wool cheques... as stakes'. Their study was backed up with further analysis by Ross Parish and Jack Duloy (1964). The arguments from this quartet of economists had some short-term success; a Reserve Price Scheme for Wool did not commence until 1974. However, it was soon obvious that the reserve price was set above industry averages in defiance of changes in market demand. As the stockpile mounted, the Tasmania Farmers Federation passed a motion in 1984 suggesting the sponsoring of a world-wide knitting contest. The mover of the motion declared that, if the contest was extensively promoted in China, Australia's wool surplus problem would be eliminated.[49] One newspaper in 1990 summed it as: 'We are selling wool to ourselves.'[50] The economists finally had their day when an inevitable accumulation of wool stock led to the system being abandoned in 1991.

Gruen and his ANU colleague Stuart Harris were two of the four co-signatories to the Whitlam Government's Green Paper on *The Principles of Rural Policy in Australia* canvassing, among other things, the idea of giving modest assistance or 'tariff compensation' to rural exporters (Harris *et al.*, 1974: 41–2). Coombs (1981, 310) had encouraged the inquiry to counter the Whitlam Government's anti-rural image, but also give it a coherent theoretical approach to rural issues. The New Zealand government had made tariff compensation an art form by intro- ducing an array of export incentives since the 1960s (Lattimore and Wooding, 1996, 320). Since tariffs for the manufacturing sector had imposed costs and reduced the profitability of rural production, they argued that there was, *prima facie*, a case for compensation. Underpinning their position were the dim pros- pects of Australia moving towards free trade. Using Meade's approach, Gruen summed up the second-best case for assistance by trying to gauge the impact which assistance to manufacturing had on rural industry and by how much resources were distorted by such support (Lloyd, 1978, 266). Besides contradict- ing the advice of the then newly established Industries Assistance Commission (IAC), tariff compensation, by offsetting the cost of protection, also contradicted the principle that, given a market distortion in one sector of the economy, it is not possible to say on *a priori* grounds whether a similar distortion in another part of the economy would improve resource efficiency. Providing such assistance to the rural sector would, in any case, be problematic since the IAC was pressing to reduce assistance levels across the board. Alan Lloyd was aware, as Copland had been in 1928, that to implement the scheme would rely on the good faith of the administrators and their freedom from political interference. Peter Lloyd spoke for the mainstream in being dismissive of tariff compensation, suggesting that it was a return to the 'protection all round' (Corden and Jayasuriya, 2006, 79). The issue was revisited by the Balderstone Committee in 1982 (agricultural economist Frank Jarrett was a member), where deregulation and greater market orientation were now seen as the way to compensate Australian farmers from the effects of protection.

Another long-held aspiration of Australian politicians was to push for the development of the vast hinterland of the continent otherwise known as 'The North'. Going against public opinion, Australian economists largely cautioned against it. The most vocal opponent of subsiding the development of the north was Bruce Davidson. An older-style agricultural economist who had undertaken his doctorate at Wye College, University of London, Davidson found employment at UWA and then Sydney University. In his book *The Northern Myth* (1965), Davidson attempted to deflate the argument that the north be developed for strategic reasons without any rigorous economic evaluation. Robust agricultural development for Northern Australia, Davidson held, should be guided by comparative advantage to develop not in terms of plentiful resources but in terms of scarce resources (Batterham *et al.*, 1994). Given this, he was critical of the capital-intensive Ord River irrigation project in the north of Western Australia that went ahead for political reasons. He told an Economic Society meeting in Canberra that the farmers involved in this particular project would become Australia's 'highest paid pensioners' given the assistance afforded them. It would be cheaper, Davidson suggested, to give each of the farmers a substantial lump sum of money than to go ahead with the irrigation project.[51] He followed up this critique by writing *Australia Wet or Dry?* (1969), wherein he stressed that water was only one of the resources needed for agricultural development and that, in any case, Australia had a reasonable supply of it without having to erect more dams, which only appealed to the ego of politicians.

Conclusion

In the post-war era, the economics profession in Australia and New Zealand regathered its strength to address new economic challenges facing both countries. As a result, there were some pioneering insights in economic thought, including advances in growth, trade and wages theory. The period saw independent economic research being undertaken by bipartisan, non-profit bodies. It also marked the establishment of Agricultural Economics as a separate field of study and one which, over time, was to infuse the wider discipline.

Notes

1　Copland to Dunababin 10/11/1952, Copland Papers, NLA.
2　Keith Hancock NLA transcript 2006
3　Noel Butlin Oral Transcript, ANU 1991.
4　Arndt to Firth 19/10/1954, Arndt Papers, NLA.
5　Downing to Prest 24/6/1946, Prest Papers, UMA.
6　Copland to Prest 24/8/1950, Prest Papers, UMA.
7　Copland to Registrar 26/9/1951, Registrar Papers, UMA.
8　Copland to Downing 31/7/1952, Downing Papers, UMA.
9　Copland to Downing 19/12/1952, Downing Papers, UMA.
10　W. S. Robinson to L. B. Robinson 13/7/1958, Robinson Papers, UMA.
11　Downing to Copland 12/1/1953, Downing Papers, UMA.
12　Downing to Williams 3/7/1963, Downing Papers, UMA.
13　Robin A. Gollan, ANU Oral History Archive.
14　Belshaw to Condliffe 1/4/1950, Condliffe Papers, UC.
15　'Economics in a changing world', April 1951, Belshaw Papers, UA.
16　Belshaw to Condliffe 2/10/1951, Condliffe Papers, UC.
17　Belshaw to Condliffe 2/22/1956, Condliffe Papers, UC.
18　Hawke had been a Rhodes Scholar in 1954 and clashed with Clark over his intended research work, which involved writing a dissertation on the Australian arbitration system. Hawke later discovered that Clark had been a leading influence in persuading Justice Kelly on the Full Bench of the Arbitration Court to ditch wage indexation in the 1953 National Wage Case on the premise that it was perpetuating inflation.
19　Arndt Oral Transcript, NLA pg. 7.
20　Karmel to Prest 28/10/1944, Prest Papers, UMA.
21　Ibid.
22　The numbers were as follows: 22 went to Cambridge, 20 to Oxford and 13 went to the LSE. The London contingent included Max Corden, Harold Bell, Gordon Bruns, Alf Hagger, Keith Hancock, Helen Hughes, Joe Isaac, Stuart Wilson, Neil Davey, David Finch, Roy Webb and Richard Snape. Bruce Davidson obtained his PhD from the University of London. The seven New Zealanders were Conrad Blyth, Rex Bergstrom, Ron Meek, Max Neutze, Malcolm Fisher (all Cambridge) Bill Phillips (LSE) and Colin Simkin (Oxford). Another New Zealander, Bryan Philpott, studied at Leeds.
23　New Zealand money, too, had financed the prototype, since Phillips's family had sent him the funds to buy materials (Bollard, 2016).
24　None of the four New Zealand university economics departments then extant acquired the MONIAC.
25　Phillips to Prest 17/11/1954, Prest Papers, UMA.
26　Firth to Prest 25/11/1949, Prest Papers, UMA.
27　Copland to Prest 1/11/1937, Prest Papers, UMA.
28　Popper was prevented from taking a position at the University of Sydney in February 1945 because he was described as 'an unnaturalised enemy alien' by conservative politicians. See Carmody, J. 2016, 'The Scurvy Treatment of Karl Popper', *Record: The University Archives*, University of Sydney pp.17–18.
29　Arndt to Harsanyi 28/4/1955, Arndt Papers, NLA
30　Arndt to P. H. Partridge 19/4/1955, Arndt Papers, NLA.
31　Arndt to Harsanyi 27/8/1957, Arndt Papers, NLA.
32　Downing to Arndt 8/6/62, Arndt Papers, NLA.
33　Downing to Tony Little 18/11/1963, Downing Papers, UMA.
34　Firth to Downing 27/6/1961, Firth Papers, UMA.
35　Firth to Arndt 22/1/1971, Firth Papers, NLA.
36　The immediate issue, in April 1957, was also noteworthy, with articles by Meade and Joan Robinson.

37 At the end of 2015 Solow's paper had over 19,000 citations, Swan's had 1,500 citations.
38 Swan was not the only Australian economist to be completely overlooked by the Nobel Prize authorities. Clark's pioneering work on national income and economic growth, too, was not recognised when Simon Kuznets won the 1971 Nobel Prize in Economics for his work in the area. When one of Clark's students, Richard Stone, won the 1984 Nobel Prize for his work on national income accounting the Swedish prize-giving authorities were unaware that he had been one of Clark's students at Cambridge and agreed that it would have been better if the two had been honoured. Communication with Peter Dixon, December 2014.
39 Interview with R. G. Gregory, NLA transcript.
40 Wellington Branch, ESANZ minute book, August 1958, ATL.
41 'Four turning points', Max Corden Economist website, http://www.maxcorden.com/life/
42 Corden's work here on the cost of protection, which he submitted to the Vernon Committee in 1964, would much later apply to international trade negotiations and estimating the producer subsidy equivalents going to agricultural producers and designing measures to contain it.
43 The Evolving Institute: 50 years of the New Zealand Institute of Economic Research, 1958–2008, https://nzier.org.nz/static/media/filer_public/da/1d/da1d1b92-5115-4e45-b787-b3e3446f8c0c/the-evolving-institute.pdf
44 Hermann Black wrote a master of economics thesis at Sydney University in 1936 looking at Sydney as a possible market for Australian produce.
45 Australia's response came from Clem Tisdell, with an article on uncertainty appearing in *Econometrica* in 1963.
46 The econometrician David Giles, the microeconomist John Riley and the applied microeconomist and game theorist John McMillan.
47 Pincus Oral Transcript, 2007, NLA.
48 Gruen staff file, Monash University.
49 F. Connors, 'The lighter side of Economics', *Canberra Times*, 2 December 1984.
50 *Sydney Morning Herald*, 21 May 1990, p. 12.
51 'Ord farmers highest paid pensioners', *Canberra Times*, 19 April 1966.

References

Arndt, H. W. 1944, *The Economic Lessons of the Nineteen Thirties*, London: Oxford University Press.
Arndt, H. W. 1976, 'R. I. Downing: economist and social reformer', *Economic Record*, 52(3): 281–301.
Arndt H. W. 1985, *A Course Through Life: Memoirs of an Australian Economist*, Canberra: Australian National University.
Arndt, H. W. 2000, 'Essays in biography: Australian economists', *History of Economics Review*, 32.
Arndt, H. W. and W. M. Corden (eds), 1963, *The Australian Economy*, Sydney: Cheshire.
Backhouse, R. 2002, *The Penguin History of Economics*, London: Penguin.
Barr, N. 1988. 'The Phillips machine', *LSE Quarterly*, 2(4): 305–38.
Bassett M. and J. Bassett, 2006, *Roderick Deane: His Life and Times*, Wellington: Viking.
Batterham, B., R. Mauldon and T. Ockwell, 1994, 'Bruce Robinson Davidson 1924–1994', *Australian Journal of Agricultural and Resource Economics*, 38(1): 121–4.
Bearman, S. 1985, *Agricultural Economics in Australia*, Armidale: Department of Agricultural Economics and Business Management, University of New England.
Belshaw, H. 1953, 'Stability and growth', in R. S. Parker (ed.), *Economic Stability in New Zealand*, Wellington: New Zealand Institute of Public Administration, 33–5.

Belshaw, H. 1955, 'Population growth and levels of consumption in New Zealand', *Economic Record*, 31(1–2): 1–17.

Belshaw, H. 1961, 'Obituary: Dr Edward Percy Neale', *Economic Record*, 37(77): 98–9.

Bensusan-Butt, D. 1964, 'Taxation in Australia: agenda for more reform', *Economic Record*, 40(90): 226–32.

Bollard, A. 2016, *A Few Hares to Chase: The Economic Life and Times of Bill Phillips*, Oxford: Oxford University Press.

Brash, D. T. 1966, *American Investment in Australian Industry*, Cambridge, MA: Harvard University Press.

Brooke, G., A. Endres and A. Rogers, 2016, 'The economists and the New Zealand population: problems and policies 1900–1980s', Working Paper in economics, Auckland University of Technology.

Brown, N. 2001, *Richard Downing: Economics, Advocacy and Social Reform in Australia*, Melbourne: Melbourne University Press.

Brown, N. 2007, 'Richard Downing (1915–1975)', in J. E. King (ed.), *A Biographical Dictionary of Australasian Economists*, Cheltenham: Edward Elgar.

Butlin, N. G. 1978, 'A fraternal farewell: tribute to S. J. Butlin', *Australian Economic History Review*, 18: 99–118.

Butlin, N. G. and R. G. Gregory, 1989, 'Trevor Winchester Swan, 1918–89', *Economic Record*, 65(191): 369–77.

Butlin, S. J. 1948, '"Of course I know no economics, but…": some comments on provision for economics teaching and research in Australia', *Australian Quarterly*, 22(3): 37–52.

Butlin, S. J. 1966, 'The hundredth record', *Economic Record*, 42(100): 508–19.

Campbell, K. O. 1985, 'Some reflections on the development of agricultural economics in Australia', Mimeo.

Chapman, B. 1998, 'F. H. G. Gruen: 1921–97', *Economic Record*, 74(225): 186–94.

Clark, C. 1962, 'Economic growth', in J. Wilkes (ed.), *Economic Growth in Australia*, Sydney: Angus & Robertson, 1–29.

Cochrane, D. 1949, 'Measurement of economic relationships', *Economic Record*, 25(2): 7–23.

Coleman, P., S. Cornish and P. Drake, 2007, *Arndt's Story: The Life of an Australian Economist*, Canberra: Australian National University Press.

Coleman, W. 2006, 'A conversation with Max Corden', *Economic Record*, 82(259): 379–95.

Coleman, W. 2015, 'A young tree dead? The story of economics in Australia and New Zealand', in V. Barnett (ed.), *Routledge Handbook of the History of Global Economic Thought*, London: Routledge: 281–93.

Coleman, W., S. Cornish and A. Hagger, 2006, *Giblin's Platoon: The Trials and Triumph of the Economist in Australian Public Life*, Canberra: Australian National University Press.

Condliffe, J. B. 1950, 'The teacher and the influence', in R. S. Allan (ed.), *Liberty and Learning*, Christchurch: Whitcombe and Tombs.

Coombs, H. C. 1959, 'A matter of prices', *Economic Record*, 35(72): 337–48.

Coombs, H. C. 1981, *Trial Balance*, Melbourne: Macmillan.

Copland, D. B. 1951, *Inflation and Expansion*, Melbourne: Cheshire.

Corden, W. M. 1957, 'The calculation of the cost of protection', in Corden (1997), *The Road to Reform*, Sydney: Addison Wesley.

Corden, W. M. 1967, 'Protection and foreign investment', *Economic Record*, 43(2): 209–32.

Corden, W. M. 1968, *Australian Economic Policy Discussion: A Survey*, Melbourne: Melbourne University Press.

Corden, W. M. 1997, *The Road to Reform*, Sydney: Addison Wesley.

Corden, W. M. 2005, 'Effective protection and I', *History of Economics Review*, 42: 1–11.

Corden, W. M. 2007, 'Fred Henry George Gruen (1921–1997)', in J. E. King (ed.), *A Biographical Dictionary of Australasian Economists*, Cheltenham: Edward Elgar, 118–23.

Corden, W. M. and S. Jayasuriya, 2006, 'Distinguished Fellow of the Economic Society of Australia, 2005: Peter Lloyd', *Economic Record*, 82(256): 77–81.

Cornish, S. 2007, 'The appointment of the ANU's first Professor of Economics', *History of Economics Review*, 1–16.

Cornish, S. and G. C. Harcourt 2013, 'Allan Barton', *Economic Record*, 89(287).

Davidson, B. R. 1965, *The Northern Myth*, Melbourne: Melbourne University Press.

Davidson, B. R. 1969, *Australia Wet or Dry?*, Melbourne: Melbourne University Press.

Dillon, J. L. 1972, 'The outlook for agricultural economics', *Australian Journal of Agricultural Economics*, 16(2): 73–81.

Dillon, J. L. and A. A. Powell, 1998, 'Obituary of Fred Henry George Gruen 1921–1997', *Australian Journal of Agricultural Economics*, 42(2): 191–6.

Downing, R. 1964, *Taxation in Australia: Agenda for Reform*, Melbourne: Melbourne University Press.

Drake, P. 2009, 'The 1960s: constrained development', in R. Williams (ed.), *Balanced Growth: A History of the Department of Economics, University of Melbourne*, Melbourne: Australian Scholarly.

Drake, P. and R. Garnaut, 1995, 'H. W. Arndt: Distinguished Fellow', *Economic Record*, 71(212): 1–7.

Driver, T. and G. Greer, 2012, '50 years of the AERU', Research Report No. 328, Lincoln University.

Duloy, J. H. and R. M. Parish, 1964, 'An appraisal of a floor price scheme for wool', *New England Marketing Studies*, No. 1, Faculty of Agricultural Economics, University of New England.

Easton, B. 2009, 'Economic growth research in New Zealand: the fathers that begat us', Paper to the New Zealand Association of Economists.

Edwards, G. and A. S. Watson, 1978, 'Agricultural policy', in F. H. G. Gruen (ed.), *Surveys of Australian Economics*, Sydney: Allen and Unwin.

Endres, A. M. and A. Rogers, 2014, 'Trade policy and international finance in the Bretton Woods era: a doctrinal perspective with reference to Australia and New Zealand', *History of Economics Review*, 59: 62–81.

Freebairn, J. 2009, 'Contributions to Australian economic policy', in R. Williams (ed.), *Balanced Growth: A History of the Department of Economics, University of Melbourne*, Melbourne: Australian Scholarly, 211–240.

Garnaut, R. 2001, *Social Democracy in Australia's Asian Future*, Canberra: Asia Pacific Press.

Garnaut, R. 2007, 'Sir John Grenfell Crawford (1910–1984)', in J. E. King (ed.), *A Biographical Dictionary of Australasian Economists*, Cheltenham: Edward Elgar, 74–9.

Groenewegen, P. 2011, '*Famous Figures and Diagrams in Economics*' (book review), *History of Economics Review*, 53: 99–102.

Gruen, F. H. G. 1960, 'Economic aspects of pasture improvement in the Australian wool industry', *Economic Record*, 36(74): 220–41.

Gruen, F. H. 1961a, 'Agriculture and technical change', *Journal of Farm Economics*, 43(4): 838–58.

Gruen, F. H. 1961b, 'Crying over spilt milk', *Economic Record*, 37(79): 352–70.

Hagger, A. and G. G. Firth, 1959, 'The Australian economy', *Economic Record*, 35(70): 1–20.

Harcourt, G. C. 1977, 'Eric Russell, 1923–77: a memoir', *Economic Record*, 53(144): 467–74.

Harcourt, G. C. 2000, 'A left Keynesian view of the Phillips curve trade-off', in Robert Leeson (ed.), *A. W. H. Phillips: Collected Works in a Contemporary Perspective*, Cambridge: Cambridge University Press.

Harcourt, G. C. 2001, *Selected Essays on Economic Policy*, Basingstoke: Palgrave.

Harris, S., J. Crawford, F. Gruen and N. Honan, 1974, *The Principles of Rural Policy in Australia*, Canberra: Australian Government Publisher.

Hawke, G. and R. Lattimore, 2005, 'Scoping the history of economics in New Zealand', New Zealand Agricultural and Resource Economics Society Conference, Nelson.

Hawke, R. J. 1962, 'Discussion', in J. Wilkes (ed.), *Economic Growth in Australia*, Sydney: Angus & Robertson, 160–5.

Higgins, B. 1951, *What Do Economists Know?*, Melbourne: Melbourne University Press.

Higgins, B. 1989, *The Road Less Travelled: A Development Economist's Quest*, Canberra Australian National University.

Hieser, R. O. 1964, 'Australian economic policy-making', *Australian Quarterly*, 36–48.

Hogan, W. P. 1999, 'Colin George Frederick Simkin, 1915–1998', *Economic Record*, 75(230): 313–22.

Holmes, F. W. 2000, 'Obituary of Bryan Philpott', *Victoria Economic Commentaries*, 17(1).

Holmes, F. W. 2011 (assisted by L. Bayliss and J. McFaul), *The New Zealand Association of Economists: Memories of its Early Years*, Wellington: New Zealand Association of Economists.

Hughes, H. 2002, 'Heinz W. Arndt: economist and public intellectual', *Economic Record*, 78(243): 479–89.

Ironmonger, D. 1972, *New Commodities and Consumer Behaviour*, Chicago: University of Chicago Press.

Ironmonger, D. and J. O. N. Perkins, 1995, 'Ronald Frank Henderson', *Economic Record*, 71(214): 284–90.

Jordan, M. 2004, *A Spirit of True Learning: The Jubilee History of the University of New England*, Sydney: NSW Press.

Karmel, P. 1959, 'Some reflections on inflation, productivity and growth', *Economic Record*, 35(72): 349–70.

Kasper, W. 2000, *Building Prosperity*, Sydney: Centre for Independent Studies.

King, J. E. 2007, 'Kurt Singer (1886–1962)', in J. E. King (ed.), *A Biographical Dictionary of Australasian Economists*, Cheltenham: Edward Elgar, 253–5.

Lattimore, R. and P. Wooding, 1996, 'International trade', in B. Silverstone, A. Bollard and R. Lattimore (eds), *A Study of Economic Reform: The Case of New Zealand*, Amsterdam: Elsevier.

Lloyd, P. 1978, 'Protection policy', in F. H. G. Gruen (ed.), *Surveys of Australian Economics*, Sydney: Allen and Unwin, 241–96.

Lloyd, P. 2006, 'Fifty years of trade policy reform', *Economic Papers*, 25(4): 301–13.

Lloyd, P. 2014, 'The path of protection in Australia since federation', *History of Economics Review*, 59: 21–43.

Lodewijks, J. 1994, 'A conversation with John Nevile', in B. B. Rao (ed.), *Essays in Economics*, Sydney: Centre for Applied Economic Research: 15–34.

Lodewijks, J. 2005, 'The ET interview: Professor Jan Kmenta', *Econometric Theory*, 21(3): 621–45.

Lodewijks, J. 2007, 'A conversation with Helen Hughes', *Journal of the Asia Pacific Economy*, 12(4): 429–51.

Lodewijks, J. 2011, 'Economists from the Antipodes: what can oral history tell us about the influences on their career development?', *International Journal of Development and Conflict*, 1(2): 283–302.

McCarty, J. 1964 'Why have we no theory of Australian economic growth?', *Economic Review*, 8: 24–5.

McClure, M. 2011, 'Thirty years of economics; UWA and the WA Branch of the Economic Society from 1963 to 1992', *History of Economics Review*, 54: 70–91.

McColl, G. D. 1965, *The Australian Balance of Payments*, Melbourne: Melbourne University Press.

McDonald, D. 2006, '150 issues of the *Australian Economic Review*: the changing face of a journal over time', *Australian Economic Review*, 39(2): 117–29.

Macintyre, S. 2015, *Australia's Boldest Experiment*, Sydney: New South.

Meade, J. 1951, *The Balance of Payments*, New York: Oxford University Press.

Metaxas, P. E. and E. J. Weber, 2016, 'An Australian contribution to trade theory: the dependent economy model', *Economic Record*, 92(298): 464–97.

Milbourne, R. 2001, 'Distinguished Fellow of the Economic Society of Australia, 2000: John Warwick Nevile', *Economic Record*, 77(238): 225–7.

Millmow, A. J. 2013a, 'Douglas Copland's battle with the younger brethren of economists', *Australian Economic History Review*, 53(2): 187–209.

Millmow, A. J. 2013b, 'How Richard Downing won the Ritchie chair', *History of Economics Review*, 58: 57–70.

Parish, R. M. 1969, 'Some thoughts on the role of the agricultural economics profession in Australia', *Australian Journal of Agricultural Economics*, 13(1): 1–7.

Perlman, M. 1977, 'The editing of the *Economic Record* 1925–1975', in J. Nieuwenhuysen and P. Drake (eds), *Australian Economic Policy*, Melbourne: Longmans.

Phillips, P. C. B. 2005, 'A. R. Bergstrom: New Zealand's first econometrician', *New Zealand Economic Papers*, 39: 129–52.

Pitchford, J. D. 2002, 'Trevor Swan's 1956 economic growth seminar: and notes on growth', *Economic Record*, 78(243): 381–7.

Powell, A. A. and K. O. Campbell, 1962, 'Revenue implications of a buffer stock scheme with an uncertain demand schedule', *Economic Record*, 38(83): 373–85.

Rattigan, G. A. 1969, 'The Tariff Board: some reflections', *Economic Record*, 45(109): 17–26.

Rattigan, G. A. 1986, *Industry Assistance: The Inside Story*, Melbourne: Melbourne University Press.

Rowe, A. P. 1960, *If The Gown Fits*, Melbourne: Melbourne University Press.

Russell, E. A. 1965, 'Wages policy in Australia', *Australian Economic Papers*, 4(1): 1–26.

Russell, E. A. and J. Meade, 1957, 'Wage rates, the cost of living and the balance of payments', *Economic Record*, 33(64): 23–8.

Salter, W. 1955, *Productivity and Economic Progress*, Cambridge: Cambridge University Press.

Salter, W. 1959, 'Internal and external balance: the role of price and expenditure effects', *Economic Record*, 35(71): 226–38.

Sanders, D. N., P. D. Jonson and M. G. Porter, 1986, 'Austin Stewart Holmes, OBE, 1924–1986', *Economic Record*, 62(179): 506–14.

Schedvin, C. B. 1992, *In Reserve: Central Banking in Australia*, Sydney: Allen and Unwin.

Skeels, C. 2016, 'The ET interview: Adrian Pagan', *Econometric Theory*, 32; 1015–94.

Snape, R. H. 1996, 'Distinguished Fellow of the Economic Society of Australia, 1995: Professor Max Corden', *Economic Record*, 72(216): 1–6.

Snooks, G. D. 1991, 'In my beginning is my end: the life and work of Noel George Butlin 1921–91', *Australian Economic History Review*, 30(2): 3–27.

Snooks, G. 2007, 'Noel George Butlin (1921–1991)', in J. E. King (ed.), *A Biographical Dictionary of Australasian Economists*, Cheltenham: Edward Elgar, 38–44.

Spencer, B. and R. W. Dimand, 2010, 'The diagram of the Solow Swan growth model', in M. Blaug and P. Lloyd (eds), *Famous Figures and Diagrams in Economics*, Cheltenham: Edward Elgar, 426–31.

Swan, T. W. 1956, 'Economic Growth and Capital Accumulation', *Economic Record*, 32(63): 334–61.

Swan, T. W. 1963a, 'Longer run problems of the balance of payments', in H. W. Arndt and W. M. Corden (eds), *The Australian Economy*, Sydney: Cheshire.

Swan, T. W. 1963b, 'Wilfred Edward Graham Salter: 1929–63', *Economic Record* 39(88): 486–7.

Tay, F. 2007, *125 Years of Economic Studies at Canterbury, New Zealand*, Christchurch: University of Canterbury.

Watt, R. D. 1955, *The Romance of the Australian Land Industries*, Melbourne: Angus & Robertson.

Weber, E, J. 2011, 'Wilfred E. G. Salter: the merits of a classical economics education', *History of Economics Review*, 54: 111–30.

Wells, G. 2011. 'Quiet Alf', *Agenda*, 18(1): 101–6.

Whitehead, D. 1973, *Stagflation and Wages Policy in Australia*, Melbourne: Longman.

Williams, B. R. 1965, 'Economics in Australian universities', *The Australian University*, 1(3): 308–18.

Williams, R. (ed.), 2009, *Balanced Growth: A History of the Department of Economics, University of Melbourne*, Melbourne: Australian Scholarly.

8   The flowering of Australasian economics

Their ways are not our ways, therefore they are a weird mob.

Nino Culotta, *They're a Weird Mob* (1957)

Introduction

The 1960s was a decade of growth and maturity for the economics profession in Australasia. There were more universities, more economics students, more economists to teach them and more journals to publish their research in. Following the recommendations of the 1957 Murray Report of the Committee on Australian Universities, the Commonwealth government provided funding for the creation of new universities which, together with a generous Commonwealth Scholarship Scheme for undergraduates, ensured that demand for new places matched the incipient supply. In New Zealand the 1959 Hughes Parry Report made similar recommendations, namely that universities played a significant role in social and economic nation-building. The Final Report spoke about the need for 'more economists', reflecting the fact that the ubiquitous Frank Holmes was a member of the Committee.

Expansion and exuberance

Nine new universities were established in Australia during the 1960s: La Trobe, Monash, Murdoch, Flinders, University of New South Wales (UNSW), Macquarie, Wollongong, Griffith and Newcastle. Across the Tasman, the University of New Zealand was dissolved in 1961, with the four constituent colleges becoming universities in their own right. A new university, Waikato, was established on the North Island at Hamilton, while the two agricultural colleges at Massey and Lincoln would eventually become universities.

It was Monash, though, which everyone was talking about. Jonathan Pincus, who went to Monash in the 1960s as a tutor, recalled that 'everyone wanted to be there' and that the Faculty was 'a really fired-up group of people' making for 'a very exciting department'. Much of the foundation for Monash's success was laid by Donald Cochrane, the Dean of the Faculty of Economics and Politics from

1961–81. He set out to make Monash a pacesetter in the fields of economics and quantitative economics in Australia. His Faculty grew quickly from 57 students in 1961 to 1,400 in 1968, making it the largest in Australia and larger, in fact, than the LSE (Davison and Murphy, 2012, 71). Michael Schneider, a lecturer at Monash in the 1960s, recalls that one of the discussions in the tea room was whether accounting should be offered as a subject at university; Cochrane was in favour of it.[1]

In a sign of things to come, Monash announced the first Chair in Econometrics in 1968, with Alan Powell, as foundation Professor, now regarded as 'the main founder of econometrics in Australia'. A graduate of Sydney and Chicago, he had been recruited to Monash by his old mentor, Fred Gruen. Cochrane wanted the brightest students 'to master the mysteries of computers and programming' (Williams and Snape, 1999, 1). One of Powell's students was Peter Dixon, who would become one of Australia's most innovative creators of economic modelling (Davison and Murphy, 2012, 72). By 1970 what had become known as 'Monash economics' was the leading economics faculty in Australia.

Meanwhile, the ANU was at last living up to its aspirations and turning out its first batch of Economics PhDs. One of the earliest of the group, Clem Tisdell completed his doctoral requirements by publishing articles in leading journals, including *Econometrica*. Eventually, his PhD thesis, 'Price uncertainty, production and profit', was published by Princeton University Press in 1968. According to one reviewer, it was largely a work in mathematical economic analysis rather than theory. In time, Tisdell would become Australia's most prolific economist, with journal articles ranging across applications of microeconomics and also making contributions in ecological, resource economics and environmental economics (Lodewijks, 2007a). Warren Hogan, a New Zealander, undertook a doctorate on growth theory with reference to capital depreciation and replacement. He detected a flaw in Robert Solow's work on technical progress, which led to an exchange with the future Nobel Prize winner (Lodewijks, 2007b, 453).

The 1960s saw a substantial increase in the number of students studying economics in Australasia. Some 50,000 students would graduate in economics between 1947 and 1986 compared with just 5,000 between 1916 and 1947 (Butlin, 1987). Between 1960 and 1980 the number of economics graduates from Australian universities increased ten-fold. Interestingly the degree regimen became 'more technical and specialised... Americanised and more attuned to rational maximising behaviour. Increasingly this training seemed to prefer efficiency to humanity' (ibid., 2). There would be another expansion in economics education in the mid-1980s commensurate with a more sustainable way to fund higher education.

So popular was the subject that publishers soon commissioned Australian adaptions of leading economic textbooks such as Samuelson or Lipsey. Australasia found itself another industry, textbooks. In this regard the local adaption of Samuelson's *Economics* in 1970 by two Flinders University economists, Keith Hancock and Bob Wallace, was certainly the most successful ever in Australia (Millmow, 2011). The two donated most of the royalties to their department. Hancock was the Foundation Chair of Economics at Flinders, where his department was situated within the School of Social Sciences rather than with business and commerce. Hancock and Wallace's adaption of Samuelson was extremely comprehensive, suiting Australian economic conditions and institutions as well as involving a substantial rewriting of Samuelson's prose to suit the local audience. They were confident enough to put special emphasis on issues specific to the Australian economy such as capital inflow, tariffs, arbitration and wages policy. There was also some coverage given to the contributions of Australian economists. When Samuelson paid a visit to Australia, he left his two Australian collaborators blushing with the remark: 'Just as Hegel said that he had not fully understood Hegelian philosophy until he read the French translation so I am led to believe that I will not understand Samuelson's *Economics* until I read the Australian version' (cited in Millmow, 2011, 555). Despite the praise, Hancock and Wallace doubted Samuelson ever read the Australian version. The next major undertaking in adapting a best-selling text for Australian students came a decade later, when two La Trobe University economists, Paul Langley and Dennis Mahoney, retitled Richard Lipsey's work *Positive Economics for Australian Students*. The relative success of the Samuelson text did, however, contribute to the adulteration of Keynesian ideas in that it replaced the Canadian economist Lorie Tarshis's text, which was an authentic rendition of Keynes's aggregate demand–aggregate supply (AD–AS) approach. Bottling that frustration was Keith Frearson, a post-Keynesian who, having encountered Samuelson at a Cambridge cocktail party, blurted out 'One cannot read the tenth edition of "Economics" without vomiting.'[2]

Adelaide, which was regarded as the spiritual home of Keynesianism in Australia, produced the textbook *Economic Activity* (1967). The text, which sprang from Peter Karmel's lecture notes to Adelaide students, rendered a rigorous introduction to Keynes. Harcourt and Wallace, the other two authors, then finessed the lectures into an attractive text published by Cambridge University Press. This book drew upon Australian experience for illustration of the Keynesian argument. It was described as a good introduction to post-Keynesian economics (King, 2002). For example, in explaining inflation it introduced mark-up pricing such that both halves of economics came together. The book was an international success, being used in Italy and Cambridge, where Harcourt lectured from it.

In a conference dinner speech celebrating his own career, Joe Isaac captured the zeitgeist of the 1960s.[3] The Great Depression and the Second World War, he argued, meant an active role for government in economic management. It meant that the scourge of mass unemployment had been solved. Greater income equality was an accepted part of economic policy. The Australian economics profession accepted, too, the idea of competitive markets, but not exclusively; sometimes markets did not operate mechanically, market failure could result when confronted by concentrations of power or ignorance. Australian economists took a pragmatic view of intervention on a case-by-case basis. Lastly, Australian economists believed their discipline was a force for good with economic growth fashionably regarded as a panacea for all material needs. Concurrent with this greater professionalism was the completion of a major report on the Australian economy to which we now turn.

Report of the Vernon Committee of Economic Enquiry

In 1963 the Menzies Government established a Commission of Economic Enquiry into the long-run prospects of the Australian economy after it had stumbled into a recession two years earlier. This was, as Max Corden shrewdly observed, typical of the Australian political habit to propose a committee of inquiry, usually staffed by economists, to deal with economic issues. Some of these inquiries did lead to change; for example, three major inquiries into the financial system undertaken in 1937, 1981 and 1997 led to major changes in the Australian financial and banking system (Edwards and Valentine, 1998). The 1981 Campbell Report into the Australian Financial System recommended the deregulation of controls upon the banking system. It drew upon considerable economics expertise, including Tom Valentine (who acted as Research Consultant), Michael Porter and Fred Argy (who acted as Secretary to the Committee). It was a report of some consequence since, just five years later, the deregulation of the Australian financial system, including the floating of the dollar, had occurred. The 1965 Vernon Report, as it became known, had indeed recommended a full-scale study of the monetary system that would become the template for the Campbell Report. Agricultural economists, however, might beg to differ about the effectiveness of inquiries and reports in terms of the power of direct lobbying (Campbell, 1985).

The Vernon Report was not to be anywhere as successful as the Campbell Report, even though it could claim to be the most exhaustive survey ever undertaken of the Australian economy. There were 14 terms of reference attached to the brief, but the theme that overshadowed it was the 'brooding pessimism' about the balance of payments. The Final Report became a minor best-seller. The businessman James Vernon was Chair, with John Crawford as deputy. Karmel was the only other economist on the Committee and his influence informed the Report. The importance of the Vernon Report was that it embraced the main themes of Australian economics, namely wages, the external account, the tariff and economic growth, which was given major attention. A line in the opening pages summed up the Committee's desiderata: 'growth endows the community with a sense of vigour and social purpose' (Vernon *et al.*, 1965, 28). Indeed, achieving a high rate of economic growth was the *sine qua non* of economic policy. This meant finding the savings to lift the investment rate for the whole economy. The Report also made recommendations such as greater scrutiny of development projects in Northern Australia, encouraging more women to enter the workforce and that Australia join the OECD.

The Committee made use of the macro-econometric model of the Australian economy developed by John Nevile. The first of a new generation of Australian economists, Nevile had received his postgraduate training at Berkeley and enjoyed a Rockefeller Foundation stint at Harvard. With an acknowledgement to Swan's model of the economy in 1943, Nevile has been since regarded as the 'father' of macro-econometric modelling in Australia (Milbourne, 2001, 225); his econometric model, comprising 18 equations, made its appearance in 1962. It had a distinctly Keynesian orientation, focusing on the efficacy of fiscal policy in dealing with endogenously driven business cycles. The Nevile model inspired Australian economists within the Federal Treasury and the Reserve Bank to begin work developing their own models of the economy (Lodewijks, 1994, 21). Besides educating Australian economics students on the nuances of fiscal policy, Nevile provided the mathematics necessary to underpin the instability principle in Roy Harrod's model of economic growth.

Most of the recommendations in the Vernon Report were ignored, mostly because, as Arndt (1968, 114) recalled, Australian economic conditions had improved. In a speech to Parliament in September 1965, Prime Minister Robert Menzies spurned the Report, not least for its focus upon economic nationalism and quasi-planning. He particularly mocked the idea of establishing an Advisory Council on Economic Growth as 'rule by technocrats' or 'government by economists'. Indeed, Australians have never warmed to the idea of systematic economic and social planning, even in subtle form.

By contrast and in passing, Wellington was far more interested in what Arndt called the *mystique de plan* and had established a number of quangos, including a Monetary and Economic Council with Frank Holmes as its first Chair. In 1962 Holmes felt there was an urgency for long-term indicative planning to help in the struggle for new exports and new markets. The Council was described as an independent, 'economic watchdog' issuing reports on the country's economic development. Bruce Ross and Bryan Philpott (1970) built a 16-sector macroeconomic projection model for the National Development Conference, another quango, which set output targets for all the major sectors of the economy.

Many years later, in 1977, the Muldoon Government established the New Zealand Planning Council which, apart from being independent, was given the broad ambit of advising the government on planning for the economic, social and cultural development of the country. Holmes was again made Foundation Chair of the Planning Council, which was charged with issuing regular reports and assessing government policy. The new body absorbed the Monetary and Economic Council and, within it, an economic monitoring group to conduct independent economic commentary. The Planning Council began to adopt a more market-orientated approach to economic policy, which irritated Muldoon. That was not hard to do. Gary Hawke described Muldoon as 'an inveterate meddler, an overconfident, self-proclaimed economic manager with a demagogic streak' (cited in Bassett and Bassett, 2006, 75). One economic journalist, Paddy McGuinness, wrote that Muldoon ruled by 'bullying and fear', with the New Zealand economy 'laden down with restrictions, licensing quotas, permits, subsidies, tariffs, instructions and threats from the government' (cited in ibid., 104). Muldoon was happy to invoke the goal of economic stabilisation to justify further meddling. That aside, most New Zealand economists in 1980 agreed that planning had been useful for the economy (O'Dea, 1981).

In Australia, Downing, Arndt and Karmel were upset at Menzies's dismissal of the Vernon Report even before it had been publically released – especially since it was perceived that this response had been strongly influenced by the Federal Treasury. In Karmel's case it would mark his last formal contribution to Australian economics as he took up an offer of becoming Vice Chancellor of the new Flinders University in Adelaide and, following on from that, the same post at the ANU. He described his change of career with the disclaimer, 'I'm no great shakes as a scholar. I just like planning and organizing.'[4]

Downing was particularly incensed at the misrepresentations of the Report, particularly the idea that economists would make policy outside the parliamentary system. He told Arthur Smithies that Menzies's speech,

> really had to be heard to be believed as reading it cannot reproduce the tone in which it was delivered. The Government has done its best to kill it stone-dead before it reaches the public. There is a strong feeling about that the Government's hatchet men had done a fairly good job with financial journalists in getting them to take an adverse view of the Report. My own feeling is that, of course, there are things to be argued about and doubted in the Report but it is obviously worth the most serious consideration now and in the future.[5]

Arndt suggested the idea to Karmel of an academic review of the Report's findings. Karmel liked the idea and divulged the projected table of contents of the Report so that the editors could quickly arrange for contributors.[6] Both an American-based (Smithies) and a British economist (Brian Reddaway) were recruited; interestingly, no one was sought from New Zealand.

In March 1966 the *Record* published a symposium on the Vernon Report with over a dozen economists contributing. Copies were sent to every Federal politician. Downing was heartened to hear from one colleague, 'I think the special number is a success and, although uneven in parts, does credit to our colleagues and to the maturity of economics in Australia.'[7] While the contributors agreed that the Report was a monumental work and likely to be the focus of attention for some years, there was sharp criticism of it. Professor Lydall (1966) of Adelaide criticised the Report's projections for its 'simplemindedness', especially the method by which a 5 per cent growth rate was obtained. The Committee's concerns about capital inflow as well as the purported rise in foreign ownership, and the corresponding flow of profits and dividends transferred abroad, turned out 'to be a figment of the imagination fed by an error of statistical manipulation' (Perkins, 1966, 119). Perkins was dismissive of arguments that foreign investment undermined Australian economic sovereignty. He reminded his colleagues that curtailing inward foreign investment simply meant a suppression of living standards and a greater effort required at generating foreign exchange. Reddaway

(1966) was equally aghast at the Report's protectionist stance and Corden was not overly impressed by the work done on the tariff.

The Committee did, at least, derive a new measure of the cost of protection in the form of a subsidy equivalent. It suggested that the import-competing sector laboured under a 30 per cent cost disability due to an over-valued exchange rate. This warranted tariffs having a benchmark level of 30 per cent (Corden, 1968, 27). However, this was an open invitation for rent-seeking. In a major advance, the Committee proposed the effective rate of protection, which Corden (1963) had perfected, as the true measure of the impact of protection on resource allocation. Corden argued that this aspect was the only truly worthwhile achievement of the Vernon Report.

Overall, the Report aged rather badly. Apart from its recondite views about foreign investment, its obsession with export pessimism meant that the rural and mining sectors were overlooked in favour of manufacturing. All this was presented, moreover, on the cusp of Australia beginning a period of large-scale mineral developments that would generate more export income and free Australia from the external constraint. Notions of export pessimism were scattered to the winds.

Menzies's rejection of the Vernon Report should not have surprised Australian economists. Three years earlier, Melville had resigned from his chairmanship of the Tariff Board because of the government's opposition to a more sober and logical approach to protection (Jones, 2016, 186). Melville's changing views on tariff reform were well captured in his 1967 Giblin Lecture in which he contrasted the Vernon Report on protection with the Brigden Report. Melville (1967) noted how both Reports were beset by the blight of trade pessimism, which he now felt no longer held; instead, there were growing trade opportunities in Asia for Australia's basket of commodities, which now including minerals. Melville felt that, in some cases, tariffs were now actually reducing Australian living standards. Further evidence of the Australian government's reluctance to expose assistance levels to scrutiny was demonstrated when the Australian Deputy Prime Minister John McEwan, one of the great proponents of 'protection-all-round', declared that 'Australia would only ever join the OECD over my dead body' (Carroll and Kellow, 2012, 516). However, even before McEwan left public office Australia was negotiating to join the OECD. And, to add insult to injury, Melville's replacement at the Tariff Board was Alf Rattigan, who was not the tame public servant that McEwan had mistaken him to be (Powell, 2000).

1966 and all that

A turning point in Australasian economics came in 1966. It had nothing to do with decimal currency being introduced in Australia on 14 February or the collapse in wool prices that jolted the New Zealand economy. Rather, it had to do with economic journals.

In Wellington, the Association of Economists unveiled their house journal, unimaginatively entitled, *New Zealand Economic Papers* (*NZEP*). It was long in the making; as early as 1946 New Zealand economists had spoken of having their own journal. One issue a year was published over the next two decades, even though the advertised intention was for two issues per year. The problem was simply that the editors were not 'deluged with copy' (Holmes, 2011, 50). In fact, the paucity of quality submissions continued for some time (Buckle and Creedy, 2016, 8). The founding editor, Frank Holmes, did not envisage any conflict with the *Record*, though, naturally enough, some local branches of the Economic Society soon decided that they should channel their support to the home-grown journal. But it went further than this: by 1974, only two branches of the Economic Society existed in New Zealand, Christchurch and Auckland; by 1982 Christchurch was the last redoubt. Membership of the Society, which had been 300 in 1970, fell to 100 just two years later (Scott, 1990, 58). The Wellington Branch, which had been the largest and most active, together with the Waikato Branch, moved to disassociate itself completely from the Economic Society of Australia and New Zealand. This rump reincarnated itself as the Economic Society of New Zealand (Inc.) in May 1975. The proceedings and the agenda resembled, however, more a business club than a gathering of economists. Fewer and fewer economists spoke at the bi-monthly meetings and, with the marked decrease in the publication and dissemination of economic material, it soon folded. In 1982, the Central Council of the Economic Society formally moved to drop New Zealand from its title. Ironically, this occurred when both countries were about to sign a Closer Economic Relations (CER) protocol.

The alienation of the New Zealand branches was exacerbated by the distance factor; the Central Council always met in Australia, with the New Zealand branches struggling to send representatives over. Another irritant was the capitation fees levied to finance the *Record*. By the 1960s these fees amounted to over 60 per cent of a New Zealand member's annual dues. The estrangement, too, might have also something to do with the poor representation by New Zealand academics in the *Record*. Over the period 1961–5 just 13 articles by New Zealand academics were published, with five of those having being commissioned on the state of the New Zealand economy (Buckle and Creedy, 2016, 7). The number of genuine research articles by New Zealanders over this period amounted to just 4 per cent of all articles drawn from 20 issues. In 1974 there were just three articles in the *Record* by New Zealanders. Overall, the drop in New Zealand authorship in the *Record* had fallen from a respectable 18.7 per cent in 1945–9 to 4.9 per cent by 1970–4 (Groenewegen, 1997, 71). The truth is that New Zealand-based economists quickly took to their new journal, having been, by far, the leading contributors to the *NZEP* over its 50-year history (Buckle and Creedy, 2016, 36). That said, the *NZEP* has not, judging from citation counts, produced any truly outstanding papers in the economics literature.[8] Nor, for that matter, did it attract the most prestigious members of the profession until the new millennium. At the outset, the journal's editorial policy was to focus upon aspects of New Zealand economics and economic history, but this focus was not always met. One editor, Gary Hawke, noticed a decline in discursive articles on the New Zealand economy and a tendency towards more quantitative and theoretical papers.

He was concerned that this would alienate some members of the Association and asked, therefore, for 'more high quality non-mathematical papers discussing trends and policies in the New Zealand economy' (Holmes, 2011, 7). This was, of course, a refrain familiar to the management involved with the *Record*. However, the editors of the *NZEP* had a far easier time, compared with those of the *Record*, since it was a journal mostly for professional economists.

In 1966 the *Record* celebrated its 100th issue and an article was commissioned in recognition of it. Downing might have felt some confidence, since the *Record* was among the first group of economic journals selected for indexing in the new *Journal of Economic Abstracts*, the forerunner to the *Journal of Economic Literature* (Scott, 1990, 36). Syd Butlin undertook the appraisal; the end result, according to the editors was, though, a 'sad, perverse piece'.[9] Butlin noted, for instance, that the *Record* was now a professional economics journal with 'an extraordinary heterogeneity of contributions', but there were 'depressingly few citations in overseas journals' to articles that had appeared in the *Record* (Butlin, 1966, 515). Too many of the articles in the journal, he noted, concerned themselves with the 'minutiae' of making small contributions to overseas work. Butlin (ibid., 38) saw 'a good deal of dabbling and dilettantism and contributions... more interested in exhibiting virtuosity in technique than in solving real problems'. While acknowledging the works of Swan and Corden, *inter alia*, Butlin echoed Clark's point that only a few economists in every generation can hope to make significant theoretical contributions to the subject. On that note, he colourfully referred to 'an air of decadence around Australian economics', with too many practitioners unprepared to invest the time and effort in making pathbreaking research (ibid., 516). Lastly, Butlin noted, too, how the journal, the house organ of the Economic Society, enjoyed 'comparative financial security', but only by dint of its membership and capitation fees – even though many of the members no longer read it. This arrangement only partly protected the journal from everyday reality; in 1967 it was reported that the *Record* had made a loss. Butlin inflicted further hurt by acknowledging that the journal sometimes accepted inferior copy simply because it was the only local means of dissemination. Put another way, Downing implicitly had to guarantee publication to an ageing professoriate not familiar with modern economic theory (Brown, 2001, 180; Arndt, 1976, 295). Prior to 1973, half of the manuscripts submitted to the *Record* were published. It fell to one third in 1973, compared with one fifth for the *American Economic Review*. In concluding, Butlin looked forward to Issue No. 200, entrusting that when that time came the *Record* would have modified its editorial policy and coverage to play its part 'reviving' Australian economics.

In a sense the *Record*'s position as the only generalist economics journal within Australasia had already prompted some action. Another economics journal had arrived on the scene in 1962. *Australian Economic Papers* (*AEP*) was affiliated with Adelaide University and, a few years later, Flinders University; these were two universities with young and vigorous Economic departments. Like the *Record*, *AEP* would be funded mostly by subscribers, supplemented by a small amount of university support. It was the brainchild of Hugh Hudson, who regarded the

Record as something of a closed shop. Hudson had been a promising doctoral student at Cambridge; Nicholas Kaldor and Joan Robinson had regarded him as the best of the Australian students in the 1950s. Returning to a position at Adelaide, he imagined the new journal to be something like an Australian version of the *Review of Economic Studies* (Harcourt, 2015, 255). It was a timely initiative when the ranks of Australian university economists were expanding. More theoretically orientated than the *Record*, *AEP* quickly established itself and proved to be more complementary than competitive to the older journal. While it would attract proportionally more foreign authorship, in a strikingly marked way, than the *Record*, it also provided the outlet for young Australian economists to make their mark (Groenewegen and McFarlane, 1990, 178). Under the fruitful editorship of Geoff Harcourt at Adelaide and Keith Hancock at Flinders, the journal, in its heyday, adopted a pluralist, cosmopolitan approach (Millmow and Tuck, 2014). Post-Keynesian articles were published alongside neoclassical offerings (King, 2002, 142). Harcourt used his marvellous ability to network to attract articles from eminent economists such as Joan Robinson and Harry Johnson.

In the debut issue, Nevile laid out his first attempt at building a Keynesian econometric model of the Australian economy; this was three years ahead of an equivalent attempt by Blyth on the New Zealand economy. It would, in time, remove much of the guesswork from macroeconomic policy (Milbourne, 2001, 225). Bob Wallace and Karmel's paper 'Credit creation in a multi-bank system' (1962) highlighted the fallacy of the now fashionable practice of using a representative agent to analyse economic behaviour.

In Australia greater university funding to handle the influx of students meant there was more time for academic research. These were the salad days for Australian economics. The Australian political scientist and economist Hugh Stretton joked that when Menzies increased funding to universities it led to a period of American salaries, British intellectual freedom and Australian study leave for local academics. There were more outlets for research with the *Record* publishing four issues a year. By 1970 there were five generalist economics journals being published in Australia, as well as several field journals; New Zealand could only muster *NZEP*. By this time, Australasian economists were also beginning to publish internationally, having realised, as Butlin alluded to in his survey, that the *Record* was not necessarily the best forum in which to place one's work.

Going international

With the professionalisation of the economics fraternity in both Australia and New Zealand, economists in the 1960s began to make their presence known in international economic journals, writing on less parochial matters. Sometimes Australasian issues were brought to the attention of a wider audience. For example, two Australasian economists, Frank Horner and Ian McDougall, writing separately in overseas journals, noted that primary producing countries such as Australia could expand the volume of exports without ruining their markets. Two high-profile Australian economists, Corden and Harcourt, published widely, but were to take up prestigious appointments abroad, at Oxford and Cambridge respectively; Harcourt was the only Australian economist ever to have teaching posts within the Cambridge Faculty.

In 1966 Corden published 'The structure of a tariff system and the effective protective rate' in the *Journal of Political Economy*. Corden now took a multi-product general equilibrium approach to the cost of protection, being far more illustrative of the economy-wide effect of protection. He has long regarded it as his best and most original work. While Corden had published in British journals earlier in his career, he knew that – in Australia, at least – what really mattered was the influence that academic research had on economic policy. In this regard, Corden contributed a total of 14 articles overall to the *Record*, most of them with a policy focus, which influenced a growing perception among policy-makers that Australia had to engage in tariff reform. The Tariff Board use of academic expertise, especially Corden's work, suggested that the acceptance of effective rates of protection 'must surely be one of the quickest movements of theory into practice in the history of Australian economics' (Webb, 1987, 357). The other significant article published during Corden's return to Australia was one demonstrating his prowess with diagrams and his ability as an expositor. Using Meade and Swan as his guide, he illustrated the conditions necessary to attain internal and external balance by using expenditure-switching and expenditure-changing policies. Corden's (1960) paper, well used as a teaching device, had been influenced by Swan's diagram, which was still not in the public domain. Another paper in that same vein, written while Corden was at the ANU, analysed recent developments in the theory of international trade from 1949–63, and was published by Princeton University. Corden believed this paper, written in a non-technical style, was sufficiently influential in helping him succeed Roy Harrod as Nuffield Reader in International Economics at Oxford. Corden would join another Australian at Oxford, the economic historian Max Hartwell, who was famous for a debate with Eric Hobsbawm over whether industrialisation had improved the material wellbeing of the English working classes. While Corden completed his work on the Australian tariff he retained an affection for Australia and always intended to return home.

Geoff Harcourt, on a two-year sojourn at Cambridge as a lecturer in Economics during the early 1960s, was of the same inclination. Earlier, as a doctoral student at Cambridge during the 1950s, he had, together with another Australian Keith Frearson, been captivated by Joan Robinson's *The Accumulation of Capital* (1956). Two New Zealand economists were there at the time. Malcolm Fisher, who had gone to Cambridge in 1950, steered well clear of the ruckus within the Faculty, working under Richard Stone on estimating household decisions on savings and consumption functions before shifting into labour supply behaviour.[10] Also removed from the theory wars at Cambridge was his countryman, Conrad Blyth, who undertook a PhD on Austrian perspectives on the theory of capital. That interest sprang from his association with Austrian economist Harro Bernardelli, who was based at Otago. Blyth would publish on capital theory in

Econometrica and also on American post-war business cycles before returning home to head up the NZIER.

Harcourt's research interests were on the Sraffa–Robinson tradition of post-Keynesianism, with the focus upon growth, accumulation and distribution. His doctoral work concentrated on the effect of 'financial prudence', namely, the writing down of assets ahead of physical user cost in oligopolistic industries. One of his earliest theoretical efforts, a paper on 'A two sector model of the distribution of income and the level of employment in the short run' (1965), published in the *Record*, was mostly overlooked. His undergraduate thesis at Melbourne pointed to a subsequent interest in the micro-foundations of macroeconomics – that is, where the firm is the basic unit of analysis and institutions matter. Harcourt's work during the 1960s was focused on developing Salter's idea of choice of technique and biases in production functions.

Besides informing readers of the *Record* about Sraffa, Harcourt would become the grand interpreter of the capital debates raging between the two Cambridges. In a 'career-changing' moment, he was invited by Mark Perlman, editor of the *Journal of Economic Literature*, to write a survey article on the controversy. The survey went to the core of the plausibility of neoclassical economic analysis. Sometimes Harcourt used the *AEP* as a platform to field contending views on the capital debates and distribution theory; for instance, Yew-Kwang Ng (1974), from UNE, wrote a defence of the marginal productivity doctrine. Today, the capital debates are seen by some in the economics profession as 'a waste of time' (Gram and Harcourt, 2015). They stemmed from Joan Robinson posing some awkward questions about the meaning of capital, its role in the production function and its influence on the distribution of income. The debates also intended to show that equilibrium was not really an effective teaching device for analysing the processes of capitalist accumulation and growth. After reading Harcourt's 1969 survey article, Terence Hutchinson told him that he could not see any 'probable operational relevance from this analysis'.[11]

In the 1960s and 1970s capital and growth theory was a major dividing line between the two contending schools of economic thought. The Cambridge approach to economics, which Harcourt articulated, placed great emphasis on the complexities of the real world and was sceptical about the ability of markets to clear. This approach recognised that individual and collective actions were shaped by institutions and by political and social forces, with the result that the picture of the world was less defined, but also less distorted, than the neoclassical vision. The neoclassical economists did concede some ground, with Christopher Bliss admitting that their 'theory of capital accumulation has no clear, or even intended, connection with economic reality' (cited in Gram and Harcourt, 2015). An Adelaide colleague, the English-born Neil Laing, with a Cambridge first in economics, made a good sparring partner since he mostly took the orthodox side on the capital debates. The two protagonists edited a volume of readings on capital and growth (Harcourt and Laing, 1971). Now almost a forgotten figure, Laing made contributions to methodology and repudiated the Friedman–Phelps line about inflationary expectations.

The expansion of the new universities augured well for the making of a new generation of locally trained economists, many of whom could undertake their doctorates without travelling further afield. Some technically trained New Zealand economists like Colin Simkin, Warren Hogan and Stephen Turnovsky moved to Australia to take up lucrative appointments just as their predecessors had done. Turnovsky was a prestigious appointment, having graduated first class in mathematics at Victoria before turning to economics.

While many Australasian economists still headed overseas to undertake their doctorates, American universities were now proving to be more glamorous than their English counterparts. In some cases Australian economists such as Pincus were warned 'Don't go to England. It's a terrible place to do economics. Go to America!'[12] Pincus duly went off to Stanford to write what would be a prize-winning dissertation on the political economy of tariff formation in the United States. His classmates there included another Australian, Michael Porter, undertaking research on exchange rate determination and the American, Arthur Laffer. One evening, Pincus was talking to the other two about his theory of the qualitative relationship between the revenue yield, and the rate of tax. To illustrate this he drew a diagram of a pregnant human belly on the board arguing that when the tax rate was zero so was the revenue. As the rate rose so did the revenue, he posited, adding that there was some tax rate above which the revenue was again zero; in between, at the umbilicus, the revenue was at a maximum. Laffer was amazed at the insight, but Pincus told him that it was well-known proposition understood by finance ministers for centuries. Laffer would later popularise the curve and, in Australia at least, would acknowledge that the foundation of the concept lay with Pincus.[13]

For Harcourt, the capital controversy had a long afterglow. When the NSW Branch of the Economic Society celebrated its 50th anniversary in 1975, it invited him to give the Jubilee Oration. He appropriately chose as his topic the significance of the Cambridge debates in capital theory and their social implications.[14] In Victoria, 200 economists gathered to celebrate the 50th anniversary of the Society, but the showpiece event was the relatively tame offering given by Jocelyn Howlett on the results of a pilot study on 'What do economists do?' Meanwhile, Harcourt would soon have another debate to engage him, involving something much more practical, Australian macroeconomic policy.

Conclusion

The 1960s marked the start of the long boom in economics education in Australasia. The *Record* celebrated a milestone, but with a lukewarm audit, while the New Zealanders felt bold enough to launch their own journal. A detailed examination of the Australian economy was summarily dismissed while New Zealand continued to toy with indicative planning. This decade also marked the turning point when economists would begin to gravitate towards North America rather than Britain to complete their education.

Notes

1 Schneider Transcript, paper given at the 29th History of Economics Thought Society of Australia Conference, Melbourne, July 2016.
2 Hatch to Harcourt 25/10/1973, Harcourt Papers, UA.
3 After dinner speech, 4/12/1997, Isaac Papers, UMA.
4 'Don with an orderly mind', *Canberra Times*, 16 March 1966.
5 Downing to Smithies 20/10/65, ESA, UMA.
6 Arndt to Downing 10/9/1964, Downing Papers, UMA.
7 Lydall to Downing, April 1966 ESA, UMA.
8 As of October 2016, the highest-cited paper in NZEP was 'Sheepskin effects and the returns to education in New Zealand: do they differ by ethnic groups?' by John Gibson of Waikato University, published in 2000.
9 Arndt to Downing 13/11/1966, Arndt Papers, NLA.
10 Malcolm Fisher Oral Transcript, UNSW Archive.
11 Hutchinson to Harcourt 24/7/1969, Harcourt Papers, UA.
12 Pincus Oral Transcript, NLA.
13 Communication with the author, July 2016.
14 J. F. Collins to Harcourt 2/10/1975, Harcourt Papers, UA.

References

Arndt, H. W. 1968, *A Small Rich Industrial Country*, Melbourne: Cheshire.
Arndt, H. W. (1976), 'R. I. Downing: economist and social reformer', *Economic Record*, 52(3): 281–301.
Bassett M. and J. Bassett, 2006, *Roderick Deane: His Life and Times*, Wellington: Viking.
Brown, N. 2001, *Richard Downing: Economics, Advocacy and Social Reform in Australia*, Melbourne: Melbourne University Press.
Buckle, R. A. and J. Creedy, 2016, 'Fifty years of New Zealand economic papers; 1966–2015', *New Zealand Economic Papers*, 50(3): 234–60.
Butlin, N. G. 1987, 'Human or inhuman capital? The economics profession 1917–1987', *ANU Working Papers in Economic History*, No. 91.
Butlin, S. J. 1966, 'The hundredth record', *Economic Record*, 42(100): 508–19.
Campbell, K. O. 1985, 'Changing institutions, processes and issues in the formulation of Australian agricultural policy', *Australian Journal of Agricultural Economics*, 29(3): 210–24.
Carroll, P. and A. Kellow, 2012, 'Fifty years of the OECD and forty years of Australian membership', *Australian Journal of Politics and History*, 58(4): 512–25.
Corden, W. M. 1960, 'The geometric representation of policies to attain internal and external balance', *Review of Economic Studies*, 28(1): 1–22.
Corden, W. M. 1962, 'The logic of Australian tariff policy', *Economic Papers*, 15: 38–46.
Corden, W. M. 1963, 'The tariff', in A. Hunter (ed.), *The Economics of Australian Industry*, Melbourne: Melbourne University Press, 174–214.
Corden, W. M. 1966, 'The structure of a tariff system and the effective protective rate', *Journal of Political Economy*, 74: 221–37.
Corden, W. M. 1968, *Australian Economic Policy Discussion: A Survey*, Melbourne: Melbourne University Press.
Culotta, N. 1957, *They're a Weird Mob*, Sydney: Ure Smith.
Davison, G. and K. Murphy, 2012, *University Unlimited: The Monash Story*, Melbourne: Allen and Unwin.

Edwards, V. and T. Valentine, 1998, 'From Napier to Wallis: six decades of financial inquiries', *Economic Record*, 74(226): 297–312.

Gram, H. and G. C. Harcourt, 2015, 'Joan Robinson and MIT', CUNY Working Paper No 9.

Groenewegen, P. 1997, 'The Australian experience', in A. W. Coats (ed.), *The Post 1945 Internationalization of Economics*, Durham, NC: Duke University Press, 61–79.

Groenewegen, P. and B. McFarlane, 1990, *A History of Australian Economic Thought*, London: Routledge.

Harcourt, G. C, 1965, 'A two sector model of the distribution of income and the level of employment in the short run', *Economic Record*, 41(93): 103–17.

Harcourt, G. C. 2015, 'AEP and me: a short(ish) memoir', *Australian Economic Papers*: 255–9.

Harcourt, G. C. and N. F. Laing (eds), 1971, *Capital and Growth: Selected Readings*, London: Penguin.

Holmes, F. W. (assisted by L. Bayliss and J. McFaul), 2011, *The New Zealand Association of Economists: Memories of its Early Years*, Wellington: New Zealand Association of Economists.

Jones, E. 2016, 'Australian trade liberalisation policy: the Industries Assistance Commission and the Productivity Commission', *Economic and Labour Relations Review*, 27(2): 181–98.

King, J. E. 2002, *A History of Post Keynesian Economics since 1936*, Cheltenham: Edward Elgar.

Lodewijks, J. 1994, 'A conversation with John Nevile', in B. B. Rao (ed.), *Essays in Economics*, Sydney: Centre for Applied Economic Research: 15–34.

Lodewijks, J. 2007a, 'A conversation with Clem Tisdell', *Economic Analysis and Policy*, 37(2): 119–30.

Lodewijks, J. 2007b, 'A conversation with Warren Hogan', *Economic Record*, 83(263): 446–60.

Lydall, H. 1966. 'The economy as a whole: policies for growth', *Economic Record*, 42(1): 149–68.

Melville, L. G. 1967, 'Tariff policy', *Economic Record*, 43(102): 193–208.

Milbourne, R. 2001, 'Distinguished Fellow of the Economic Society of Australia, 2000: John Warwick Nevile', *Economic Record*, 77(238): 225–7.

Millmow, A. J. 2011, 'The green and gold revolution: the story behind the Australian adaption of Paul Samuelson's classic textbook', *Economic Papers*, 30(4): 546–56.

Millmow, A. J. and J. Tuck, 2014, 'A tale of two Australian economics journals', *Economic Papers*, 33(2): 186–201.

O'Dea, D. J. 1981, 'A survey of what economists think: recent research results', Wellington; NZIER: 41–6.

Perkins, J. O. N. 1966, 'Overseas investment, trade policy and balance of payments', *Economic Record*, 42(1): 105–28.

Powell, A. A. 2000, 'Probity before pragmatism: Alf Rattigan 1911–2000', *Economic Record*, 76(234): 301–4.

Reddaway, W. B. 1966, 'An English economist's view', *Economic Record*, 46(1): 13–26.

Ross, B. J. and B. P. Philpott, 1970, 'Indicative economic planning with a sixteen sector projection model of the New Zealand economy', *Australian Economic Papers*, 9(14): 108–26.

Scott, R. H. 1990, *The Economic Society of Australia: Its History 1925–1985*, Melbourne: Economic Society of Australia.

Vernon, J., Crawford, J. G., Karmel, P. H., Molesworth, D. G. and Myer, K. B. 1965, *Report of the Committee of Economic Enquiry*, Canberra: Commonwealth of Australia.

Wallace, R. H. and P. H. Karmel, 1962, 'Credit creation in a multi-bank system', *Australian Economic Papers*, 1: 95–108.

Webb, R. 1987, 'Review of G. A. Rattigan "Industry Assistance: The Inside Story"', *Economic Record*, 63(183): 356–8.

Williams, R. and R. H. Snape, 1999, 'Distinguished Fellow of the Economic Society of Australia, 1998: Professor Alan Powell', *Economic Record*, 75(228): 1–4.

Yew-Kwang Ng 1974, 'The neoclassical and neo Marxist–Keynesian theories of income distribution: a non-Cambridge contribution to the Cambridge controversy in capital theory', *Australian Economic Papers*, 13(22): 123–32.

9   Hardly the Age of Aquarius

Introduction

The speaker for the dinner at the 1974 Conference of Economics held in Canberra was Bob Hawke, then the President of ACTU. Irrespective of his station, it was a strange choice since Hawke had, in a public lecture, scolded economists the year before for their opposition to price controls to combat inflation. His draft notes for the occasion were marked 'not usual after dinner speech'. Scribbled on the back of his speech notes was Joan Robinson's famous dictum about the need to study economics to avoid being deceived by economists. That night, an irascible Hawke relished the opportunity to harangue economists about the inflation rate, which had been forecast to reach 20 per cent. He referred to Deputy Prime Minister, Jim Cairns's suggestion that the process of metric conversion be deferred as a means of containing inflation. Yet there was another element of metric conversion that interested Hawke, namely the conversion of economists to econometrics. This conversion, Hawke argued, had the effects of making economists more aloof and worsened the communication problems between experts and laymen. Economists, he feared, would retreat into the unreal world of esoteric models. Hawke was being unrealistic; it was a vain hope that Australian economists would turn away from modelling. The period was marked by great activity in building economy-wide models in which Australian economists were to be pioneers. Indeed, designing an anti-inflation policy would become predominantly econometric in character, with the RBA and the Federal Treasury contributing their own models of the Australian economy. In the mid-1960s a whole econometric cottage industry had sprung up dedicated to fitting a Phillips curve for Australian data (Hagger, 1978, 136). While the audience at the Conference dinner found Hawke's vitriolic attack on econometrics gratuitous, the rest of his speech made reasonable sense. He suggested that inflation was tearing at the fabric of society and proposed an anti-inflationary economic policy including his preference for a prices–incomes policy reached by consensus between unions and business.[1] In his earlier, more militant days, Hawke would argue since it was not their economic system the workers were entitled to exert their industrial muscle as much as they could.

The economic backdrop to that conference was surreal; inflation and unemployment were rising sharply and economists scurried to explain what had gone wrong. Paul Samuelson saw it as a sea-change in economic philosophy: 'We live in the age after Keynes. Electorates all over the world have eaten of the fruit of the tree of modern economics knowledge, and there is no going back to an earlier age' (cited in Silk, 1974, 21). Many economists were confounded by events, in despair about the value of economics and trying to gather their wits. To others, it was year zero, time to fashion a new wisdom for a new age. In Australia there was a bewildering turbulence of events in the first five years of the 1970s with one Federal Treasurer Bill Snedden stating that 'what we need is a new Keynes'. To take one Australian statistic: between 1973 and 1974 average male wages rose by 27 per cent, female wages by 33 per cent. The year after, unemployment reached 5 per cent and inflation hit 20 per cent. Simply put, Australia and New Zealand were facing their worst peacetime economic crisis since 1930. However, there was some good news. Economists were not only being listened to, but also given more econometric firepower to embellish their models about the economy. Moreover, Australia had joined the OECD in 1971, meaning that all aspects of its economic policy now bore greater international scrutiny, even if the commentary was written by Australian Treasury officials.

This chapter looks at how the Australasian economics profession responded to these unprecedented challenges. Stagflation certainly presented new research opportunities on macroeconomic stabilisation and Australian economists were advantaged, at least, as in 1930, by having at their disposal a centralised wage determination system which might be moulded to contain cost inflation. Visiting Australia in 1969, Henry Phelps Brown (1969, 121) commented upon how fortunate Australia was in already having the makings of an incomes policy with its centralised wage determination system. Moreover, it could also work under floating exchange rates. Ironically, he made these comments when Australian unions and firms were engaging in direct bargaining. It was an age when the Australasian economics profession underwent a sea-change in economic philosophy, with the Keynesian consensus and pluralist approach to economics being replaced by an often intolerant neoclassical paradigm. There was also a marked rise in the use of econometric models for both macroeconomic policy and analysing trade and structural change issues.

Reflecting that change in philosophy were some dramatic changes within the *Record*, with, in effect, a replacement of the old editorial guard. The journal became more internationally respectable, although this drew a vociferous local reaction. Students, too, a few years earlier began voicing dissent over the economics being offered at some universities, especially at Sydney University (Butler *et al.*, 2009).

The permissive economy

In 1969 Richard Downing, once described as the 'Australian economist of his generation', told a gathering of economics teachers that it was hard to see how the post-war story of comparatively rapid economic growth could be subverted (Brown, 2001, 247). The following year he told businessmen that the trade cycle had been subdued by macroeconomic policy and that all that was needed to complement productivity and efficiency was 'a popular enthusiasm for economic growth' (ibid., 248). Downing had spoken too soon; by the end of the decade inflation began to accelerate and was stronger than for most other countries. Wages rose faster than productivity, meaning that the share of company profits in GDP began to shrink. Wage inflation was accelerating with the Commonwealth Conciliation and Arbitration Commission seemingly powerless to deal with it. In 1971 the Labor Party placed on its party platform a commitment promoting collective bargaining. Keith Hancock (1971) feared that it was the end of Australian wage policy. Essentially, workers, advantaged by expansionary economic conditions, were winning pay rises through collective bargaining. Nevile (1971, 308) detected an inflationary psychology emerging. La Trobe University economist Donald Whitehead was perhaps the first Australian economist to use the term 'stagflation' in describing the Australian situation at the start of the 1970s. Ronald Henderson of the Melbourne Institute also drew attention to stagflation and proffered incomes policies as a first solution (Williams, 2012, 41). Following the collapse of the Bretton Woods Agreement in 1973, the US dollar was no longer convertible into gold and became a source of inflationary pressure. Two years earlier, in 1971 a group of Australian economic professors, led by Trevor Swan, concerned at the undervalued exchange rate, wrote an open letter urging that the Australian currency be revalued in a bid to stop the huge inflow of capital and, more importantly, inflationary pressures from building.

However, the Australian government turned a deaf ear to these arguments. Downing admitted that the pursuit of full employment came at the cost of inflation and his 'worry' was that if no way could be found to control inflation within one or two decades, 'You'll get a backlash, you'll get a revolution of some sort, either from the Right or the Left, and my worry would be that in a country like Australia that revolution is likely to come from the Right' (cited in Brown, 2001, 252). While he was no longer the leading source of economic advice, Downing was prophetic in assessing how long it would take to kill the inflation dragon, but incorrect in anticipating political revolution. His only solution was to require that the public moderate its demands, perhaps by indexing wages to the inflation rate, warning of the economic and political consequences if they did not.

Downing blamed the process of an escalating increase in average earnings on 'not only a much more permissive society but also a permissive economy. The old inhibitions – the fear of unemployment, the fear of loss of markets which supplied some of the rigidities which could curb inflation are crumbling' (cited in ibid., 255). His old colleague, Joe Isaac, who in 1974 was invited to join the Conciliation and Arbitration Commission as a Deputy President, could only agree. He saw the wages explosion first-hand and concluded that decentralised wage bargaining had been a disaster. With occupational and industry differentials being tied together, the pursuit by one sector of a wage rise would trigger action for comparative wage justice by other sectors, with the result that wage increases soon outpaced productivity (Isaac and King, 2015, 68–9).

New Zealand was experiencing similar wage pressures as both employers' groups and unions moved towards direct bargaining in defiance of the Arbitration Court (Maloney and Savage, 1996, 175). With Australian and New Zealand industry protected from international competition, and fiscal and monetary policy mostly accommodative, there was little resistance from employers to wage hikes. Isaac quickly saw that the only solution was to restore central authority on competing income claims. In both Australia and New Zealand big hikes in real wage outcomes were the product of economic boom and accommodating economic policy. In both countries relative income shares were being skewed in favour of labour.

The arrival of a serious inflation problem and the drift of the Phillips curve from its moorings was a boon for macroeconomics research. Simkin (1972) undertook one of the first surveys to identify whether inflation in Australasia was demand-pull or cost-push derived, concluding the latter. However, this finding was disputed by Jonson, who blamed it on foreign inflation and the corollary that Australia had a fixed exchange rate. Simkin was pessimistic about the effectiveness of wage and price controls in both countries, preferring instead fiscal policy, cutting tariffs, imposing punitive taxes on companies that ignored wage restraint and, lastly, having the public sector set an example in wage deals.

In this period, student activism was challenging conventional wisdom – particularly about what was taught in university economics courses. Monash was the first campus to erupt, becoming a hotbed of student radicalism in the late 1960s. There was considerable challenge to the 'bourgeois economics' taught there. Fred Gruen, a classic liberal at heart, sought to unravel the student grievances (Chapman, 1998, 188). He attempted to tell his charges that mainstream economics had plenty to offer, including a useful set of tools, yet his attempt at bridge-building was rebuffed by both students and staff alike. Monash had been the first Australian economics department to become internationally focused and to invite a large number of American-trained economists to visit the department. It also became Chicago-focused, even if there were not many staff who had studied there. One man who had was Ross Parish, who arrived at Monash in 1973. He had an interest in what was then called 'the new political economy' microeconomic analysis, with a particular emphasis on applying the basic principles of price and resource allocation theory to other spheres of economic and social activity like non-price rationing mechanisms, the environment, product promotion, student finance and consumerist issues (Hogbin, 2007). Parish's long-term goal was to make the Monash department aware of the power of free markets to promote human welfare by creating incentives for producers to satisfy the demands of consumers. In this it can be said that he largely succeeded since the agitation by students at Monash about mainstream economics ebbed away.

It was a different story at the University of Sydney, where there was student unrest over the revamped economics degree being introduced. Hitherto, the only controversy within the Sydney Faculty had been about abandoning evening lectures in 1966, a move which disadvantaged part-time students. One of them, Max Walsh, the future journalist, wrote a letter to the press saying the move was a misallocation of resources and contrary to the spirit of the democratisation of economics. The newly appointed Vice Chancellor, Bruce Williams, a Melbourne-trained economist, triggered the revolt by asking Colin Simkin and his old Auckland-trained colleague, Warren Hogan, to revise and modernise the economics degree. They wanted to introduce more mathematical and quantification techniques into the curricula and rid it of its hitherto descriptive bias (Lodewijks, 2007). This induced a counter-reaction from some of the staff, led by Frank Stilwell and Ted Wheelwright, *inter alia*, to introduce a course in radical economics in 1973. One of their colleagues, Geelum Simpson-Lee, also objected to the changes because he believed they signi-fied the emergence of the 'go-getting academic' or 'publish or perish' ethic (Groenewegen, 2009, 118).

The subsequent feud was to result in a long acrimonious campaign and would fracture the Sydney Faculty between opposing factions. Peter Groenewegen (2009, 159), a member for more than 50 years, concluded that the department 'suffered enormously' from the feud, which ran, intermittently, for more than three decades – a conclusion shared by one of the disputants, Hogan (Lodewijks, 2007, 450). One upshot, though, was the creation of a political economy course which commenced in 1975 (Butler *et al.*, 2009). In his survey of Australian economics, Withers (1978, 76) noted that 'relatively little substantive analytical work' emanated from that department, a view shared by Groenewegen (1979) in his survey of radical economics. Groenewegen was a trifle optimistic in his prediction that mainstream economists would have to accept the legitimacy of radical economics as a legitimate field of study.

Fighting stagflation

When the Whitlam Labor Government was elected to office at the end of 1972 it inherited an economy beset by incipient stagflation; the previous Coalition Government had refused to revalue the currency with the result that the country was awash with liquidity. Wage inflation had also been allowed to run unchecked, as well as expansionary budgets which fuelled inflationary pressures. The prob-lem was later exacerbated when Commonwealth public servants were granted huge pay rises.

For all its faults, the Whitlam Government had a reformist agenda and adopted a technocratic approach to economic policy, hiring university economists to serve on various committees and advisory bodies. Gough Whitlam was the first Australian leader to bring economic rationalist policies to the fore. Whitlam had Fred Gruen, Brian Brogan and Trevor Swan within earshot as advisors. He had a group of academic economists seconded to the Priorities Review Staff, which was part of the Prime Minister's Department. It was, in effect, Australia's first economics think-tank. This body, aimed at providing advice on the economic feasibility of various ministerial proposals, existed from mid-1973 until 1975. Two leading members were Austin Holmes and Michael Porter, both seconded from the RBA. While the Priorities Review Staff was only in existence for two years it was influential in suggesting changing Australian economic policy towards a more outward and competitive setting.

Whitlam held that protection had been in place for too long and to the detri-ment of Australian living standards. Anticipating this major change in protection policy, the Whitlam Government therefore replaced the Tariff Board with a new economic agency that would be staffed by economists. John Crawford assisted in crafting a new bill which would culminate in the establishment of the Industries Assistance Commission in 1974. Whitlam equipped the Commission with powers of independent enquiry on all matters of assistance to Australian industries, though the government was not obliged to act upon its recommendations (Powell, 2000, 303). The IAC was provided with a wider framework of enquiry into assistance levels and charged with improving the efficiency with which the nation's productive resources were used. Whitlam appointed Rattigan as its first Chairman (Jones, 2016, 184). Bob Gregory noted the Commission's 'intellectual apparatus' was built upon Corden's analytical approach to assistance.[2] The IAC philosophy was to draw a close association between economic growth and structural change and, in turn, that structural change was a means by which resources would shift from less to more productive pursuits; protection inhibited structural change and therefore growth. The role of this independent, impartial source of advice in grappling with the phrase 'economic and efficient' and pushing the case for tariff reform cannot be underplayed (Lloyd, 2006, 311).

Monash supplied so many of the personnel going to advisory positions during the Whitlam years that Frearson jibed: 'Everyone at Monash seems to be policy-making in some way or another. I think the time is ripe for an article on the "The Economic Effect of Economists"!'[3] ANU economists, too, provided the Australian government with expertise. These were the glory days for Australian economics as economists saw their research work materialise into practical policy.

The Minister for Social Security in the Whitlam Government, Bill Hayden, guest speaker at the 1975 ANZAAS Conference, joked that Australia's new universal health care system, Medibank,

> was coming along since its conception. On July 1 (1975) two doctors who have been working very hard on the delivery will be presiding over its birth and they will be very proud. They are two economists, but real doctors, Scotton and Deeble.
>
> Wallace, 1976, 253

What Hayden did not say, though, was that the two originators, Richard Scotton and John Deeble, whose original paper had been entitled 'A scheme of universal insurance' (1968), felt that patients should pay a modest fee for receiving medical service. Scotton and Deeble, both from the Melbourne Institute, were also introducing Australian economists to the brand new province of health economics (Norman, 2007, 9–10). It would be another growth area in Australian economics and, as such, Gruen commissioned two Adelaide economists, David Richardson and Bob Wallace, to review it for his *Surveys of Australian Economics*. They reported that there had, so far, been a relatively meagre contribution by Australian economists. The next audit of the area by Jane Hall (2003, 70) could report significant contributions on the demand for health insurance, the comparative efficiency of public and private health providers, welfare assessment, and economic evaluation.

The Whitlam Government made a good start in dealing with the external maladjustment by appreciating the currency and then, in 1973, implementing an across-the-board tariff cut – an action that Australian authorities had previously considered as politically impracticable. Gruen was, together with Rattigan and others, a proponent behind Australia's 25 per cent general tariff cut in 1973 as a counter-inflationary measure which aimed to increase aggregate supply and improve resource allocation (Lloyd, 1978, 258). This decision was less than a year after the OECD survey on Australia concluded that a uniform cut in tariffs was 'impracticable' (Sheehan, 1973, 650). The *Australian Financial Review* hailed it as a 'watershed in Australian economic history' and 'as a vast step towards economic maturity' (Sheehan *et al.*, 1979). When it came to dealing with stagflation, university economists had been vocal in commenting on a referendum on a prices and incomes policy (Sheehan, 1973). Indeed, Australian economists had 'reached an impressive consensus' on a 'package' of prices and incomes policy made workable by 'carrots and sticks' (Hagger, 1978, 175). This was a way of anchoring the Phillips curve such that notions of a trade-off between inflation and unemployment might still be valid (Hagger, 1978).

The RBA, ambitious for a new approaches to tackling persistent inflation, had invited the English monetarist economist Michael Parkin, from the University of Manchester, to be its visiting Research Fellow for 1973. To the research economists within the bank, such as Peter Jonson, Parkin was a breath of fresh air; he announced with certitude that restricting money supply growth would overcome inflation (Guttmann, 2005, 78). His confidence was in stark contrast to the more guarded university economists (ibid., 17). In the 1973 Giblin lecture given at the ANZAAS conference, Parkin argued that the Phillips curve relationship to which the bank had first been exposed in 1959, had broken down. This development would not have surprised most university economists since they had already been sceptical of the curve's applicability to Australian conditions (Beggs, 2015). Parkin invoked Giblin in his argument that the money supply should be controlled by a central bank free from government control (Guttmann, 2005, 19). He pushed for monetary targeting and for the RBA to be given the goal of price stability. He promoted tailoring the rate of money supply growth to output growth. While the RBA did not adopt monetarism it did adopt Parkin's inflationary expectations argument, one with which it had been sympathetic since the era of Coombs (1959). Overall, Parkin's monetarist views were not taken seriously by mainstream Australian economists (Beggs, 2015). The monetary economist David Rowan, who earlier had been Foundation Professor of Economics at UNSW, warned Downing that it would be a mistake 'to let him influence policy directly' and to persuade the RBA 'to get some more sensible English visitors'.[4]

Most Australian economists were still Keynesians and, like Rowan, confirmed in their belief in the efficacy of fiscal policy (Nevile and Stammer, 1972, 9). While macroeconomic policy up to that point had been 'impressive', Australia's growth record had been less striking. Monetarism was still something of a 'minority taste' (Hughes, 1980, 44). The exceptions included economists such as Warren Hogan, Michael Porter, Ian Sharpe and Johannes Juttner. Even Bruce

McFarlane had, in an earlier guise, attributed the blame for cost-push inflation to excessive monetary expansion by the RBA, drawing support from the University of Queensland's John Gifford in his lonely quest in the area, well before Milton Friedman introduced Monetarism to Australia. Across the Tasman, Frank Holmes (1972) could write in a textbook: 'We do not appear to have in New Zealand any simple, straight-forward or enduring relationship between money, near moneys and the GNP,' though he did concede that money mattered.

Two groups of Australian economists proposed policy packages to deal with inflation. The Melbourne Plan, put out by the Melbourne Institute – essentially Duncan Ironmonger and Peter Sheehan – was a radical progression from past policies. The Institute resisted the idea of disinflation, calling, instead, for a policy of cooperation and consensus. It proposed a prices and income accord between the Federal government, unions and employers. There would be modest fiscal stimulus to reinforce the agreement (Williams, 2012, 41), with wages to be indexed by 3 per cent per annum (Guttmann, 2005, 21). Companies would be penalised if they granted wage rises in excess of the 3 per cent. The Institute was also prepared to countenance money supply targets in its policy mix.

The 1974 Adelaide Plan, prepared by Harcourt and Russell, together with two Flinders University economists, Philip Bentley and Barry Hughes, focused on wages and price-setting practices as a gradual way of reducing inflation while maintaining high levels of employment and external balance. The four economists knew that wage indexation could exacerbate inflation by disrupting existing relativities and perpetuating inflation. The Plan recommended that company tax be used as a means to penalise companies which earned profits above a set level and that wage increases above a permissible level be disallowed as a tax deduction. This would be an effective form of price control but was adjudged unworkable. The Plan also mooted the possibility of swapping income tax reductions for a reduced National Wage increase. These expedients did have some consequence; the year after, in April 1975, Australia moved to adopt full wage indexation as a means to control wages growth, much to the consternation of the Treasury which feared that this would lock in real wages. The Conciliation and Arbitration Commission had been reluctant to take the move as a means of restraining wages but, not long after, employers and unions abided by it.

Meanwhile, two eminent economists, Joan Robinson from Cambridge, and Milton Friedman from Chicago, visited Australia in 1975 to propose measures to deal with stagflation and to discuss the academic status of the Phillips curve. Its originator, Bill Phillips, had only recently died in Auckland, worn out by ill-health and dismayed at how his life-long quest to find the recipe for economic stability had fallen foul of the identification problem in econometric modelling. Lionel Robbins told Conrad Blyth that Phillips was 'one of the real geniuses of his age'.[5] It was entirely coincidental that Robinson and Friedman were visiting Australia in 1975, the jubilee year of the Economic Society. Robinson had spent a term at Monash but had found it too rabidly neoclassical for her liking. Like the ANU, Monash was becoming trenchantly libertarian; with pockets of resistance in the Department of Economics being increasingly marginalised. Robinson gave lectures to capacity audiences at both Monash and Sydney University on the 'The Economic Crisis'. Her view of inflation was to regard the autonomous wages push that lay behind it as a reflection of the struggle between labour and capital, and about relative income shares. Meanwhile, Friedman's short visit was instigated and financed by Sydney stockbrokers who wanted him to air his views on the monetarist cure for inflation.

Both economists appeared on Australian television, reflecting the public's interest in inflation. Friedman proved the better performer with the positive message that there was a solution available. When asked about the importance of the control of the money supply in curing inflation, Robinson replied 'Well, very much less than Milton Friedman makes out!'[6] Friedman's great attraction was that inflation was caused by the quantity of money 'so you don't have to face this deep and divisive political problem, and that is why people clutch at straws'.[7] Robinson accused Friedman of engaging in a sleight of hand by deliberately confusing the money supply with money expenditure so as to recommend deflationary economic policy.[8]

Some Australian economists were – initially, at least – 'overawed' by Friedman's presence. Ironmonger, the Deputy Director of the Keynesian-inclined Melbourne Institute, conceded that 'a lot of what you are saying is agreeing with a lot of what we're saying. A lot of sense is being said which is comfort to us' (Hughes, 1980, 43). Two of the old guard, Arndt and Clark, bewildered by towering inflation, sided with Friedman (Coleman *et al.*, 2007, 170). Clark was amused to see a communist trade union leader take heart from Friedman's suggestion that unions did not cause inflation (Clark, 1980, 42).

Other Australian economists were not swept away by Friedman's media blitz; Barry Hughes criticised Friedman's 'pretty pictures' of correlations between money supply growth and GDP (Hagger, 1978). Indeed, one Australian economist had, the year before, mocked Friedman's work. Owen Covick, a young English economist who had taken up an appointment at Flinders, parodied Friedman's definitive article on a restatement of the quantity theory of money by swapping money for drink; Covick came up with 'The quantity theory of drink: a restatement' (1974).[9] It was a witty send-up, Covick having been exposed to ardent monetarists Parkin and David Laidler at the University of Essex. Covick had sent the paper to the *Journal of Political Economy* (*JPE*) to be considered for the Miscellany section, but the editors did not share his humour so he redirected it to the *AEP*. Friedman was not amused when shown it.[10]

Ironically, it was the reformist Whitlam Government which extinguished the last embers of Keynesianism in fiscal policy. In his 1975/6 budget speech the Federal Treasurer, Bill Hayden, announced an 'inflation first' focus, proclaiming that Australia was no longer living in 'the simple Keynesian world in which some reduction in unemployment could, apparently, always be purchased at the cost of more inflation. Today it is inflation itself which is the central policy problem. More inflation simply leads to more unemployment' (cited in Guttmann, 2005).[11] The words were written, however, by John Stone, a senior Treasury official. This puritan approach was later described as the first 'economic rationalist' budget

(Hughes, 1980). The year after a new conservative government introduced Australia to money supply targeting, despite this experiment being incompatible with a fixed exchange rate and interest rate controls – one reason why the RBA remained 'mildly agnostic' about it (Schedvin, 1992, 518). The Federal Treasury was primarily behind monetary targeting, seeing it as a new anti-inflationary tool and the means to build up confidence with the financial markets and general public. Corden pinpointed the two problems with the new practice, namely 'controllability' and 'predictability' (Cornish, 2016, 339). Undeterred the Treasury would soon play a leading role in introducing another economic dogma during this period, one that would split asunder the Australian economics profession.

The real wage overhang debate and the fight against stagflation

The Australian experience

In May 1975 Richard Snape, Chairman of the Economics Department at Monash, gave a graduation address defending mainstream economics against the 'stirring' words of dissidents. Essentially a non-mathematical economist, specialising in trade and applied microeconomics, Snape had been recruited to Monash in 1962 to work with Fred Gruen on estimating the demand for Australia's rural exports, and then, later, with Alan Powell to study the effects of protection in Australia. Snape, together with Corden, Powell and Gruen, lent public support in the 1960s to the Tariff Board Chairman Alf Rattigan in his campaign to develop a rational economic framework for tariff-making (Banks *et al.*, 2003).

Snape had undertaken his doctorate at the LSE under Basil Yamey. His analysis of the international sugar industry was regarded as a definitive work on protection in agricultural markets. Part of it was quickly published in *Economica*, which inspired Harry Johnson, in turn, to contribute an article entitled: 'Sugar protection and the export earnings of less developed countries: variations on a theme by R. H. Snape' (1966). Snape's name was in the title of a journal article almost before he had a publication to his name; few economists could boast such a dream start to their academic career as this.

Not adverse to public advocacy, Snape was soon defending the profession's incoherent responses to stagflation. It was unfair to attack mainstream economics, he held, when there was 'no politically feasible solution to the problem at the moment', but coyly added, 'however I hazard the view that political feasibility will be changed by the process of inflation'.[12] Snape was correctly reading the political tea-leaves, predicting that Australian economic policy would shortly succumb to the monetarist agenda of defusing cost-push inflation by disinflation. He was also alluding to what would later become known as the real wage overhang thesis, positing that Australian real wages had grown faster than labour productivity. Snape would become a strong supporter of that thesis and, while serving on the Treasurer's Panel of Economists, his advice proved particularly influential with Treasury officials (Banks *et al.*, 2003). Yet Snape did not envisage how the real wage issue would divide the Australian economics community. This view was not popular with Keynesians, who blamed unemployment on demand restraint.

The senior Treasury official Stone said the imbalance between real wages and productivity 'was the central and most difficult problem facing the Australian economy' (cited in Whitwell, 1986, 217). The Treasury argued that this imbalance induced employers to substitute capital for labour (Hughes, 1980); higher real wages also depressed the profit share, which acted negatively upon investment spending. The Treasury was adamant that the solution to unemployment was money wage restraint; but it wanted more than just for the wage and profit shares to be restored, arguing that there needed to be a correction to bring about a sustained rise in business investment (Whitwell, 1986, 223). The Treasury's sights were focused on the wage determination system, especially the role of the Arbitration Commission, being especially scathing of quarterly wage indexation which had been introduced in 1975. This arrangement impeded the so-called natural order of things, the Treasury argued, in the sense that the imbalance could not be corrected by market forces. Given this philosophical outlook, the Treasury grew sceptical of the effectiveness of stabilisation measures and, in 1978, rejected Keynesian ideas outright (ibid., 225). Stone, who was Secretary of the Treasury (1979–84), moved to embrace a rational expectations view of economic policy; budget deficits and fiscal stimuli would be counterproductive and have a negative effect on expectations; economic agents were now more sensitive to price changes. The Treasury emphasis was on the government setting a good example by reining in the budget deficit and exhibiting fiscal restraint (ibid., 226–7).

Some economists followed in this wake by agreeing that the huge wage hikes in 1974/5 had a grievous impact upon job creation. Certainly, the job losses in the 1974 recession were disproportionately large against the fall of output; this suggested that the real wage impact was crucial (ibid., 222). University economists began to focus upon the measurement of real wage costs. The overhang argument was appealing to those with a marginal productivity outlook but its method of application was jarring. Quite simply, a cut in real wages was seen as a precondition of recovery rather than a consequence of recovery. The idea was that a real wage cut would assist employment directly, by encouraging employers to hire labour, and indirectly, by restoring profits and thus investment (ibid., 23).

To other economists, though, the Treasury's argument was reminiscent of the 1930s. Lamenting 'Will we ever learn?', Colin Clark drew comparisons with 1931, when the Arbitration Court had attempted unsuccessfully to cut real wages – an experiment which Keynes made note of in the *General Theory*. Clark (1979, 6) said that the idea of a real wage cut prompting industry to increase its output was 'a resuscitation of Say's Law'. Some economists, such as Harcourt (2001, 19), strongly criticised moves within the Australian professoriate, orchestrated by Arndt, to adopt some of the Paish–Phillips doctrine of developing slack in the economy to dampen money wage increases.

Bob Gregory, the ANU labour economist, and Ron Duncan, an economist in the public service, suggested that the higher unemployment was due to an upsurge in labour supply which had pushed up the labour participation rate. It had nothing to do with how employers were using labour in the production process (Hughes, 1980, 164–5). Even more damning of the real wage overhang argument was the fact that female employment had risen, despite their relative wages rising markedly more than for men (Gruen, 1979; Whitehead, 1977). Gregory recollected how personally rewarding this work had been in identifying how institutional and legal arrangements were just as important as economic factors in shaping labour market outcomes.[13]

In his address as President of the Economic Society of Australia and New Zealand given at the 1978 Conference of Economists, Max Corden (1979) sought to encapsulate the wage debate among Australian economists. He explained that, while he was still a Keynesian in the short run, centralised wage determination could result in unemployment caused by unions pushing wages up too high. Corden called it 'union voluntary unemployment', or classical unemployment, reminding those who advocated 'popular Keynesianism' that the level of real wages mattered even with a prior expansion in demand. Corden's speech was a significant intervention in changing attitudes about the importance of real wages. Simply put, if real wages were inflexible downwards and the economy was subject to decreasing returns, then expansionary economic policy would only increase the rate of inflation, not real output. Paddy McGuinness said the address marked the 'gradual conversion' of the Australian economics profession to the proposition that real wages had to fall temporarily if unemployment was to fall (cited in Millmow, 2011, 93). Dixon *et al.* (1979), Higgins (1979), Holmes (1979) and Snape (1979) were all of the view that real wages had become a significant constraint on employment.

Corden was also pessimistic about the possibility of wage restraint under economic recovery. He was scathing of the Melbourne Institute's view, issued in the *Australian Economic Review*, arguing that it was time for a 'mighty' Keynesian response. Corden replied that it would result in a 'mighty' balance of payments deficit and an equally 'mighty' devaluation.[14] In a rare outburst, Swan entered into the debate, posing 'some very hard schoolboy questions' of the Melbourne Institute's prescription of expanding the budget deficit with tax cuts. Swan was worried by the size of the deficit and at how the tax cuts might feed into wages, profits and higher interest rates due to greater deficit-financing. He concluded that 'the vice of misplaced and uncosted compassion is none the less dangerous for its high-sounding virtue'.[15] Gruen's position on real wages was to suggest that a reduction was a necessary but not a sufficient condition for a reducing unemployment. There had been a change in economic circumstances, such as the external account or structural change, meaning that the real wage level necessary for near full employment may have changed. However, Gruen was not prepared to dispense with the Keynesian legacy. Neither was Whitehead (1977), who disputed the contention pushed by Corden and Snape that unemployment was more Pigovian than Keynesian in character (Corden, 1977, 30). Technically, Keynesians such as Harcourt and Whitehead felt the real wage overhang issue would dissipate because of the pro-cyclical nature of productivity accompanying reflation. Peter Sheehan *et al.* (1979), too, argued that labour productivity had been reduced by the recession and that an expansion in employment caused by an increase in aggregate demand would increase productivity and so reduce the size of the wage share.

Australian economists grew restless with the Treasury's policy of fiscal restraint and the 'fight inflation first' strategy, arguing that it was not working (Whitehead, 1977, 30). Some now turned to incomes policies and tax–wage bargains as a means of defeating stagflation. As we saw earlier, the Melbourne Institute advocated indirect tax cuts together with wage restraint, emphasising their anti-inflationary effect; unionists would maintain their real after tax incomes.

J.O.N. Perkins of Melbourne University, who composed ditties in his spare time using Gilbert and Sullivan as a reference, was, to use one of his own songs, 'the very model of a modern macro economist' (McDonald, 2016). He put forward his own plan to beat stagflation. This macroeconomic policy mix of tax reductions, cuts in government spending and tight monetary policy would result in the maintenance of an unchanged level of employment, but at a much lower level of money prices and costs due to a positive supply-side effect coupled with fewer demand pressures. Workers would not press for money wage increases if inflation was contained or if take-home pay increased by a reduction in direct taxation. Tight money would reduce cost-push pressures and give a signal to unions about the dangers of pushing for further wage rises. Perkins's mix promised that inflationary expectations would be quelled. Yet without the notion of a permanent incomes policy, Meade (1980) was not entirely convinced that Perkins had conceived the cure for stagflation. There were concerns, for instance, that this mix would only have a one-off effect unless the deal was renegotiated with unions every year. The government would soon run out of fiscal bargaining chips and have to contend with a deterioration on both its fiscal and external accounts.

Another critic, Malcolm Rimmer, reminded Perkins of the perversity of expectations. Nevile (1983, 8), too, was not entirely convinced about how much anti-inflationary effect could be generated by cutting tax rates. Using the ORANI general equilibrium model of the Australian economy, Corden and Dixon (1980) tested whether a wage restraint with tax cut bargain would deliver a 'free lunch' in the form of employment gains and a revenue neutral outcome. While, theoretically, it would, Corden remained sceptical, insisting that more employment would only come with lower real wages. Nevile, a long-time advocate of fiscal policy, also argued that the conventional policy of 'fighting inflation first' was proving ineffective. Nevile had established a Centre for Applied Economic Research at UNSW to encourage discussion on policy issues (Lodewijks, 1994, 33). Nevile posited that only an incomes policy could tame inflationary expectations, simply because he saw inflation as primarily a conflict over income shares among different groups in society and that low growth intensified that struggle. An incomes policy, he argued, would ensure that the inflationary consequences, possibly devaluation, following a fiscal stimulus would be counteracted. Buttressing Nevile's stance was research showing that rapid rises in the rate of inflation had a diabolical effect on business investment. Also unimpressed with the disinflation-ary approach, Whitehead (1977) supported Nevile's view that an incomes policy, together with reflation, was the only way to break the deadlock; however, he remained pessimistic that a workable solution could be devised without major institutional reform of the wage determination system and changes in the attitudes and militancy of union leaders. This view was a widely shared one. Colin Clark (1979) did not think that incomes policies were effective and suggested that moderate downward pressure on demand was the only antidote to breaking the inflationary spiral of prices and wages. Historically, he recalled how the inflation-ary outbreaks of 1920 and 1951 were followed by price stability after deflationary surgery (ibid., 3). Recycling his 1945 views, Clark (1975) linked inflation with excessive government expenditure, even if it was fully covered by taxation. His reasoning was that government expenditure created an immediate demand effect while the effects of taxation on private consumption are subject to considerable time lags and may not eventuate at all when tax rates become high and bite into savings. The remedy for inflation, he believed, was a large reduction in govern-ment expenditure followed by reductions in direct and indirect taxation.

The real wage debate came to a resolution when another round of wage hikes in 1981, predicated upon a coming resource boom, resulted in a marked rise in unemployment. While the rise in unemployment was a statistical aberration, as more workers became self-employed contractors, the correlation was hard to dislodge from policy-makers' minds. When the new Hawke Labor Government took office in March 1983, it was prepared to negotiate a prices and incomes policy between government and unions which went hand-in-hand with a modest Keynesianism. Harcourt and Prue Kerr had been involved in the Labor Party's 1979 National Committee of Inquiry, which formulated a new economic strategy built on post-Keynesian lines upon Labor's return to government (Hatch and Rogers, 1997). One should also acknowledge the work of Gerard Firth, who, in a pamphlet entitled 'Economic policy in 1979', described inflation as primarily a distributional phenomenon driven by the anxiety of interest groups to preserve or increase their respective shares of output. It largely anticipated what Harcourt would write two years later.[16] After being shown the pamphlet, Coombs opined that 'the only possibility for breaking the wage–price spiral is either brutal defla-tion or some form of social control'.[17] Both Joe Isaac and Keith Hancock were also pessimistic about Firth's plan.

In 1979 Harcourt had drafted an economic policy framework for a future Labor government which encompassed fixed exchange rates, a commitment to tariffs, nationalisation and a prices–incomes policy: in short, a blueprint for a small, open economy with institutional peculiarities in its product and labour markets. Harcourt's faith in these principles has never wavered, much to the astonishment of his mainstream colleagues. There were supporting adjacent measures including prices surveillance, structural reform including lower assistance and intervention-ist industry policy, but Harcourt was disappointed that his blueprint was not fully acted upon. The centrepiece of economic policy in the Hawke Labor Government was, however, the Prices and Income Accord, which, over the next eight years,

1983–91, subtly engineered a real wage decline, the largest decline in Australia during the twentieth century. Peter Sheehan of the Melbourne Institute, joint author of the Melbourne Plan, was a key influence behind this Accord. It worked because the government encouraged unions to be involved in national goals and to achieve them in an efficient and equitable way. Workers would be compensated by a 'social wage' in the form of compulsory superannuation, Medicare, education and training and the possibility of wage–tax trade-offs. Just as the Premiers' Plan arguably pulled Australia out of the Great Depression in 1931, the Accord, as a piece of economic architecture, rescued Australia from stagflation. It was so successful, in fact, that Labor politicians like Ralph Willis adamantly declared that it was their creation, not economists (Goldfinch, 1999, 8).

For Australian economists, the Prices and Incomes Accord was a useful vehicle for applied research on a range of labour and macroeconomic issues. This included issues such as wage determination, trade union membership, demographics, strike activity, absenteeism, unemployment and other labour market issues. Using the Accord as his case study, Gruen found that it succeeded because the number of groups which needed to be accommodated in the bargain were small, making it more likely that negotiators for each group could come to some agreement (Chapman, 1998, 190).

The New Zealand experience

New Zealand, too, had its own version of the real wage gap, which took hold from 1978 – as evidenced by econometric research, particularly by economists within the RBNZ. This research calculated that real wages had risen by 24 per cent while productivity had grown by 10 per cent over the period from 1969 to 1980. The culprit was the wage determination system which awarded wage raises beyond the external capacity to pay beholden as it was to upholding wage relativities, commonly known as comparative wage justice. Real wages had risen despite the New Zealand economy stagnating while a balance of payments constraint ruled out demand stimulation. The RBNZ's research on real wages was contested by Haywood and Moore (1983) among others. Like McGuinness in Australia, Easton (1990) saw the episode as involving 'a paradigmatic shift' by New Zealand economists. Before 1984 New Zealand's wages system had reverted to a centralised system where equity considerations mattered more than market pressures. The Muldoon Government broached the idea of a wage–tax trade-off with the Federation of Labour in 1982 but negotiations were unsuccessful. Moreover, the idea of wage–price controls met with a lukewarm response by local economists (O'Dea, 1981). Rebuffed, the Muldoon Government moved to implement a comprehensive incomes and prices freeze within the economy, including directors' fees, interest rates, rents and even the exchange rate. New Zealand economists, like their counterparts abroad, had a strong aversion to this expedient (ibid.). While the freeze reduced inflation, fiscal and monetary policy, together with the economy itself, were made 'hostages' of the freeze (Dalziel and Lattimore, 1996, 19).

Anticipations of a sea-change

In a move that suggested a significant change in economic strategy, Hawke appointed Ross Garnaut as his economic advisor instead of sticking with the Harcourt blueprint. A little hurt, Harcourt would later joke that Hawke followed his programme for at least a good half-hour! It was more, though, than just the symbolic passing of the torch to the younger man. While Garnaut was, like Harcourt, a social democrat, he subscribed to a different set of economic policies. His appointment signalled that it would be the ANU, not Adelaide or Melbourne University, which would play a formative part in changing the intellectual basis of Australia's trade and industry policy. That appointment signified that the Australian political elite had at last recognised that Asia's galloping industrialisation meant that protectionist and regulatory attitudes in Australia were no longer tenable. Moreover, Garnaut relished rolling up his sleeves and getting involved in policy work if he felt the government was genuine about economic reform.

Garnaut came from the RSPacS at the ANU, having undertaken a doctorate on Australia's trade with Southeast Asia (Hill, 2010, 282). As Hal Hill (ibid., 286) recalls, not many leading Australasian economists have launched their careers from Papua New Guinea (PNG). Garnaut did, advising the newly independent PNG government about developing a credible macroeconomic framework. It was while working there that Garnaut had made an early theoretic contribution by helping to devise a means of taxing the mineral wealth of a developing country without impeding production and further exploration. This came from having worked with Anthony Clunies Ross, a development economist employed at the University of PNG. This country had very wealthy deposits of copper which went mostly untaxed, so Garnaut and Clunies Ross came to the rescue by devising a system of mining taxation that would generate large revenue flow from highly profitable mines without deterring investment in marginally profitable ventures. This resource rent tax was an outstanding example of a theoretical contribution by Australian economists which found expression in a practicable form of taxation. It resulted in an article in the *Economic Journal* and the monograph, *The Taxation of Mineral Rent*.[18]

Garnaut's work on the 1979 Crawford Committee Study group on structural change had brought him to Hawke's attention. He had already written to the incoming Labor government advising them to float the dollar and to deregulate financial markets. The Hawke Government had already been forced to devalue the dollar upon taking office in March 1983. Hawke's new direction was made manifest in his Stan Kelly lecture to the Victorian Branch of the Economic Society. Hawke confirmed that protectionism had been a mistake and that Australia was now committed to a more dynamic and outward-looking economy.[19] This was recognition that the very nature of international commerce was changing with the liberalisation of controls on trade, capital and exchange rates. Most economic historians consider the floating of both the Australian dollar and the New Zealand dollar to be the most major change for either economy in the modern era. For Australia and New Zealand it meant no longer being enslaved to concerns about the current account and worrying about having sufficient foreign exchange reserves (Endres and Rogers, 2014, 74). However, it would take policy-makers some time to appreciate the new rules of the game in international commerce (Endres and Rogers, 2014).

Garnaut came from a department originally headed up by Crawford and then Arndt, which included names such as Max Corden, Helen Hughes, Peter Lloyd, Stuart Harris and Peter Drysdale. The Department's earlier focus had been on development economics and Asia; however, when Corden took over from Arndt in 1981 international economics and open economy macroeconomics became the new priority. This switch of research focus brought home the divide within the Department between the theorists and the 'muddy boots' practitioners with their field research. Corden did not think it appropriate that the RSPacS should limit itself to field studies or a particular region. Garnaut (2006, 136) conceded that Corden was the one who most influenced his approach to economic analysis, especially on trade and tariffs. Now, by a process of intellectual germination, 'beachheads of advanced scholarship in trade and development' sprang up in Adelaide, with Kym Anderson and Chris Findlay leading the way, and at the UNE, with Peter Drake and Malcolm Treadgold (ibid., 134). Monash had already gone down that road with Snape, Ian McDougall, Garry Pursell, Gary Sampson and Michael Porter leading the charge.

In the 1970s Snape, also inspired by Corden's work, had focused on the under-developed nature of Australia's exchange rate system. At that time Australia was hampered by fixed exchange rates which, with a huge capital inflow, led to monetary disorder (Porter, 1977); that is, external monetary forces were leading to domestic economic turbulence. Revaluing the currency was opposed by rural interests. Snape (1970) found the idea of flexible exchange rates attractive, given that fixed exchange rates, then under the Bretton Woods arrangements of adjust-able pegs, made easy profits for speculators. A floating currency would assist policy-makers and would reflect the development of Australia's maturing finan-cial system.[20] Porter added his weight with his portfolio balance model of the exchange rate, co-authored with the Finnish economist Peniti Kouri. It built upon his Stanford doctorate, which had enquired into 'Interest rate differentials inter-preted as behaviour towards exchange rate expectations' (Porter, 1971). However, Simkin (1974), one of the last of the old guard, had reservations about flexible exchange rates.

Serendipitously, with the election of the Labor government, Nevile (1983) had an article published in the *Record* arguing the case for fiscal stimulus, provided that a workable and effective incomes policy could be put in place. Nevile's wishes were met by an agreement between ACTU and the government with the Arbitration Commission reintroducing centralised wage determination and indexation. The Accord aimed to realign factor shares in favour of capital, discounting the real wage for domestic expansion (Mitchell, 1998). At first, economists such as Gruen and Hancock doubted that any type of incomes policy would work, given the history of union militancy in Australia. However, real wage resistance was replaced by real wage flexibility. As such, workers were assured that they would enjoy redistribution through the public sector (increases in the social wage) if they complied with money wage restraint. The fact that employment growth and a falling wage share of national income were now concurrent was further proof of the real wage overhang thesis. When a team of North American economists from the Brookings Institution, together with the ANU's Centre for Economic Policy Research, organised a forum on aspects of Australian economic policy, they sanctioned approval of the Hawke Government's mix of fiscal stimulus and incomes policy to deal with unemployment. Hughes (1985, 412) noted that this particular 'view from the north' dominated the conference proceedings because it challenged the prevailing will of the Treasury. The other key finding of the visitors was to posit that Australia was still very much a rent-seeking society (Caves and Krause, 1984, 12). The originator of that concept, Anne Krueger, was a regular visitor to Australia, particularly at Monash and the ANU. While it was a fair comment in an economy constrained by government regulations and financial repression, Australia, as we shall see, was on the cusp of change.

The rise of the economic modellers

The 1970s in Australasia was a decade marked by the arrival of highly technical computable general equilibrium (CGE) economic models. There were also econometric models on macroeconomics forecasting being developed within the Treasury and RBA, as well as academic models looking at more esoteric structural issues facing the Australian economy (Gruen, 1979, 232–5; Williams, 2012, 47–50). Gruen (1979, 234) felt that forecasting models advanced an understanding of the economy because they traced out, in a systematic and precise way, the interactions and interdependencies within the economy. One of the designers of the Treasury's model was Chris Higgins, who had studied under Lawrence Klein at the University of Pennsylvania. An economist who mixed in academic as well as policy circles, Higgins introduced the Treasury and the local economics profession to the importance of inflationary expectations, supply-side economics, financial crowding-out and the implications for economic performance of a growing public sector (Fitzgerald, 1991, 258).

In a 1977 report on *Some Issues in Structural Adjustment*, the Industries Assistance Commission dismissed the idea that structural change be suspended whenever there is high unemployment. Instead, it argued that the resulting gains from achieving allocative efficiency would provide the wherewithal for the pursuit of equity and welfare. Not many academic economists would have gone that far.

Economists, too, led by Corden, Gruen, Melville and Perkins, felt that when Australia had abundant international reserves and balance of payments surpluses conditions were ripe for lowering protection, particularly for highly assisted industries. The phenomenon of newly industrialising countries in Asia meant that the prospects for trade liberalisation for Australia looked promising. Some manufacturers were unhappy with Rattigan and his constant review of tariff assistance. One manufacturing spokesman complained that tariff policy was being 'led by the nose by theorists' with their 'arithmetical cut-off points and other fancy economic theories' (cited in Jones, 2016, 185). Hitherto, much of the windfall benefit that would follow from Australia lowering its protection levels and undertaking meaningful structural change had only been asserted, never quantified. This was all about to change.

The IAC was equipped with an applied general equilibrium econometric model called the Impact Project. This would allow the development of an analytical framework making it possible for officials to obtain an overview of the effects of policy changes, most especially changes in assistance levels (Lloyd, 1978, 274). The Impact Project was managed by Alan Powell, who was later seconded to the IAC. The model was the brainchild of Powell and Peter Dixon, the latter having undertaken a Harvard dissertation supervised by Wassily Leontief on general equilibrium, which was subsequently published by North Holland in their *Contributions to Economic Analysis* series (Dixon, 1975).

It must be noted that Powell and Dixon followed on the work by H. David Evans at Monash, who had been the first to model the general equilibrium effects of protection upon the Australian economy. His results showed that a differential tariff structure in Australia depressed output and real incomes. Peter Lloyd (1978, 274) regarded Evans's work 'as the most important single contribution' in Australian economic thought since the 1960s, while another reviewer said that he had advanced effective protection analyses 'by a couple of light years' (cited in Lloyd, 2014, 31). Following a first-class honours degree at UWA, Evans had undertaken a dissertation at Harvard in the mid-1960s on the effect of the Australian tariff upon income distribution. His supervisor, Leontief, described him 'as a real economist, not a disguised mathematician'.[21] Hired by Donald Cochrane, Evans was soon working as a senior research fellow on a Monash research project – which was led by Gruen and Powell and funded by the Australian government – preparing an econometric analysis of protection. In 1973, exhausted by his labours on that project, Evans applied for study leave to visit the Institute of Development Studies at University of Sussex and chose not to return to Australia. Meanwhile, the Monash model of protection was about to become the predecessor to something more audacious.

The Impact Project comprised four modules of computable general equilibrium modelling, one of which, ORANI, a multi-sectoral model of the Australian economy, became 'the workhorse of CGE modellers in Australia' (Williams and Snape, 1999, 3). It was used in many applications, not merely about tariff cuts and their optimal timing but also about structural change or agricultural issues and even, in one instance, the effectiveness of a 'Buy Australian' campaign (Horridge *et al.*, 1987). ORANI put to death the idea that protection positively affected employment levels. The model was a landmark in applied quantitative research into the Australian economy and its inherent features made it unique in the world of CGE modelling. It spawned a huge literature. In 1979 Dixon, Powell and Brian Parmenter published *Structural Adaptation in an Ailing Macroeconomy*, which used the ORANI model to analyse the effects on the Australian economy of various policy simulations mostly in combatting unemployment.

The book's title summed up the Australian predicament of necessity for structural change but in an unfavourable economic setting. Despite the work of Rattigan, effective rates of protection had failed to budge during the 1970s, partly because of macroeconomic factors. Indeed, some protected industries enjoyed even higher rates of protection because of quantitative import restrictions. Some economists took a dissident line about the push for lower protection, especially in a poor economic climate. Neville Norman at Melbourne emphasised that tariff reductions delayed business investment and that the assumed law of one price did not hold. Hugh Hudson (1982) suggested that those economists inclined towards free trade overlooked complications such as factor immobility, infrastructure costs, changes in asset values, the differential timing of costs and benefits and distributional income effects following a tariff change. These combined factors, he argued, pushed up the rate of discount applying to future benefits and costs with the effect of lowering the net benefit from reduced protection. Another dissident was the political economist Hugh Stretton, who, in 1999, published – after 15 rejections from publishers – an alternative economics textbook which drew some notoriety.

Meanwhile, Powell and Dixon were gathering up the glittering prizes; Powell took the Ritchie Chair at Melbourne in succession to Downing at the beginning of 1979 and Dixon was awarded a Chair at La Trobe. Interestingly, Harcourt had also applied for the Ritchie Chair but the election of Powell signalled that applied economy-wide modelling was more appreciated than post-Keynesian theory. As Harcourt observed, Melbourne felt there was more 'future' in Powell's work 'than my type of economics'.[22] The IMPACT model was relocated to Melbourne (Williams, 2012, 49); Dixon, too, would end up at Melbourne, but his appointment there, as we shall see, caused some controversy.

Harcourt was not the only one to be affected as Australian economics became more mainstream. At Monash the pluralist tradition that had once characterised the Economics Department was being snuffed out. One extreme case was that of labour economist Peter Riach, whom Joe Isaac regarded as the 'outstanding Australian exponent of income distribution theory'.[23] Riach had made significant contributions to showing, first, the Australian arrangements on wages partly governed by productivity bargaining and, second, female participation in the labour market. Feeling unappreciated at Monash, not least, because some of the units he taught were removed from the curriculum, Riach left for a position in England.

The Gregory thesis

Australia lived up to its status as the 'Lucky Country' following the OPEC oil crises of the 1970s, when its vast energy resources promised a comfortable future. Moreover, the increased cost of energy made Australia an attractive location for energy-related projects such as aluminium production. The prospect of a mineral export boom led to expectations not only of enhanced living standards, but also that Australia, finally, would be free of its external constraint. While working in the IAC as a consulting economist, Gregory, like Corden before him, learned not just the value of applying simple economics, but also how rewarding it was to dwell upon Australian economic problems. It was economic circumstances that lay behind Gregory's great discovery. During 1972–4, Australia experienced an appreciation in its real exchange rate, a balance of payments surplus despite large import flows. Gregory could see the consequences, but struggled to capture them in a model that would be easy to understand. With Australia recording rapid increases in mineral exports, he postulated that the increase in the real exchange rate would be the equivalent of an all-round tariff cut in the import-competing sectors. This was the nub of the Gregory thesis, which considered how an appreciation of the real exchange rate, brought about by the mining boom and associated capital inflow, would affect different parts of the economy – in particular, the agricultural and manufacturing sectors. It is interesting to note that, while Gregory finalised the paper in the United States, he chose not to send it to any local journals there, given that it focused on an Australian issue using Australian data. This went against the conventional practice of placing one's best research in the most prestigious journals.

The paper, eventually published in *AJAE* in 1976, was among his earliest publications; he had already published a well-received article on import demand functions in the *American Economic Review*. While the choice of journal meant that Gregory's research was overlooked by overseas audiences, in Australia it was a different story. As Coleman notes, 'the story sold itself' simply because the thesis was timely and easy to understand. One Federal politician called it the 'greatest idea since Keynes' (Coleman, 2009, 78). When the article was published, Gregory, still in the United States, found himself the subject of attention from the Australian media. He later referred to it as 'the 4 weeks I was in Parliament' (cited in Chapman, 2003, 130). Some economists pointed out that Gregory had overlooked the growth in real incomes resulting from the resource boom and that a rise in the effective real exchange rate was not axiomatic. This would also become a never-ending story since Australia was to experience another mineral export boom towards the end of the twentieth century, fuelling China's industrialisation with copious amounts of iron ore and coal.

Professionally, the article was Gregory's highest cited paper and a precursor to the literature on 'Dutch Disease' or the booming sector problem. Gregory was the first economist to see the potential implications of such resource booms. His thesis was fortified by Snape (1977), identifying what would become known as the 'resource movement effect', where the booming sector attracts labour to it because of the higher marginal product.

It was here, too, that Max Corden struck it rich in terms of citations. He had been at Oxford in the early 1970s when the prospect of North Sea oil revenue first began to register an impact on British manufacturing. Back in Canberra, Corden revisited the subject with his former student, Peter Neary, and, in 1982, they developed the classic economic model describing 'Dutch Disease'. Corden synthesised earlier work in the field to describe how the resources boom affected an economy in two ways. First, there was, as mentioned, a 'resource movement effect', as the booming sector dragged labour away from the lagging and non-tradeables services sectors of the economy. Second, there was also a 'spending effect', as a result of the revenue flowing to the booming sector. This increased demand for labour in the services sector would put pressure on the lagging tradeables sector, which would also suffer further deindustrialisation from the increase in the real exchange rate (Corden and Neary, 1982).

A little local difficulty

During the 1970s the leadership of Australasian economics departments began to place a premium on theoretical work rather than on policy analysis and applied economics. There was a greater emphasis on research capacity and achievement in selecting staff for promotion, while applicants with overseas qualifications, preferably from the United States, were also favoured. All this had implications for the *Record* and its future orientation. In May 1973 Richard Downing resigned as editor and Scott (1990, 37) records that his resignation was received with regret. Downing was praised for having raised the reputation, frequency and popularity of the journal. He had realised that it was the *Record* which was the common link holding the membership of the Society together (ibid., 39); that binding became frayed with his departure. Alan Boxer had served as joint editor with Downing since 1969 and was reluctant to continue when he heard of Downing's resignation, complaining that he 'had been left out on a limb'.[24]

Downing had taken up an appointment as Chairman of the Australian Broadcasting Commission, telling Arndt it was 'the maddest thing I have ever done, two days a week for a ten day a week job' (Brown, 2001, 267). Downing was also, at the time, President of the Australian Academy of the Social Sciences. Near the end of his editorship of the *Record*, he had been assisted by four associate editors, all from the Faculty in Melbourne. There were complaints about this from the other branches, as there had been about editorial policy. Downing continued his fine balancing act of publishing a journal that met the needs of specialist and generalist audiences. A new editorial team was assembled for the *Record*, with three joint editors, namely, Boxer and Roy Webb, both from Melbourne, and Steven Turnovsky of the ANU, as well as three other associate editors in tow. Boxer soon left, concerned that the new technical focus of the journal under Webb and Turnovsky would further alienate the broader readership.

The enlargement of the editorial team and the use of referees rather than relying on the Editorial Board underscored the new professionalism of the journal. As Scott (1990, 38) noted, this new practice was to ensure that the *Record* could maintain a place in 'the international community of professional economists'. By the mid-1970s the *Record* had become more internationalist in its content. However, this ambition set the new editors on a 'collision course' with the business community, who had an interest in applied economics relating to domestic policy issues. The old guard decided to mount one last protest. Encouraged by David Bensusan-Butt, Heinz Arndt wrote to all the branches of the Society noting how the post-Downing issues of the *Record* had become 'a publication outlet for academic producers of mathematical and econometric papers indistinguishable from similar overseas journals'.[25] He felt that the editorial change would have 'a high price to pay' in terms of lost readership and suggested that the Central Council of the Economic Society open negotiations with the editors of the *AEP* so that it would become 'the primary vehicle' for technical papers. Geoff Harcourt, who was at the time President of the Economic Society and involved with the *AEP*, remained mute on the idea. If this proposal was agreed to, the *Record* could 'revert' to the formula that Downing had established over the last 20 years. It was a vain hope, but the issue of the readability of the *Record* festered. The Central Council had established a Publications Committee to review the range, content and organisation of the *Record*. Moreover, in another concession, purely theoretical or econometric articles were to be written in such a way that their results were accessible; such articles were to include a brief introduction indicating the nature of the subject matter and a brief conclusion stating the significance of the findings, with lengthy proofs placed in an appendix. Turnovsky and Webb revealed their ambitions for the *Record* when they disapproved of a plan by the Central Council to introduce a submission fee. This was one way of dealing with the bugbear of non-academic members of the Society having to subsidise a scholarly journal. Turnovsky was concerned that the cross-elasticity of demand for a place in the *Record* was weak and that authors would take their copy elsewhere.[26] Simply put, the *Record* was not yet sufficiently established internationally to insist on a submission fee.

In 1977 the Publications Committee of the Society noted that the *Record* was one of the few internationally recognised economic journals with a substantial proportion of articles which were literary in style. The Committee wanted the *Record* to adopt the standard of analysis and sophistication of other economics journals. Following that preference, of course, would merely antagonise the broader readership. To be fair, the Committee had already moved to commission annual survey articles in areas of economic theory or analysis of topical Australasian economic issues. The NSW Branch, supported by a strong element of business economists, had already complained that many of its members found too many of the articles appearing in the journal of little interest because of their highly theoretical nature and practical irrelevance. Ultimately, some of these broke away to form their own association of business economists, echoing what the Wellington Branch of the Society had already done in 1974. The West Australian Branch of the Society suggested that membership fees should not include compulsory capitation fees to finance the *Record*. Things went from bad to worse when that Branch made noises about seceding from the Society over this issue and general feelings of isolation. Corden, the new President of the Society in 1978, made great efforts to prevent any such breach by personally attending to their grievances. The Queensland Branch had already expressed displeasure with the Society by establishing its own generalist journal *Economic Analysis and Policy* in 1970. This catered for empirically based papers on areas such as taxation reform, environmental and natural resources, government intervention and an analysis of Queensland economic problems (Duhs, 2000).

Corden again undertook to examine the readability of the *Record* by analysing the contents of the journal between 1974 and 1979 (Scott, 1990, 39). He described the conundrum as basically one of 'mathematics versus the market'. He also investigated whether the journal's content embraced Australasian economic issues. On this aspect the journal scored well, with 98 out of 186 articles on Australasian economics, though some 53 of them were deemed unreadable to the non-specialist. Interestingly, Corden noted that the *Record* had a high proportion of articles that could be described as 'pure theory' – higher, in fact, than comparable journals. He proposed three plans of action: a campaign to encourage members to support the journal; changing the contents formula to suit popular demand; and focusing upon marketing and pricing arrangements. A fourth proposal, already floated, was for the Society to put out a second journal dedicated to policy analysis. *Economic Papers* was to be the solution. It had been in existence since 1941, initially published by the NSW Branch of the Society and from 1964, put out by the Victorian and NSW Branches of the Society. It concerned itself with practical aspects of Australian economic policy, especially stabilisation and economic development, and relatively little with economic theory (Groenewegen, 1976). Corden's diplomacy kept the Australian branches of the Society in harmony at a time when the loss of the New Zealand branches was still being absorbed (Scott, 1990, 40). Another salve to the Society was the glowing success of the annual Conference of Economists, which first began in 1970. The surpluses from these conferences helped offset the cost of producing the *Record* and gave the weaker branches a financial lifeline (Millmow, 2011).[27]

Conclusion

This chapter demonstrated how Australasian economists responded to the convulsive changes in the world economy of the 1970s and early 1980s. It was an age in which the Keynesian consensus and pluralist approach of the post-war years was replaced by a more inflexible neoclassical paradigm. Concurrent with this was a marked rise in the use of econometric modelling in macroeconomic policy.

Notes

1 'Speech notes, 1974 Conference of Economists', Hawke Papers, University of South Australia Archives.
2 Gregory interview with Corden, NLA, p. 68.
3 Frearson to Harcourt 1973, Harcourt papers, UA. The fact that the economics profession was expanding in Australia while economic performance was deteriorating and the misery index was shooting upwards lent proof to Zauberman's Law (named after the LSE economist) which suggested a country's economic performance was inversely related to their reliance upon economists. It could be said, of course, that the direction of causation ran the other way, with poor performing countries turning to economists for assistance.
4 Rowan to Downing 20/10/1974, Downing Papers, UMA.
5 Robbins to Blyth 13/3/1975, Robbins Papers, LSE.
6 Monday Conference ABC-TV Transcript, 28 April 1975.

7 Ibid., p. 7.
8 Ibid., p. 4.
9 The quantity theory of drink may, in another sense, apply to the scourge of alcoholism and how it affected the research productivity of promising Australian economists. The most tragic case here is that of Ronald Hieser, who had to quit the ANU in 1963 because of his drinking. He had been supervised by Trevor Swan, who did not suffer fools. Apart from educating Bob Hawke in economics, Hieser produced a dozen theoretical articles in the *Record*, ranging from distribution theory, wage bargaining, imperfect competition, neo-Keynesian growth models to his last effort, in 1973, looking at the negative economic consequences of zero population growth. Richard Downing praised them for their outstanding quality in substance and in comparison with other contributions appearing in the *Record*.
10 Communication with Covick, 2015.
11 Over a year later the British Prime Minister James Callaghan told the 1976 Labour Party Annual Conference essentially the same thing, namely, that Keynesianism, in an inflationary environment, would only inject 'a bigger dose of inflation into the economy, followed by a higher level of unemployment'.
12 Ibid.
13 R. G. Gregory Transcript, NLA.
14 'Professor critical of analysis', *Canberra Times*, 8 August 1978.
15 'Economist prescription attacked', *Canberra Times*, 18 August 1978.
16 'Economic policy in 1979', pamphlet written in June 1977, Firth Papers, NLA.
17 Coombs to Firth 30/7/1977, Firth Papers, NLA.
18 One of Garnaut's colleagues at the ANU, Helen Hughes, had used rent theory in the early 1960s to win more income entitlement for the people of Nauru from phosphate mining (Byrne, 2005, 2).
19 The Stan Kelly lectures, which started in 1977, were in memory of a farmer who railed against the cost of protection. His son Bert became a Federal MP and wrote a weekly column in the *Australian Financial Review* called 'The modest member' highlighting the everyday deceptions and abuses of tariff protection.
20 Snape was an inspiring teacher and the Monash Economics Students Society circulated a bumper sticker which read 'Free the Exchange Rate Now!'
21 Leontief to J. D. Butchardt 7/7/1967, Evans staff file, Monash Archives.
22 Harcourt to A. Singh 2/3/1978, Harcourt Papers, UA.
23 Riach staff file, Monash University Archives
24 Boxer to Downing 31/5/1973, Downing Papers, UMA.
25 Arndt to B. Parmenter, secretary of the Victorian Branch of ESANZ, May 1975, Downing Papers, UMA.
26 Turnovsky to Harcourt 4/9/1974, Harcourt Papers, UA.
27 Notes of the publications committee, 1977 ESANZ, Harcourt Papers, UA.

References

Banks, G., K. Clements and P. Kenyon, 2003, 'Distinguished Fellow of the Economic Society: Richard Hal Snape 2002 (1936–2002)', *Economic Record*, 78(241): 159–64.
Beggs, M. 2015, *Inflation and the Making of Australian Macroeconomic Policy, 1945–85*, London: Palgrave Macmillan.
Brown, N. 2001, *Richard Downing: Economics, Advocacy and Social Reform in Australia*, Melbourne: Melbourne University Press.
Butler, G., E. Jones and F. Stilwell, 2009, *Political Economy Now!*, Sydney: Darlington Press.
Byrne, G. 2005, 'Distinguished Fellow of the Economic Society of Australia, 2004: Helen Hughes', *Economic Record*, 81(252): 1–5.

Caves, R. and L. Krause, 1984 (eds), *The Australian Economy: The View from the North*, Sydney: Allen and Unwin.

Chapman, B. 1998, 'F. H. G. Gruen: 1921–97', *Economic Record*, 74(225): 186–94.

Chapman, B. 2003. 'Distinguished Fellow of the Economic Society of Australia, 2001: Robert G. Gregory', *Economic Record*, 78(241): 129–35.

Clark, C. 1975, 'Inflation: the cure', *Quadrant*, June, 15–22.

Clark, C. 1979, 'The persistence of stagflation', *Economic Analysis and Policy*, 9(1): 1–14.

Clark, C. 1980, 'Do trade unions raise wages?', *Economic Analysis and Policy*, 10(1): 40–2.

Coleman, P., S. Cornish and P. Drake, 2007, *Arndt's Story: The Life of an Australian Economist*, Canberra: Australian National University Press.

Coleman, W. 2009, '"The Power of Simple Theory and Important Facts"; A Conversation with Bob Gregory', *Agenda*, 16(2): 61–89.

Coombs, H. C. 1959, 'A matter of prices', *Economic Record*, 35(72): 337–48.

Corden, W. M. 1977, 'Macro-economic policy options for Australia', in Corden, 1997, *The Road to Reform*, Sydney: Addison Wesley, 136–46.

Corden, W. M. 1979, 'Wages and unemployment in Australia', in Corden, 1997, *The Road to Reform*, Sydney: Addison Wesley, 147–76.

Corden, W. M. and P. Dixon, 1980, 'A tax-wage bargain; is a free lunch possible?', in Corden 1997, *The Road to Reform*, Sydney: Addison Wesley, 177–95.

Corden, W. M. and J. P. Neary, 1982, 'Booming sector and deindustrialization in a small open economy', *Economic Journal*, 92: 825–48.

Cornish, S. 2016, 'Monetary targeting in Australia', in R. A. Cord and J. D. Hammond (eds), *Milton Friedman*, Oxford: Oxford University Press, 334–55.

Covick, O. 1974, 'The quantity theory of drink: a restatement', *Australian Economic Papers*, 13(23): 171–7.

Dalziel, P. and R. Lattimore, 1996, *The New Zealand Macroeconomy*, Melbourne: Oxford University Press.

Dixon, P. B. 1975, *The Theory of Joint Maximisation*, Amsterdam: North Holland.

Dixon, P. B., A. P. Powell and B. R. Parmenter (1979), *Structural Adaptation in an Ailing Macroeconomy*, Melbourne: Melbourne University Press.

Duhs, L. A. 2000, 'Economic analysis and policy: a thirtieth birthday retrospective', *Economic Analysis and Policy*, 30(1): 1–10.

Easton, B. 1990, 'The real wage debate, 1978-90', Working Paper 101, Victoria University of Wellington.

Endres, A. M. and A. Rogers, 2014, 'Trade policy and international finance in the Bretton Woods era: a doctrinal perspective with reference to Australia and New Zealand', *History of Economics Review*, 59: 62–81.

Fitzgerald, V. W. 1991, 'Chris Higgins' early career: the establishment of economic modelling in the Australian Treasury', *Economic Record*, 67(198): 257–60.

Garnaut, R. 2006, 'Real Australian in economics', in B. Lal and A. Ley (eds), *The Coombs: A House of Memories*, Canberra: Australian National University Press, 125–48.

Goldfinch, S. 1999, 'Remaking Australia's economic policy: economic policy decision-makers during the Hawke and Keating Labor governments', *Australian Journal of Public Administration*, 58(2): 3–20.

Gregory, R. G. 1976, 'Some implications of the growth of the mineral sector', *Australian Journal of Agricultural Economics*, 20(2): 92–102.

Groenewegen, P. 1976, 'The fiftieth issue of *Economic Papers*', *Economic Papers*, 52: 46–51.

Groenewegen, P. 1979, 'Radical economics', in F. H. Gruen (ed.), *Surveys of Australian Economics*, Vol. 2, Sydney: Allen and Unwin, 171–223.

Groenewegen, P. 2009, *Educating for Business, Public Service and the Social Sciences: A History of the Faculty of Economics at the University of Sydney 1920–1999*, Sydney: Sydney University Press.

Gruen, F. H. G. (ed.), 1979, *Surveys of Australian Economics*, Vol. 2, Sydney: Allen and Unwin.

Guttmann, S. 2005, *The Rise and Fall of Monetary Targeting in Australia*, Melbourne: Australian Scholarly Press.

Hagger, A. 1978, 'Inflation', in F. H. G. Gruen (ed.), *Surveys of Australian Economics*, Vol. 1, Sydney: Allen and Unwin, 133–85.

Hall, J. 2003, 'Health economics', in I. McAllister, S. Dowrick and R. Hassan (eds), *The Cambridge Handbook of Social Sciences in Australia*, Melbourne: Cambridge University Press, 60–73.

Hancock, K. 1971, 'Wage policy and inflation: Australia's experience under Compulsory Arbitration', *Australian Economic Review*, 4(4): 9–14.

Harcourt, G. C. 2001, *Selected Essays on Economic Policy*, Basingstoke: Palgrave.

Hatch, J. and C. Rogers, 1997, 'Distinguished Fellow of the Economic Society of Australia, 1996: Professor Emeritus Geoff Harcourt', *Economic Record*, 73(221): 97–100.

Haywood, E. and C. Moore. 1983, 'An examination of the Reserve Bank real wage–employment relationship', *New Zealand Economic Papers*, 17(1): 59–68.

Higgins, C. 1979, 'Policy relevant models for the 1970s', *Australian Economic Review*, 12(1): 75–80.

Hill, H. 2010, 'Distinguished Fellow: Ross Garnaut', *Economic Record*, 86(273): 281–8.

Hogbin, G. 2007, 'Ross McDonald Parish (1928–2001)', in J. E King (ed.), *A Biographical Dictionary of Australasian Economists*, Cheltenham: Edward Elgar: 209–12.

Holmes, A. 1979, 'What do we now know?', *Australian Economic Review*, 12(1): 81–7.

Holmes, F. 1972, *Money, Finance and the Economy: An Introduction to the New Zealand Financial System*, Auckland: Heinemann.

Horridge, M., B. Parmenter and P. Warr, 1987, 'Buying Australian', *Economic Record*, 63(3): 231–46.

Hudson, H. 1982, 'The case against reduced protection for Australian manufacturing industry', *Economics*, December: 5–11.

Hughes, B. 1980, *Exit Full Employment*, Sydney: Allen and Unwin.

Hughes, B, 1985, 'Brookings on the Australian economy', *Economic Record*, 69(1): 405–14.

Isaac, J. 1973, 'Incomes policy: Unnecessary? Undesirable? Impractical?', *Journal of Industrial Relations*, 15(3): 237–58.

Isaac, J. and J. E. King, 2015, 'A conversation with Joe Isaac', *History of Economics Review* 62: 58–74.

Johnson, H. G. 1966, 'Sugar protection and the export earnings of less developed countries: variations on a theme by R. H. Snape', *Economica*, 33(129): 34–42.

Jones, E. 2016, 'Australian trade liberalisation policy: the Industries Assistance Commission and the Productivity Commission', *Economic and Labour Relations Review*, 27(2): 181–98.

Lloyd, P. 1978, 'Protection policy', in F. H. Gruen (ed.), *Surveys of Australian Economics*, Vol. 1, Sydney: Allen and Unwin, 241–96.

Lloyd, P. 2006, 'Fifty years of trade policy reform', *Economic Papers*, 25(4): 301–13.

Lloyd, P. 2014, 'The path of protection in Australia since Federation', *History of Economics Review*, 59: 21-43.

Lodewijks, J. 1994, 'A conversation with John Nevile', in B. B. Rao (ed.), *Essays in Economics*, Sydney: Centre for Applied Economic Research: 15–34.

Lodewijks, J. 2007, 'A conversation with Warren Hogan', *Economic Record*, 83(262): 446–60.

Maloney, T. and J. Savage, 1996, 'Labor markets and policy', in B. Silverstone, A. Bollard and R. Lattimore (eds), *A Study of Economic Reform: The Case of New Zealand*, Amsterdam: Elsevier.

McDonald, I. 2016, 'Obituary of J. O. N. Perkins', *Academy of the Social Sciences of Australia*, available at http://www.assa.edu.au/fellowship/fellow/deceased/248

Meade, J. E. 1980, 'Review of J. O. N. Perkins: the macro-economic mix to stop stagflation', *Economic Record*, 56(152): 99–100.

Millmow, A. J. 2011, 'Australian Conference of Economists at 40: the state it's in', *Agenda* 18(3): 87–108.

Mitchell, W. F. 1998, 'Macroeconomic policy in Australia 1983–1996', Working Paper No 98-03, Centre of Full Employment and Equity, University of Newcastle.

Nevile, J. W. 1971, 'The Australian economy, August 1971', *Economic Record*, 47(119): 305–14.

Nevile, J. W. 1983, 'The role of fiscal policy in the eighties', *Economic Record*, 59(184): 1–14.

Nevile, J. W. and D. W. Stammer (eds), 1972, *Inflation and Unemployment: Selected Readings*, Ringwood: Penguin.

Norman, N. 2007, 'The contribution of Australian economists: the record and the barriers', *Economic Papers*, 26(1): 1–16.

O'Dea, D. J. 1981, 'A survey of what economists think: recent research results', Wellington; NZIER: 41–6.

Phelps Brown, H. 1969, 'Balancing external payments by adjusting domestic income', *Australian Economic Papers*, 8(13): 111–21.

Porter, M. G. 1971, 'Interest rate differentials interpreted as behaviour towards exchange rate expectations', PhD thesis, Stanford University.

Porter, M. G. 1977 'Monetary management 1970–75: a review', *Economic Papers*, 54: 124–36.

Powell, A. A. 2000, 'Probity before pragmatism: Alf Rattigan 1911–2000', *Economic Record*, 76(234): 301–4.

Richardson, D. and R. Wallace, 1983, 'Health economics', in F. H. G. Gruen (ed.), *Surveys of Australian Economics*, Vol. 3, Sydney: Allen and Unwin, 124–86.

Schedvin, C. B. 1992, *In Reserve: Central Banking in Australia*, Sydney: Allen and Unwin.

Scott, R. H. 1990, *The Economic Society of Australia: Its History 1925–1985*, Melbourne: Economic Society of Australia.

Scotton, R. and J. Deeble, 1968, 'Compulsory insurance for Australia', *Australian Economic Review*, 68(4): 9–16.

Sheehan, P. 1973, 'Review of economic survey of Australia, 1972, OECD', *Economic Record*, 49(128): 650–3.

Sheehan, P., B. Derody and P. Rosendale, 1979, 'An assessment of recent empirical work relevant to macro-economic policy in Australia', *Australian Economic Review*, 12(1): 33–61.

Silk, L. 1974, 'Economists among the inflation wounded', *Australian Financial Review*, 28 June.

Simkin, C. G. F. 1972, 'Inflation in Australia and New Zealand', *Economic Record*, 48(124): 465–82.

Simkin, C. G. F. 1974, 'Reflections on foreign exchange rates', *Economic Papers*, (43): 1–12.

Snape, R. H. 1970, 'A foreign exchange market for Australia?', *Economic Record*, 46(115): 297–311.

Snape, R. H. 1977, 'Effect of mineral development on the economy', *Australian Journal of Agricultural and Resource Economics*, 21(3): 147–56.

Snape, R. H. 1979, 'Productivity, costs and employment', *Australian Economic Review*, 12(2): 65–7.

Stretton, H. 1999, *Economics: A New Introduction*, Sydney: UNSW Press.

Wallace, R. H. 1974, 'The changing role of monetary policy since 1956', *Economics*, September, 44–9.

Wallace, R. H. 1976, 'Review R. B. Scotton Medical Care in Australia: an economic diagnosis', *Economic Record*, 52(2): 253–6.

Whitehead, D. 1977, 'The economic crisis in Australia: a non-monetarist view', Paper given at Sixth Conference of Economists, University of Tasmania.

Whitwell, G. 1986, *The Treasury Line*, Sydney: Allen and Unwin.

Williams, R. 2012, *The Policy Providers*, Melbourne: Melbourne University Press.

Williams, R. and R. H. Snape, 1999, 'Distinguished Fellow of the Economic Society of Australia, 1998: Professor Alan Powell', *Economic Record*, 75(228): 1–4.

Withers, G. 1978, 'The state of economics', *Australian Quarterly*, December: 74–80.

10 The age of economic reform

Introduction

The state of the Australian and New Zealand economies on the cusp of the 1980s provoked a flurry of scholarship urging reform and rejuvenation. This was prompted by each economy's relative economic performance being among the worst in the OECD (Norton and McDonald, 1981; Massey, 1995, 10–13). The editor of the *Australian Financial Review*, Max Walsh, greeted the arrival of the 1980s by bemoaning Australia's complacency about its future. Echoing Donald Horne's (1964) classic summation of Australia in the 1960s, Walsh (1979, 226) commented:

> Australia will be enormously handicapped through the eighties despite its wealth of natural endowments. It will be a willing quarry for the rest of the world, but little more than that... It will be a quaint, provincial outpost with many of the external trappings of material success.

Australia would, he said, 'muddle along, enjoying its version of the good life... We are destined to remain a poor little rich country.' Walsh was lamenting the lack of economic vision by the Coalition Government, driven by little else, it seemed, than expediency. It was a gloomy time; Australia was still struggling with stagflation, budgetary imbalance and a reluctance to engage in meaningful economic reform other than to commission an inquiry into the financial system. The Fraser Government (1975–83) had actually increased tariff protection for Australia's labour-intensive industries such as textiles, clothing and footwear, as well as motor vehicles. The IAC pointed out that the degree of structural change, particularly in the Australian manufacturing sector, was lower than in the OECD countries (Lloyd, 1978, 290).

Some economists criticised Australia's sense of complacency and inaction on economic reform. Austin Holmes, in his 1980 Giblin lecture entitled 'The Good Fight', spoke about 'the struggle to get good sense (economic rationality, if you like) into our economic affairs and, more specifically, into the economic policies which influence those affairs' (Holmes, 1981, 1). Holmes had, by that time, become a proponent of market-determined interest rates and floating of the exchange rate. He had a profound influence on thinking about economic policy both within the RBA and outside it, including persuading Roderick Deane of the RBNZ of the unintended consequences of financial regulation. Austin Holmes gave encouragement to Michael Porter and Richard Snape in establishing an entrepreneurial research centre in economic policy at Monash University. Later retitled the Centre for Policy Studies, it was deemed a centre of research excellence and received federal funding to supplement the assistance from the business sector. It used conferences, debates and lectures from guest economists rather than academic articles to hammer home the need for economic reform.

Five economists, with Wolfgang Kasper (1980) as lead author had, in a book entitled *Australia at the Crossroads: Our Choices to 2000*, argued that Australia faced two paths, one called 'the mercantilist trend', the other 'the libertarian agenda'. The latter path was a manifesto pushing for eliminating restrictions on trade and capital flows, deregulation of markets and reducing the role of government in the economy. Kasper, a German-born economist who had worked for the German Council of Economic Advisors, promised that the libertarian strategy would result in a more dynamic economy with economic outcomes superior to the mercantilist path (Berg, 2015, 201–2). Some private conservative think-tanks, such as the Centre for Independent Studies (1976) and the New Zealand Business Roundtable (1985), had emerged and began to push the case for economic liberalisation. The New Zealand Planning Council, made up of public sector economists including Frank Holmes and Rodney Smith, put out reports pushing market liberalisation (Bertram, 1993, 37–8). Two papers were harbingers of the future. One of them, on New Zealand's welfare system mooted the idea of reducing the size of the public sector. The other paper, by Rodney Smith and Rodney Deane, issued in 1980, was to become hugely influential within the Wellington policy-making establishment. It was critical of the role of activist fiscal policy, arguing that it had, in effect, been pro-cyclical. They recommended that fiscal policy adopt a medium-term outlook (ibid., 39).

The economic profession, would be taken by surprise by just how rapidly Australia and New Zealand engaged in comprehensive economic reform and even more at the fact that this was undertaken by Labor/Labour governments. The former OECD economist David Henderson (1996, 13), said the New Zealand reforms, compressed into a decade, amounted to 'one of the most notable episodes of economic liberalisation that economic history has to offer'.

The big question, though, is where did the academic economics profession in each country stand in all this upheaval? One gets the distinct impression that, certainly in New Zealand, it was economists within the Treasury and the RBNZ who did the lobbying (Dalziel and Lattimore, 1996). There were claims made, too, that New Zealand was importing whole-sized chunks of economic doctrine from North American universities. To some extent the reforms were inevitable: international economic pressures, the example of successful economies elsewhere, technology and an erosion in the ineffectiveness of controls were the driving factors. Looking at opinion surveys of New Zealand, academic economists might clarify matters. Of course, articles and commentaries advocating economic reform and liberalisation had long been 'in the air', but the relationship between university economic analysis and economic development is a tenuous one (Brooke *et al.*, 2016, 2). Nor was it always clear who would be the direct beneficiaries of such reform, though economists had certainly pointed out the damage done by over-regulation and protection. Anticipating the future, the Deputy Governor of the RBNZ, Rodney Deane (1981, 45) followed up his earlier work on fiscal policy by publicly expressing his frustration about excessive policy variability and how new classical economic analysis had 'barely been tapped in New Zealand'.

In some cases, Australia and New Zealand had no choice but to undertake economic liberalisation. They had been slow in undertaking structural reform to become much more outward-looking economies; there were other more pressing matters. In the election campaign preceding the Labour Party's electoral victory in New Zealand, there had been a massive run against the currency which left the RBNZ scrambling for lines of international credit. The reform process launched by the fourth Labour government met, as we shall see, with a mostly negative reaction from university economists (Bertram, 1993).

This chapter briefly discusses the economic reform processes of the 1980s and how Australasian university economists reacted to them and the extent of their influence. The 1980s was undoubtedly a decade when, after an initial burst of Keynesianism by the Australian Labor government, the prevailing economic philosophy was neoliberalism or, in the Australian vernacular, one of economic rationalism. In New Zealand it was known as 'Rogernomics' after the Finance Minister, Roger Douglas. This change in philosophy was already infusing university economics departments: the ANU and Monash in Australia and Canterbury in New Zealand. Melbourne was still the sentimental home of old-style Keynesianism, but that, too, was coming under challenge. We focus here on one particular episode at the Melbourne Institute where a feud raged over two different econometric models of the Australian economy and the philosophy that underpinned them.

Modelling wars

In the 1980s, a dispute broke out within the Faculty of Economics and Commerce of Melbourne University over which large-scale structural model best described the Australian economy. Until 1984 the Melbourne Institute used a unique econometric model of the Australian economy called the IMP (Institute Multi-Purpose) model. The creator of the model was Peter Brain; he had developed it with a distinctly Keynesian view of the economy (Williams, 2012, 44–7). The model placed importance, for instance, on unemployment and social issues ahead of economic efficiency and resource allocation. It was the only detailed Keynesian model being used for long-term policy analysis and was seen as an alternative to that used by the Federal Treasury. The Institute's work and its annual assessment of Federal economic policy, including scrutinising the budget forecasts, carried great weight. Earlier, the Institute had opposed the thesis that the real wage overhang was the leading cause of unemployment. The IMP model was part-funded by the University and partly by business corporations along with various state and welfare bodies. The Victorian government was a keen supporter. The trade union movement used the Institute's modelling to justify its wage submission before the Arbitration Commission.

So when Melbourne University appointed Peter Dixon as Director of the Melbourne Institute in March 1984 there was some concern that he would favour an image of the economy captured in the alternative ORANI model which he had developed nine years earlier with the Federal government's IMPACT project team. This model emphasised resource allocation and efficiency and the economic bounty resulting from deregulation and liberalisation. By contrast, the IMP model generated results that justified protecting the manufacturing sector contrary to the arguments of many mainstream economists (ibid., 49). The IMP model was criticised for insufficient documentation of its underlying assumptions and its lack of scrutiny in academic journals. However, the ORANI model was accessible to all and had been published in the prestigious North Holland series *Contributions to Economic Analysis* (ibid., 73). One criticism of the ORANI model has been that it embodies assumptions about the tendency of the economy towards full employment equilibrium, the flexibility of prices and wages and the central importance of markets.

There had already been a plenary session about the two models at the 1979 Conference of Economists but this had resulted in a stalemate. One economic journalist at the Conference, Paddy McGuinness, was annoyed that there had been no blood on the floor. The two protagonists, Brain and Dixon, were convinced that their particular model of the Australian economy was superior to the other. At issue was not merely economic forecasting but perceptions of how the Australian economy actually operated.

The upshot, then, was that there were two distinct schools of thought, and econometric models, about the Australian economy. The fact that Alan Powell had brought the ORANI model along with him to Melbourne University meant that the Melbourne Faculty had now two large-scale structural models of the Australian economy on different floors of the one building. As Williams (ibid., 50) coyly observed, the Melbourne Faculty's research in model-building 'was not in equilibrium'.

Upon his appointment as Director of the Institute, Dixon ideally wanted to make a rigorous comparison of the two models and integrate the strengths of each to build an even more robust model. But the attempt at rapprochement failed. Brain and the principal IMP researchers left the Institute, some half of the staff, taking their clients with them. They quickly set themselves up as a private research and consulting group known as the National Institute of Economic and Industrial Research. While this won financial backing from unions, private companies and state and local governments, it would never achieve the comparable status of the Institute. Dixon experienced an unsettled first few years at the Institute. Some 30 government and private organisations loyal to the Keynesian IMP model had initially petitioned the University about his appointment and threatened to withdraw almost half a million dollars in funding. Brain and Dixon never reconciled their differences with each other or their beloved models. There would be a sequel in the 1990s, but this time involving other players and other models mostly about which large scale econometric models were the best predictor of Australia's macroeconomic performance.

An irrelevance of economists?

In 1982 the Economics Editor of the *Australian Financial Review* (*AFR*), Paddy McGuinness, who regularly attended the annual conference of economists and, indeed, had contributed to the *Record*, wrote a scathing editorial about Australian university economists, criticising their passivity and lack of worldliness. In 1979 he had complained how, at the 8th Annual Conference of Economists, its participants were ignoring issues such as inflation, unemployment, technological change and structural adjustment.[1] Now, in 1982, he suggested that economists were surrendering commentary on contemporary economic matters to commentators, choosing to focus, instead, on 'trivial subjects upon which they can publish unreadable papers in recondite journals to further their own careers among their own kind'. This was not a cheap, populist shot at economists; there was, according to McGuinness, a 'real malaise' within the profession, especially about the performance of large econometric models, and he pondered overall whether the public purse was being well spent on the increasing 'irrelevance of the academics economic profession'.[2] Richard Snape, now editor of the *Record*, fired back in a public letter that, while the *AFR* editorial would have been 'great fun to write', he rejected the idea that economists had said nothing about issues like unemployment or wages by citing the recent contributions of Nevile, Corden and Hancock. Snape added that it was not the duty of academics to be writing in the press as 'their comparative advantage is in longer and deeper analysis'. He derided McGuinness's claim that little relevant research was being undertaken in Australia by listing some of the major economic research centres. With regard to stagflation, Snape warned that economists knew there would be no quick fix. He concluded by noting that while economists are strong at diagnosis and specification of options, 'implementation of policy is not an area where economists can claim an advantage'.[3] Yet McGuinness was prophetic about university economists leaving the field of economic commentary and ideas to others: a pattern that would become entrenched in the 1990s with the socialisation of economics in the form of market economists and those working with think-tanks. It was commensurate with the trend for university economics to become more technical and esoteric. Coleman and Hagger (2001) also attribute it to economists becoming more reluctant to engage in public fora. But McGuinness was entirely wrong about the productivity and versatility of Australian university economists.

At the time, the academic economics profession within Australia was at its largest. Conference papers abounded and the profession, like a mighty river, had tributaries feeding into it; tributaries such as the work of econometricians, agricultural economists, labour economists, health economists, historians of economic thought, heterodox economists and economic historians. Some of these specialisations, such as agricultural economics, already had their own societies, field journals and conferences; others would follow suit. The econometricians, too, held their first Australian meeting at Monash in 1983. In 1988, Australia's bicentennial year, all the economic societies assembled fittingly at the ANU for the Australian Bicentenary Economic Congress, with over 1,000 delegates attending. This marked the apogee of the Australian economic profession, certainly in terms of quantitative strength, with over 1,000 academic economists employed at local universities – representing, at the time, almost 10 per cent of total Australian full-time university staff (Groenewegen, 1989, 101). Meanwhile, the Society had dug into its financial reserves to fund guest speakers for the jamboree, including Joe Stiglitz, Clive Granger, Angus Deacon, Alan Blinder, Jeffrey Williamson and William Parker. The Congress was opened by Prime Minister Hawke, who reminded delegates of how Australia was undergoing a period of reform and reconstruction but still to face its next challenge, namely not to become too reliant on a narrow range of commodity exports. At the time delegates marvelled at the amount of economic reform being undertaken in both Australia and New Zealand.

The crucible of reform

A significant year for Australasian economics was 1984, simply because Australia and New Zealand embarked upon an astonishing burst of economic reform, which was to span a ten-year period. In Australia, Bob Hawke held a National Economic Summit, with representatives drawn from state and federal governments, the union movement, academics, employer and major industry groups to discuss his themes of reconciliation and reconstruction. The Summit issued a communique adopting the Prices and Incomes Accord as well as the creation of an Economic Planning Advisory Council (something which the Vernon Report had recommended in 1965). There was also to be a new approach to industry policy, with protection being phased out along with an extensive programme of microeconomic reform measures.

However, it was New Zealand that captured the imagination of the world's economists, as it was about to experiment with what Blyth (1966, 44) called 'the competitive model, efficiency style'. Not long after winning power, the new Prime Minister of the fourth Labour government, David Lange, convened a National Economic Summit in September 1984 to discuss the precarious state of the economy and to endorse the necessity for reform. Precarious was not too harsh a word; the country faced a gaping deficit on its external account and the budget deficit was 6.5 per cent of GDP; inflation was persistent while growth and productivity remained subdued, despite considerable overseas borrowing by Wellington. New Zealand's per capita productivity had sunk to the lowest of OECD countries. In 1950 its per capita national income was 25 per cent above the OECD average; 40 years later it had slumped to 25 per cent below the OECD average (Silverstone *et al.*, 1996, 5). Between 1974 and 1979 per capita income fell by 11 per cent. Since the early 1960s New Zealand economists had been concerned at the low growth rate and stagnation in real income that had become all too evident in the 1970s. The Muldoon Government's 'Think Big' development programme in 1982–3 to reduce energy dependence on foreign supplies, associated with a wide range of economic controls, had been wasteful. Ordinary New Zealanders, too, suspected, that they had been living in a 'fools' paradise'. There was, then, 'a certain inevitability' about the need for economic reform, to try something different – whether it was theory-driven or pragmatic (Blyth, 1987).

To empathise the gravity of the situation, Lange took the unprecedented move of 'opening the books'; that is, publicly releasing the briefings given to him by the Treasury. That briefing raised great commotion; it read like the Spanish Inquisition, listing five specific examples of economic mismanagement, but only echoed what the Treasury had been advising the Muldoon Government three years earlier. Yet the Treasury's indictments were levied at every New Zealand government since 1935. These were, first, the failure to adjust the economy to changing external conditions. Second, New Zealand governments had been incoherent and erratic in the assignment of policies to targets. Third, governments had done little in pushing competitive reform. Fourth, New Zealand governments had been structurally negligent in their embrace of insulation and an overvalued exchange rate. Lastly, the Treasury accused governments of engaging in the political trade cycle (Dalziel and Lattimore, 1996, 23–4). Like their counterparts in Canberra, Treasury officials lamented the lack of wage flexibility within the economy generally and linked it to unemployment (Maloney and Savage, 1996, 182).

At the end of the conference a communique was issued confirming that New Zealand would pursue five macroeconomic goals; yet the most remarkable statement was to signify that the paradigm of insulation was over. The communique also noted that New Zealand had 'an unacceptable level of poverty' and that this particular failure to match resources with performance had been the case for the past 30 years (Dalziel, 2002, 44). As such, Finance Minister Douglas had *carte blanche* in his first budget for what he called 'comprehensive economic and social reform' which would be 'the hallmark of the fourth Labour Government' (Dalziel and Lattimore, 1996, 7). It was accepted that the reforms would, in the short term, lead to lower growth and considerable economic disruption.

The few university economists at either economic summit were like spectres at the feast, given their long advocacy for economic reform. In Australia, Hawke and Keating had two academic economists, Ross Garnaut and Barry Hughes, serving as personal advisors. The previous prime minister, Malcolm Fraser, had Cliff Walsh, an Adelaide University economist specialising in competition policy and regulation, as his principal economic advisor (1981–3). Meanwhile, the bulk of the Australian economic profession was mostly in favour of the economic reform programme now unfolding. Some economists though, such as Harcourt, Hudson and Isaac, were never convinced by economic liberalism, believing it was 'peculiarly unsuited' for Australia (Hatch and Rogers, 1997, 98). In New Zealand, Rosenberg and Sutch would have bristled at the shift towards liberalism but they had long departed the scene. What, though, about the remainder of the academic economics community there? An opinion survey of 118 New Zealand economists conducted in 1980, drawn from academe, business and the public sector, unanimously agreed that the country's manufacturing sector had been over-protected from international competition (O'Dea, 1981). Matching this response was that the same economists strongly agreed with the proposition that tariffs and quotas had the effect of reducing economic welfare but that, of these two, tariffs were the lesser evil.

The debate was only just beginning; the next stage was in assessing the net results of the reform programme. One group of proponents, Lewis Evans, Arthur Grimes, Bryce Wilkinson and David Teece loftily proclaimed in the *Journal of Economic Literature* that New Zealand, at the end of the reform process, will 'once again' emerge from 'the laboratory from which results will animate debate and policy throughout the world' (Evans *et al.*, 1996, 1895). 'Laboratory' it certainly was, but where were the results? Before answering that question it is useful to note the actual reforms which New Zealand undertook. Within a year of coming to office, the Lange Government had deregulated interest rates, floated the currency and abandoned all controls on capital flows. Quotas were phased out, replaced by tariffs (this process had actually started in 1981). Domestically, most agricultural subsidies and export tax incentives were phased out on the premise that a lower New Zealand dollar would be of assistance for the export sector. There was a revolution, too, in domestic competition policy in favour of contestability, together with all government trading enterprises being instructed to conduct themselves along private business lines in readiness for privatisation. At the macroeconomic policy level, the RBNZ was granted independence in 1989, becoming the first central bank in the world to focus purely on price stability. After a change of government in 1990 the reforms continued with the deregulation of the labour market, the centralised system which had lasted for nearly a century being replaced by a decentralised, individual contract system. The Employment Contracts Act of 1991 was described as legislation concerning individual contracts between employer and employee designed to promote an efficient labour market.

David Henderson told the Business Roundtable, an influential New Zealand lobby group, that while New Zealand,

> was just one of a crowd... in no other OECD country has there been so systematic an attempt at the same time (1) to redefine and limit the role of government, and (2) to make public agencies and their operations more effective, more transparent, and more accountable.
>
> Cited in Bates, 1997, 351

Equally, the Governor of the RBNZ, Don Brash (1996, 15), told the Fifth IEA Annual Hayek Memorial Lecture in London that 'The revival of the New Zealand economy in the last few years follows one of the most remarkable economic liberalisations of modern times.' Painting the reforms in a Hayekian light, Brash (ibid., 19–20) observed that the reforms had only proceeded because there had been 'a spectacular collapse of the mental defences against the intellectual counter-revolution which Hayek had begun in the 1940s'.

What were the theoretical origins behind these reforms? Was Victoria University economist John Zanetti correct in saying that the reforms were instigated by 'inside' economists? Alan Bollard (1994) certainly conceded in a study on economic reform that it was inside economists that were driving the reforms. And, more pointedly, were critics such as Kelsey (1995), Bollard (1988), Bertram (1993), Easton (1988) and Goldfinch (2000) correct in attributing the ideas that powered New Zealand's economic revolution to overseas economic expertise, especially American economists? There was certainly no 'native economic wisdom' about the economic ideas behind the supply-side reforms; they sprang from the neoliberal economics being taught at the Ivy League universities in America. A country, therefore, that had zealously practised import licensing had no reservations about digesting chunks of economic ideas from abroad without thought of filtering them for domestic application. The New Zealand reforms were theoretically grounded, characterised by the application of new conceptual frameworks in microeconomics including elements of contestable markets, principal agency relationships and public choice theory (Silverstone *et al.*, 1996, 7). Equally, the new macroeconomic paradigm to replace economic controls included elements of rational expectations theory, policy transparency and credibility and an expectations-augmented Phillips curve (Bates, 1997, 352). More specifically, the new paradigm included Demsetz and Coase on the theory of the firm, Williamson on transactions costs, Baumol on contestability theory, Buchanan and Tulloch on political influence and public choice, Friedman's monetarism leavened with rational expectations insights from Kydland and Prescott (Kelsey, 1995, 54).

Evans *et al.* (1996, 1862) summed up the New Zealand reforms as the 'pursuit of coherent policies on a broad front: credibility and time consistency; a comparative institutional approach; and efficient contracting arrangements'. Economic institutions such as the RBNZ and Treasury would be allowed to pursue theoretically derived policy free, on the surface at least, from vested interests. Underpinning all these reforms was a philosophical shift away from the Keynesian consensus towards neoliberalism; the balance of economic policy shifted away from distribution and stabilisation towards the allocation of resources (Blyth, 1987, 4).

The political scientist Shaun Goldfinch (2000), in a survey of 87 respondents, found that the theoretic ideas powering the economic reforms were considered very important. In writing about the 'policy entrepreneurs' behind the reforms, he found that some of the 'intellectual elites', or 'change agents' as Jane Kelsey (1995, 54) calls them, were graduates of North American economics departments working within either the Treasury or RBNZ. When asked to nominate the sources of ideas influencing the radical new economic policy, the response was that they hailed from neoclassical economics. While Colin Clark had labelled New Zealand a 'veritable museum of economic errors', she had now become, 50 years later, the world's showcase for neoliberal economic policies. The fact that these ideas bore the imprimatur of the IMF, OECD and World Bank lent support to their legitimacy. The fact, too, that the lacklustre performance of the New Zealand economy in terms of a poor growth rate had long been analysed meant it could equally provide a ready-made set of simple and attractive solutions (Goldfinch, 2000, 20). Some commentators claimed that New Zealand's political and economic leaders simply adopted a pragmatic response to dire economic conditions rather than displaying conviction; yet this does not explain why one path was chosen over another. There had, in official circles, been, as discussed, a considerable dissatisfaction with activist demand management, over-regulation and the suppression of the market prices for labour, foreign exchange, capital, energy and resources (Bassett and Bassett, 2006, 90–1). For some time economists within the RBNZ had been advocating financial deregulation and the floating of the dollar. At the same time Treasury economists were 'intensively following' the latest developments in microeconomics (Evans *et al.*, 1996, 1862; Goldfinch and Roper, 1993). All these influences now culminated in the Treasury's post-election briefing papers given to the Lange Government in 1984.

Interestingly, only a few of the 87 'thought leaders' whom Goldfinch interviewed were academics. He found, in fact, that only a few local academic economists were contributors to ideas. Indeed, some of the respondents in the survey were frank in pointing out just how minor a role academics played in the process. This was with the exception, though, of the University of Canterbury, where, under Richard Manning's leadership, it became New Zealand's equivalent of the Chicago School, with prestigious visitors like Gerard Debreu, Clive Granger and Charles Kindleberger. Some of Canterbury's graduates played critical roles in the implementation of the neoliberal monetarist reforms of the late 1980s. Goldfinch attributed the discard of local academic opinion to top public servants already having exposure to postgraduate economics and the old familiar argument that New Zealanders did not attach a high value to theoretical and policy debate by academics. Goldfinch found that it was the official thinking within the Treasury and RBNZ, together with the Business Roundtable, which was instrumental in convincing policy-makers to adopt the new reform programme. While there is little to challenge the view that 'inside' economists led the crusade for reform we must make allowances for pragmatism and the tide of events. In terms of identities, Roderick Deane at the RBNZ and two high-level Treasury officials, Graham Scott and Roger Kerr, have been cited as the key players, along, of course, with the *force majeure*, Roger Douglas (Goldfinch, 2000, 11–12; Kelsey, 1995). Evans *et al.* (1996, 1862) also cited the same persons, noting how Douglas, when in Opposition in 1980, pondered the need for a different economic approach to what the Muldoon Nationalist Government had been attempting.

The economists fight back

Kelsey overstates the case in saying that there was a 'critical void' among academic economists about the 1984 New Zealand economic reforms. There were, as we shall see, critics of the reforms including the 'Victoria Seven', as well as Bryan Philpott, Paul Dalziel and Tim Hazledine. Kelsey is more correct in the sense that the academic dissent never achieved the public prominence it did in Britain and America. This was due to the prevailing intellectual culture and the perceived role of universities in the country (Bertram, 1993, 46). After the Labour Party had won power and began to recast economic policy, some university economists were plainly apprehensive about what the Treasury and RBNZ had in store for the country. Seven economists from the Victoria University, led by Zanetti (1984), were not swept away by the ideology of either the Treasury or the RBNZ about the proposed new economic order. Indeed, where the Victoria Seven could identify Treasury briefings, they found them too doctrinaire, set within a neoclassical framework 'unmodified by any recognition of the highly idealised nature of the model or the fact that its adjustment mechanisms are now much questioned'. Treasury, Zanetti *et al.* argued, was prone therefore 'to express conclusions from the abstract model as though they were statements of empirical fact'. The Treasury, therefore, was in danger of offering facile solutions to persistent economic problems such as inflation and the trade deficit. The economists favoured 'accounts of adjustment mechanisms which make sense in terms of known institutional structures and processes' (Bertram 1993, 44–5). Neither were the economists impressed by the Treasury's monetarist explanation of inflation or the tendency to visualise the labour market as just like any other market. While the Victoria Seven were not opposed to the idea of financial deregulation, including floating the currency, they saw no sense in wanting 'to plunge into an orgy of deregulation in the expectation that the economy will slide smoothly into the elegant harmony of general equilibrium' (Zanetti *et al.*, 1984, 28).

These protests did not go unchallenged as the frank exchange of views between Treasury and academic economists at the 1985 Conference of Economists demonstrated. Easton described it as 'a clash of cultures' regretting how a chance for cooperation became one of conflict.[4] However, it was unlikely that the two parties could come together. The Treasury (1985) chided the academics for both misinterpreting their report and misrepresenting their views. The university economists seemed unaware that the Treasury paper articulated a possible framework for approaching economic management, an options paper rather than recommendations for action. The Treasury wanted more stability in policy and a mutually reinforcing balance between policies, which it believed was best achieved by 'harnessing and supplementing markets rather than suppressing them' (ibid., 96). Zanetti *et al.* (1984) drew comfort from the official advisors, being 'at pains to resist the monetarist label and to disassociate themselves from the formalism of monetarism', but noted that there were other references in their briefings that spoke of monetarism. This left Zanetti thinking there was still considerable ambiguity about the theoretical basis of the advice being tendered to the Treasury. By the time Zanetti published his argument, New Zealand's unemployment was reaching unprecedented levels as the reform programme began to take effect. A land, then, which had once enjoyed an enviable mix of inflation and unemployment was no more. It had also been a torrid time, with considerable economic dislocation.

Douglas and the Treasury probably knew that the critique by academic econo-mists was coming. Before being elevated to Finance Minister in 1984, Douglas had canvassed local academics about policy alternatives, but was left unim-pressed by their unwillingness to find common ground or come to some compro-mise with Treasury economists. A conference had already been held in Wellington in 1983 between government economists and economists drawn from Victoria and Auckland universities. Bertram (1993, 41) reports that the academics were of broadly neo-Keynesian or of a structuralist persuasion, while the Treasury and RBNZ economists were monetarist or new classicalist. There was even some disagreement between the economists from the two universities over whether New Zealand's fundamental problem was not enough savings or not enough foreign exchange.

Paul Dalziel (1986, 50), from Lincoln University, had already taken to task the vagueness about the weights given to each of the economic objectives agreed at the 1984 Summit. The listed objectives approved were: sustainable economic growth; full employment; price stability; external balance; and an equitable distribution of income – all this while 'fully respecting social and cultural values and avoiding undue environmental costs'. However, some groups at the Summit were partial towards one objective over the others and, in seeking to reach a compromise, might not have revealed their true preferences.

At the 1986 annual conference of economists Bryan Philpott predicted from his econometric model of the New Zealand economy that Rogernomics would result in slow growth and high unemployment. So it proved. For his trouble, the Treasury bluntly responded by cutting funding for his CGE work (Easton, 2007, 111). After his appointment as Macarthy Professor at Victoria in 1970, Philpott shifted his views on protection. From his modelling, Philpott now concluded that New Zealand would not benefit from ending protection. He had reached, by scientific means, the Sutch–Rosenberg position that New Zealand could not rely on its pastoral exports for all the foreign exchange it needed (Easton, 2001, 220–1). Easton (ibid., 223) credits him with successfully forecasting that the 1984 economic reforms, when implemented, were unlikely to deliver what its proponents promised. Philpott articulated that his own 'median' approach, inspired by James Meade, encompassed incomes policies, employment growth targets, lower protection and economic planning (ibid., 214). Two of Philpott's colleagues at Victoria, David Sheppard and Jan Whitwell, were concerned that the RBNZ's plans to control the quantity of money via control over primary liquidity of the financial system was ill-founded.

Apart from these contributions the general perception was that the input of the academic economists was minor. Brian Easton (1988), an economic commentator who wrote for the weekly news magazine *The Listener*, attributes this to the academic community being relatively small, isolated and marginalised. He argued elsewhere that academic criticism of the economic reforms was muted because of a degree of self-censorship (Easton, 2007, 110). There was also the trademark academic reserve. Susanne Snively (1988, 142), an American econo-mist who had migrated to New Zealand, was struck by the way university economics departments suffered 'the typical lack of confidence of an insular group' and 'looked to the overseas journals for their affirmation'. Moreover, the compact, policy-making community in Wellington did not allow for much dissent to gather (Goldfinch, 2000, 19). As noted the Treasury and RBNZ were significant sources of economic research, having invested considerable resources in that regard. Deane, for instance, had gone to some lengths to equip the RBNZ with a macroeconomic model of the economy (Scobie, 2013).

Stalwarts such as Conrad Blyth (1964, 15) and Frank Holmes had already modelled how the New Zealand economy would fare under a liberalised environment with no protection, no export incentives and the trade account dealt with by adjusting the exchange rate. Their modelling was all fanciful since no one ever took it seriously the fact that New Zealand would move in that direction. Around the same time, Wilfred Candler, in an unsigned piece in *The Economist*, lampooned New Zealand as a country going through Rostow's stages of growth in reverse order, moving from a developed to a less developed country (Lattimore and Wooding, 1996, 324).

If Zanetti felt that he had been patronised by Treasury economists it was nothing compared to the way in which RBNZ economists responded to objections, raised by their university counterparts, about the proposed legislation giving the Bank independence solely to pursue price stability:

> The economists consulted... are out of date with mainstream economics thinking, both in academe and in the wider world. We expect that the general approach to monetary policy being adopted in New Zealand does not enjoy wide support in the New Zealand academic economics community. However, given the broader international support received, we suggest that the lack of local academic support says more about the state of New Zealand academic economics than about the correctness of the Reserve Bank and the Government's approach to monetary policy.
>
> Cited in Kelsey, 1995, 161–2

The reactions of Zanetti and his colleagues to the mooted policy reforms were echoed in a survey of academic opinion organised by Coleman (1992) eight years after the Summit. He found that New Zealand academic economists were not strong advocates of monetarism, unlike those at the RBNZ. The most striking finding from the survey was that university economists were considerably less sympathetic to market advocacy than business or public sector economists (ibid., 54). Equally, Coleman found that the proportion of university economists agreeing with the proposition that Rogernomics was 'basically sound' was far smaller than among business and public sector economists. Coleman (ibid., 56) also uncovered a 'generation gap' in his survey of New Zealand economists' opinion. The young, he noticed, were more market-inclined, more monetarist, more in favour of privatisation, more likely to support the tenets of Rogernomics than their older counterparts. An example of this was Philpott's lament that all his postgraduate students were much more market-orientated than he was (Holmes, 2000).

Midway through the reform programme in 1990, when the new Nationalist government had to deal with a deterioration in its fiscal position by cutting expenditure in the midst of recession, there was more academic reaction. Fifteen Auckland university economists wrote a public letter to the editor of a leading newspaper in June 1991 stating that the deficit-cutting strategy was 'fatally-flawed... and can only depress the economy further' (cited in Evans *et al.*, 1996, 1861). It was, perhaps, a smaller version of the episode in Britain in 1981 when 365 economists signed a public letter in *The Times* condemning the Thatcher Government's embrace of fiscal rectitude while in recession. The then Finance Minister, Ruth Richardson, called the 15 members of the Auckland Economics Department 'shallow and unscholarly' because they dared to publicly criticise the government's deflationary policies as being likely to intensify a recession (Goldfinch, 2000, 15). These economists would be later embarrassed to learn that strong GDP and employment growth dated from that time. Before the reforms some university economists had been apprehensive about the uncritical accept-ance of a barrow-load of overseas economic dogma.

When it comes to gauging the economic outcomes of the New Zealand reforms it could be said that it depends upon whom one consults. The first eight years of New Zealand's economic experiment had resulted in a fairly anaemic economic performance; a budget deficit and inflation complicated the process. One common point among analysts was to suspend commentary on the net outcomes until well over a decade after the reforms had taken place, if not longer. For instance, defenders of the reforms stress that the RBNZ did not have its price stability target in place until 1989 and that the labour market was not deregulated until 1991. The latter delay was considered one of the main reasons why adjustment costs were high; the policy-making authorities readily admitted an error in the timing and sequencing of the reforms. For instance, some urged that the reform of product and labour markets should take place before financial deregulation otherwise it would lead to a net capital inflow and an appreciation of the real exchange rate, thus making it harder for a reallocation of resources to move to exports. Reforming the labour market much earlier would have stirred agitation from the union movement and perhaps undermined the whole programme. The expatriate New Zealand economist John McMillan (1997) noticed how the 'textbook-perfect' reforms inflicted considerable and unanticipated suffering before they began to work. Evans *et al.* (1996) argued that the international economics community would benefit from the experiment, especially mature western economies including Australia. There were some lessons to be drawn; not reforming the labour market earlier had added to transition costs since lower real wages and lower exchange rates may have been achieved much earlier. The importance of the sequencing of reforms could be overridden by engaging in simultaneous reforms where gains to the sector without assistance could be achieved from reforms elsewhere. The scale of the New Zealand experiment, including outsourcing, privatisation and the elimination of both export subsidies and import licensing, as well as competition policy reform showed that market solutions could work far more efficiently than many observers had envisaged.

Lastly, New Zealand had undertaken fiscal consolidation and a wave of public sector efficiencies at a rate far greater than most would have considered feasible (ibid., 1894).

The New Zealand reforms included two important pieces of economic legislation which were the first of their kind in the world. First, in 1989 the RBNZ was, as mentioned, given independence to design policies to address 'the single goal of achieving and maintaining stability in the general level of prices' (Dalziel and Lattimore, 1996, 44). Gone were the days when a prime minister could speak of 'absolute authority over the Bank' (Bassett and Bassett, 2006, 91). Second, in 1994 the Fiscal Responsibility Act introduced transparency and integrity into the country's public accounts with a net public debt target set around 20–30 per cent of GDP. The government was also expected to outline its long-term objectives and short-term strategies, explaining how they accord with responsible fiscal management (Dalziel and Lattimore, 1996, 59–60). These two measures signalled the end of the New Zealand government's ability to use macroeconomic policy for political ends. More importantly, measures were put in place to secure the revolution in economic policy, thereby making it irrevocable (Blyth, 1987, 18).

The study by Evans *et al.* (1996), together with the account by Silverstone *et al.* (1996, 20), sought to inform the world that the New Zealand economic reforms had, for the most part, been a success. The latter study was 'cautiously optimistic that the reforms have contributed to sustainable economic growth', before going on to remark that the country's reform programme 'may still rank as one of the more successful by world standards', with a marked improvement in economic wellbeing. Somewhat extravagantly, Evans *et al.* (1996, 1985) concluded that 'After decades of policy error and investment blunders, New Zealand appears to have finally diagnosed its predicament appropriately and is on a trajectory to maintain its economy as a consistent high performer among the OECD'. Silverstone *et al.* (1996, 13) believed that the reforms began to pay dividends by 1992, though it was too early to state whether the improved economic performance would be sustained. They add that New Zealand had followed, almost to the letter, John Williamson's seven-point 'checklist' for successful economic reform, one of which, was to have a team of government economists with a clear and coherent view of what needs to be done, backed by the executive power to do it (ibid., 19).

Contradicting the view that the process had delivered positive economic outcomes, Jane Kelsey (1995) was adamant that, after a decade of reforms, New Zealand had become a more unequal, less cohesive society. Moreover, the country had performed worse in economic terms than most other countries. In the mid-1990s Bob Gregory wondered why both countries' decade-long engagement with microeconomic reform had not led to 'unambiguously better macro outcomes in Australia and New Zealand' (cited in King, 2003, 40). Later, in appraising the net benefit of the New Zealand reforms, Gregory was fairly damning, suggesting: 'Indeed it is perhaps difficult to believe that the outcomes could have been worse if there were no reforms at all' (cited in Nobbs, 2014, 25). Dalziel (2002) found, after running some econometric tests, that New Zealand incurred a significant diminution of real GDP per capita in undertaking its economic reform programme. This meant that New Zealand's real GDP per head diverged from the Australian rate, a gap that grew wider as the millennium approached. This was a development which Goldfinch (2000) and Kelsey (1995) also drew attention to in their individual assessment of the outcomes from the reforms; the Australian economist John Quiggin (2000) corroborated these findings. Moreover, Dalziel found that the average unemployment rate was higher after 1988 and that labour productivity growth declined after 1992. Low-income households were not protected from the upheaval, with their income 3 per cent lower than it was in 1984. From this evidence Dalziel concludes that the reforms did not reach their core objective of lifting more New Zealanders out of poverty. Only the new millennium would confirm whether proponents of the reform such as Evans *et al.* or the detractors were correct. External factors – not least, global economic conditions – would always have an influence, meaning that judgement on the net outcomes of the reforms always had to be qualified.

From a political economy perspective, the reforms had melded together the rural sector, services sector and business classes, all of whom were mostly in favour of free trade. Manufacturers and workers, as well as the social welfare lobby, were against the reforms. The Lange Government's (1984–90) 'big bang' approach to reforms had – by stripping away import licensing, subsidies, tax wedges and other privileges – split asunder the network of lobby groups that had captured previous governments. The beneficiaries were now the Business Roundtable and exporters, including tourism and the financial services sector. By contrast, in Australia, the distributional conflict over income shares was muted by the Labor government adopting a gradualist and consensual approach with unions and the business sector.

An economist at Auckland University, Tim Hazledine (1997, 287), would have agreed with Evans *et al.* (1996) that his country was, indeed, supplying a 'public good' to the rest of the world by demonstrating what happens to a small economy when it is 'flooded' with overseas economic dogma. Hazledine suggested that the rest of the world would be anxious to see how New Zealand fared under the rigours of a radical neoliberal economic experiment.

The debate over economic rationalism in Australia

A 'turning point' in Australian economic history came in 1991, not just because it was the year the country finally rid itself of inflation or the year China entered the global economy (Schedvin, 2008). It was also the year that Australia began its privatisation programme by selling off the first tranche of the Commonwealth Bank, once known as 'The People's Bank'. The authority and reach of the Arbitration Commission was restricted to safety net adjustments and its role monitoring enterprise bargaining restricted by not being allowed to apply its 'public interest' test to private deals. For economists it was to be a testing year, with Australia still mired in recession. In 1991 a social scientist raised a commotion, and a long-lasting one at that, within the economics profession. Michael Pusey published a book entitled *Economic Rationalism in Canberra* (1991) claiming that 'inside' economists had hijacked economic policy and pushed it in a stridently neoclassical direction. Canberra, Pusey claimed, was being 'swept by a locust strike of economic rationalism' (ibid., 1). He advanced the thesis that, as was the case in New Zealand, it was usually young, ANU-trained officials or 'econocrats' within the 'central agencies' such as Treasury and the Department of Finance that were behind the economic reform programme. Pusey had the temerity to publish an earlier précis of his book in *Economic Papers* (Pusey, 1990).

The phrase 'economic rationalism', first used innocently in the 1970s to denote orderly, rational economic process – particularly in agricultural economics – now assumed a pejorative intent. Pusey (1993, 14) defined it as 'a doctrine that says markets and prices are the *only reliable* means of setting a value on things, and, further, that markets and money can *always*, at least in principle, deliver better outcomes that states and bureaucracies' (his emphasis). He argued that the econocrats were mostly young, laissez faire economists opposed to the mixed economy and that their brand of economics had led to bad economic and social outcomes. His work attracted a diversity of supporters, some of them sociologists keen to take up the charge against classical liberalism and modern economics (Manne and Carroll, 1993; Horne, 1992). Economic rationalism, then, was not just seen as a new economic creed, but also as a term of abuse directed at market-orientated economic policy. Academic economists were unsettled by the debate since most, by their definition of economic rationalism, abided by it (Schneider, 1998). Indeed, to oppose it was to be classified as an economic irrationalist, which Coleman and Hagger (2001) made great play of in their critique of Pusey. Some economists were reluctant to enter the debate because they felt that some economic rationalists did not assign a high priority to addressing unemployment or an equitable distribution of income. Other economists, having some doubts about financial liberalisation, were not prepared to dismiss Pusey's claims totally. There were reservations, too, about relying on market forces to address every area of human need. Harcourt (2001) warned, for instance, that because of cumulative causation and stocks dominating over flows, optimal outcomes do not always ensue for foreign exchange, financial assets and housing markets.

However, the economics profession decided to fight back. Two volumes of collected articles, (one of them being King and Lloyd, 1993) were published defending mainstream economics against the charge that it was tainted. However, as one reviewer, Jenny Stewart observed, it was an unedifying experience since the economists, and their critics, were basically 'talking past each other' (cited in Schneider, 1998, 51). Economists complained that their critics did not understand the intricacies of the subject, including the possibilities of market failure. A Canberra-based public sector economist, and then President of the Economic Society, Fred Argy pointed out that Pusey was overstating things and that the economic rationalists in policy-making circles were neither as monolithic, homogeneous nor as doctrinaire as had been made out. In other words, Argy said Pusey was attacking a straw man. Argy (1992, 84) also questioned the thoroughness and integrity of survey methods engaged by Pusey, as did a later critique by Coleman and Hagger (2001). Moreover, it was essential to note that it was not econocrats who shaped policy, but politicians – a conclusion also borne out by Goldfinch's (1999) analysis of the key decision-makers behind the Hawke and Keating governments' economic policy. Goldfinch discovered that there were other players, apart from the central agencies, behind the formulation of economic policy, including ministers, their advisors and even union officials.

In his critique of Pusey, Fred Argy teased out the collective state of opinion of Australian university economists during the early 1990s. He documented four areas were the econocrats were inclined to be more interventionist than their peers in academe. Argy noted, for instance, that the then head of the Federal Treasury, Tony Cole, remained a stern opponent of floating the currency. Second, despite macroeconomic fine-tuning being discredited within academe it still attracted strong support within government circles. Third, while 'inside' economists regarded the current account deficit as an appropriate target of macroeconomic policy, ANU economists had now concluded that this approach was entirely wrong-headed. Lastly, key economic officials, even a reluctant Treasury, supported the Australian Labor Party (ALP)–ACTU Accord (Argy, 1992, 85). On microeconomic and industry policy, Argy again concluded that Pusey was making a 'gross exaggeration'. Equally, he said Pusey was wrong to link rationalism with social inequality simply because rationalism was, by definition, concerned primarily with efficient resource allocation and effective economic management. Another reviewer, less tolerant than Argy was Richard Blandy (1992, 101) who found Pusey's tome 'a riotous farrago of fact and fantasy, insight and prejudice, distortion and perceptiveness, jargon and elegance'. Blandy noted that Pusey tended to confuse mainstream economics with laissez faire economics.

Nonetheless, Pusey's book reminded Australians of a sea-change in political and economic philosophy towards a smaller public sector, openness, deregulation and marketisation. He was broadly correct in that, since the mid-1970s, Australian economics had begun to adopt libertarian or market-inclined economics, a melange of Austrian–Chicago style economics which emphasised the virtues of decentralised markets and was suspicious of government and cartels (Withers, 1978, 77).

Besides the efforts of Australian economists in promoting economic reform, Mancur Olson's book *The Rise and Decline of Nations* (1982) had considerable appeal in Australia thanks to Gruen (1986), who drew upon it. Olson spoke of how a pattern of urban-based cartels of manufacturers and unions and their lobbies had been weaned on protection and regulated markets; this enfeebled a country's economic vitality. From his 'preliminary investigations', Olson felt his theory could explain the Australasian economies' poor growth performance in recent times. He stressed that property rights, open markets and sensible economic policy were just as important as basic resources in explaining economic growth (Olson, 1982, 135).

Olson's work had some resonance with those who favoured public choice theory, though Pincus (2014) had doubts about its penetration in the Australian polity. He related Australia's microeconomic reforms more to welfare economics and more sophisticated economic modelling like Peter Dixon's ORANI model, which disclosed the costs of assistance and over-regulation (ibid., 87). John Quiggin argued that, contrary to the Olson thesis, strong governments could stand up to special interests. David Clark (1995, 142) suggested that microeconomic reform was prompted more by the failure of the Accord to deliver the necessary productivity for Australia to lift its trade performance. In New Zealand, Roderick Deane, too, saw how regulation led to unintended adverse consequences and that it was microeconomic policy which was 'fundamental' to shaping economic outcomes (Scobie, 2013).

The timing of Pusey's book gave it impetus; Australia was then in recession. Besides having the highest rate of unemployment since 1930, Australia also suffered structural dislocation due to tariff cuts. There was a gaping current account deficit caused by a real appreciation in the exchange rate. Hindsight would reveal that the Hawke Government had erred in using high interest rates and tight fiscal policy to correct the current account deficit.

The phrase 'economic rationalism' became so controversial that economists within the Federal Treasury were instructed not to use the term. Later, Argy (1999) defused the issue by coining a better lexicon; those who believed that market forces were best left unhindered and blamed government failure rather than market failure were described as the school of 'hard liberalism', later known as neoliberalism. In contrast, 'progressive liberals' were those who believed, like Argy that government can play a supplementary role in terms of economic management and distribution. The 'statists' were those from the left who preferred old-style intervention and regulation. Argy (1999) and John Nevile (1994) qualified the grounds for the debate by noting that the economic rationalists' claim that their policy prescriptions all devolved from standard economic analysis, and not from value judgements, was not entirely correct. Nevile reminded economists that they could sometimes reduce the quality of their analysis by the 'wrong-headed introduction of inappropriate policies on the basis of ideology rather than rational economics' (Lodewijks, 1994, 28).

The popular reaction to Pusey's critique of rationalism foreshadowed a difficult time for the Australian economics profession. Hancock's comment that his countrymen had a dislike of 'scientific economics (still more) scientific economists' came back to haunt them. Pusey was a sociologist and the impact that his work had on the profession was, in a sense, poetic revenge for Copland's dismissal of sociology in the 1920s. Long after the rebuttals by Argy and Blandy, economists such as Coleman and Hagger (2001), infuriated by the success of Pusey's book – which they argued was media-orchestrated – penned a sharp, sarcastic critique against it. Even though Pusey's book had not stopped the economic reform programme, they felt that that the economics profession had not acquitted itself well in responding to the attack. Coleman and Hagger (2001, 300) saw Pusey's book as part of a broader campaign of reviving the old tradition of anti-economics sentiment, of undermining the moral authority of economists and of turning the public opinion against the need for economic reform. It is interesting that an opinion survey among Australian economics professors at the time that ranked those academics who knew the least about economics had academic sociologists placed in last spot (Anderson and Blandy, 1993, 495). While economists would have drawn psychic comfort from that barb, the authors conceded that the collective opinion of the Australian economics professoriate was now more aligned with the market-orientated US–German–Swiss culture than the interventionist culture of French and British economists.

Notes

1 'Australia grapples with inflation, unemployment… while La Trobe conference deals with yesterday's issues', *AFR*, 11 September 1979.
2 'An irrelevance of economists', *AFR*, 3 September 1982.
3 R. H. Snape 'Letter to the editor', *AFR*, 9 September 1982 (copy in the Arndt Papers, NLA).
4 'Advice and dissent', B. Easton, *The Listener*, 4 February 1995.

References

Anderson, M. and Blandy R. (1993), 'Academic economists on trial: the value of econo-mists' opinions', *Australian Quarterly*, 65(1): 482–97.

Argy, F. 1992, 'Review of Michael Pusey economic rationalism in Canberra', *Economic Papers*, 11(1): 83–90.

Argy, F. 1999, *Australia at the Crossroads: Radical Free Market of a Progressive Liberalism?*, Sydney: Allen and Unwin.

Bassett M. and J. Bassett, 2006, *Roderick Deane: His Life and Times*, Wellington: Viking.

Bates, W. 1997, 'The New Zealand model of economic reform: a review', *Agenda*, 4(3): 351–64.

Berg, C. 2015, 'Classical liberalism in Australian economics', *Economic Journal Watch*, 12(2): 192–220.

Bertram, G. 1993, 'Keynesianism, neoclassicism and the state', in C. Rudd and B. Roper (eds), *State and the Economy in New Zealand*, Auckland: Oxford University Press.

Blandy, R. 1992, 'Multiple schizophrenia: economic rationalism and its critics', *Australian Quarterly*, 64(1): 101–6.

Blyth, C. A. 1964, *The Future of Manufacturing in New Zealand*, London: Oxford University Press.

Blyth, C. A. 1966, 'The special case: the political economy of New Zealand', *Political Science*, 18: 38–51.

Blyth, C. A. 1987, 'The economists' perspective on economic liberalisation', in A. Bollard and R. Buckle (eds), *Economic Liberalisation in New Zealand*, Wellington: Allen and Unwin.

Bollard, A. (ed.), 1988, *The Influence of United States Economics on New Zealand: The Fulbright Anniversary Seminars*, Wellington: NZIER.

Bollard, A. 1994, 'New Zealand', in J. Williamson (ed.), *The Political Economy of Policy Reform*, Washington, DC: Washington Institute of Economic Progress.

Brash, D. T. 1996, *New Zealand's Remarkable Reforms*, London: Institute of Economic Affairs.

Brooke, G., A. Endres and A. Rogers, 2016, 'Does New Zealand economics have a useful past? The example of trade policy and economic development', *New Zealand Economic Papers*, 50(3): 281–302.

Clark, D. 1995, 'Microeconomic reform', in P. Kriesler (ed.), *The Australian Economy*, Sydney: Allen and Unwin, 142–69.

Coleman, W. 1992, 'Concord and discord amongst New Zealand economists; the results of an opinion survey', *New Zealand Economic Papers*, 26(1): 47–81.

Coleman, W. and A. Hagger, 2001, *Exasperating Calculators: The Rage against Economic Rationalism and the Campaign against Australian Economists*, Sydney: Macleay Press.

Dalziel. P. 1986, 'The 1984 Economic Summit conference: a search for policy objectives', *New Zealand Economic Papers*, 20(1): 41–51.

Dalziel, P. 2002, 'New Zealand's economic reforms: an assessment', *Review of Political Economy*, 14(1): 31–46.

Dalziel, P. and R. Lattimore, 1996, *The New Zealand Macroeconomy*, Melbourne: Oxford University Press.

Deane, R. S. 1981, 'Reflections on fiscal policy', *New Zealand Economic Papers*, 15(1): 28–49.

Easton, B. 1988, 'From Reaganomics to Rogernomics', in A. Bollard (ed.), *The Influence of United States Economics on New Zealand: The Fulbright Anniversary Seminars*, Wellington: NZIER.

Easton, B. 2001, *The Nation Builders*, Auckland: Auckland University Press.

Easton, B. 2007, 'Brian Easton', in L. Simmons (ed.), *Speaking Truth to Power*, Auckland: Auckland University Press, 105–26.

Evans, L., Grimes A., Wilkinson B. and Teece, D. 1996, 'Economic reform in New Zealand 1984–95: the pursuit of efficiency', *Journal of Economic Literature*, 34: 1856–902.

Goldfinch, S. 1999, 'Remaking Australia's economic policy: economic policy decision-makers during the Hawke and Keating Labor governments', *Australian Journal of Public Administration*, 58(2): 3–20.

Goldfinch, S. 2000, 'Paradigms, economic ideas and institutions in economic policy change: the case of New Zealand', *Political Science*, 52(1): 1–21.

Goldfinch, S. and B. Roper, 1993, 'Treasury's role in state policy formulation during the post-war era', in B. Roper (ed.), *State and Economy in New Zealand*, Auckland: Oxford University Press, 50–73.

Groenewegen, P. 1989, 'The development of economics in Australia: a tale of two centuries', *Economic Papers*, 8(3): 97–108.

Gruen, F. H. G. 1986, 'How bad is Australian economic performance and why?', *Economic Record*, 62(177): 180–93.

Harcourt, G. C. 2001, *50 Years a Keynesian and Other Essays*, London: Palgrave.

Hatch, J. and C. Rogers, 1997, 'Distinguished Fellow of the Economic Society of Australia, 1996: Professor Emeritus Geoff Harcourt', *Economic Record*, 73(221): 97–100.

Hazledine, T. 1997, 'Economizing on morality', *Landfall*, 194: 280–91.

Henderson, D. 1995, 'The revival of economic liberalism; Australia in an international perspective', *Australian Economic Review*, 1: 59–85.

Henderson, D. 1996, *Economic Reform: New Zealand in an International Perspective*, Wellington: New Zealand Business Roundtable.

Holmes, A. 1981, 'The good fight', *Economic Record*, 57(156): 1–11.

Holmes, F. W. 2000, 'Obituary of Bryan Philpott', *Victoria Economic Commentaries*, 17(1).

Horne, D. 1964, *The Lucky Country*, Melbourne: Penguin.

Horne, D. (ed.) 1992, *The Trouble with Economic Rationalism*, Melbourne: Scribe.

Kasper, W., R. Blandy, J. Freebairn, D. Hocking and R. O'Neil, 1980, *Australia at the Crossroads: Our Choices to 2000*, Sydney: Harcourt Brace.

King, S. 2003, 'Competition policy and regulation', in I. McAllister, S. Dowrick and R. Hassan (eds), *The Cambridge Handbook of Social Sciences in Australia*, Cambridge: Cambridge University Press.

Kelsey, J. 1995, *Economic Fundamentalism*, Auckland: Auckland University Press.

King, S. and P. Lloyd (eds), 1993, *Economic Rationalism: Dead End or Way Forward*, Sydney: Allen and Unwin.

Lattimore, R. and P. Wooding, 1996, 'International trade', in B. Silverstone, A. Bollard and R. Lattimore (eds), *A Study of Economic Reform: The Case of New Zealand*, Amsterdam: Elsevier.

Lloyd, P. 1978, 'Protection policy', in F. H. G. Gruen (ed.), *Surveys of Australian Economics*, Sydney: Allen and Unwin, 241–96.

Lodewijks, J. 1994, 'A conversation with John Nevile', in B. B. Rao (ed.), *Essays in Economics*, Sydney: Centre for Applied Economic Research: 15–34.

McMillan, J. 1997, 'Review of Silverstone *et al.* A study of economic reform: the case of New Zealand', *Journal of Economic Literature*, 35(4): 2094–5.

Maloney, T. and J. Savage, 1996, 'Labor markets and policy', in B. Silverstone, A. Bollard and R. Lattimore (eds), *A Study of Economic Reform: The Case of New Zealand*, Amsterdam: Elsevier.

Manne, R. and J. Carroll, 1993, *Shutdown: How Economic Rationalism Failed Australia*, Melbourne: Text.

Massey, P. 1995, *New Zealand: Market Liberalization in a Developed Economy*, Basingstoke: Palgrave Macmillan.

Nobbs, C. 2014, *The Failure of Free Market Economics and the Future of New Zealand*, Auckland: Chris Nobbs.

Norton, W. and R. McDonald, 1981, 'Implications for Australia of cross-country comparisons of economic performance', *Economic Record*, 57(159): 301–18.

Nevile, J. W. 1994, 'Economic rationalism', *Australian Quarterly*, 66(1): 25–43.

O'Dea, D. J. 1981, 'A survey of what economists think: recent research results', Wellington; NZIER: 41–6.

Olson M. 1982, *The Rise and Decline of Nations*, New Haven: Yale University Press.

Pincus, J. J. 2014, 'Public choice theory had negligible effect on Australian microeconomic policy, 1970s to 2000s', *History of Economics Review*, 59: 82–93.

Pusey, M. 1990, 'The impact of economic ideas in public policy in Canberra', *Economic Papers*, 9(4): 80–90.

Pusey, M. 1991, *Economic Rationalism in Canberra: A Nation-Building State Changes its Mind*, Melbourne: Cambridge University Press.

Pusey, M. 1993, 'Reclaiming the middle ground... from new right "economic rationalism"', in S. King and P. Lloyd (eds), *Economic Rationalism: Dead End or Way Forward*, Sydney: Allen and Unwin.

Quiggin, J. 2000, 'Free market reform in New Zealand: an Australian perspective', *Victoria Economic Commentaries*, 17(2): 35–42.

Schedvin, C. B. 2008, 'Primary phases of Australian economic development in the twentieth century', *Australian Economic Review*, 41(4): 450–5.

Schneider, M. 1998, '"Economic rationalism", economic rationalists and economists', *Quadrant*, 42(10): 48–53.

Scobie, G. 2013, 'An interview with Roderick Deane', *Asymmetric Information*, 46.

Silverstone, B., A. Bollard and R. Lattimore (eds), 1996, *A Study of Economic Reform: The Case of New Zealand*, Amsterdam: Elsevier.

Snively, S. 1988, 'Labour markets and social policy: reversing the roles', in A. Bollard (ed.), *The Influence of United States Economics on New Zealand: The Fulbright Anniversary Seminars*, Wellington: NZIER.

The Treasury, 1985, 'Opening "the books"; a reply', *New Zealand Economic Papers*, 19(1): 95–115.

Walsh, M. 1979, *Poor Little Rich Country*, Melbourne: Penguin.

Williams, R. 2012, *The Policy Providers*, Melbourne: Melbourne University Press.

Withers, G. 1978, 'The state of economics', *Australian Quarterly*, December: 74–80.

Zanetti, G. N. 1966, 'The New Zealand economy 1966: the failure of policy', *New Zealand Economic Papers*, 1(2): 5–15.

Zanetti, G. N. *et al.* 1984, 'Opening the books: a review article', *New Zealand Economic Papers*, 18(1): 13–30.

Zanetti, G. N. 1985, 'Opening "the books": reply', *New Zealand Economic Papers*, 19(1): 123–5.

11 Australasian economics at century's end

Introduction

By the turn of the 1990s the economics profession in Australia and New Zealand had shed the Keynesian paradigm and discarded the vestiges of protection, regulation and centralised wage fixation. The profession's disenchantment with the performance of the Australian and New Zealand economies and its despair over the post-war political economy was replaced by optimism and excitement. What Conrad Blyth and Frank Holmes (1962) could only dream of in the 1960s was coming to fruition. A new type of economy beckoned and with it a whole new research agenda. Economists could now focus their research on issues such as privatisation, the deregulation of the product, labour, capital and foreign exchange markets and the attendant issues that flowed from these. Fathoming out competition policy and its practicalities attracted the finest minds. The efficacy of fiscal and monetary policy in a deregulated environment was another issue worth investigating. The new buzz word of 'globalisation' not only superseded economic rationalism, but also conveyed the message of unrelenting change. Australasia's engagement with Asia was timely, even forward-looking, given the shift in the centre of gravity of economic power towards East Asia.

While the Economic Society chose not to celebrate its 75th anniversary in 2000, the Australian economics profession was, in terms of publications, in relative health. A study showed that Australia's share of the total journal citations for economics between 1981 and 1997 was 3.3 per cent compared to 10.7 per cent for Britain and 64.8 per cent for the United States (McAllister *et al.*, 2003, 4). Of course, just because papers are being produced does not mean they are of much consequence. An audit undertaken by Pomfret and Wang (2003) showed that the great majority of Australian university economists generated little research. Nonetheless, the last two decades of the twentieth century were marked by innovations in economic theory and practice; some will be showcased in part two of this chapter.

There were also some detours on the road to economic reform; indeed, it became fashionable, towards the end of the century, to talk of reform fatigue. Some economists also questioned the bounty from the reforms; these concerns will also be discussed later in this chapter.

Another development was the fading away of heterodox tradition in economics and the snuffing out the last pockets of pluralism within Australian university economic departments. The wellspring of radical economics that once fed and infused the mainstream was no longer. One might refer here to post-Keynesian economics, which did not sustain the impetus it had shown in the 1970s and which led Peter Groenewegen (1979, 206) to give it such an upbeat assessment of its prospects. After a bright start, post-Keynesian economics, together with other branches of heterodox economics, began a 'pronounced and continuing decline' caused by the Americanisation of the profession in the form of recruitment, publishing and research degree practices (King, 2002, 144). Reviewing John King's *Post Keynesian Economics: An Annotated Bibliography* (2002), Groenewegen (1995) said it marked the gravestone of that school's contribution. Geoffrey Harcourt had always attributed the decline of the Keynesian consensus to the way in which economics had been taught at Australian universities – for instance, the fact that the Samuelson's textbook, and its subsequent clones, were a popular teaching resource. Tim Thornton (2016) wrote on the narrowing of the agenda of Australian university economics degrees, dating it, in the first instance, from the 1980s. By narrowing, he meant not just at the expense of political economy but also in units such as economic history, the history of economic thought and comparative economic systems.[1]

The Groenewegen–MacFarlane (1990) prophesy of the 'fatal embrace' of North American economics was borne out in the hiring practices of Australian and New Zealand economics departments. It became standard practice for leading university departments to recruit directly from abroad, sometimes overlooking locally trained candidates. This 'internationalisation' of the profession, as it was politely termed, meant that many younger academic economists looked more to the American Economics Association as the exemplar rather than the Economic Society or the New Zealand Association of Economists. This attitude would hit both the Society and the Association hard in the new millennium not just in academic membership, but also in where one would pitch and place their research publications.

There was another interesting development about to envelop Australasian university economics departments. In 1956 Syd Butlin had gone on a study tour to America to examine the intriguing development of business schools. He came away unimpressed because they used the 'case method' as the main form of training. Many American business deans told Butlin (1957) that the 'fatal error' with business schools was their separation from 'academic' subjects such as economics, which had come about because economics departments had largely refused to become involved. Butlin concluded that this 'separation' had been bad for economics: first, because economics departments had missed out on an applied area; and, second, because business education was little more than a mass of case studies and descriptive material. Forty years on, Butlin would have cause to regret his sentiments. Towards the end of the millennium the trend in Australia, at least, was for economic departments to be swallowed whole into business schools, with some economists reduced to a marginalised existence doing service teaching to business and accounting students; business school deans even began to ponder whether economics should continue to be taught alongside business electives. This rise of business schools gathered pace as vocationally driven students flocked to do business degrees. This switch in tastes and the subsequent impact on faculties of commerce would challenge the integrity and independence of some university economics departments. As enrolments in economics degrees languished, the Economic Society commissioned an audit of the problem (Lewis and Norris, 1997). New Zealand, too, had a decline in economics degree enrolments during the 1990s.[2]

Latter-day contributions to economic thought

In the last two decades of the twentieth century the regimen of the *Record* included issues such as competition policy, distribution, international comparisons of living standards, trade, Asian economies, unemployment, the labour market experience for migrants, human capital and taxation. Broadly, the top five subjects were: labour and demographics, microeconomic issues, macroeconomics and monetary economics, international economics, health and education and welfare (Millmow and Tuck, 2013). There were several new outstanding areas of research and policy practice to which we now turn.

The balance of payments

While Australia had liberalised its capital account in 1983 with the float of the dollar it had not emancipated Australian policy-makers' minds from concerns about Australia's balance of payments. Australia was traditionally a capital-importing country, which meant running persistent current account deficits offset by capital account surpluses. The historic balance of payments 'problem' had risen substantially concurrent with foreign indebtedness. This led to concerns about Australia's vulnerability to external shocks and long-run solvency. In May 1986, just three years after the float, Paul Keating, the Federal Treasurer, spooked markets by warning that Australia was in danger of becoming a 'banana republic' because of the problem. It was feared that the foreign debt would impose a constraint on economic growth and expose the economy to external turbulence. Conventional thinking at the time was that capital markets could not be trusted and that the foreign debt was a threat to Australia's economic security; the external deficit was seen by the RBA as a symptom of excess aggregate demand.

In line with the 'twin deficits thesis' fiscal policy was tightened to reduce Australia's call upon foreign savings. A tight monetary policy bore down upon inflation and import demand. However, interest rates were kept high for too long and so, instead of the mooted 'soft landing', Australia stumbled into recession. While Australia improved its budgetary position the current account deficit persisted, causing an exasperated Keating to colourfully disparage the twin deficits thesis. It would take some time for policy-makers to free themselves from the 'traditional view' about the current account deficit.

An academic's insight led to enlightenment all round. John Pitchford (1989) advanced the view that the current account deficit should be seen not as a macroeconomic imbalance but as the outcome of private behaviour, specifically economic agents making inter-temporal utility-maximising consumption and savings decisions. In short, the current account balance was the net result of saving and investment decisions within the economy. If these decisions were rational the resulting current account deficit, or surplus, should not be a cause for macroeconomic concern *per se*. A deficit meant that households wanted to consume now rather than later while firms wanted to borrow to take advantage of business opportunities within Australia. Both parties, and the foreign agent prepared to finance both activities, were confident in the capacity to repay. In other words, the deficit was the result of 'consenting adults' and so macroeconomics policy to check the current account deficit was completely unnecessary. Pitchford pointed out that those who took umbrage at Australia's rising foreign debt obviously did not like foreign investment. The inflow of capital to Australia was the result of foreign investors seeking higher returns (Belkar *et al.*, 2007, 14–15). The idea that the current account deficit was a restraint on growth was discarded; instead, it was seen as a means for financing more growth. The only role for policy-makers was to monitor any distortions or regulations impeding capital flows. There were some reservations about the thesis – for instance, the presumed rationality of agents, adverse swings in the sentiment of foreign investors and, lastly, that excessive borrowing from abroad meant a higher risk premium for all transactors within Australia. Kearney (1995, 91–2) noted that the two critical assumptions underpinning Pitchford's analysis were that all production throughout the world occurs under constant returns to scale and that all markets were perfectly competitive. These assumptions, especially if realised, have sometimes been called into question by modern trade theorists (ibid., 92).

At the ANU Arndt and Gruen (1986) strongly disagreed with Pitchford's thesis. Arndt believed the foreign debt was fanning consumption expenditure and that the float of the dollar was not a clean one. Gruen also argued that the value of the Aussie dollar was sending the wrong signals to the economy and encouraging investment in the non-traded parts of the economy.[3] Earlier Gruen (ibid., 23) had been concerned that the growth in the foreign debt was the result of the decline in Australia's terms of trade, low level of savings and the high level of public borrowings. Despite these reservations, the 'intellectual weight' of the Pitchford thesis was acknowledged by the RBA, which quickly re-assigned monetary policy to containing inflation and made the current account deficit a medium-term concern (Belker *et al.* 2007, 16). Even with continuing current account deficits and rising foreign liabilities, it became apparent that the foreign debt problem was, as one commentator put it, 'the dog that didn't bite'. Even the unconvinced within academe conceded that Pitchford had established the fact that, despite the possibility that the current account deficit might still be a valid concern, the government did not necessarily have the degree of knowledge to guarantee that the results of its policy actions would be better than if it had refrained from acting in the first instance.

The funding of higher education

The Whitlam Government abolished university tuition fees in 1974 on the pretext that it would make tertiary education accessible to all. One year later, in preparing the 1975/6 budget, the Treasurer Bill Hayden had seriously considered tapering that support as a budgetary savings measure. The rising demand for tertiary education funded from taxation prompted economists such as Colin Clark and Michael Porter to point out that the scheme was regressive since the beneficiaries were mostly drawn from the middle classes. In the era before free tertiary education, Donald Cochrane (1968) proposed an extensive expansive loans scheme which graduates would repay after completion of their studies. In search of a more sustainable funding model, the Hawke Government established the Wran Committee on Higher Education Funding (1988) to inquire into the matter. The nub of the issues, as Gregory recalled, was 'How can the government introduce university fees and collect substantial sums of money without appearing to introduce student fees?'[4] The Committee recommended seeking contributions from those directly benefiting from education. The idea of income-contingent loans, first mooted by Milton Friedman in 1955, came from another ANU labour economist who had been a consultant to the Committee. Bruce Chapman's (1997) intellectual contribution was around the issue of income-contingent funding usually in the form of loans. This was a more equitable way for funding growth of the system, he argued, than asking taxpayers to pay the cost. Students, rather than their parents, were given the autonomy to make the decision whether to undertake higher education. Student contributions would be made through the tax system whereby once they had reached a threshold income they would pay an additional 2 per cent tax until 20 per cent of the cost of their education had been met. This solution put the idea of reintroducing university fees to bed. The Committee also recommended three different levels of contributions dependent on the nature of the cost of the degree undertaken.

Chapman's idea led the precedent of income-contingent funding of Australian higher education based on what became the Higher Education Contribution Scheme (HECS). The advantage of the income-contingent repayment was that it did not constitute a financial barrier to low-income students and, moreover, these students had the autonomy to make the decision of whether or not to participate in further education (ibid., 738). The scheme was quickly adopted by the Australian government, with interest expressed by other countries about the funding model. Earlier, Helen Hughes serving on a Committee reviewing Australia's aid programme in 1984, recommended that foreign students coming to Australia should pay full fees. While the vice chancellors opposed this, it saw the beginnings of one of Australia's top export earning industries. Hughes supplemented that work by serving on another common immigration policy committee with a focus on recruiting skilled migrants who had previously studied in Australia (Byrne, 2005, 3).

Trade and development

Given the ANU's Research School in Pacific Studies' expertise in trade and development, it is unsurprising that a coterie of economists there were to make significant contributions in this area. Arndt wanted the department to study the theoretical and applied problems of economic growth and trade with specific reference to East Asia and the Pacific. Helen Hughes, one of the few women honoured by the Economic Society, was among the first economists to see the significance of export-led industrialisation as the means to rapid and equitable economic development. Before doing so, she had to take apart the Presbisch–Singer model of import substitution industrialisation. It was another dagger blow to the doctrine of export pessimism. Hughes also argued the merits of economic openness, including flows of capital and people (ibid., 2). Fittingly, her last appointment at the ANU was to establish the National Centre for Development Studies, which became a leading centre for economics studies in the Asia Pacific. These achievements were all the more satisfying since, at the start of her career, Hughes had suffered blatant discrimination in employment with full-time positions closed off to her by fellow economists (Lodewijks, 2007).

After Garnaut returned to the ANU to take up the chair once occupied by Crawford, Arndt and Corden, he was asked by Hawke to write a report on how Australia should respond to the economic transformation occurring in East Asia. In *Australia and the Northeast Ascendancy* (1989), Garnaut concluded that Australia would enjoy more rapid economic growth if it engaged in trade liberalisation with East Asia and stressed the complementarity between those economies and Australia's resource base. It also meant that, domestically, the government had to accept rapid structural change as an inevitable part of economic progress (Garnaut, 2001, 91). In his report, Garnaut recommended that Australia remove all its trade barriers without waiting for reciprocation from its trading partners. This astounded some but he reminded critics that protectionism always weakened the importing country and that, since the Asian countries were liberalising their economies, there was no need for formal discussions (Hill, 2010, 284). Hawke has also requested that Garnaut assist the work of his ANU colleague Peter Drysdale in laying the intellectual foundations for the establishment of APEC (Asia Pacific Economic Cooperation).

The idea of a multilateral free trade bloc, or open regionalism, among the Pacific Rim countries had long been the dream of Drysdale. A graduate of UNE, Drysdale had come to ANU to undertake a doctorate supervised by Corden on Japanese–Australian trade. He would spend his career working on regional integration and helped establish the Australia–Japan Research Centre at the ANU in 1980. Since the late 1960s Drysdale had been arguing for a pan-Pacific economic integration, with Australian and New Zealand participation, and the formation of an organisation for trade aid and development.[5] Drysdale referred to the transformation in Australian trading patterns towards Asia and America, despite its trade preferences still favouring Britain. Australia, he argued, already had a strong interest in closer Pacific cooperation. Drysdale mooted that the move to free trade should be gradual, that incomes would rise from growing trade volumes and the dynamic benefits of integration, and that trade diversion costs would be low. A high degree of protection would also become exposed. Drysdale felt that bilateral government-to-government relations and negotiations would be best expedited within the framework of such an organisation.[6] The foundation of APEC sprang from a Pacific Economic Community seminar at the ANU, commissioned by the Australian and Japanese governments. While Australian politicians claimed the glory, the intellectual architect of the forum was Drysdale encapsulated in his prize winning book *The Economics of International Pluralism: Economic Policy in East Asia and the Pacific* (1988).

On a less grand scale, Peter Lloyd (1991) and Frank Holmes (1966), working independently, forged an interest in market integration between Australia and New Zealand. This was one of the first subjects of the research papers put out by the NZIER. It bore early fruit with the 1965 New Zealand–Australia Free Trade Agreement which provided for the gradual elimination of tariffs on some products traded between the two countries. But it only went so far: Australia vetoed butter and New Zealand vetoed manufactured goods. In a study for CEDA, Peter Lloyd (1991) proposed a single market as a means of strengthening the bond between the two countries. Eventually, in 1983, Australia and New Zealand signed a free trade agreement, the Closer Economic Relations (CER). Some New Zealand economists raised the possibility of a joint currency to further economic integration, possibly to be called the ZAC. However, the idea of a common currency was a bridge too far (Grimes and Holmes, 2000).

While on leave from Monash and working at the World Trade Organization, Richard Snape, assisted by his compatriot Gary Sampson, developed a framework for analysing barriers to international trade in services. This became the foundation for the WTO's General Agreement on Trade in Services of the Uruguay Round. Snape also championed a rules-based multilateral format for existing regional and bilateral trading agreements.

Unemployment and the labour market

In the 1970s a veritable Australasian industry developed as economists empirically measured and applied the Phillips curve to local data. Just as Phillips attempted to construct an Australian Phillips curve in 1959 (Perry, 1994, 44–8), most studies have focused on the causal factors underpinning it, such as the level of unemployment benefits, union militancy, import price inflation and the degree of domestic competition. The end objective of all this Phillips curve modelling was to estimate the NAIRU. The official view from the Federal Treasury and the RBA was that this rate was around 5 per cent for Australia. Some post-Keynesian economists such as Geoff Harcourt, John King, Peter Kriesler and John Nevile would have felt that this rate was too high. Ian McDonald, a new Keynesian economist at the University of Melbourne, came to the same conclusion, finding that there was a range of rates of unemployment at which the rate of inflation remained constant and that the short run Phillips curve did not apply. Before that, McDonald had collaborated with Robert Solow on identifying the conditions in which trade union behaviour, mixed in with some insights from behavioural economics, resulted in real wage rigidity. McDonald and Solow (1981) realised that the wage employment outcome in the union monopoly model was not actually a Pareto optimal outcome. This led to their 'efficient bargains' model between a union and firm, where wages were set higher than the marginal revenue product of labour. Their highly cited paper was published in the *American Economic Review* and was the foundation for bargaining models in many areas of economics, as well as industrial relations. Bob Gregory continued his work on the segmentation of the labour market based on gender, age and location and how it related to inequality in household and individual income.

Econometrics

Possessing one of the world's first econometricians in Bill Phillips and one of the world's best-known econometricians in Peter C. B. Philips, New Zealand has certainly punched above its weight in this field. Credit for this legacy lies with pioneers and teachers such as Bergstrom for its rich legacy in cultivating first-rate econometricians. Australia too can boast of Adrian Pagan, who had a Chair in Economics at RSSS at the ANU from 1992 and is now Professor of Economics at Sydney. In the 1970s and 1980s there was a cluster of academics dispersed around several departments at the ANU, including Ted Hannan, Ray Byron, Deane Terrell and Pravin Trivedi, which made for a centre of excellence in econometrics. Pagan's early work at the ANU on the use of econometrics to solve real-world problems engaged him in areas such as time series analysis, the estimation and specification of single equation models, nonparametrics, macroeconometrics and financial econometrics. He became something of a 'Swiss army knife' of econometrics (Skeels, 2016, 1056). One innovation, developed with one of his doctoral students Trevor Breusch (1978), was to design a test for heteroscedasticity in a linear regression model.[7] In more recent times Pagan has examined the validity of real business cycle models and the efficacy of monetary policy on the economy. In that, he followed in the footsteps of other ANU economists Melville, Swan and Gregory by being invited to serve on the RBA Board deliberating over monetary policy. There Pagan learned all about reading the economy with 'big data' and the importance of having a simple framework for analysing monetary policy (Skeels, 2016, 1073). Currently there are eight Australian and three (non-resident) New Zealanders who are Fellows of the Econometric Society.

Microeconomic reform and its critics

Given that both New Zealand and Australia engaged in wide-ranging economic reform programmes in the 1980s, an assessment of the outcomes makes a useful contribution to economic knowledge. Some commentators have argued that it is too early to make a judgement but, after 15 years of reform, economists such as John Quiggin (2000) felt justified in taking an audit about what had been achieved. An integral part of these measures known as 'microeconomic reform' – to improve the efficiency of public and private sectors of the economy – included not just privatisation of government-owned business enterprises but also the deregulation of product, finance and labour markets (Borland, 2015). In New Zealand the privatisation process, preceded by corporatisation of state-owned enterprises, was the most comprehensive and systematic of any in the world. For older generations of economists such as Geoff Harcourt or Russell Mathews, the privatisation of the state assets went against their beliefs that public spending on infrastructure underpinned a country's economic development (Barton and Grewal, 2000, 407).

Fred Argy, who had been Secretary to the Campbell Committee (1980) and a signatory to the Final Report recommending extensive deregulation of the Australian financial system, was, a decade later, beginning to share second thoughts. The financial markets, he argued, had too much influence over the bearing of macroeconomic policy, especially over budgetary settings. The Federal government was being made hostage, 'trying to second-guess what financial markets will do in response to macroeconomic policy'.[8] The financial markets were 'obsessed' with reducing the size of the public sector and dictating what programmes should be cut. The danger, then, was that financial markets were reducing the authority of governments to set social and economic policy. Argy did not seek to return to regulation, urging, instead, that the players behind financial markets differentiate between malign and benign budget deficits. The markets, he argued, should become more enlightened about 'the interaction between social equity, social cohesion and economic growth'.[9] Economic policy, he said, should be concerned with improving society not just economic outcomes and should give due regard to distribution, quality of life and the environment even if this meant sacrificing economic growth.

Another sceptic of the benefits of microeconomic reform was John Quiggin, who adopted the curate's egg position in arguing that benefits of the reforms have been overstated, but that, overall, they had been 'positive and significant'. He did not agree with critics of economic rationalism that the reforms had led to a reduction in social welfare.

Australian economists assumed that privatisation should have no effect on the public sector net worth, which was known as the equivalence proposition; violations of this proposition would arise if the price for the asset sold differs from its market value or the value of the asset in public ownership differs from its value in private ownership. Quiggin argued that, overall, most privatisations left the public worse off since public assets and public enterprises had been sold for less than the present value of the future stream of earnings they would have generated under continued public ownership. Specifically, Quiggin (2003, 22) found that the interest savings derived from the sale of the Commonwealth Bank and Telecom New Zealand used to repay public debt were less that the revenue forgone from the privatisations. Quiggin's findings did not go uncriticised. The net conclusion from the debate was that the fiscal viability of privatisation depended largely on perceptions of whether risk is borne better by the government or the private sector. Another feature of the Australian debate on privatisation was to focus upon the distributive outcomes. In New Zealand, Ian Duncan (1996, 418) of the NZIER said that that the equivalence proposition test could not be addressed because 'the arithmetic is constantly changing'. However, from a policy perspective he stated that the public sector reforms can be judged a success by, first, improving the performance of the economy by improving good and services provision and that the framework was 'sufficiently robust and flexible' to deal with many different market and regulatory circumstances.

Quiggin's (1996, 222) other key observation was to note that the rage for microeconomic reform had become a mania, driven by 'a dogmatic commitment towards competition and the private sector' without much analytical forbearance. On the net effect of the New Zealand reforms, Quiggin (2000) noted that it was in the 1980s that the economic trajectories of the two economies diverged, with Australian per capita incomes being 35 per cent higher by the end of the century. However, he attributed this outcome to poor macroeconomic management rather than the furious rate of structural reform in New Zealand. Another aspect of microeconomic reform was the need for competitive regulation over infrastructure facilities since mere access to these was unlikely to guarantee any improvement in the welfare of consumers (King and Maddock, 1996, 3). Regulatory authorities overseeing privatised utilities needed to capture the benefits of scale economies while constraining the tendency towards monopoly power.

Mesoeconomics

In the 1990s two Australian economists at Monash, Yew Kwang Ng and Xiaokai Yang, drew world attention for breaking into the new field of mesoeconomics and inframarginal economics of specialisation. The Sydney-trained Kwang already had a distinguished record in contributing to welfare economics and was known for breaking with tradition and making new approaches (Corden *et al.*, 2008). He teamed up with Yang to focus on an ambitious programme of rebuilding the core of economic analysis with mesoeconomics that would reconcile microeconomics with macroeconomic analysis in a simplified general equilibrium setting. The first thing was for Kwang to help Yang publish his Princeton PhD as *Specialisation and Economic Organisation* (1993). Yang's approach wanted to recast economics by switching attention away from resource allocation to economic organisation. He wanted to formalise classical economic thought on the role of the division of labour and show how it promoted growth and the shaping of economic organisation. Mesoeconomics would allow macroeconomic analysis to be set free from the confines of perfect competition. Their model could generate increasing returns at the firm level and at the economy level arising from the division of labour and would positively affect productivity, economic performance and the shape of economic organisations.

Conclusion

In the years since the founding of the Economic Society, in 1925, the Australasian economics profession has made a respectable contribution to world economic literature. One could list significant contributions in trade and protection theory, agricultural economics, econometrics, macroeconomics, growth theory, immigration economics, public finance, microeconomics, labour economics and even in a field we did not cover – how the indigenous peoples of Australia and New Zealand interact, and indeed fare, within the broader economy.

Australian libraries, archives and universities, along with historians of Australian economic thought have done an excellent job in preserving the legacy and work of their forbears. The bibliography of primary sources, listing the records, archives and interviews with Australian economists, points to the fact that this book has been somewhat Australia-centric, that there are still gaps in telling fully the story of New Zealand economic thought. Yet that 'wee' country, with its rich tradition of exporting human capital, has punched above its own weight in contributions to economic thought to deserve a separate account. It is hoped that the likes of Tony Endres, Geoffrey Brooke and Alan Rogers will go on to furnish us with a more complete history of New Zealand economic thought.

It can be argued that Australasian economics has lost not just its distinctiveness, but also its identity; as William Coleman (2015, 290) says, 'there is no Australia in economics any longer. Australian economics is at an end.' That is sad. In the same way that Australians as a society are no longer the 'weird mob' that Nino Culotta (pseudonym of author John O'Grady) observed in 1957, Australian academic economists are no longer the 'peculiar tribe' that Giblin spoke of in the 1930s. As a whole, they are now more qualified and professional and no less persuasive in influencing government decision-making. By contrast, as this book has suggested, New Zealand academic economists have consistently struggled to make an imprint on national policy, including the two major economic upheavals over the past 50 years; the sad fact is that many of their finest econometricians and economists, beginning with Copland and Fisher, were lured overseas. Arguably, the small size of the academic economics profession there has militated against it having a critical mass. However, it should take credit for the fact that there are more locally trained economists within the public service than ever before. Those inside economists were attracted to the idea of using neoliberal economic theories to overhaul the New Zealand economy. There was also a neoliberal transformation of the Australian economy, but the imported economic dogma was filtered to some degree by a sceptical university profession.

There is an element of success in our story that met the challenge Craufurd Goodwin set for historians of Australasian economic thought some years ago. The sociology of the academic economics profession in both Australia and New Zealand is, like the societies they serve, a diverse and multi-faceted one. That fact, in itself, is tribute to the way in which the profession in these two countries has, like their economies, became integrated with the global economy. In complete contrast with 1925, or even 1965, Australia and New Zealand now have the most open economies in the world in terms of goods, services, ideas, capital and people.

Notes

1 While there is a Society of Heterodox Economists that has an annual and well-attended conference in Sydney, it has not made much penetration into the curricula of Australian economic departments.
2 'Dismal interest in the dismal science', *Asymmetric Information*, October 1998 (3).
3 'The economics professors great debate', *Canberra Times*, 27 April 1991.
4 R. G. Gregory Transcript, 2002, NLA.
5 'Australia in a Pacific free trade area', *Canberra Times*, 13 January 1968.
6 'Call for Pacific trade grouping', *Canberra Times*, 15 April 1972.
7 Breusch can also claim to have the highest cited paper to have appeared in *Australian Economic Papers* on the same topic.
8 I. Henderson, 'Bringing his deregulation to heel', *Canberra Times*, 18 March 1995.
9 Ibid.

References

Barton, A. D. and B. J. Grewal, 2000, 'Russell Lloyd Mathews: an appreciation', *Economic Record*, 76(235): 401–11.

Belkar, R., L. Cockerell and C. Kent, 2007, 'Current account deficits: the Australian experience', *Research Discussion Paper*, RBA.

Borland, J. 2015, 'Microeconomic Reform' in S. Ville and G. Withers (eds.) *The Cambridge Economic History of Australia*, Melbourne: Cambridge University Press: 419–37.

Breusch, T. 1978, 'Testing for autocorrelation in dynamic linear models', *Australian Economic Papers*, 17(31): 334–51.

Butlin, S. J. 1957, 'Business schools in American universities', *Economic Review*, 2: 13–15.

Byrne, G. 2005, 'Distinguished Fellow of the Economic Society of Australia, 2004: Helen Hughes', *Economic Record*, 81(252): 1–5.

Chapman, B. 1997, 'Conceptual issues and the Australian experience with income contingent charges for higher education', *Economic Journal*, 107(442): 738–51.

Cochrane, D. 1968. 'The cost of university education', *Economic Record*, 44(2): 137–53.

Coleman, W. 2015, 'A young tree dead? The story of economics in Australia and New Zealand', in V. Barnett (ed.), *Routledge Handbook of the History of Global Economic Thought*, London: Routledge: 281–93.

Corden, W. M., P. Forsyth and C. Tombazos, 2008. 'Distinguished Fellow of the Economic Society of Australia, 2007: Yew-Kwang Ng', *Economic Record*, 84(265): 267–72.

Drysdale, P. 1988, *The Economics of International Pluralism: Economic Policy in East Asia and the Pacific*, Sydney: Allen and Unwin.

Duncan, I. 1996, 'Public enterprises', in B. Silverstone, A. Bollard and R. Lattimore (eds), *A Study of Economic Reform: The Case of New Zealand*, Amsterdam: Elsevier.

Garnaut. R. 1989, *Australia and the Northeast Ascendancy*, Canberra: Australian Government.

Garnaut, R. 2001, *Social Democracy in Australia's Asian Future*, Canberra: Asia Pacific Press.

Grimes, A. and F. Holmes, 2000, *An Anzac Dollar? Currency Union and Business Development*, Wellington: Victoria University Press.

Groenewegen, P. 1979, 'Radical economics', in F. H. Gruen (ed.), *Surveys of Australian Economics*, Vol. 2, Sydney: Allen and Unwin, 171–223.

Groenewegen, P. 1995, 'Post-Keynesian economics: a memorial?', *History of Economics Review*, 24: 137–9.

Groenewegen, P. and MacFarlane, B. 1990, *A History of Australian Economic Thought*, London: Routledge.

Gruen, F. H. G. 1986, 'Our Present Discontents: Presidential address to the Economic Society, 1986', Centre for Economic Policy Research: ANU.

Hill, H. 2010, 'Distinguished Fellow: Ross Garnaut', *Economic Record*, 86(273): 281–8.

Holmes, F. W. 1962, *Planning for Growth in a Freer Economy*, Wellington: NZIER.

Holmes, F. W. 1966, *Free Trade with Australia*, Wellington: NZIER.

Kearney, C. 1995, 'The balance of payments and international debt', in P. Kriesler (ed.), *The Australian Economy*, Sydney: Allen and Unwin: 80–100.

King, J. E. 2002, *A History of Post Keynesian Economics since 1936*, Cheltenham: Edward Elgar.

King, S. and R. Maddock, 1996, *Unlocking the Infrastructure: The Reform of Public Utilities in Australia*, Sydney: Allen and Unwin.

Lewis, P. and K. Norris, 1997, 'Recent changes in economics enrolments', *Economic Papers*, 16(1): 1–13.

Lloyd P. 1991, *The Future of CER: A Single Market for Australia and New Zealand*, Wellington: Victoria University Press.

Lodewijks, J. 2007, 'A conversation with Helen Hughes, *Journal of the Asia Pacific Economy*, 12(4): 429–51.

McAllister, I., S. Dowrick and R. Hassan (eds), 2003, *The Cambridge Handbook of Social Sciences in Australia*, New York: Cambridge University Press.

McDonald I. and R. Solow, 1981, 'Wage bargaining and unemployment', *American Economic Review*, 71(5): 896–908.

Millmow, A. J. and J. Tuck, 2013, 'The audit we had to have: the *Economic Record* 1960–2009', *Economic Record*, 89(284): 112–28.

Perry, L. J. 1994, 'Inflation and unemployment', in B. B. Rao (ed.), *Essays in Economics*, Sydney: Centre for Applied Economic Research: 35–81.

Pitchford, J. 1989, 'A sceptical view of Australia's current account and debt problem', *Australian Economic Review*, 22(2): 5–14.

Pomfret, R. and L. C. Wang, 2003, 'Evaluation the research output of Australian universities' economics departments', *Australian Economic Papers*, 42(4): 418–41.

Quiggin, J. 1996, *Great Expectations: Microeconomic Reform and Australia*, Sydney: Allen and Unwin.

Quiggin, J. 2000, 'Free market reform in New Zealand: an Australian perspective', *Victoria Economic Commentaries*, 17(2): 35–42.

Quiggin, J. 2003. 'Privatisation', in I. McAllister, S. Dowrick and R. Hassan (eds), *The Cambridge Handbook of Social Sciences in Australia*, New York: Cambridge University Press: 17–30.

Skeels, C. 2016, 'The ET interview: Adrian Pagan', *Econometric Theory*, 32: 1015–94.

Thornton, T. 2016, *From Economics to Political Economy*, London: Routledge.

Yang, X. and Y.-K. Ng, 1993, *Specialisation and Economic Organisation*, Amsterdam: North Holland.

Appendix 1

Distinguished Fellows of the Economic Society of Australia, 1987–2016*

1987	Colin Clark Trevor Swan	National income statistics, growth theory, external and internal balance
1988	Sir Roland Wilson	Balance of payments theory, economic management
1989	Murray Kemp	International trade theory, welfare economics
1990	Noel Butlin	Australian economic history
1992	Sir Leslie Melville	Central banking, monetary theory
1994	Heinz Arndt	Monetary economics, history of economic thought, development economics
1995	Max Corden	Applied international trade, open economy macroeconomics
1996	Geoff Harcourt	Post-Keynesian economics, capital and growth theory
1997	Fred Gruen	Agricultural economics, welfare economics
1998	Alan Powell	Econometrics, CGE model-building
1999	Adrian Pagan	Econometrics
2000	John Nevile	Econometrics and policy-orientated macroeconomic theory
2001	Bob Gregory	Labour economics, international economics
2002	Richard Snape	Trade theory and open economy macroeconomics
2003	Peter Dixon	CGE econometric model-building
2004	Helen Hughes	Development economics
2005	Peter Lloyd	Trade theory: theoretical and applied
2006	Maureen Brunt	Law and economics
2007	Yew Kwang Ng	Welfare economics, microeconomics, mesoeconomics
2008	Alan Woodland	Applied econometrics
2009	Ross Garnaut	Australian integration with Asian economies, resource rent tax
2010	Peter Groenewegen	Public finance and history of economic thought
2011	John Quiggin	Microeconomic theory
2012	John Pitchford	Balance of payments theory
2013	Geoff Brennan	Public choice theory
2014	John Freebairn	Tax theory, agricultural economics and welfare economics
2015	Bruce Chapman	Funding of higher education, labour economics
2016	Joe Isaac	Labour economics and industrial relations

Note: *There was no award made in 1991 and 1993

Distinguished Fellows of the New Zealand Association of Economists 2004–16

2004	Conrad Blyth	Economic growth
2004	Sir Frank Holmes	Economic leadership, economic planning
2004	Roderick Deane	Economic policy and public sector reform
2004	Peter Phillips	Econometric theory
2005	Brian Easton	Economic journalism
2005	Lewis Evans	Completion policy and network economics
2005	Garry Hawke	Economic history
2005	John McMillan	Microeconomics and game theory
2006	John Gould	Economic history
2006	Peter Lloyd	Trade theory
2007	Don Brash	Economic governance
2012	Leslie Young	Econometrics and trade theory
2012	Stephen Turnovsky	Macroeconomic stabilisation
2013	John Riley	Microeconomics and asymmetric information
2014	David Giles	Econometrics and CGE model-building
2015	Arthur Robson	Microeconomics
2016	Bruce Ross	Agricultural economics

Appendix 2

Corden (1968)	Gruen (1978, 1979, 1983)	McAllister, Dowrick and Hassan (2003)
Wages policy	Monetary policy	Privatisation
Balance of payments issues	Wages policy	Competition policy and regulation
Tariff policy	Inflation	Economics and the environment
Banking, monetary and fiscal policy	Agricultural policy	Health economics
Public finance	Protection policy	Immigration
Immigration and foreign investment	Income distribution, poverty and redistributive policies	Labour market and industrial relations
Agricultural economics	Urban economics	Income distribution and redistribution
The Vernon controversy	Economics of education	Taxation
	Radical economics	Innovation
	Australian economics 1968–78	Trade and industry policies
	Economics of regulation	The macro economy
	Resources and economic development	Money and banking
	Health economics	
	Taxation policy	

Bibliography of primary sources

Sir Douglas Copland Papers, National Library of Australia (NLA).
Sir James Hight Papers, MacMillan Brown Library, University of Canterbury (UC).
Albert Tocker Papers, MacMillan Brown Library, UC.
Horace Belshaw Papers, University of Auckland.
Faculty of Economics and Commerce Papers, University of Melbourne Archives (UMA).
Economic Society of Australia, Victorian Branch, memoranda and correspondence, UMA.
Hermann Black Papers, University of Sydney Archives.
Wilfred Prest Papers, UMA.
Registrar Papers, UMA.
Alan Ritchie Papers, UMA.
J. B. Condliffe, 1973, *Autobiography*, Macmillan Brown Library, UC.
J. B. Condliffe Papers, Bancroft Library, University of California, Berkeley.
Edwin Cannan Papers, British Library of Political and Economic Science, LSE.
Lionel Robbins Papers, British Library of Political and Economic Science, LSE.
Royal Society of Economics Papers. British Library of Political and Economic Science, LSE.
Gerald Firth Papers, NLA.
Colin Clark Papers, Fryer Library, University of Queensland.
Gordon Wood Papers, NLA.
John La Nauze Papers, NLA.
William S. Robinson Papers, UMA.
Monash University Staff Records.
Otago University Staff Records.
R. J. L. Hawke Papers, University of South Australia Archives.
Economic Society of Australia and New Zealand, Wellington Branch, minute books, 1946–84, Alexander Turnbull Library, Wellington, New Zealand.
Wolfgang Rosenberg Papers, Alexander Turnbull Library, Wellington, New Zealand.
Heinz Arndt, ANU Oral History Archive transcript.
Noel Butlin, ANU Oral History Archive transcript.
Robin Gollan, ANU Oral History Archive transcript.
Keith Hancock, Oral Transcript, 2006, NLA.
Jonathan Pincus, Oral Transcript, 2007, NLA.
Robert Gregory, Oral Transcript, 2002, NLA.
Malcolm Fisher, Oral Transcript, 1992, University of New South Wales Archives.
Joe Isaac Papers, UMA.
Leslie G. Melville, Oral Transcript, 1973, NLA.

Index

Douglas, Major C. H. and Social Credit
  economic reform movement 36, 94
Douglas, Roger 5, 210, 213, 215
Downie Stewart, William 76
Downing, Richard 22, 43, 131, 164,
  176–7, 196; appointed Ritchie Chair
  of Economics, Melbourne University
  123–4; and reaction to Keynes' *General
  Theory* 87–9
Drake, Peter 191
Drysdale, Peter 191, 232
Duncan, Ron 186
'Dutch Disease' 195
Dyason, Edward 53

early 20th-century economic characteristics
  of Australia and New Zealand 22–8
Easton, Brian 189, 214
Econometrica 145
econometrics 146–7, 175, 192, 234
economic modelling 128–30, 163, 168,
  175, 187, 192–4, 206–8
Economic Papers 198, 219
Economic Planning and Advisory Council
  (Australia) 209
economic rationalism 183–4, 206,
  219–23
Economic Record 6, 41, 42–4, 50, 81, 90,
  104, 120, 124, 126, 128, 130–1, 133,
  140, 164, 166, 167, 169, 170, 176, 191,
  196–8, 208, 229
economic reforms of 1970s and 1980s: in
  Australia 175–98, 204–6, 209–13; in
  New Zealand 175–98, 205–6, 209–13,
  234–6
Economic Society of Australia and New
  Zealand 1–2, 5, 6, 14, 42–4, 70–1, 141,
  166, 171, 182, 190, 197, 227
Economic Stabilisation Committee (New
  Zealand) (1942) 99, 107
economic thought in Australasia: earlier
  attempts at documentation 12–13;
  general characteristics 14–19, 237
economics profession in Australia,
  development in post-war period 121–33
economics textbooks 160, 175–6, 228
Economists' Committee (New Zealand)
  (1932–33) 74–8
Eggleston, Frederic 60
Employment Act (New Zealand)
  (1944), 108
Employment Contracts Act (New Zealand)
  (1991) 211

European Common Market 28
Evans, Henry David 193
exchange rate *see* balance of payments
export pessimism 25–6, 165

Finance and Economic Committee
  (Australia) 105–6, 108
Firth, Gerald 1, 38–9, 107, 129,
  132, 188
fiscal federalism 59–60
Fiscal Responsibility Act (New Zealand)
  (1994) 218
Fisher, Allan G.B. 57; *The Clash of
  Progress and Security* (1935) 79;
  response to Keynes' *General Theory* 89;
  response to Report of the Economists
  Committee 78–9, 95
Fisher, Malcolm 146, 169, 210
floating of Australian and New Zealand
  currency 190–1, 229
Forgan Smith, William 92
formal economics instruction, beginnings
  of 28–9, 36–42
Fraser Government (Australia) (1975–83)
  204
Fraser, Peter 32
Frearson, Keith 161, 180
Friedman, Milton 182–3, 230
full employment idealism, post-war in
  Australia 107–10

Garland, J. M, 'Pete' 86, 88
Garnaut, Ross 51, 149, 190, 210, 232;
  Australia and the Northeast Ascendancy
  (1989) 232
Giblin, Lyndhurst Falkiner 1, 5, 8,
  50, 59, 69, 80, 87, 106, 108; and
  Brigden Report (1929) 52–4; and
  Economic Society of Australia and
  New Zealand 42–4; *Letters to John
  Smith* (1930) 73; 'Major Giblin's
  multiplier' 57–9; Member of Finance
  and Economic Committee 105–6; role
  in establishment of formal economics
  instruction in Australia 39–41; on tariff
  reform 165
Gifford, John 147, 182
'globalisation' 227
Gold Standard 68
Goldfinch, Shaun 212–13
Goodwin, Craufurd: *Economic Enquiry in
  Australia* (1966) 12, 237